ECONOMIC DEVELOPMENT AND SOCIAL CHANGE IN SRI LANKA

A SPATIAL AND POLICY ANALYSIS

Economic Development and Social Change in Sri Lanka

A Spatial and Policy Analysis

Edited by
PAUL A. GROVES

MANOHAR
1996

First Published 1996

ISBN 81-7304-100-9

Published by Ajay Kumar Jain for
Manohar Publishers & Distributors
2/6, Ansari Road, Daryaganj, New Delhi - 110002

Lasertypeset by A J Software Publishing Co. Pvt. Ltd.
305, Durga Chambers, 1333, D.B. Gupta Road,
Karol Bagh, New Delhi - 110005

Printed at Rajkamal Electric Press, G.T. Karnal Road, Delhi

CONTENTS

LIST OF FIGURES

LIST OF TABLES

ACKNOWLEDGEMENTS

This collection of ten original self-contained essays on economic and social change in Sri Lanka by American and Sri Lankan academics is the result of a series of University of Maryland at College Park- sponsored group projects to Sri Lanka. Supported by Fulbright- Hays grants from the U.S. Department of Education, university and college faculty visited Sri Lanka during the summers of 1983, 1984 and 1987. The directors for these visits were Valerie Woolston (1983), James Björkman and Marta Axelson (1984), and James Björkman and Paul Groves (1987). During each visit Sri Lankan scholars, from both universities and research institutes, were intimately involved in the program and gave unstintingly of their time by providing local expertise on resources, giving orientation lectures on the social, economic and political aspects of Sri Lankan development, and leading field excursions throughout the southern two-thirds of the island. Some of these scholars, dominantly from the University of Peradeniya, are represented by chapters in this book.

Of the many scholars, administrators and support staff involved in this project there are several who demand special acknowledgement. In Sri Lanka, Stanley Kalpage, Leslie Panditharatne, and the staff of the American Studies Center provided critical help. At the University of Maryland at College Park, special thanks are due to William E. Kirwan (President) for his institutional support and to the following members of the Department of Geography: Vivre Koomanoff, Gavin Keith and Alan Eney of the Computer Graphics Laboratory for producing the maps: Pat Leedham for her extraordinary word processing skills and patience: and to John Townshend, Chair, for providing access to departmental resources. In particular, Kenneth Corey should be commended for his energy and enthusiasm in the initial development of this project. Without his efforts during the early gestation period it is unlikely that this material would have been published.

Thanks are due also to *Urban Geography* and the *International Journal of Group Tensions* for permission to reprint the chapters by Kenneth E. Corey and Kingsley M. de Silva, respectively, which originally appeared in those journals.

Finally, the efforts of John Adams and Ramesh Jain are appreciated. Through the process of editing and publishing they have been unfailingly supportive.

Paul A. Groves
College Park, MD.
October, 1994.

NOTES ON CONTRIBUTORS

James Warner Björkman, educated in political science at the University of Minnesota (B.A. *Summa Cum Laude*, 1966) and Yale University (M. Phil. 1969; Ph. D. 1976), is Professor of Public Policy and Administration at the Institute of Social Studies, The Hague, as well as Professor of Public Administration at Leiden University, The Netherlands. He is also the Executive Director of the International Institute of Comparative Government in Lausanne, Switzerland. Having previously held appointments in Sweden (University of Linköping), England (University of Essex), Pakistan (Institute of Development Economics), India (Institute of Economic Growth) as well as Yale University, he served during 1987-1990 as Director of the American Studies Research Center, Hyderabad, India. His books include *Federal-State Health Policies and Impacts* (1978), *The Politics of Administrative Alienation in India's Rural Development Programs* (1979), *Changing Division of Labor in South Asia: Women and Men in Society, Economy and Politics* (1985), *Fundamentalism, Revivalists and Violence in South Asia* (1987), and *Controlling Medical Professionals: The Comparative Politics of Health Governance* (1988). He has also published over 40 journal articles. During 1985-1990 he conducted a major comparative study of national health policies and politics in South Asia.

Kenneth E. Corey is Dean of the College of Social Science and Professor of Geography and Urban Planning at Michigan State University. His work on Asia began in 1979 when he initiated a research project on planning for the metropolitan area of Seoul, Korea. Since that effort he has returned to Korea and has researched urbanization in Sri Lanka and urban planning processes in Singapore. He was a Fulbright Research Fellow at the Institute of Southeast Asian Studies in Singapore and has taught at Peking

University, the University of Maryland at College Park, University College of Wales at Aberystwyth, the University of Rhode Island and the University of Cincinnati. Currently he is investigating the role of information technology in the development planning of Singapore. He is co-author and co-editor of *The Planning Change*, third edition.

Kingsley M. de Silva is Foundation Professor of the History of Sri Lanka at the University of Peradeniya, Sri Lanka; he was a member of the University Grants Commission, Sri Lanka from 1979 to 1989 and its Vice-Chairman from 1985-89. His publications include *A History of Sri Lanka* (1981), *Managing Ethnic Tensions in Multi-Ethnic Societies; Sri Lanka 1880-1985* (1986) and (with W. Howard Wriggins) *J.R. Jayewardene of Sri Lanka; A Political Biography*, Vol. I 1906-1956 (1983). He is a graduate in History of the University of Ceylon, Peradeniya and holds a Ph. D. from the University of London. He was been a Visiting Fellow in Commonwealth Studies and Visiting Fellow of Clare Hall, Cambridge; and Fulbright Scholar in Residence and Visiting Professor of History at Bowdoin College, Maine.

Kurt Finsterbusch is on the faculty of the Department of Sociology, University of Maryland, College Park. He is currently working on development issues in the Third World and rural America. On Third World development his pubications include (with Jerald Hage) *Organizational Change as a Development Strategy* (1987) and he has edited (with Jasper Ingersol and Lynn Llewellyn) *Methods for Social Analysis in Developing Countries* (1990). His publications on rural development include *Understanding Social Impacts* (1980) and (edited with Lynn Llewellyn and C.P. Wolf) *Social Impact Assessment Methods* (1983).

Paul A. Groves, educated in geography and economics at the University College, London (B.Sc. Econ., 1956) and at the University of California, Berkeley (Ph.D., 1969), is currently on the faculty at the Department of Geography, University of Maryland,

College Park. He has held appointments in Canada (University of Manitoba), Scotland (University of Edinburgh) and England (University of Hull). He was a member of the University of Maryland Group Project Abroad to Sri Lanka in 1983 and was the co-director of a similar group to that nation in 1987. His publications are focussed on the social geography of the American city, migration patterns in Third World countries, and the historical geography of North America. His most recent book is *North America. The Historical Geography of a Changing Continent* (edited with Robert D. Mitchell)

James C. Hanson is a Farm Management and Marketing Specialist for the Department of Agricultural and Resource Economics at the University of Maryland, College Park. He has been involved in designing appropriate educational programs for farmers and students with his current extension appointment and previously as a Lecturer at the Institute of Applied Agriculture, a postsecondary technical school for agricultural training at the University of Maryland, College Park. He visited Sri Lanka as a member of a Fulbright Group Project to study the supply and demand of technical agricultural workers in that country. He has written numerous articles on farm management, agricultural marketing, sustainable agriculture, and extension programs, and is a frequent speaker at farm meetings. He also teaches as a Professorial Lecturer for the School for Advanced International Studies, The Johns Hopkins University, Washington D.C.

Leslie B.L. Panditharatna is currently affiliated with the Ceylon Mineral Sands Corporation, a member of the University Grants Commission, and Professor of Geography at the University of Peradeniya, Sri Lanka, where he formerly held the position of Vice-Chancellor. His research specialty is in Sri Lankan urban-rural studies and he has published extensively on those themes in both Sri Lankan and foreign journals.

G.H. Peiris is Chairman and Professor of Geography at the

University of Peradeniya, Sri Lanka. He has been a visiting teacher/fellow at the University of Western Australia, the University of British Columbia, and the University of Maryland, College Park and has served as a research consultant to several international agencies. His research writings are mainly in the fields of social geography and agrarian affairs and include monographs on *Basic Needs and the Provision of Government Services in Sri Lanka, Irrigation and Water Management in a Peasant Settlement Scheme in the Dry Zone of Sri Lanka,* and *Planning for Rural Development in Sri Lanka* (co-author V.M. Rao).

S.W.R. de A. Samarasinghe is Director of the International Centre for Ethnic Studies, Sri Lanka. He holds a Ph. D. from Cambridge University and was a Takemi Fellow at Harvard University in 1985-86, Visiting Fellow at the Center for International Development and Conflict Management, University of Maryland, College Park in 1986, and Julien and Vernon Cornell Visiting Professor at Swarthmore College, Pennsylvania in 1989-1990. He is the co-editor of *Secessionist Movements in Comparative Perspective and Economic Dimensions of Ethnic Conflicts* and has published widely on Sri Lanka and South Asian economic and political issues.

Vidyamali Samarasinghe, is currently on the faculty of the School of International Service, The American University, Washington D.C. having spent most of her academic career with the Department of Geography, University of Peradeniya, Sri Lanka. She has also held academic appointments at the University of Maryland, College Park and as the Julien and Virginia Cornell Visiting Professor at Swarthmore College, Pennsylvania. She is co-editor of *Women at the Crossroads: A Sri Lankan Perspective* and recently headed a research team investigating the maternal nutrition and health status of Sri Lankan plantation workers.

PART ONE

SETTLEMENT DYNAMICS IN SRI LANKA

Chapter I

THE DEVELOPMENT OF THE SRI LANKAN SETTLEMENT SYSTEM

B.L. Panditharatna
University of Peradeniya, Sri Lanka

This chapter presents an analysis of the salient features, dynamics, development strategies, problems and trends of contemporary settlement in Sri Lanka. This is accomplished by reviewing Sri Lanka's structural features and cultural factors during the ancient and colonial periods with specific attention to their connectivity to the developing settlement pattern.

Sri Lanka is a tropical island, in size about 25,330 square miles, situated at the southern tip of India but separated from it by the Palk Straits. It has a central mass of highlands and mountains where most of the rivers originate and drain radially towards the surrounding lowlands and the coast. Rainfall is the most important element in the island's climate. It is seasonally derived from the Southwest and Northeast monsoons. On the basis of rainfall, the island is divided into a Dry Zone (those areas receiving rainfall of less than 75 inches, occupying about 60% of the nation) and Wet Zone (receving more than 75 inches, mostly confined to the Southwestern parts of the island) (Fig. 1.1).

HISTORICAL BACKGROUND

Sri Lanka's settlement has a rich, varied and continuous history dating back to about 500 B.C. (Mahavamsa), a span of nearly 2500 years. The economy and associated settlement have been subject to three distinct phases of development (i.e., hydraulic,

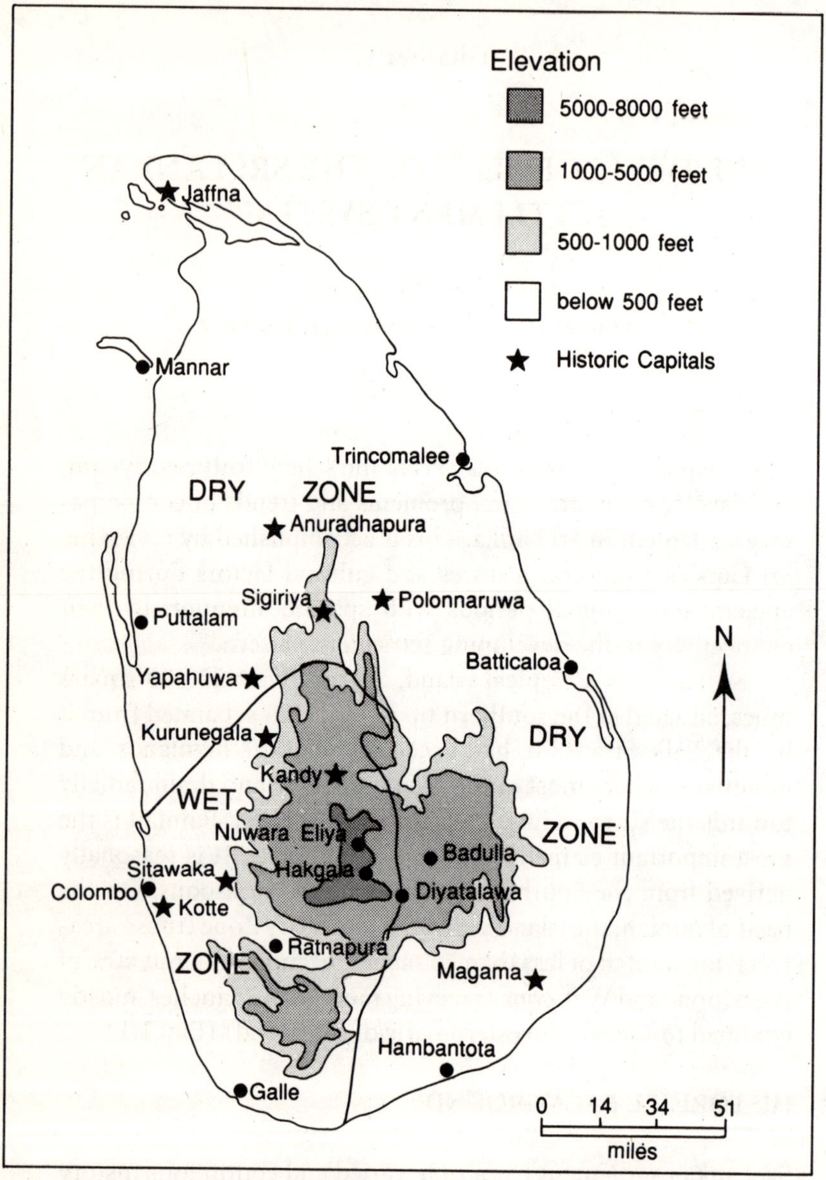

Fig. 1.1 Orientation Map of Sri Lanka

colonial and national) resulting in locational changes in capital cities, core areas and settlement patterns developed in several environmental zones.

During the ancient period (up to 100 A.D.) of *hydraulic civilization*, the settlement pattern spread along the river valleys consequent on the development of the hydraulic infrastructure (i.e., dams and reservoirs) occupying the Northern plain and Southeastern lowlands of the Dry Zone. These were politically organized as the Kingdom of Rajarata centered at Anuradhapura as the first capital city (300-1017) and the Kingdom of Rohuna with Magama as the capital.

Under the rule of the Portuguese (1505-1658) and Dutch (1658-1796) *European colonial powers*, the Dry Zone settlements and the irrigation system declined. Along the coast, port and fort settlements along with trading functions became prominent. Irrigation-based agriculture gave place to rainfed crops such as cinnamon and spices. As a result, the Southwest lowlands became increasingly populated. The British ruled the whole island from the early nineteenth century until independence but the intensity of their administrative efforts decreased from the core to the periphery. Their developmental policies were focused on Colombo as the capital and chief port. Through Colombo the products of the hinterland (tea, rubber and coconut) were exported and manufactured goods imported. Overdevelopment of Colombo and the cash crop producing hinterland and the relative neglect of the Dry Zone rice economy were the inevitable results of this colonial phase of settlement.

A national phase of settlement was ushered in after independence in 1948. National planning was centralized and articulated in various national plans (i.e., The Ten Year Plan, 1959; The Five Year Plan, 1971-76; Public Investment, 1983-87) which emphasized an all-island spatial-sectoral development. The objectives of these plans were to:

(a) reduce the uneven regional development and establish a balance in regional development and population distribution by the resettlement of the Dry Zone.

(b) diversify the economy and settlement by agricultural modernization, crop diversification, and industrialization.

(c) monitor the trends of population growth, urbanization, and suburbanization.

(d) improve and develop rural and estate sector settlement.

Several features of the ancient and colonial settlement have relevance and connectivity to the contemporary settlement. First, the so-called golden age of hydraulic civilization (300-1200) reflected a political system of absolute control of the factors of production (land, labor and capital) coupled with centralized organization management but with implementation decisions effectively decentralized at the regional and local levels. In many respects, the administration of the hydraulic civilization resembled the Wittfogelian model of oriental despotism (Wittfogel, 1957). The present administrative structure based on centralized planning and bureaucratic controls at the regional level resembles the traditional system except that it attempts as far as possible to place decision making and management at the grass roots levels.

Second, the ancient hydraulic infrastructure of river systems, dams, reservoirs, canals, directional canals and field canal systems, provided a model upon which to base modern projects. Restoration of the village *wewas*, rehabilitation of the *purana* villages, the reconstruction of the major irrigation works, resettlement in colony settlements, and even the construction of multipurpose river valley development projects (Gal-Oya, Walawe, Mahaweli, Lunugamvehera and Nilwala) provide examples of linkage between the old and the new. In the Accelerated Mahaweli River Development Project, the ancient dams of the Mahaweli River (Kalinga Nuwara, Minipe, Hattota, Elahera and Angamedilla) and associated irrigation network have influenced the micro and macro aspects of project planning (Madduma Bandara, 1985). For example, the site chosen for the construction of the modern Madura-Oya dam is identical to that of a large ancient earthfill dam. The Mahaweli project in many ways is restructuring the former connections and augmenting the supply of water to the ancient irrigation network. This is all intended to usher in a reactivated phase of contemporary hydraulic civilization.

Third, the location of ancient capital cities, the distribution of central places, and the infrastructure of these settled areas provide useful guidelines and insights for settlement planning and regional development. Anuradhapura, the historic capital city and one of the great Buddhist centers, has been redeveloped into a "Sacred City" and focal "New Town" for the Northern plain. It has the attributes of centrality, historic, religious, cultural and regional importance to potentially develop as a kind of second national capital. Other historic capital cities (Sigiriya, Polonnaruwa, Kandy) and several religious archaeological sites will be key nucleii in modern settlement planning and regional development when restored and developed.

Symbolic of the synthesis of religion and the economy, the traditional settlement had at its base the *gama* with *wewa* and the *dagoba* as its central features (Ganawardena, 1979). In the past, although such villages had functioned as autonomous, agricultural republics (Brohier, 1935), linkages were maintained with the market villages (*niyangamas*), the regional centers (*nuwaras*), and the ports (*patunas*). Anuradhapura (the *aganuware*) as the first capital city was at the apex of the settlement hierarchy; the seat of royality, the sacred city of Buddhism, the center of administrative, military, commercial and institutional functions. Structurally the contemporary settlement retains these features although the economic, institutional and cultural bases have been modernized.

Colombo the typical "colonial city", chosen by the Portuguese as the capital and retained by the Dutch, has faced several changes in its morphology but has retained certain "colonial features" as relic forms in the modern city. Similarly the port-fort towns (Galle, Matara, Negombo, Jaffna, Mannar, Batticaloa, Kalpitiya) retain the ramparts, moats, esplanades and monumental buildings in their redeveloped morphology.

The British improved the infrastructure and broadened the economic base of the urban areas and central places. The salient features of the British settlement system were:

(a) the development of Colombo as the capital city and chief port and its growth as the metropolis.

(b) the development of Trincomalee as a naval base for their Eastern Empire.

(c) the division of the island into nine provinces and twenty districts as the basis for decentralized regional administration and the subsequent growth of the capital cities of these provinces and districts.

(d) the development of the tea and rubber plantations and, as the road and railway network spread, the growth of several junction centers in the Southwest lowlands and Jaffna peninsula rather than in the Dry Zone.

Fourth, religion has always played a significant role in settlement. Buddhism enjoyed the status of a national religion during the ancient period. The *sangha* were not merely the preachers of the *dharma* but were also the privileged advisors to the king and the mediators between the king and society. The *viharas* and temples functioned as centers in the diffusion of learning and the arts (literature, philosophy, art, architecture, sculpture and painting). Although the status of Buddhism was played down during the colonial period, it has reassumed national standing and coexists in harmony with Hinduism, Islam, and Christianity. Hinduism, the religion of the majority of Tamils, is concentrated in the north and east and has influenced Buddhist worship patterns, ritual and ceremonial aspects. The Roman Catholic religion introduced by the Portuguese is concentrated along the West Coast between Moratuwa and Chilaw. Islam is the religion of the Moors (Muslims) and the Malays and is concentrated in the Eastern Province and in urban areas. These four major religions have coexisted throughout the centuries and a degree of ecumenism seems evident. Further, the constitution of Sri Lanka safeguards its citizens from any form of discrimination on the grounds of race, creed, or religion.

Fifth, the geographical distribution of ethnic groups in Sri Lanka's multi-ethnic society is related to historical circumstances. The Sinhalese have been geographically widespread since ancient times in the Kingdoms of Rajarata, Rohuna and later in the Kingdoms of Kotte, Kandy and Sitavaka. Tamils, associated with the Dravidians of South India, inhabited the northern areas and established the Kingdom of Jaffna in the 13th century. The Moors (Muslims) were descendants of the Arabs who had indulged in coastal trade from early times (about 5 A.D.), settled down and intermarried with the local population but retained their ethnic identity as Muslims. The Indian Tamils were brought by the British in the 19th century to work in the estates and are geographically isolated and culturally segregated from both the Sri Lankan Tamils and the Sinhalese of the highlands. Ethnic groups such as the Malays and Burghers are small in number.

CONTEMPORARY SETTLEMENT

Contemporary settlement is classified as rural, estate and urban. The village is the basic unit of rural settlement; of the total national population of 14.85 million, about 10.72 million (72.2%) lived in some 18.500 villages in 1981. Estate settlements accounted for 0.93 million (6.3%), and 135 urban areas contained the remaining 3.2 million (21.5%) (Census of Sri Lanka, 1981). The distribution of the rural, estate and urban population in Sri Lanka's 24 districts is indicated in Table 1.1.

More than 90% of the population live in villages in the districts of Kurunegala, Anuradhapura, Polonnaruwa, Moneragala, Mullaitivu and Hambantota: and more than 70% in Kandy, Galle, Kalutara and Kegalle districts (Fig. 1.2). The estate settlements are confined generally to the plantation districts of Nuwara Eliya, Badulla and Ratnapura. Colombo District is the most urbanized of all districts with 74% of the population living in urban areas. Jaffna has about one-third living in urban areas. Gampaha and Trincomalee Districts' urban population is above the national average of 21.5%. In all the other districts the urban ratio is below the national average (Fig. 1.3). Sri Lanka's population increased at the rate of 1.7% per year during 1971-81. The rural rate of increase was 1.8% per year and urban rate 1.2% per year for the

TABLE 1.1

Population and Settlement Types (Sectors) in Districts, 1981

	Total	Urban		Rural		Estate	
District	No.	No.	%	No.	%	No.	%
Sri Lanka	14,850,001	3,194,879	21.5	10,721,671	72.2	933,451	6.3
Colombo	1,698,322	1,261,998	74.3	427,354	25.2	8,970	0.5
Kalutara	827,189	176,985	21.4	605,686	73.2	44,518	5.4
Kandy	1,126,296	147,436	13.1	848,365	75.3	130,495	11.6
Matale	357,441	37,908	10.6	289,050	80.9	30,483	8.5
Nuwara Eliya	522,219	37,866	7.3	171,696	32.9	312,657	59.8
Galle	814,579	168,120	20.6	625,579	76.8	20,880	2.6
Matara	644,231	71,547	11.1	552,607	85.8	20,077	3.1
Hambantota	424,102	41,416	9.8	381,205	89.9	1,481	0.3
Jaffna	831,112	270,601	32.6	560,476	67.4	35	0.0
Mannar	106,940	14,469	13.5	91,759	85.8	712	0.7
Vavuniya	95,904	18,531	19.3	77,393	80.7	—	—
Batticaloa	330,899	79,565	24.0	251,154	75.9	180	0.1
Amparai	388,786	53,603	13.8	335,183	86.2	—	—
Trincomalee	256,790	83,262	32.4	169,693	66.1	3,835	1.5
Kurunegala	1,212,755	43,898	3.6	1,157,937	95.5	10,920	0.9
Puttalam	493,334	61,774	12.5	428,661	86.9	2,959	0.6
Anuradhapura	587,822	41,675	7.1	544,649	92.7	1,498	0.2
Polonnaruwa	262,753	20,759	7.9	240,110	91.4	1,884	0.7
Badulla	642,893	51,478	8.0	430,071	66.9	161,344	25.1
Moneragala	279,743	6,048	2.2	265,067	94.8	8,628	3.0
Ratnapura	796,468	59,199	7.4	629,700	79.1	107,569	13.5
Kegalle	682,411	53,502	7.8	566,694	83.0	62,215	9.2
Gampaha	1,389,490	386,057	27.8	1,001,392	72.1	2,041	0.1
Mullaitivu	77,512	7,202	9.3	70,240	90.6	70	0.1

Source: Sri Lanka, Department of Census and Statistics. 1985. *Census of Population and Housing 1981*. Colombo: Ministry of Plan Implementation.

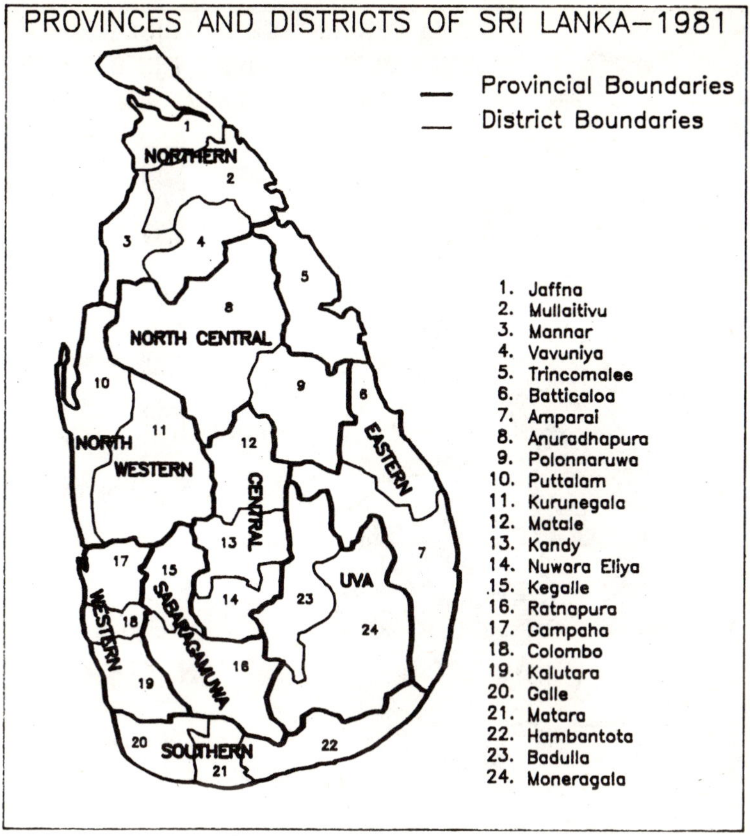

Fig. 1.2 Provinces and Districts: Sri Lanka, 1981

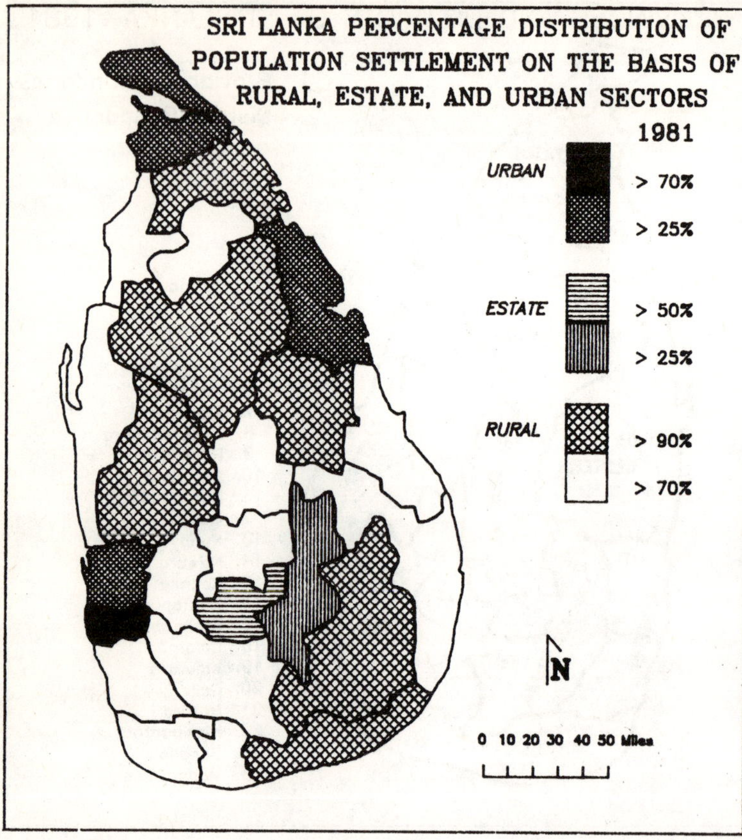

Fig. 1.3 Rural, Estate and Urban Sector Populations: Sri Lanka, 1981

same period. Table 1.2 indicates the growth rates of the district populations for the period 1971-81. The salient points are:

(a) The Southwest coastal districts (Colombo with more than 10% of the national population; Kalutura, Galle and Matara with more than 5%) recorded growth rates below the national average of 1.7% per year.

(b) Very low growth rates (below 1%) were recorded in the Central Highland districts of Kandy, Kegalle, and Badulla.

(c) A negative growth rate (-0.3) was recorded in Nuwara Eliya because of the repatriation of Indian labor to India and outmigration from the district.

(d) The highest growth rates (above 5% per year) were found in the relatively remote but fast developing Dry Zone districts of Mullaitivu, Vavuniya and Mannar (although the population in each of these districts was less than 1% of the national population)

(e) Other Dry Zone districts (Anuradhapura, Polonnaruwa and Moneragala) recorded high growth rates of more than 4% per year.

Sri Lanka's society is multi-ethnic, multi-linguistic and multi-religious. The Sinhalese who speak Sinahala and who are predominantly Buddhist in religion constitute 74% of the total population. The Sri Lankan Tamils who speak Tamil and are mostly Hindu in religion represent 12.6% and the Moors (Muslims) who profess Islam as their religion 7.7%. The Indian Tamil group, mostly Hindu in religion, account for 5.6% of national population; Malays and Burghers are small ethnic groups.

Sinhalese are widespread and are the majority group in all the districts except those in the north (Jaffna, Mannar, Vavuniya, Mullaitivu) and one district in the east (Batticaloa). The Sri Lankan Tamils are concentrated and are the majority group in the north districts (as mentioned above) and Batticaloa. The Indian Tamils are confined to some of the plantation districts and are in the majority in Nuwara Eliya District. The Moors (Muslims) constitute a large proportion of the population in the east (in Amparai, Trincomolee and Batticaloa districts they account,

Table 1.2
Population Distribution in the Districts and Inter-Censal Rates of Growth 1971-1981
POPULATION

District	1971		1981		Average Annual Rate of Growth 1971-1981
	Number	Percentage of Total	Number	Percentage of Total	
Sri Lanka	12, 689,897	100.0	14, 850,001	100.0	1.7
Colombo	1,498,393	11.8	1,698,322	11.4	1.3
Gampaha	1,173,872	9.3	1,389,490	9.4	1.8
Kalutara	729,514	5.7	827,189	5.6	1.4
Kandy	1,096,737	8.6	1,126,296	7.6	–0.3
Matale	314,841	2.5	357,441	2.4	1.4
Nuwara Eliya	541,466	4.3	522,219	3.5	0.3
Galle	735,173	5.8	814,579	5.5	1.1
Hambantota	340,254	2.7	424,102	2.9	2.4
Jaffna	696,664	5.5	831,112	5.6	1.9
Mannar	74,125	0.6	106,940	0.7	3.9

Mullaitivu	43,625	0.3	77,512	0.5	6.3
Batticaloa	256,721	2.0	330,899	2.2	2.7
Amparai	272,605	2.1	388,786	2.6	3.8
Trincomalee	188,245	1.5	256,790	1.7	3.3
Kurunegala	1,025,633	8.1	1,212,755	8.2	1.8
Puttalam	378,430	3.0	493,344	3.3	2.9
Anuradhapura	388,770	3.1	587,822	4.0	4.5
Polonnaruwa	163,653	1.3	262,753	1.8	5.1
Badulla	615,405	4.8	642,893	4.3	0.5
Moneragala	193,020	1.5	279,743	1.9	4.0
Ratnapura	673,558	5.3	796,468	5.4	1.8
Kegalle	642,538	5.1	682,411	4.6	0.6
Vavuniya	60,212	0.5	95,904	0.6	5.1
Matura	586,443	4.6	644,231	4.3	1.0

Source: Sri Lanka, Department of Census and Statistics. 1985. *Census of Population and Housing 1981*. Colombo: Ministry of Plan Implementation.

respectively, for 42%, 30% and 24% of the total population) and are numerically strong in Colombo and Kandy Districts. Malays and Burghers are predominantly in urban areas.

The distribution pattern of ethnic groups identifies areas of geographic concentration (Fig. 1.4). For example, the South Indian ethnic group has remained geographically and culturally isolated from the surrounding populations. With increasing migration and settlement in the developing areas of Trincomalee, Amparai and Vavuniya, ethnic settlements have developed while preserving their own traditions, customs and ethnic identities. The "Kandyan Sinhala enclaved villages" in the plantations or the "Muslim enclaved villages" in the Sinhala country remain relatively isolated and unassimilated with other ethnic groups in the region.

In the urban areas, ethnic identities are preserved despite greater mixing and participation of the groups in different sectors of activity. For instance, Colombo City's population is a mix of ethnic groups (Sinahala 50.1%, Sri Lankan Tamils 22.2%, Moors 21%, Malays 2.2%, Indian Tamils 1.9%, Burghers 1.3% and others 1%) whilst the employment structure is likewise ethnically heterogeneous.

Rural Settlement

The village is ubiquitous and identified by its place name. It occupies an area to which the residents have an attachment and a sense of belonging and share a village tradition, attitude and outlook, factors which matter in the development process and change. For administrative purposes, a village (or groups of villages) was formerly under a headman but he was replaced by the *gramasevaka niladari*; for developmental purposes, the former *Gamsabhawa* was replaced by *Gramodaya mandalaya* (see Appendix 1).

In general, the village economy is characterized by predominantly peasant-scale organization and management of rice agriculture in relatively small-size land holdings (85% less than one

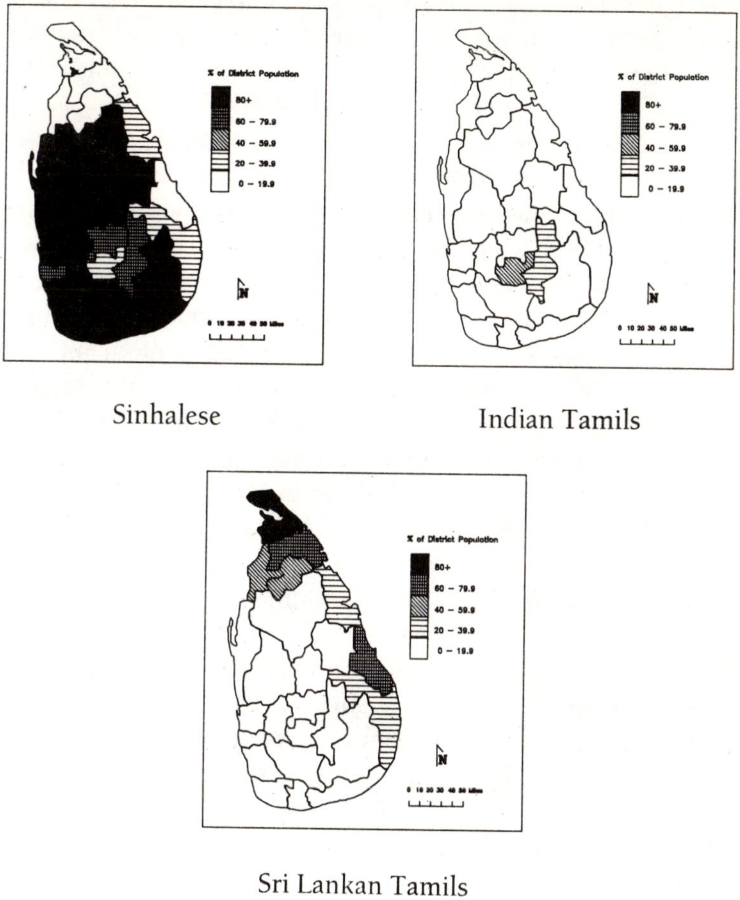

Fig. 1.4 Distribution of Ethnic Groups by District: Sri Lanka, 1981

acre), low levels of technology and capital investment, and agricultural production partly for subsistence and partly to cater to the domestic market combined with petty commerce and retail trading.

Villages vary in size, layout, land use, tenure, population numbers, density, socio-economic and housing characteristics in the different geographical regions. In the Dry Zone, for example, the *purana* village which derives its water from the village *wewa* has a morphology characterized by the *wewa,* rice fields, homestead area, chena and jungle. The colony settlement differs in that it has a more uniform rice field and homestead allotment size (although this varies in the old and new colonies), that land is inalienable, and that the source of water is through directional and field channels. Certain modifications of the layout and orientation of field system and household lot have been introduced in the planned cluster system of hamlets, villages and townships of the areas under the Mahaweli Settlement Authority. In the Jaffna peninsula, villages are different to the Dry Zone types. The underlying miocene limestone does not permit surface drainage and the villages depend on wells for water. The villages are small, compact and contiguous. In the Wet Zone, villages depend on rainfall or the river systems directly for water. In the *deniya-duwa* landscape of the Wet Zone the lowlying areas (the *deniyas*) are under rice and the *duwas* under homesteads and mixed tree crop cultivation (coconut, rubber, spices, homegarden crops, etc.). Along the Southwest coastal lowlands the small, compact, densely populated and contiguous villages are increasingly becoming residential and urbanized. The coast is dotted with fishing settlements in a linear pattern.

In the Central Highlands, the typical riverine Kandyan village has to adjust to the contours of the landscape. The paddy plots occupy the flood plain, the homesteads occupy the higher tier (above the flood level), the low slopes are under homegarden tree crops, and the higher slopes either under pasture or forest. Ribbon development is a characteristic feature along the transportation route system. In the tea plantations, several "enclaved villages" are confined to the valley bottoms with tea occupying the higher slopes.

The estate is involved in the production of tea for export. Tea estate settlement has a distinctive morphology recognizable by the factory and the offices, the superintendent's bungalows, the staff quarters and the "cooly lines" (*sic*) - the residential quarter for the South Indian labor force. In the rubber and coconut estates the settlement is dispersed.

The non-agricultural rural settlements comprise fishing villages located along 1100 miles of coastline and few settlements whose economies are based on the utilization of locally available raw materials such as clay for pottery, coral for lime, cane and reeds for cottage crafts, or specialization in traditional crafts.

Urban Settlement

An urban area in Sri Lanka is not based on any definite criteria as regards the size of population, density, proportion of the male population in non-agricultural occupations or status of civil administration. The Minister of Local Government has the discretion either to create new towns or raise the status of existing ones. As an administrative unit urban areas were hierarchically categorized in 1981 into 12 municipalities, 36 urban councils, and 90 town councils.

The rate of urbanization was about 3.5% per year up to 1971 but decreased to 1.1% per year during the 1971-81 decade. Natural increase of population continued to be the chief factor. Migration increases however were particularly significant in the towns of the Colombo and Gampaha Districts and colonizing Dry Zone areas. Since 1963, the creation of 45 towns and the extension of town limits in three municipalities has also increased the urban population.

Spatially the rates of urbanization vary considerably. Colombo City recorded a growth rate of 2% per year until 1963 which declined to 1% during 1963-71 and fell to 0.4% in 1971-81. A similar decreasing trend has been recorded for four other large Sri

Lankan cities (100,000 + populations). Dehiwala-Mt. Lavinia decreased from 4.2% per year in 1953-63 to 1.3% in 1971-81. During the same periods, Jaffna declined from 2.2% to 1% per year; Kotte from 3.5% to 0.8%; and Kandy from 1.9% to 0.9%. Towns in the Colombo-Gampaha region recorded growth rates of more than 4% per year and Dry Zone towns high rates of above 8% per year.

Three phases can be identified in the Sri Lankan urbanization process. First, a phase of polarization on Colombo City as the capital city and chief port. Second, a phase of depolarization from Colombo City related to the implementation of a policy of decentralized location of industries from Colombo City and the provision of countermagnets through the improvement and upgrading of the institutional infrastructures of regional and district towns. Third, a phase of decentralized urbanization through implementing several counterurbanization measures reflected in (a) the shift of the political capital from Colombo to Sri Jayawardenapura, (b) the devolution of administration by the establishment of district development councils for the 24 districts, (c) the creation of several administrative agencies, namely, the Urban Development Authority, the Greater Colombo Economic Commission, the Central Environmental Authority, and the National Housing Development Authority to regulate, direct, monitor, plan and integrate urban development and (d) Dry Zone development measures reactivating the growth of the ancient cities, central places, and new towns as centers of the evolving agricultural regions.

Colombo, the capital, is the largest city with a 1981 population of 585,776 which represents 18% of the total urban population and 4% of the national population. Five large towns have more than 100,000 in each. Three, Dehiwala-Mt. Lavinia, Kotte and Moratuwa are located in the Colombo metropolitan region while Kandy and Jaffna are capitals of the Central and Northern Provinces respectively; 34 towns have populations between 100,000-20,000; 35 towns have between 20,000 and 10,000 inhabitants, and 59 towns have populations below 10,000. (Table

1.3). The spatial impact of urbanization has resulted in:

(a) Colombo City at the apex of the national urban system performing the highest level functions and services (including those of the capital city and chief port) and acting as the focus of the regional metropolitan area.

(b) Rapidly developing domitory-industrial townships in the Colombo-Gampaha Districts.

(c) Increased suburban growth and the emergence of urbanized villages along the southwest coast and around Kandy and Jaffna.

(d) Reactivated growth of towns in the plantation sector reflecting reorganizational measures in the plantations.

(e) Rapidly developing towns in the Dry Zone. Functionally the urban hierarchical system in this region is characterized by:

   (i) Small towns and junction centers with populations below 10,000 at the lowest order of the hierarchy.

   (ii) Medium-sized towns with populations of 10,000-30,000 performing mid-level to high-level functions, and

   (iii) The large towns, especially the provincial capitals of Kandy and Jaffna.

A large number of small towns widely distributed at route-junctions function as low-order service centers catering to the basic needs of their residential populations and those in their hinterlands. Recently, cinemas, bus-stop facilities, doctor's clinics and the state's low-order offices have enhanced their functional significance.

Medium-sized towns with populations of 10,000-20,000 are mostly in the Dry Zone. A few district and provincial capital towns of the Dry Zone and a large number of towns in the Southwest lowlands have populations of 20,000 to 50,000. These provide the local populations with a wide selection of retail goods, personal and professional services. The public institutions include secondary schools, hospitals, banks, state offices and

TABLE 1.3
Size of Towns (By Population Size), 1953-1981

Categories (Pop. in (000s)	1953 Nos. of Towns	1953 Population	1953 % of Total U.Pop.*	1963 Nos. of Towns	1963 Population	1963 % of Total U.Pop.*	1971 Nos. of Towns	1971 Populations	1971 % of Total U.Pop.*	1981 Nos. of Towns	1981 Populations	1981 % of Total U.Pop.*
500+	—	—	—	1	510,947	25.4	1	563,705	19.8	1	585,776	18.3
100-499.9	1	426,127	34.4	1	111,631	5.5	2	260.093	9.1	5	631,054	19.8
50-99.9	6	383,038	30.9	5	379,265	18.8	5	411,311	14.4	3	195,094	6.1
20-49.9	6	154,727	12.5	18	487,986	24.2	25	781,874	27.5	31	976,957	30.6
10-19.9	15	213,150	17.2	21	278,153	13.8	34	499,561	17.5	35	511,138	16.0
5-9.9	4	29,691	2.4	23	158,280	7.9	30	215,848	7.6	28	199,189	6.2
0-4.9	11	32,400	2.6	30	90,023	4.5	38	114,914	4.1	31	95,671	3.0
All Towns	43	1,239,133	100.0	99	2,016,285	100.0	134	2,848,116	100.0	134	3,194,879	100.0

*U. Pop. = urban population

Source: Sri Lanka, Department of Census and Statistics. 1981. *Census of Population and Housing 1981*. Colombo: Ministry of Plan Implementation.

cinemas. In district and provincial capitals, there is a concentration of mid-level state functions and services such as the *kachcheri* (secretariat) of the government agent and district development council, courts of law, municipal or urban council offices, government hospitals, "A" grade post offices, banks, insurance firms, established secondary schools, junior technical colleges and a variety of commercial, institutional, cultural, secretarial and religious services serving populations of around 120,000-150,000 in the hinterlands of Dry Zone towns and 250-300,000 in the Wet Zone towns.

Kandy and Jaffna, the provincial capitals of the Central and Northern Provinces (with populations of more than 100,000) occupy a third tier but owing to locational, historical, religious and cultural factors perform high-order functions. Dehiwala-Mt. Lavinia, Kotte and Moratuwa although their populations exceed 100,000 do not enjoy the status of high-order functional centers because such functions are subsumed by Colombo.

SETTLEMENT DYNAMICS AND STRATEGIES OF DEVELOPMENT

It is estimated that the population of Sri Lanka in 2001 will be 20 million; the rural component will account for 14 million (70%) and the urban about 6 million (30%). Nearly 12 million (60%) of the population will be in the Wet Zone and 8 million (40%) in the Dry Zone. Mahaweli settlement systems will absorb around 4-5 million of the Dry Zone population.

By 1986, death rates in Sri Lanka had been reduced to 7 per 1000, birth rates to 22 per 1000, and consequently the rate of natural increase was below 2% per annum. Checks on fertility resulting from the rising levels of education among females, the postponement of the age of marriage to about 22-24 years, increasing participation of females in employment, and the successful implementation of family planning policies are likely to decrease birth rates in the future. Continued urbanization and internal migration are likely to be the dominant demographic trends until the end of this century.

By 2001, urban population will almost double (from 3.2 million to 6 million) reflecting substantial natural increases in the towns of the Colombo Region, migration into the Dry Zone towns, and administrative decisions in raising the urbanized villages and rural townships to urban status. This suggests a trend towards a more decentralized pattern the salient features of which will be:

(a) Decentralization from Colombo City as emphasized in the Colombo Master Plan will continue. The Colombo conurbation will be the most urbanized zone with a population of 2 to 2.5 million. Sri Jayawardenapura as the new political capital will develop rapidly as it acquires more institutional functions. Towns in the Colombo, Gampaha and Kalutara Districts (Western Province) will experience rapid growth tied to improvements in their infrastructures and development measures implemented by the Urban Development Authority. Industrialization will be an added stimulus to urban growth, particularly in the export-oriented industrial townships of the Free Trade Zones (Katunayake and Biyagama) and the local market-oriented industrial towns. Promotion measures aimed at stimulating the tourist industry will contribute to the development of the Southwest coastal towns.

(b) An accelerated phase of urbanization in the Dry Zone will be focused on the newly created services cum-agro-industrial based townships of the Mahaweli settlement systems. The old towns of Anuradhapura and Polonnaruwa will be reactivated as administrative, route, historic, religious or archeological centers. Trincomalee will be developed as the port of the East coast and grow as an industrial center. Development of rural agro-based industries tied to rural electrification will stimulate the growth of several junction centers and rural townships.

(c) The devolution of administrative powers to the provinces (Provincial Councils Act), will stimulate growth and expansion of the provincial capitals (excluding Colombo City), district capitals, and several newly created regional administrative centers.

(d) Suburbanization and rural development have been stabilizing forces and will continue to be significant factors in counterurbanization. Suburbanization is conspicuous in the Southwest coastal lowlands and in the environs of the provincial capitals of Kandy, Jaffna and Kurunegala; proximity to places of work, relatively cheap land, availability of regular bus services and access to shopping and community services have all promoted suburban residential growth. Residential land use is characterized by the increasing subdivision of agricultural property into residential lots offered for sale to a proliferating class of state and private sector employees who are eligible for housing loans on concessional terms. Residential quality, however, shows considerable variation in size, quality, and architectural style related to land values, access to work and amenities, and transportation frequency.

Rural Development

Rural development has always been a primary concern of Sri Lanka's policy makers. Some of the earliest developmental measures were directed towards the control of malaria, eradication of endemic diseases, improvement of rural health services, restoration of *purana wewas* and villages, rehabilitation of major irrigation works and associated settlement colonization and village expansion schemes. Several laws (Paddy Lands Act of 1958, Land Reforms of 1972 and 1975) were implemented with the objectives of extending social justice and egalitarianism in the rural sector. In many ways Sri Lanka affords a model for the Third World for the peasants, by extended participation in the production process, have improved their incomes and standards of living.

The present integrated rural development policies, projects and strategies implemented by State agencies (Mahaweli Development Authority, District Development Councils, National Housing Development Authority and several departments of ministries) are directed at:

(a) improving the infrastructure of rural areas through improved roads, water supply, sanitation, housing, education, health and community services;

(b) increasing agricultural productivity and promoting self employment utilizing locally available raw materials;

(c) eradicating poverty, increasing levels of income, and improving standards of living.

The colonization schemes were the principal instrument of Dry Zone development and settlement from 1930 to 1980. In the 1980s, there were 104 major colonization schemes with a total of 100,611 allottees and 382,118 acres developed (Table 1.4).

The Accelerated Mahaweli Development Project, the most ambitious and comprehensive program of land development and settlement undertaken in Sri Lanka, provides irrigable water to 364,000 hectares enabling the settlement of 150,000 families and the capacity to generate 508 MW of hydroelectric power. The Mahaweli new settlement structure is hierarchical, based on the concept of settlement clusters; 100 settler family units to form a hamlet, 4-5 hamlets will be consolidated into a "village," and 4-5 villages will form a "township". A hamlet provides basic amenities such as a primary school and cooperative store; a village serves the other basic needs; and the town is a service center for the population of surrounding hamlets and villages totaling around 2,000-3,000 families (20,000 people) and provides educational, medical, postal, banking and trading services. The state has invited private sector participation in secondary and tertiary sectors to generate employment.

Programs of agricultural modernization are combined with

TABLE 1.4
Settlement and Land Development in Major Colonization Schemes
(as of the end of 1980)

District	Number of Schemes	Number of Allottees	Extent of Land Developed Paddy	Highland
Kandy	1	1,982	5,425	3,454
Matale	4	3,785	7,992	5,290
Nuwara Eliya	1	152	152	152
Hambantota[1]	3	2,127	4,631	1,922
Uda Walave Scheme	1	10,835	n.a	n.a
Kurunegala[2]	9	6,610	15,172	9,631
Puttalam	10	2,358	6,276	7,282
Anuradhapura[3]	9	20,381	52,038	23,806
Polonnaruwa	7	14,687	52,287	24,089
Badulla	9	4,128	9,566	4,996
Monaragala	9	2,114	5,365	2,158
Ratnapura	1	552	1,318	379
Mannar	3	587	1,761	1,174
Vavuniya	4	1,439	4,257	2,510
Mullaitivu	9	5,286	8,812	11,482
Jaffna	9	3,054	8,548	6,134
Trincomalee	6	6,325	18,105	8,938
Batticaloa[4]	8	3,394	11,763	4,819
Amparai[5]	1	10,815	32,643	11,798
ALL DISTRICTS[6]	104	100,611	247,111	135,007

Sources: Land Commissioner's Department
Uda Walave Scheme data, from the Agricultural Research Station at Angunukolapelessa

Notes: 1. Hambantota data exclude those on Uda Walave Scheme.
2. Kurunegala data include the Left Bank unit of the Rajangane Scheme.
3. Anuradhapura data include the Right Bank unit of the Ranjagane Scheme.
4. Parts of the Gal-Oya Scheme located in Batticaloa District are added to the district total.
5. Amparai data refer to those portions of the Gal-Oya Scheme located in that district.
6. There are no 'Major Colonization Schemes' in the Districts of Colombo, Gampaha, Kalutara, Galle, Matara and Kegalle.

the improvement of village infrastructure. Changes in cultivation practices by improved seed selection, water mangement, and the reduction and postharvest losses have increased yields from 25-30 bushels to 40-50 bushels per acre. Further, improvements in rural transportation and marketing, subsidies for inputs, guaranteed prices for rice, institutionalized rural credit facilities and extension services have given an impetus to the farmer to increase production.

The Jaffna farmer has organized the cropping system to market-oriented high price crops such as tobacco, onions, chillies, potatoes, vegetables and fruits and has also mechanized by using kerosene powered pumps to draw water from the wells to irrigate the intensively cultivated small plots. Crop diversification in the plantations has brought the marginal lands under minor crops (spices, fruits and vegetables) and combined about 12,000 hectares allocated to the Kandyan landless peasants in a scheme of highland colonization for homesteads and cash crop cultivation. In general, the agricultural modernization programs have created a sense of self-reliance and viability in the rural sector.

In the estate settlements, a comprehensive development package includes the improvement of conditions in housing, education, health, welfare and employment. The Janavasa program (Ministry of Plantation Industries) proposes to integrate the estate and the village in the plantations by offering greater opportunities to the village to participate in estate activities and combine the estate and the village under one administrative umbrella.

The Integrated Rural Development Programme (IRDP) implemented in 12 relatively underdeveloped and backward districts which are unlikely to benefit from large schemes has as its objectives the improvement of the living standards of the poorest of the poor (household below the poverty level), of backward villages, and of vulnerable groups particularly female-headed households and public assistance recipients. The Janasaviya Program (implemented in stages) provides the organizational framework and financial backing for folk-oriented poverty eradication through self-motivated sustainable activities directed at improving standards of living.

The projects focus on activities based on the utilization of locally available resources to generate imployment and self-employment. Vocational trainging is provided to improve skills in masonry, carpentry, sewing, livestock farming, home gardening and home crafts. The improvement of sanitation particularly water supplies and toilet facilities, the more widespread introduction of family planning, continued efforts aimed at curbing malnutrition, and several non-governmental *shramadana* projects have incrementally improved village life.

In the coastal fishing settlements around 18,000 householders have a similar economic and social status as the rural landless laborers (F.A.O. Report, 1982,) Some 75% of the fishermen (22,000 units) operate with small traditional craft and receive fluctuating incomes. A fishery modernization program has been implemented by the mechanization of craft to replace the traditional outrigger (31/2 ton mechanized craft and fiber glass boats), the adoption of nylon nets, and improved methods and techniques of fishing in order to augment fish production. This is coupled with institutional changes in marketing, trasportation, financing, insurance and welfare aspects. State sponsored and private enterprises associated with the supply of motor machines, boat building and repairs, sales of nets, artifacts and related industries have proliferated.

Levels of education, housing conditions, social status, attitudes and values of the fishermen have improved in the fishing villages. Contrary to the notion of "illiterate fishermen" in the 1950s, the fishermen of the 1980s were literate and receptive to the innovations and challenges of modernizing industry. As mechanization of craft gave them better control of the elements and a sense of security, improved methods produced a better catch and their incomes increased. A new homeowning fishermen class has emerged side-by-side with the traditional land and houseowning class. The state has also improved the infrastructure and welfare services of the fishing villages. The morphology and the socio-economic configuration of the fishing villages are changing rapidly (Panditharatna, 1983).

Housing

Housing units, the dominant land use in any settlement, experienced an increased rate of growth of 2.5% per year for 1971-81 exceeding the population rate of 1.7% per year for the same period. In 1981, there were 2,811,406 housing units for a population of 14,850,001 giving an occupancy rate of 5.2 persons per housing unit (Table 1.5). Urban sector housing increased by 21%, the rural sector by 33.7% while the estate sector decreased by 8.5% during the 1971-81 period (Sri Lanka, Census of Population and Housing, 1981). Three broad house types (permanent, semi-permanent and improvised) based on the principal materials used in the construction of the floor, walls and roof are identified in Sri Lanka. In the rural sector (village) the semi-permanent type with mud walls and cadjan roofs accounted for 56.1% and the improvised type 6.7% in 1981. In the estate sector, semi-permanent types dominated (75.8%) as most of the housing units had mud floors although the walls were of bricks, cabook or cement and the roofs of metal sheets. In the urban sector permanent housing types accounted for 68% of the total (Table 1.6). At the national level the average number of rooms per housing unit was 2.5 (Census of Population and Housing, 1981). In the estate sector it was below the national average with 1.7 rooms per unit. In all the sectors one-third of the housing units were one roomed houses.

The majority of housing units (73.1%) obtained water from wells (which at times are a source of contamination and spread waterborne diseases) and 7% from other sources namely the rivers and *wewas*. At the national level only 17.3% of the housing units were served with pipe water on tap; in the estate sector 65.6% were similarly provided, in the urban sector 46.5% but in the dominant rural sector less than 6% of had access to piped water (Table 1.7). The rural and estate sectors had 34.8% and 28.1% of their housing units without any toilet facilities and even in the urban sector 16.4% units were without such amenities. The construction of pit latrines in the rural and estate sectors (54.5%

TABLE 1.5
Growth of Population and Housing by Sectors, 1971 and 1981

Sector	Population 1971	Population 1981	Population % Increase	Occupied Housing Units 1971	Occupied Housing Units 1981	Occupied Housing Units % Increase
All Sectors	12,689,897	14,850,001	17.0	2,217,478	2,811,406	26.8
Urban Sector	2,848,116	3,194,879	12.2	421,155	509,459	21.0
Rural Sector	8,707,455	10,721,671	23.1	1,558,765	2,084,496	33.7
Estate Sector	1,134,326	933,451	-17.7	237,558	217,451	-8.5

Source: Sri Lanka, Department of Census and Statistics. 1985. *Census of Population and Housing 1981*. Colombo: Ministry of Plan Implementation.

TABLE 1.6
Distribution of Occupied Housing Units by Type by Sectors, 1971-1981

		1971 Number	1971 %	1981 Number	1981 %
All Sectors	Total	2,217,478	100.0	2,811,406	100.0
	Permanent	785,949	35.4	1,173,995	41.8
	Semi-Permanent	1,271,232	57.3	1,457,329	51.8
	Improvised	160,297	7.2	180,078	6.4
Urban Sector	Total	421,155	100.0	509,459	100.0
	Permanent	264,787	62.9	346,623	68.0
	Semi-Permanent	118,368	28.1	124,013	24.3
	Improvised	38,000	9.0	38,820	7.6
Rural Sector	Total	1,558,765	100.0	2,084,496	100.0
	Permanent	492,700	31.6	776,450	37.2
	Semi-Permanent	950,252	61.0	1,168,549	56.1
	Improvised	115,813	7.4	139,496	6.7
Estate Sector	Total	237,558	100.0	217,451	100.0
	Permanent	28,462	12.0	50,922	23.4
	Semi-Permanent	202,612	85.3	164,767	75.8
	Improvised	6,484	2.7	1,762	0.8

Source: See Table 1.5.

TABLE 1.7
Percentage Distribution of Occupied Housing Units by Source of Water Supply by Sectors, 1971 and 1981

Source	All Sectors		Urban Sector		Rural Sector		Estate Sector	
	1971	1981	1971	1981	1971	1981	1971	1981
Piped water on Tap	20.1	17.3	45.3	46.5	4.8	5.1	74.7	65.6
Well	68.8	73.1	50.0	48.7	81.9	84.5	15.4	20.4
River, Tank or other source	8.9	7.0	2.0	1.1	11.0	8.5	7.3	5.8
Not Stated	2.3	2.7	2.1	3.7	2.3	1.9	2.1	8.1
Total	100.0	100.0	100.0	100.0	100.0	100.0	100.0	100.0

Source See Table 1.5.

and 32.5% respectively) and water seal type (17.5% in the rural sector in 1981) have improved the sanitary conditions in those areas. In the urban sector, flush toilets accounted for only 15.6%, water seal type 38.9% and bucket type 8.8% in 1981. (Table 1.8).

The majority of housing units (82.4%) continue to use kerosene for lighting despite the expansion of rural electrification to some 3500 villages. Even in the urban sector only 45.9% of the housing units have electricity; the rural and estate sectors had only 8.3% and 5.6% respectively. Firewood is the fuel used by 94.1% of the households for cooking; kerosene is used by only 2.3%. Use of firewood poses a greater fire-hazard in relatively crowded urban housing than in rural areas.

Since the 1980s housing has received special attention in the *Gamudava* movement, which has two aspects; the *Model Villages* and the *One Million Housing* program. There are currently more than 400 model villages. In its early stages, houses were supplied to the needy with the supporting infrastructure but, as the program gained momentum, the concept of the self-reliant homebuilder with the state providing only technical advice and limited financial support has been introduced. The concept is similar to Gandhi's *Gamraj*, "the need to develop the country by developing the village". The "One Million Housing" program involves rural, urban, Mahaweli area and private housing and attempts to develop a sense of individual civic consciousness and interest in the potential houseowner so that his own efforts are maximized and he expects minimum State support and intervention.

Despite considerable improvements in the socio-economic conditions and the morphology of the settlement, there is evidence of poverty although in Sri Lanka this is difficult to quantify as data on rural and urban informal sector incomes are not available. The farmers and those self-employed in the urban informal sector often report no income although they manage their homes, eat, buy clothes, attend religious services, make pilgrimages to Anuradhapura and Kataragama, and spend on the social commitments of the family (puberty, marriage, death and

TABLE 1.8
Percentage Distribution of Occupied Housing Units by Type of Toilet by Sectors, 1971 and 1981

	All Sectors		Urban Sector		Rural Sector		Estate Sector	
Type of Toilet	1971	1981	1971	1981	1971	1981	1971	1981
Flush toilet	6.7	4.8	22.8	15.6	2.2	2.1	8.2	4.9
Water Seal	14.3	21.9	19.2	38.9	9.9	17.5	33.9	24.2
Pit Type	38.8	37.9	18.3	17.0	44.4	43.5	38.2	32.3
Bucket Type	4.8	2.0	19.4	8.8	1.0	0.3	4.1	2.1
None	34.3	30.9	19.1	16.4	41.5	34.8	13.4	28.1
Unspecified	1.2	2.5	11.3	3.4	1.0	1.7	2.2	8.5
Total	100.0	100.0	100.0	100.0	100.0	100.0	100.0	100.0

Source: See Table 1.5.

almsgivings). Absolute poverty is absent as the basic needs of food, primary education and health are provided by the State. However, nearly four million or about 22% of the population are in receipt of food stamps. On the other hand the physical quality of life index (PQLI) is above average for a natíon like Sri Lanka with a low per capita income of $400 per year (World Development Report, 1989). Nevertheless there are substantial differences within the nation. On the basis of twelve major socio-economic indicators for selected districts, Jaffna District was above average in all criteria except water supply; Nuwara Eliya and Kandy were below average for housing, nutrition, infant and child mortality; Galle and Kurunegala were adequate in respect of all the criteria and Batticaloa District fared below average as regards most of the criteria (Table 1.9).

PROBLEMS AND TRENDS

Land hunger is one of the most serious problems. In the Dry Zone, since colony allotments are inalienable, the possession and ownership of land by the second generation poses several questions. If the land allotments are given to either the first son or any one son or any one descendant of the original allottee, what are the prospects for other descendants of the second generation? Will there be sufficient irrigable land available to be offered or will the secondary and tertiary sector activites develop fast enough to absorb them? If the parcellation of land in the allotments is permitted among the heirs of the original allottees, will it result in excessive subdivision reducing with a reduction in the viability of the holdings?

In the plantation sector, the land problem has two dimensions. First, the claims of the Kandyan peasantry for land on the basis of displacement from their traditional homelands consequent on British land policy is compounded by population increases and the recent dislocations of villages caused by earth slips and landslides. Second, the inevitable increasing demand for land for homesteads from the domiciled South Indian ethnic

TABLE 1.9

Status of Selected Districts in Relation to some Major Socio-Economic Indicators, 1979
(C = Average, C+ Better than average, C- = Worse than average)

		Jaffna	Batticaloa	Kandy	N' Eliya	Galle	Kurunegala
1.	Infant Mortality	C+	C-*	C-	C-	C	C+
2.	Child death rate	C+	C-	C-	C-	C+	C
3.	Nutritional levels	C+	C-	C	C-	C+	C
4.	Life Expectancy	C+	C-	C-	C-	C+	C+
5.	Literacy	C+	C-	C	C	C+	C+
6.	Nature of Housing	C+	C-	C-	C-	C+	C
7.	Owned Housing	C+	C+	C-	C-	C+	C+
8.	Water Supply (Tap and Well)	C-	C-	C+	C+	C	C
9.	Electricity	C+	C+	C+	C+	C+	C-
10.	Toilets	C+	n.a	C+	C+	C	C
11.	Primary School enrollment	C+	C-	C+	C+	C+	C+
12.	Primary School dropout	C+	C-	C+	C+	C+	C+

* Batticaloa Infant Mortality Rate is recorded at 35.5 in 1979, a significant improvement over 1977 (50.8) and 1978 (45.6).

Source: Sri Lanka, Dept. of Census and Statistics. 1983. Socio-Economic Indicators of Sri Lanka. Colombo: Ministry of Plan Implementation.

group who are presently housed in the "cooly (sic)" line settlements. With the high rates of natural population growth, together with increases in the levels of education, political consciousness and bargaining power, their demands for land, employment, and participation in political, social, and administrative decision-making will produce inevitable difficulties.

In the urban and suburban areas, housing will continue to be a civic problem despite the successful implementation of several state programs and policies. It continues to be a problem in Colombo City where nearly one-third of the city's residents live in substandard houses. In the large towns, slums and shanties have spread quickly and encroached on public property adversely affecting the urban environment. The present economic circumstances appear to reduce the likelihood of a broad based house-owning urban proletariat and increase the probability that urban housing will continue to remain a reality for an exclusive bourgeois domain.

The infrastructural facilities and services in urban areas namely water, sewerage, electricity, and garbage disposal cannot meet increasing demands and are excessively overloaded. The state has been responsible for financing these infrastructures as the local tax bases have been relatively insufficient. But as state resource allocations for development are based on priorities, it appears that urban development may not be placed high on the priority list.

The ethnic problem has assumed crisis proportions, almost a civil war between the majority Sinhalese and the minority Sri Lankan Tamils, costing the state nearly 25% of its total budget for defense and security and seriously affecting the life and economy of the north and east areas, in particular, and the entire country in general. Provincial autonomy confers devolution of power to the provinces to manage land settlement, colonization, agriculture, industry, internal civic affairs such as education, health, police and all other local matters. New settlements however have to be based on the ethnic ratios of the respective localities as registered by the Census of 1981. Although provincial autonomy may be presented as an acceptable strategy to settle the ethnic problem, the possibility that it may also lead to increasing provincialism, regionalism, communalism and other fissiparous tendencies impairing the development of a Sri Lankan identity cannot be ruled out.

If peace can be established and the country restored to normalcy, the positive developmental trends of the past decade auger well for the future. The successful implementation of a) developmental efforts in agricultural, industrial, urban and rural sectors: b) population policies resulting in decreasing rates of growth; c) improvements in the quality of life and standard of living; and (d) advances in education, health, welfare, mass media and communications, provide Sri Lanka with a solid economic foundation for development. With its experience as a model democracy and welfare state since independence and with its highly literate, politically conscious population and relatively efficient bureaucracy, Sri Lanka should be able to establish a balanced, viable and stable economy, and institute harmonious relationships between the different ethnic groups.

REFERENCES

Madduma Bandara, C.M. 1985. Catchment Ecosystems and Village Tank Cascades in the Dry Zone of Sri Lanka. A Time-Tested System of Land and Water Resource Management in *Strategies for River Basin Management*. ed. J. Lundqvist, U. Lohm and M. Falkenmark. Lancaster: D. Reidel.

Brohier, R.L. 1935. *Ancient Irrigation Works in Ceylon*, Vol. I, II, III. Colombo: Government Press.

Gunawardena, R.A.L.H. 1979. Robe and Plough: Monasticism and Economic Interest in Early Medieval Ceylon in *The Assoc. of Asian Studies Monograph Series No. 35*, Tucson: University of Arizona Press.

Panditharatna, B.L. 1983. The Negombo Fisherman: A Study of the Impact of Mechanization of Craft on Rural Change and Development, *13th Quinquennial Commonwealth Universities Congress*, Birmingham: University of Birmingham.

Sri Lanka, Department of Census and Statistics. 1981. *Census of Population and Housing*, Colombo: Ministry of Plan Implementation.

United Nations, F.A.O. 1982. *Agrarian Reform and Rural Development in Sri Lanka*. Rome: F.A.O

Wittfogel, K. 1957. *Oriental Despotism*. New Haven: Yale University Press.

World Bank. 1989. *World Development Report*. New York: Oxford University Press.

APPENDIX I

English rendering of words italicized in the text
(in alphabetical order)

aganuwara:	capital city
dagoba:	a Buddhist religious building (dome shaped)
deniya:	low lying wet areas suitable for rice cultivation
dharma:	docterine (Buddhism)
duwa:	dry upland areas like islands suitable for homesteads and home garden crops
gama:	village
gamsabhawa:	village council
gamudava:	village reawakening movement
gramsevaka niladari:	village service officer
gramodaya mandalaya:	council of villages
niyangama:	market village
nuwara, nagaara:	town
patuna:	port
purana:	ancient
sangha:	Buddhist monks
vihara:	Buddhist temple
wewa:	reservoir or tank

Chapter II

URBANIZATION AND MIGRATION: PATTERNS AND PROCESSES

Paul A. Groves
University of Maryland, College Park

Sri Lanka, as measured by economic, social and demographic indicators, has a distinctive place in the economic development literature (Vining, 1985: Sen, 1981). Within the context of the low-income economies, those identified by the World Bank in 1983 as having a GNP (Gross National Product) per capita of less than $400, Sri Lanka has experienced (a) a decline in the primacy of Colombo since 1963, (b) only modest increases in the level of urbanization from 1953 to 1981, (c) a major rural-urban migration to Colombo but an even stronger migration stream destined for the colonized rural Dry-Zone districts of Anuradhapura and Polonnaruwa (Fig. 2.1), and (d) a continued improvement in "the physical quality of life"; an indicator which places Sri Lanka above its low-income economy cohort (Table 2.1). "In terms of relation with per capita GNP, Sri Lanka's actual value of i) life expectancy, ii) adult literacy, iii) infant mortality, and iv) fertility, all lie comfortably away from their expected values...Sri Lanka's record in removing poverty and providing a higher quality of life is quite remarkable" (Sen, 1981, 301).

The unusual relationship between Sri Lanka's low per capita GNP and physical quality of life can be more fully appreciated by examining one indicator - life expectancy. Of the 71 countries identified in 1983 as low or lower middle-income (per capita GNPs $1,640 to $ 6,850) only nine exceeded the average life expectancy level of Sri Lanka's population (World Bank, 1985, 174-175). Using the life expectancy indicator, Sri Lanka is

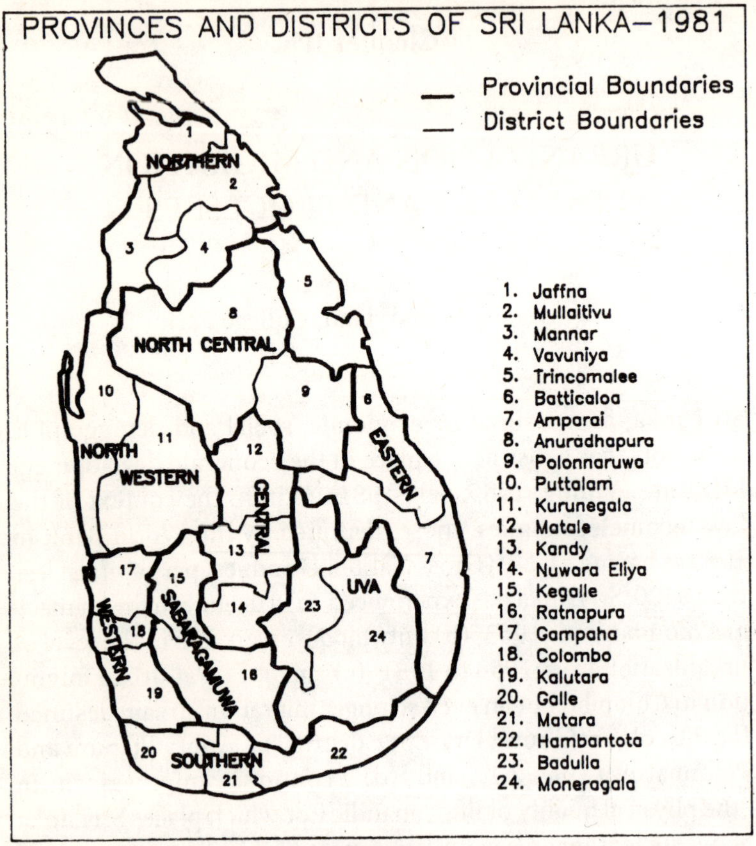

Fig. 2.1 Provinces and Districts: Sri Lanka, 1981.

TABLE 2.1.
Basic Demographic and Economic Indicators: Sri Lanka and Selected Areas

	Population (millions) mid-1983	GNP per capita ($s) 1983	Life expectancy at birth (years) 1983	Crude birth rate per 1000 population (1983)	Crude death rate per 1000 population (1983)	Urban population average annual growth rate (per cent)		Urban population as percentage of total population		Average annual growth of population (per cent)	
						1965-73	1973-83	1965	1983	1965-73	1973-83
Sri Lanka	15.4	330	69	27	6	2.0	1.7	20	26	3.4	2.9
India	733.2	260	55	34	13	2.3	2.3	18	24	4.0	4.2
Burma	35.5	180	55	38	13	2.3	2.0	21	29	4.0	3.9
Bangladesh	95.5	130	50	42	16	2.6	2.4	6	17	6.6	7.6
Pakistan	89.7	390	50	42	15	3.1	3.0	24	29	4.3	4.3
Low-Income Economies[a]	583.0	200	51	43	16	2.6	2.6	13	21	5.2	5.0

[a] Countries with GNP per capita less than $ 410 in 1983 (excluding China and India).

Source: *World Development Report 1985*

comparable with economies where per capita GNP is five to twenty times greater. It should also be noted that within Sri Lanka disparities between districts (with the notable exception of Nuwara Eliya with its high concentration of Indian Tamil population) are modest by Third World standards. This phenomenon is usually explained by the high rates of public expenditure in rural districts (Moore, 1984, 103) and, concomitantly, by the relatively sophisticated social infrastructure and effective delivery system of social welfare benefits (Samarasinghe, 1984, 4).

A further effect of such public expenditure allocations is the very low rate of net rural-urban migration since independence (1948) when compared with other low-income economies. Sri Lanka is similar to most developing countries in that a significant migration to its primate city (Colombo) has occurred since 1946. However, it is not as powerful a stream as is found in other Third World nations. An extreme example is presented by South Korea. A national population increase of 16 million between 1955 and 1980, created a 9 million population increase in Seoul and the surrounding province (Vining, 1985, 1). Thus, while Colombo and its suburbs have experienced modest population increases from 825 thousand (1963) to 1.1 million (1981), their proportionate share of the total Sri Lankan population has declined from 7.8% to 7.1% over the same period (Mendis, 1981, 28). A far rarer phenomenon for developing countries is the presence of other, even stronger, migration flows. The Sri Lankan government since independence has placed considerable emphasis on public investment in peasant agriculture. Irrigation systems, many of ancient origin, that had fallen into disrepair have been rehabilitated and new land brought under cultivation. By 1953, 48,000 hectares of land had been colonized in the Dry Zone by close to 17,000 families (Farmer, 1957, 165). Between 1953 and 1968, a further 71,000 hectares in the Dry Zone had been colonized by an additional 43,000 families. As a result of such long-term colonization schemes and the recent impact of the Accelerated Mahaveli Project, the Dry Zone has experienced a lifetime inmigration which exceeds that of Colombo. Based on 1981 data (Sri Lanka,

Census of Housing and Population, 1982), the Colombo region (Fig. 2.2) has experienced a net lifetime inmigration of 206, 000 (inmigrants 463,000, outmigrants 257,000) while the Dry Zone attracted a net lifetime migration of 458,000 (601,000 inmigrants, 144,000 outmigrants).

Thus, two countervailing migration forces have been operating in Sri Lanka. First, in line with the general experience of less-developed countries, there has been a significant migration stream to the capital city of Colombo. Second, unlike most developing countries, a powerful rural-to-rural migration stream to the Dry Zone is identifiable, with the Wet and High Country Zones experiencing heavy outmigration.

Sri Lanka, therefore, exhibits less urban bias than most countries of similar economic status. Government policy has narrowed traditional urban and rural disparities by "emphasizing equality in development and thereby paying particular attention to agricultural-rural development" (Mera, 1982, 187). This has been reinforced by the lack of dramatic structural change in the Sri Lankan economy. The percentage of the labor force in agriculture has declined minimally since 1960 from 56% in that year to 54% by 1981. Over the same period, the proportion of gross domestic product accounted for by agriculture declined by only five percentage points to 27% (World Bank, 1985, 178). Thus, structural change toward a more strongly industrial and service-oriented economy with the potential for more urban employment and urban growth has been missing. Against this background, this chapter will examine in turn 1) the role of Colombo in the Sri Lankan urban system, 2) the pattern of migration in Sri Lanka, and 3) the structural and spatial characteristics of Sri Lankan urbanization.

COLOMBO

The traditional role of Colombo as the major dominating urban area of Sri Lanka is linked to the development of the plantation economy under a colonial administration. While coffee, as a

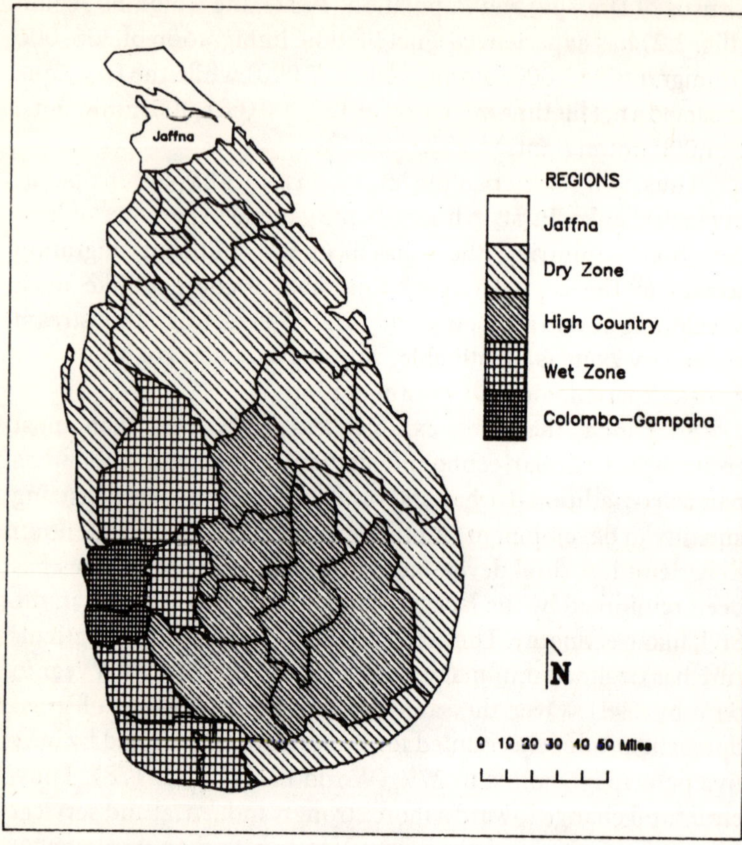

Fig. 2.2 Regional Groupings of Districts: Sri Lanka, 1981.

plantation crop, was eradicated by disease in the 1870s, the plantation crops of today - tea, rubber and coconut - were the keystones of that economy by the early twentieth century. Dependence of such products on overseas markets required efficient transportation to Colombo and from Colombo to foreign ports. Thus, trading, administrative, and service functions were strongly concentrated in Colombo from the early days of British rule to independence (1948). The dominant role of Colombo in the Sri Lankan urban system is clearly identified in the pattern of transportation networks. The development of road and rail networks displayed a marked bias towards the plantation districts and Colombo but the latter was the focus for each system. Colombo as a primate city in a developing country shares the general characteristics of such cities. They are "seaboard cities - points of contact with overseas metropolises, sites of power of former colonial administrations, inlets of modern influence and technology, and at the same time, outlets from the interior of the country" (Brutzkus, 1975, 635).

That Colombo is a primate city is not in dispute (Table 2.2). The primacy index attributed to Jefferson (1939) measures the relationship between the largest city (invariably the capital city) and the next largest urban place. This has been modified by Berry (1961) whose calculations compare the largest city against the total of the next four largest cities. The index, whether using Jefferson's or Berry's methods, identifies the same general trend in Colombo's relationship to other Sri Lankan cities. Both indexes identify the highest level of primacy in the 1960s with a significant reduction in primacy since 1971. The primacy level in 1981 is less than in 1946. Colombo, by this measure at least, is experiencing declining dominance over the Sri Lankan urban system; whether this trend will continue is an open qustion.

The decline in primacy of the Colombo core region is distinctive within an Asian context. The metropolitan regions of South Asia have exhibited growth rates equal to or greater than the growth rates of their national populations from 1950 to the present. In three of the four inter-censal periods since 1946

(1963-71 being the exception), the Colombo region (Colombo and Gampaha Districts) experienced lower than national rates of growth (Vining, 1985, 498). "Outside of the communist bloc countries, such as Cuba, North Korea, Vietnam and Kampuchea, no country in the developing world besides Sri Lanka has experienced long-term deconcentration away from its core region...only Sri Lanka has managed to combine a solar energy-based economy (emphasizing tea, rubber and coconut production) with a relatively adequate standard of living throughout the national territory, without developing a manufacturing base with all of the attendant ills of population concentration and urban primacy" (Vining, 1985, 508).

TABLE 2.2

Sri Lanka: Primacy, 1946-1981

Date	Jefferson Index	Berry Index
1946	9.9	3.0
1953	9.1	3.1
1963	10.9	3.4
1971	10.4	3.6
1981	7.8	2.4

*Primacy measures use Colombo plus suburbs as primate 'city'.

Source: Samarasinghe, 1982 and Sri Lanka, Department of Census and Statistics. 1981. *Census of Population and Housing 1981.* Colombo: Ministry of Plan Implementation.

Within the Colombo metropolitan area (Colombo City plus suburbs) differential growth has occurred. Since 1963, the population of Colombo City has increased by 74,000, while the suburban population experienced a 156,000 person addition (Mendis, 1981, 28). Suburban growth has been encouraged by an overly-congested Colombo City, availability of cheap public transportation, relatively inexpensive suburban land, and the expansion of an industrial sector northwards to Kochchikade and southwards to Aluthgama. The Colombo metropolitan area accounted for a smaller percentage of the total national population in 1981 as compared with 1963. Nevertheless, one of every three residents of Sri Lanka lived in the Colombo metropolitan area in 1981. The pattern, therefore, is one of reducing primacy (though overall dominance), and more rapid growth of suburbs versus city.

The unique character of Colombo's declining primacy together with a more general characteristic of suburban growth does not mean than Colombo has escaped the problems of the Third World city. Housing has been one of the city's major problems. In Colombo, 257,000 people (44% of the city population) live in substandard housing, classified as either shanties or slums (Urban Development Authority, 1981). The 1981 survey identified nearly 16,000 shanties and 17,000 slums. Slums are located generally in the inner portions of the city and represent deteriorated housing. Shanties are built of any available material (metal sheets, jute, plants) and constructed by unauthorized occupation of private or public land. These structures are found mostly on the periphery on the city. Both types of housing have poor (or non-existent) sanitary facilities and are overcrowded. While the overall occupancy rate for housing has declined from 7.8 persons per housing unit in 1971 to 6.8 in 1981, the rate for substandard housing remained in 1981 at 7.8 (Urban Development Authority, 1981). Given such housing conditions, the incidence of poverty is high. It is estimated that 19% of Colombo's households have incomes that place them below the poverty line (Rs 100/- per capita per month) and that an additional 30% operate at minimal subsistence levels (Panditharatne, 1985, 24-5). In addition, substandard housing units have the lowest frequencies of electricity, piped water and flush toilets.

Decreasing rates of concentration in the primate urban center sets Sri Lanka apart from most developing nations of the world. It has been argued that when developing countries pass a threshold of development (identified as a per capita GNP of c. $ 4,000 in 1980) there is a slowing in the rate of population redistribution to the core urban centers (Vining, 1985, 508). Clearly Sri Lanka does not belong to this group with its low per capita GNP in 1983 of $330 (Table 2.1). Rather, the decline in Colombo's primacy is the result of dispersed production, equality of access by the population to physical quality of life factors, modest structural changes in the economy during the past three decades, and lack of industrial development. The latter has traditionally been linked with urbanization yet Sri Lanka's industrial base is weak and its relative absence tends to reduce the potential for population concentration.

MIGRATION

Changes in the size and distribution of the Sri Lankan population are a function of differential rates of natural increase between areas, migration across the national borders, and migration within the country. It is the latter of these components that is addressed most fully but brief comments on the other two factors are necessary.

Crude death rates exhibit smaller differences than crude birth rates between rural and urban Sri Lanka. While for the nation the crude birth rate in 1983 was about 27 per 1,000 and the crude death rate 6 per 1,000 (a 2.1% annual increase in population), for Colombo the rates in 1980 were 19 and 7 producing an annual rate of increase of only 1.2% (Table 2.1 and Panditharatna, 1985, 26). Rural areas exhibit higher rates of natural increase than do the larger urban centers and this translates into generally higher rates of natural increase in the Dry Zone districts (Abeysekara, 1980b, 65-6).

Migration of Sri Lankans seeking employment, rather than education, outside of the country is a comparatively recent phenomenon which started in the later 1960s (Korale, 1983, 1). Flows of professional manpower acclerated in the 1970s. Short-term migration to the Middle East, particularly Saudi Arabia, by unskilled and semi-skilled male and female labor is of more recent origin. It is estimated that in 1978, close to 20,000 Sri Lankans were employed in the Middle East earning salaries of from 5-15 times their potential earnings in Sri Lanka (Ruhunage, 1979, 1-11); by 1981, the number had increased to 58,000 (Korale, 1981, 2) and by 1988 to approximately 200,000 (Institute for Society and Religion, 1988). In 1988, some 70% of Sri Lankans in the Middle East were maids earning up to 30 times more than their home-based counterparts and only tea brought in more in foreign earnings than the repatriation of salaries of such workers. The migration of such Sri Lankans to the Middle East has provided, therefore, a considerable source of much needed foreign exchange; a source dramatically terminated as a result of the Persian Gulf War.

The dominant factor in population redistribution is internal migration. The internal migration data for this study are of two types: a) lifetime migration data derived from the 1981 Census of Population and Housing, and b) 1971-81 migration by Ukwatta (Ukwatta, 1982). It is important to recognize that the first data set is consistent and accurate; the second data set is derived from calculations using place-of-birth, vital statistics, or forward survival ratio techniques and there is a fairly large variation in the estimates arrived at by these methods (Vamathavan, 1961). Greater emphasis in the analysis is placed on lifetime migration streams as providing the most accurate picture possible. It should be noted that this approach hides any inter-censal migrations, as well as seasonal movement from the Wet to the Dry Zone by migratory labor (Crooks and Ranbanda, 1981).

While migration flows are of great importance in redistributing the population of developing countries overall levels of migration are often lower than in the western world. In 1981, the percentage of the Sri Lankan population residing outside their district of birth was only 15.6. In the United States, one of the most mobile societies in the world, almost one-half of the population does not live in their state of birth.

Lifetime migration streams in Sri Lanka for 1981 were organized initially by regions (Fig. 2.2). These regions attempt to reflect climate (particularly the division between Wet and Dry Zones), topography, and, in the case of Jaffna, unique ethnic composition. The lifetime migration flows between these regions are comprised, in all cases, of the reciprocal movement of people. For example, the Colombo region was the lifetime destination of 462,885 people but was also the origin of 256,577 persons who migrated to other parts of Sri Lanka. Even those zones, therefore, with high net inmigration levels (Colombo and the Dry Zone) or that experienced net outmigration (Wet Zone, High Country and Jaffna) had both incoming and outgoing populations (Table 2.3). Migration flows between the five designated zones (Table 2.3) and the net migration flows and population totals by zone for 1981 (Table 2.4) more clearly define the dominant migration flows.

The inmigrant zones are the Dry Zone and Colombo in that order of importance. The Dry Zone in 1981 had a net inmigration flow of 457,251, whilst Colombo's inmigration level stood at 206,308. The major zones providing migrants to the Dry Zone were the Wet Zone and High Country, with Colombo and Jaffna being of considerably lesser significance. This indicates that such flows are predominantly rural to rural in nature. Migrants to Colombo came from the same major zones of origin that fed the Dry Zone but this flow was dominantly a rural to urban one. The impact of such migration on population distribution is evident. The population of Sri Lanka grew by 2.1 million between 1971 and 1981; 51% of that population increase took place in the Dry Zone, with Colombo accounting for only 8% (Table 2.4). This evidence supports a more powerful argument than has hitherto been made concerning the attraction of the Dry Zone for migrants and the decreasing strength of Colombo as a migrant destination.

A finer-grained analysis can be undertaken by mapping the net migration levels for 1981 by district (Fig. 2.3). As of 1981 there were 24 districts in Sri Lanka, an increase of two over 1971. It should be noted that changes in district boundaries make pre-1981 and 1981 comparisons difficult, particularly in the High

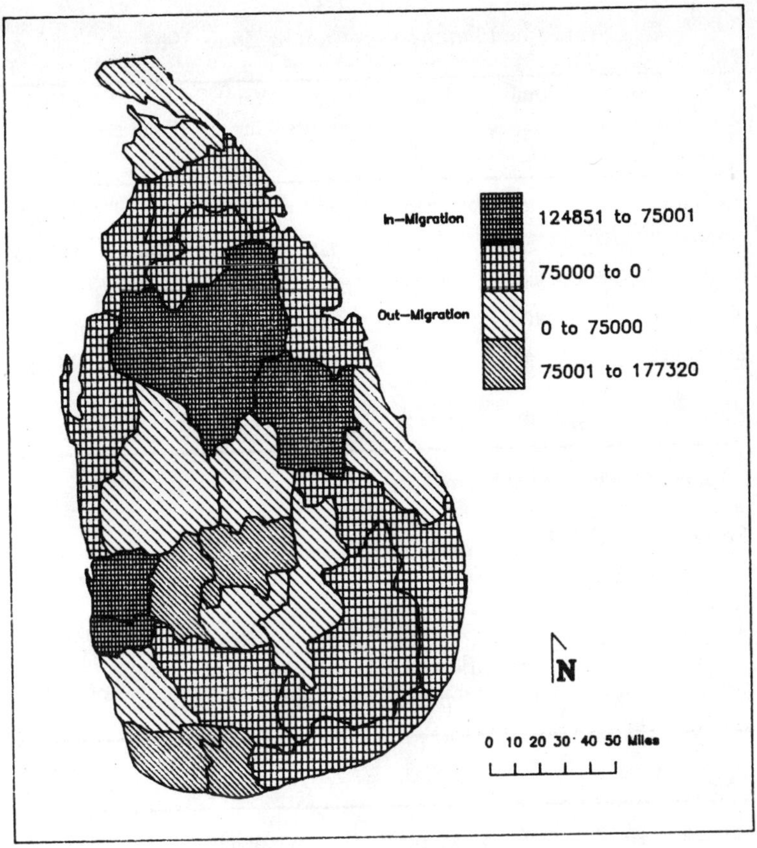

Fig. 2.3 Net Lifetime Migration by District: Sri Lanka, 1981.

TABLE 2.3
Sri Lanka: Lifetime Migration by Zone, 1981

Origin \ Destination	Colombo	Jaffna	High Country	Wet Zone	Dry Zone	Totals
Colombo*	—	3,792	52,496	101,811	98,478	256,577
Jaffna*	25,335	—	5,929	2,721	51,970	85,955
High Country*	133,800	12,272	—	77,792	204,761	428,625
Wet Zone*	262,406	4,246	142,232	—	246,109	654,993
Dry Zone*	41,344	9,937	48,254	44,532	—	144,067
Total	462,885	30,247	248,911	226,856	601,318	1,570,217

*Regions are identified in Figure 2.2.

Source: See Table 2.2.

TABLE 2.4
Sri Lanka: Population (1971 and 1981) and Lifetime Migration by Zone

Zone	Population 1971	Population 1981	Lifetime Migration
Colombo	2,672,265	2,846,842	+206,308
Jaffna	701,603	827,851	-55,708
High Country	3,422,813	3,706,196	-179,714
Wet Zone	3,731,515	4,174,230	-428,137
Dry Zone	2,161,701	3,245,442	+457,251
Total	12,689,897	14,800,561	

Source: See Table 2.2.

Country and northern sections of the Dry Zone. Examination of district data shows four major districts of net lifetime immigration; namely (in rank order), Anuradhapura, Polonnaruwa, Gampaha, and Colombo. The first two are districts of traditional colonization that have experienced considerable recent inmigration as the Accelerated Mahaveli Project nears completion. The latter two contain the Colombo urban area (Colombo plus suburbs) and maintain, albeit in modified form, their traditional roles as primate city and migrant destination. These districts are equally balanced in number by four major outmigrant districts. These are (in rank order) Kandy, Matara, Galle, and Kegalle.

While such analysis identifies districts of net loss and gain as a result of migration, it does not determine for each area compared with all districts the origins and destinations of migrants. In order to accomplish this goal, the districts with the greatest in- or outmigration totals were grouped in the following manner, a) Colombo and Gampaha Districts, b) Anuradhapura, Polonnaruwa and Trincomalee Districts, c) Galle and Matara Districts, d) Kandy District, e) Jaffna District, and f) Kegalle District. For each of the six groups, data were organized (Table 2.5) and maps produced (Fig. 2.4-2.9) to identify for inmigrant areas the origins of migrants, and for outmigrant areas their destinations.

These data have been organized to identify origins and destinations within the six group matrix. It should be noted that Colombo/Gampaha attracted net migration from every other area except Anuradhapura/Polonnaruwa/Trincomalee. On the other hand, the latter area (A/P/T) received population from all other areas. Galle/Matara was such a strong outmigration area that Kandy, Jaffna, and Kegalle were net recipients of population from those districts. Other outmigration areas - Kandy, Jaffna, and Kegalle - experienced only modest interaction amongst themselves, with Kegalle attracting minimal inflows from Kandy and Jaffna.

The migration flows identified in the matrix (Table 2.5) account for about one-half of all lifetime migration in Sri Lanka as of 1981, and together with the maps (Figs. 2.4-2.9) provide a detailed picture of population redistribution. However, some important flows (10,000 plus) are missing from the matrix and are identified below. The Colombo/Gampaha area experienced significant net inflows from Kalutara, Nuwara Eliya, Badulla, and

Ratnapura and an important net outflow of population to Puttalam. Anuradhapura/Polonnaruwa/Trincomalee drew migrants in large numbers from Kurunegala, Matale, and Nuwara Eliya. Galle/Matara provided populations to Hambantota, Ratnapura, Moneragala, Kalutara, and Amparai. No additional significant flows exist for Kandy, and Kegalle had one additional outmigration to Kurunegala. Finally, Jaffna experienced important outmigration to Mullaitivu and Vavuniya. The identification of these additional migrant flows supports the contention that much migration is 'local' in character, i.e. to districts that share common boundaries with the origin/destination district. More than one-half of the "additional" flows were to adjacent districts.

The inter-censal data for the 1971-1981 period (Ukwatta, 1981) generally support the analysis derived from lifetime migration information. In comparing the data, two relative changes are noteworthy. First, inmigration to Colombo during the 1971-81 period was less important than lifetime flow; 11 per cent of all Sri Lankan migration versus 16% life time. While Colombo received

TABLE 2.5.
Sri Lanka: Lifetime Migration
Between Selected Areas, 1981
(Figures in 000s)

Origin \ Destination	C/G	A/P/T	G/M	Kandy	Jaffna	Kegalle	Total
C/G	—	39	—	—	—	—	39
A/P/T	—	—	—	—	—	—	0
G/M	118	28	—	6	1	1	154
Kandy	41	61	—	—	5	—	107
Jaffna	22	8	—	—	—	—	30
Kegalle	24	34	—	2	1	—	61
Total	205	170	0	8	7	1	391

Note: C/G =Colombo/Gampaha Districts
A/P/T = Anuradhapura/Polonnaruwa/Trincomalee Districts
G/M = Galle/Matara Districts.

Source See Table 2.2

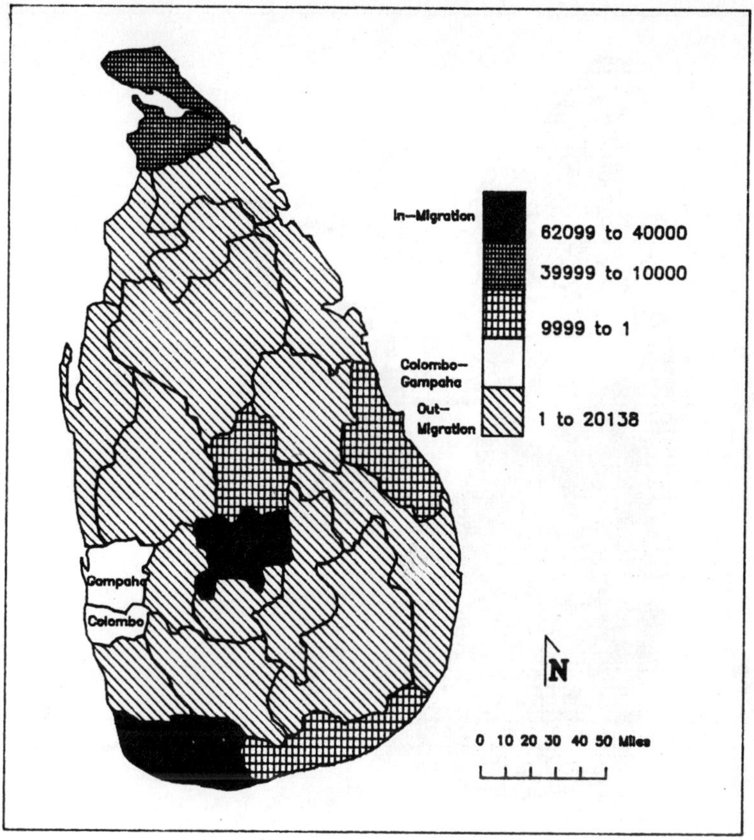

Fig. 2.4 Net Lifetime Migration: Colombo-Gampaha Districts, 1981

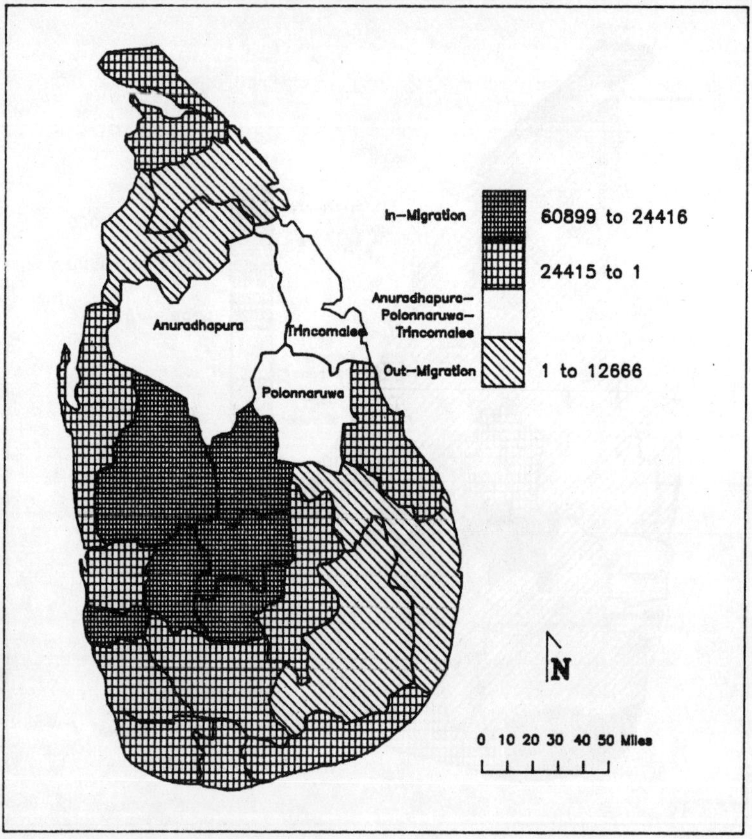

Fig. 2.5 Net Lifetime Migration: Anuradhapura-Polannaruwa-Trincomalee Districts, 1981.

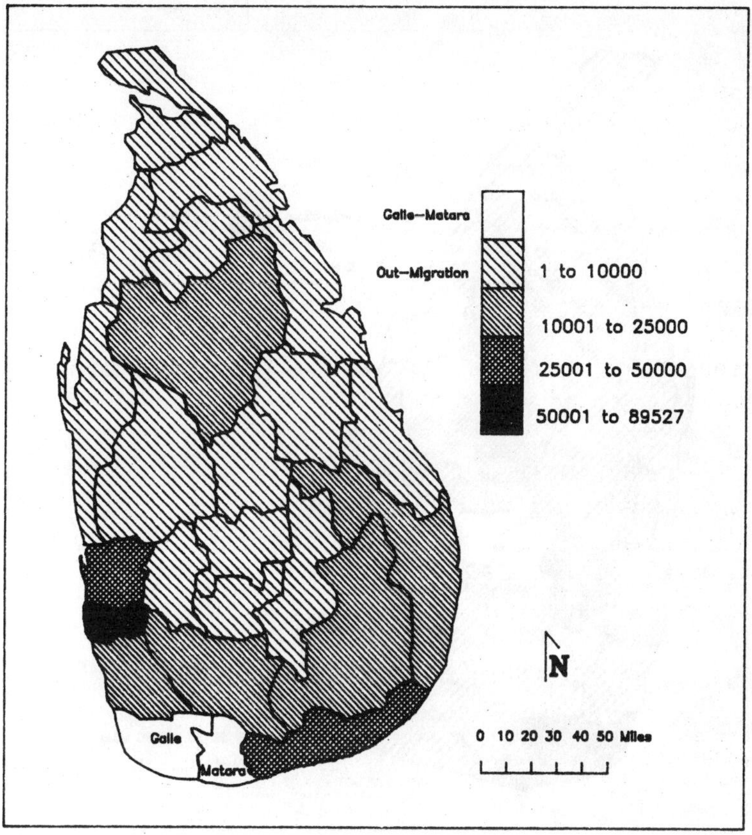

Fig. 2.6 Net Lifetime Migration: Galle-Matara Districts, 1981.

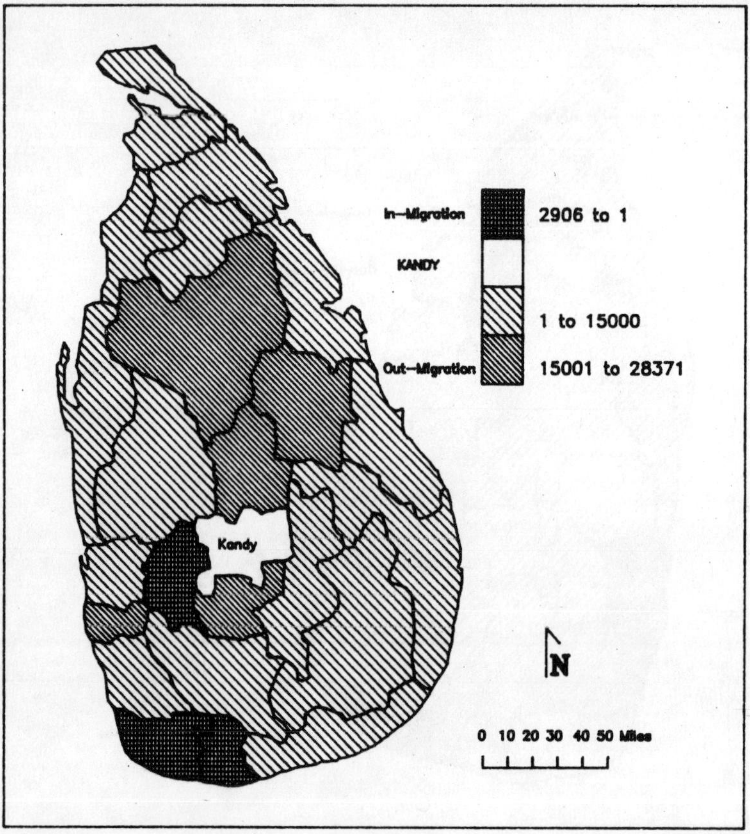

Fig. 2.7 Net Lifetime Migration: Kandy District, 1981.

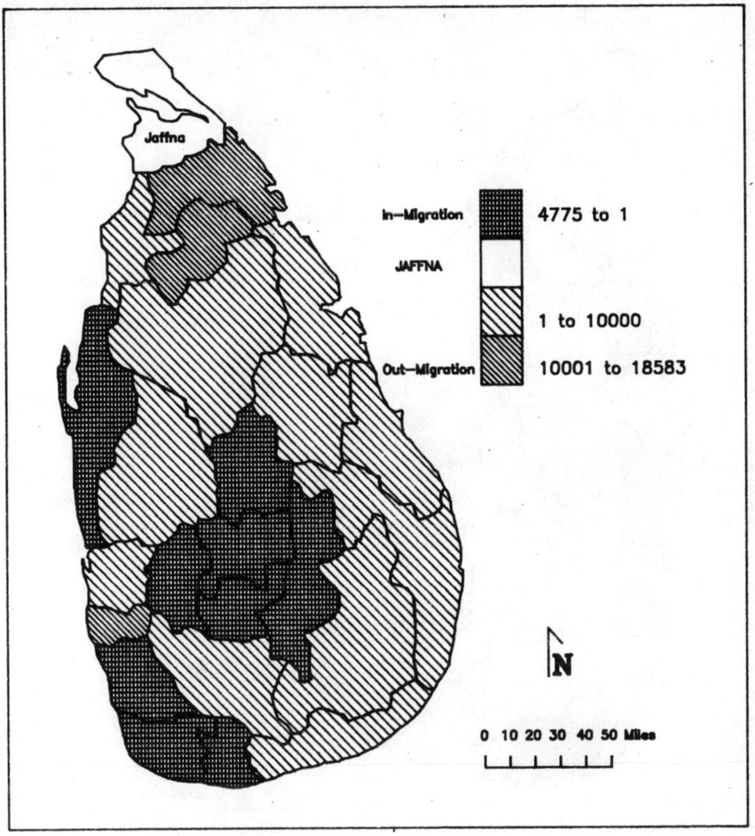

Fig. 2.8 Net Lifetime Migration: Jaffna District, 1981.

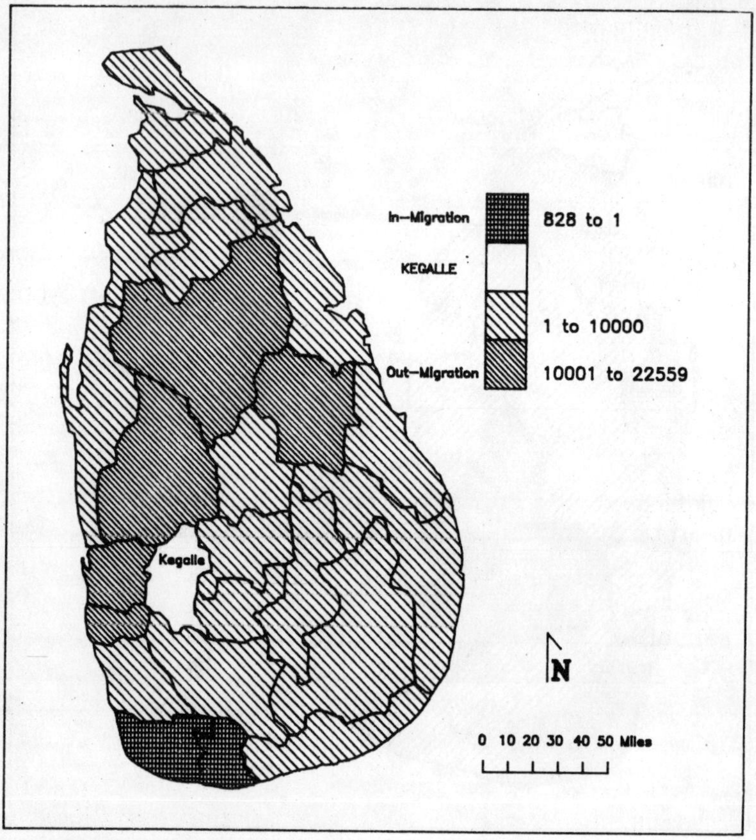

Fig. 2.9 Net Lifetime Migration: Kegalle District, 1981.

flows of 5,000 plus from six districts between 1971 and 1981, three flows from Colombo (to Jaffna, Anuradhapura, and Polonnaruwa) exceed that figure. Second, the greatest relative change in migration by zone is found in the Wet Zone (38% of 1971-81 migration versus 32 per cent lifetime). The Wet Zone has intra-zone movement (for example, Galle to Kalutara) but its most important overall flows were to the Colombo area, particularly from the southern section (Galle, Matara, Kalutara). The northern section of the Low Country showed migration in the 1971-81 period to both Colombo and the Dry Zone.

It is important to note that migration flows are selective on the basis of sex and ethnicity. Three major patterns of changing sex ratios as a function of migration have been distinguished (Kearney and Miller, 1984, 9-10). The first pattern is of a fairly balanced sex ratio: Colombo/Gampaha as the largest urban area in Sri Lanka and as a long-term recipient of migrants had a sex ratio of 106 in 1981 compared with a national figure of 103. Evidence suggests that the Colombo pattern has higher proportions of males in the younger age groups but that this balances out through time. The second pattern is strongly male preponderant. The Anuradhapura/Polonnaruwa/Trincomalee area had a sex ratio of 118 in 1981. This results from males migrating into the colonizing areas of the Dry Zone. The third pattern is of female-dominated areas. This is most firmly established in the Galle/Matara area where the 1981 sex ratio was 94, nine points below the national level. In general there is a very high correlation between lifetime net inmigration districts and sex ratios. All 11 districts with sex ratios above the national average in 1981 were net lifetime inmigration districts, ranging from Polonnaruwa (130) to Hambantota (104); all 13 districts with sex ratios below the national level, with the exception of Gampaha and Puttalam, were outmigration districts.

The ethnic factor in Sri Lanka is most evident in the case of Sri Lankan Tamil concentration in Jaffna. From 1971-81, the total population of Jaffna increased by 129,502 while its Sri Lankan Tamil population concentration rose from 92.1% of

Jaffna's population in 1971 to 95.3% in 1981. While migration data are not available by ethnic group, several inferences can be drawn from existing lifetime and inter-censal migration data. Lifetime outmigration flows from Jaffna are dominantly to Colombo, Mannar, Trincomalee, Mullaitivu, and Vavuniya. Each of these districts has either large absolute numbers of Sri Lankan Tamils and/or that group accounts for the majority of the population. The attraction of Mannar, Mullaitivu and Vavuniya "which do not come under any of the sectoral policies is due to the availability of land for settlement and agriculture to the Tamil ethnic group" (Samarasinghe, 1984, 18) and proximity to Jaffna.

Migration data support four basic themes. First, the continuing and increasing importance of the Dry Zone, and, in particular, Anuradhapura and Polonnaruwa Districts as major recipient areas. Long-term colonization schemes as well as the more recent post-1978 Accelerated Mahaveli Programme have produced a new "pole" of settlement, albeit largely rural in character. Second, the relative demise of the Colombo metropolitan area as a recipient area. Colombo is still a major destination for migrants but now shares that role with the Mahaveli region. Third, in line with migration theory, short-distance migration flows are of continuing importance. Adjacent districts are often better known, easier to reach, and may involve less economic risk as migrant destinations. Finally, the great outmigration area is in the Wet Zone, particularly Galle and Matara Districts. The question remains as to whether such migration petterns have radically altered the level of urbanization in Sri Lanka and, concomitantly, the growth and development of its urban places.

URBANIZATION

While a major migration stream is focused on Colombo, the contribution of migration to urban growth in Sri Lanka is modest. Estimates are not widely available but a study of the 1963-71 period calculated the contribution of migration to urban growth in Sri Lanka at 22% (ESCAP, 1980). The same study, commenting on the minor role played by migration, stated that the relatively small socio-economic differences between the urban and rural contexts was the major reason for this finding and added that poor housing and health services, unemployment and low incomes combined to make the urban areas unattractive. By contrast, in 25 Asian and Latin American countries for which estimates are available, the contribution of migration to urban growth was calculated at between 35 and 50% (ESCAP, 1980).

The share of the urban population in the total population increased by only 2.4 percentage points during the 18 year period from 1963 (19.1%) to 1981 (21.5%). In addition, the annual growth rate of the urban population of Sri Lanka declined from the 1965-73 period to 1973-83, a contrast with the experience of its South Asian neighbours (Table 2.1).

As in most countries, the definition of "urban" in Sri Lanka is contentious. The most recent national census (1981) defined as urban all persons living in Municipal, Urban and Town Council areas. Urban place populations range from less than 2,000 to more than 585,000 in the case of Colombo City. Two basic definitional problems arise. First, that the urban classification lacks consistency "in demographic, occupation, sociological or morphological terms" (Jones and Seevaratnam, 1970, 199). Second, that there are many so-called "urbanized villages" with populations exceeding 5,000 which "are comparable to most Town Councils in terms of urban character, but which have not been accorded Town Council status" (Jones and Selvaratnam, 1970, 200). Such problems cannot be realistically resolved through adjustments to census data. As a result, the analysis that follows accepts Sri Lankan census definitions while recognizing their limitations.

"Cities are the instruments whereby specialized sub-regions are articulated in a rational space-economy. They are the centers of activity and innovation, focal points of the transport network, locations of superior accessibility at which firms can most easily reap scale economies and at which industrial complexes can obtain the economies of localization and urbanization" (Berry,

1971, 115). This concept has been focused recently on the role of secondary cities in alleviating problems in the larger cities, reducing regional inequalities, stimulating rural economies, increasing administrative capacity, and reducing urban poverty (Rondinelli, 1983, 31-41). Within the context of the Berry and Rondinelli arguments, Sri Lanka plays an uneasy role. First, the country is small and public transportation relatively cheap. Thus, migration to urban centers is less necessary than in countries operating at larger scales. Second, the number of urban places that would qualify currently for secondary city status is negligible. Outside of Colombo and Gampaha Districts, only Kandy and Jaffna meet the Rondinelli criterion as secondary cities (namely "urban places other than the largest city with a population of 100,000 or more") (Rondinelli, 1983, 49). The growth patterns of urban places since 1946, indicate a growing role for medium-sized towns (Table 2.6). Since 1946, the number of such towns has increased from 18 to 66, accounting for 34 and 47 per cent of total urban population. It would appear, therefore, that it is this level of urban place in the Sri Lankan context that "articulates relations among regions" (Berry, 1971, 115) and not the larger 100,000 plus secondary cities of larger (spatially and economically) nations.

Yet, there is contradictory evidence. The rural region of greatest lifetime inmigration (Anuradhapura/Polonnaruwa/Trincomalee Districts) in 1981 had only five medium-sized towns and three small towns. This may be a result of the "urbanized village" factor, but may also be more functionally tied to the nature of colonization in that part of the country. Regardless, large inmigrations obviously do not result necessarily in a dramatic expansion of the number and size of urban places. Outside of Jaffna and the Colombo/Gampaha complex, urban Sri Lanka is characterized by small- and medium-sized towns; sixteen of the 24 districts (1981) have less than 15% of their populations living in urban places (Fig. 2.10).

In any defined urban hierarchy Colombo is the primary city. It is only in Colombo/Gampaha Districts and Jaffna that urban populations exceed one-third of the total population. The large urban centers of 50,000 or more inhabitants may be viewed as performing *regional* functions. By contrast, Colombo performs *national* functions; political, administrative and commercial. The regional centers are (in rank order) Jaffna (118,000 population in 1981), Kandy (101, 000) and Galle (77,000). All other large urban centers are found in the Colombo or Gampaha Districts and are, in effect, part of the functional Colombo metropolitan

TABLE 2.6.
Sri Lanka: Number of Urban Places
by Size Category, 1946-1981

Size of Urban Place	1946	1953	1963	1971	1981
Large (50,000+ inhabitants)	5(57)	7(65)	7(50)	8(43)	9(44)
Medium (10,000-49,999 inhabitants)	18(34)	21(30)	39(38)	59(45)	66(47)
Small (less than 9,999 inhabitants)	19(9)	15(5)	53(12)	68(12)	59(9)

Note: Percent of total urban population in parentheses.

Source: Mendis, 1982b and Mendis, 1981.

area (Table 2.7). Much of the Sri Lankan urban system is composed of small- and medium-sized towns. At this level of the urban hierarchy, the administrative function of the district capital is particularly important. District capitals range in size from Colombo (586,000) to Monaragala (6,000). However, excluding the larger cities already identified, 19 of the 21 remaining district capitals have populations of between 10,000 and 50,000. Thus,

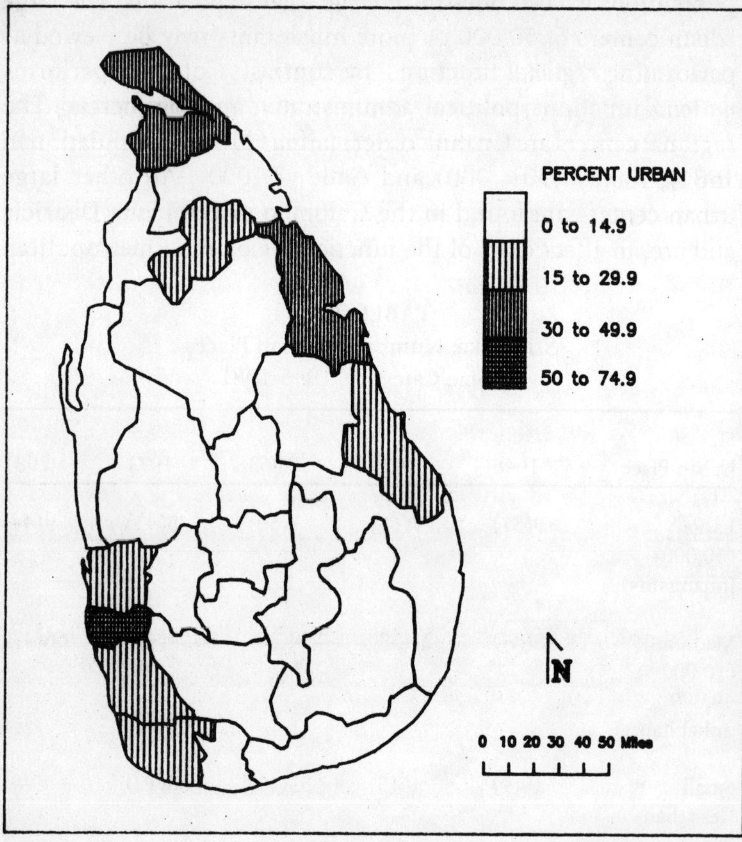

Fig. 2.10 Urban Population by District: Sri Lanka, 1981.

a third level of the Sri Lankan urban hierarchy is composed of district capitals plus additional medium-sized towns functionally related to district capitals or to larger cities.

The medium- and, to a lesser extent, the small-sized towns are of particular importance in Sri Lanka. Since 1946 their numbers have increased from 37 (1946) to 125 (1981) and their proportion of the total urban population from 43 to 56%. Again, the medium-sized town is the focus. In the 1946-81 period, their numbers increased from 18 to 66, and their share of the urban population from 34 to 47% (Table 2.6 and Fig. 2.11). As Mendis has noted "they comprise a vital link for supporting rural producers and accommodating the surplus rural labour. By such means they thus demonstrate urban-rural complementary which is necessary for effective rural development" (Mendis, 1982b, 32). The retention of rural populations in *locus* is the product of central government investment in the agricultural sector. It has also enabled the growth of small- and medium-sized settlements to serve as centers for trade and administration and, to an extent, acted as an effective screen against migration.

TABLE 2.7.
Sri Lanka: Distribution of Large, Medium and Small Towns by Zone, 1981

	Small Towns		Medium Towns		Large Towns	
Zone	No.	Population	No.	Population	No.	Population
Colombo	5	29,752	17	503,058	6	1,053,869
Jaffna	3	19,159	9	133,227	1	118,215
High Country	20	75,030	7	164,524	1	101,281
Wet Zone	17	93,110	17	343,759	1	77,183
Dry Zone	14	77,829	16	335,527	0	-
Total	59	294,880	66	1,480,095	9	1,350,548

Source: See Table 2.2.

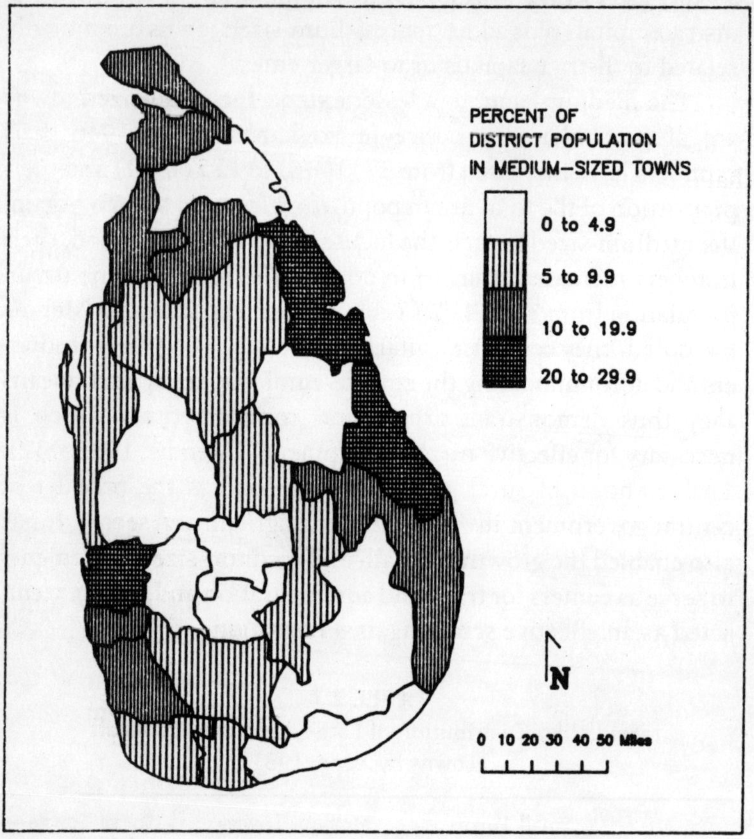

Fig. 2.11 Medium-Sized Towns by District: Sri Lanka, 1981.

Sri Lanka has experienced, particularly in contrast with most developing countries, a relatively slow rate of urbanization. The role of migration in urban growth is less than in other Asian and Latin American countries. Colombo has experienced decreasing primacy during the past twenty years, and national urban growth that is occurring is more pronounced in the medium- and small-sized towns. The slower growth rate of urbanization and its comparative non-primate city focus separates Sri Lanka from the model experience of developing countries.

The findings of an ESCAP study, supported by the later work of Abeysekera, identify six factors that have influenced the pattern of urbanization in Sri Lanka since the country's independence (ESCAP, 1976, 74-6; Abeysekera, 1980a, 31-2). They are that population concentration has resulted from commerce and trade rather than industrialization; the processing of tea and rubber was carried out on the rurally located plantations; successive Sri Lankan governments have strongly encouraged peasant agriculture through public investment policies; public expenditure had the effect of equalizing living standards between rural and urban areas; structural bottlenecks to the development of peasant agriculture (insecurity of land tenure and an impoverished landless proletariat, for example) were modest; and, finally, that a well-developed network of state-owned roads and railways made travel within the country relatively easy and inexpensive. The majority of Sri Lanka's rural population live within 30 miles of a town of 20,000 or more inhabitants and employees are able to commute from rural areas to towns rather than taking up residence in the urban area (Jones and Selvaratnam, 1970, 210).

CONCLUSIONS

Sri Lanka presents a case study of a traditional dual economy where government public investment policies have contributed toward the redress of emphasis on the primate city of Colombo through agricultural and rural development. Slow rates of urbanization combined with powerful migration streams into the Dry

Zone, and in particular to the Accelerated Mahaveli Project (AMP) region, have created on unusual scenario for a developing country. Investment in the Accelerated Mahaveli Project calls for irrigation of some 350,000 acres of land, the settlement of over 100,000 landless or nearly landless farm families on one hectare plots, and the generation of 750 Mwhs of hydroelectric power to be distributed locally and nationally. The Accelerated Mahaveli Project in particular and the Integrated Rural Development Programme (IRDP) to a lesser extent have created economic opportunities for peasant farmers that provide an alternative to rural to urban migration (Figure. 2.12). The latter migration flow is typical of the developing nations of the world.

Alternatively, the major urban areas have "a limited number of entry points to the rural labour surplus who have therefore opted to remain unemployed or underemployed in their own villages rather than squat or live in slums in the cities" (Mendis, 1981, 24). What has emerged is a lower than expected level of pull by urban areas and a lower than expected level of push from rural areas. Urban areas have experienced little industrial growth which is classically associated with an increased level of urbanization. For example, much of the employment attracted by the Greater Colombo Economic Commission (GCEC) into the Investment Promotion Zone (20 miles north of Colombo) since its inception in 1978 is in the garment industry. This industry uses imported raw materials and its product is exported. There is little incentive to forge inter-industry linkages, for example, which would produce further manufacturing growth and increased employment.

Social welfare policies have produced smaller than expected (in relation to other developing countries) spatial disparities. If Colombo is viewed as a magnet for migrants, it is worth noting that a majority of the remaining districts have higher physical quality of life indices and include those districts central to the Accelerated Mahaveli Project. The counter-magnet to Colombo found in the Dry Zone has produced only minimal urbanization below the district capital level. "The degree of polarization of socio-economic activities in Colombo had its peak around 1953

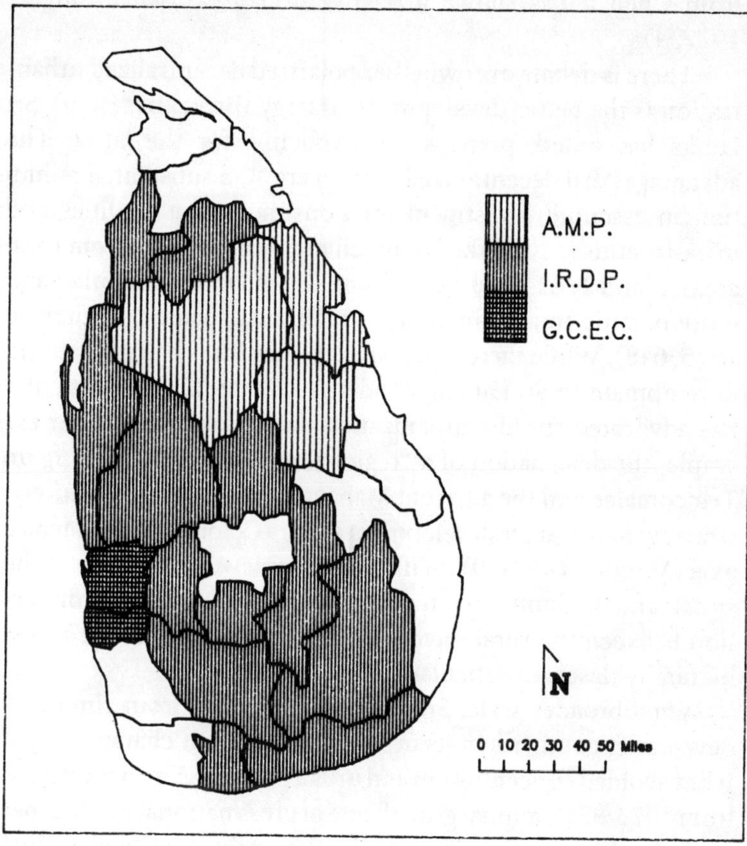

Fig. 2.12 Major Districts Impacted by AMP, IRDP, and GCEC Policies: Sri Lanka, 1981.

from when it has shown a relative decrease" (Samarasinghe, 1977, 4).

There is debate over whether polarized decentralized urbanization is the better development strategy (Brutzkus, 1975). Sri Lanka has opted, perhaps not explicitly, for the latter. The advantages of a decentralized pattern are "I) a substantial reduction in essential investment for housing, urban facilities and infrastructures . . . . linked to much more commuting from rural areas. . . and 2) in social and cultural terms a much smoother and more organic transformation of traditional society" (Brutzkus, 1975, 648). While there is no explict policy for urban growth and development in Sri Lanka, Mendis (1982a: 1982b) in particular has advocated specific urbanization policy formulation; for example, the designation of a "regional growth area" focusing on Trincomalee and the adjacent Mahaveli area as part of a national strategy to encourage development along a Colombo-Trincomalee axis (Mendis, 1982a, 9). Within this framework, the role of the small- and medium-sized towns as the critical points of connection between the rural sector and the upper levels of the urban hierarchy deserve particular attention.

On a broader scale, Sri Lanka stands aside from almost all developing countries in its urban and migration characteristics. It has avoided concentration and urban primacy. Yet in the period from 1973-83 its annual growth rate of gross national product per capita has been modest, its annual inflation rate high, and its level of unemployment high (World Bank, 1985, 174). "Sri Lanka can be considered as not particularly noteworthy from the point of view of economic development, but as a success from the point of view of achieving urban rural balance, attaining social welfare, and the elimination of poverty" (Mera, 1982, 193). Within this context, the direction and size of migration flows and the lack of dramatic short-term changes in the Sri Lankan urban system, at least until the civil disturbances of the mid-and late-1980s, are more readily understandable.

REFERENCES

Abeysekera, D. 1980a. *Urbanization and the growth of small towns in Sri Lanka, 1970-71*. Papers of the East-West Population Institute, No. 67. Honolulu: Hawaii.

Abeysekera, D. 1980b, *Determinants and consequences of internal migration: the rural wet zone to rural dry zone stream in Sri Lanka*. Ph. D. dissertation, Department of Sociology, Brown University, Providence Rhode Island.

Berry, B.J.L. 1961. A Statistical Analysis in *An Atlas of Economic Development*, ed. N. Ginsburg. University of Chicago, Department of Geography, Research Paper No. 68. Chicago: University of Chicago.

Brutzkus, E. 1975. Centralized versus Decentralized Pattern of Urbanization in Developing Countries: An Attempt to Elucidate a Guideline Principle. *Economic Development and Cultural Change* 23: 633-652.

Centre for Society and Religion. 1988. Sri Lankan Workers in the Middle East. *South Asia Bulletin* 10: 61-62.

Crooks, G.R. and Ranbanda, H.A. 1981. *The Economics of Seasonal Labour Migration in Sri Lanka*. Agrarian Research and Training Institute, Research Study Series: 46. Colombo: Agrarian Research and Training Institute.

Economic and Social Commission for Asia and the Pacific (ESCAP). 1976. *Population of Sri Lanka*. ESCAP Country Monograph Series, No. 4. Bangkok: United Nations.

Economic and Social Commission for Asia and the Pacific (ESCAP). 1980. *Migration, urbanization and development in Sri Lanka*. Bangkok: United Nations.

Farmer, B.H. 1957. *Pioneer Peasant Colonization in Ceylon*. Oxford: Oxford University Press.

Jefferson, M. 1939. The Law of the Primate City. *Geographical Review* 29: 226-232.

Jones, G.W. and Selvaratnam. 1970. Urbanization in Ceylon, 1946-63. *Modern Ceylon Studies* 1: 199-212.

Kearney, R.N. and Miller, B.D. 1984. *Sex Differences in Patterns of Internal Migration in Sri Lanka*. Working Papers on Women in International Development, No. 44. East Lansing, MI: Michigan State University, Office of Women in International Development.

Korale, R.B.M. 1981. *Middle Eastern Migration*. Colombo: Ministry of Plan Implementation.

Mendis, M.W.J.G. 1981. Urbanization in Sri Lanka. The Demographic Perspective. *Progress* 1: 23-32.

Mendis, M.W.J.G. 1982a. An Analysis of the Inter-Censal Growth of Towns in Sri Lanka: Its Relevance in Urban Planning and Development. *Development Planning Review* 1: 1-13.

Mendis, M.W.J.G. 1982b. Small and medium towns in Sri Lanka: a situational analysis and their planning significance. *Economic Review* 8: 27-33.

Mera, K. 1982. Industrial Development Strategies and Rural-Urban Imbalances: Case Studies and an Overview. *Environment and Development in Asia and the Pacific*. United Nations Environment Programme, 187-226. Nairobi: United Nations.

Miller, E.W. and Miller, R.M. 1989. *The Third World: India, Sri Lanka and Nepal, A Bibliography*. Monticello, Illinois: Vance Bibligraphies, Public Administration Series, Bibliography 2654.

Moore, M. 1984. Categorizing Space: Urban-Rural or Core-Periphery in Sri Lanka. *Journal of Development Studies* 20: 102-122.

Panditharatna, B.L. 1985. *Colombo City, Sri Lanka: Infrastructure and Access to Basic Public Services*. Urban Studies Working Paper No. 4. College Park, MD.: Institute for Urban Studies.

Robinson, F., ed. 1989. *The Cambridge Encylopedia of India, Pakistan, Bangladesh, Sri Lanka, Nepal. Bhutan and the Maldives*. New York: Cambridge University Press.

Rondinelli, D.A. 1983. *Secondary Cities in Developing Countries: Policies for Diffusing Urbanization*. Beverly Hills, California: Sage Publications.

Ruhunage, L.K. 1979. *Migration of Sri Lankans to the Middle Eastern Countries*. Colombo: Ministry of Plan Implementation.

Samarasinghe, S.W.R. de A., ed. 1977. *Agriculture in the Peasant Sector of Sri Lanka*. Peradeniya: Ceylon Studies Seminar.

Samarasinghe, V. 1982. Spatial Polarization of Colombo - A Study of Regional Inequality. *Journal of Social Sciences* 5: 75-95.

Samarasinghe, V. 1984. Government Policy and Regional Development in Sri Lanka - Recent Trends. Discussion Paper to the Staff Studies Seminar, University of Peradeniya, Sri Lanka.

Sen, A. 1981. Public Action and the Quality of Life in Developing Countries. *Oxford Bulletin of Economics and Statistics* 43: 287-319.

Sri Lanka, Department of Census and Statistics, 1981. *Census of Population and Housing, 1981*. Colombo. Ministry of Plan Implementation.

Sri Lanka, Department of Census and Statistics, 1982. *Census of Population and Housing, 1981*. Preliminary Release No. 2. Colombo: Ministry of Plan Implementation.

Sri Lanka, The Survey Department of Sri Lanka. *The National Atlas of Sri Lanka*. 1988. Colombo: Sri Lanka.

Ukwatta, S. 1982. *The Patterns of Internal Migration in Sri Lanka during the period 1971-1981*. Diploma of Population Studies thesis, Demographic Training and Research Unit, University of Colombo.

Urban Development Authority, Sri Lanka, 1981. *Colombo City: Residential and Non-Residential Buildings and Sub-Standard Housing*. Colombo: Urban Development Authority.

Vamathavan, S. 1961. *Internal Migration in Ceylon, 1946-1953*. Colombo: Department of Census and Statistics.

Vining, D.R., Jr. 1985. The Growth of Core Urban Regions in Developing Countries. *Population and Development Review* 11: 495-514.

The World Bank. 1985. *World Development Report*. New York: Oxford University Press.

Chapter III

DEVELOPMENT IN SRI LANKA: A MODEL FOR COUNTERURBANIZATION POLICIES AND PLANNING

Kenneth E. Corey
Michigan State University

Sri Lanka's current population of nearly 15 million people is approximately 20% urban. This small island state has maintained a similar urban-rural ratio for 20 years or so. Indeed, for over 100 years, Sri Lanka never has been more than 22.4% urban. Such a pattern of stable, low-level urbanization is increasingly unusual in the developing world. Until 1983, Sri Lanka often was cited as a model of third-world development. Therefore, it may be useful to examine the potential transferability of urban-development lessons from Sri Lanka to other developing countries that seek to control their own high rates of urbanization.

The research reported here was undertaken to answer two specific questions. (1) What role has government policy played in producing the pattern of urbanization in Sri Lanka? (2) To what extent is Sri Lanka a model for other developing countries as they plan policies and programs to address their urbanization problems?

BACKGROUND

Urbanization Issues

There is a pervasive popular view that developing countries are undergoing rapid rates of urbanization. Urbanization "is a process of population concentration. . .it implies movement from a state of less concentration to a state of more concentration" (Berry, 1976, 17). Population forecasts that have Mexico City exceeding 30 million inhabitants in the next generation are reported frequently in the press. There is also a growing body of scholarly literature on urbanization in developing countries. Some researchers are concerned with analyzing and modeling urban growth in developing countries (Kelley and Williamson, 1984). Others have focused on policies for third-world cities (Linn, 1983). and some others have addressed national urbanization policies in developing countries (Renaud, 1979). Still other scholars and urban-development officials have been struggling to find ways to stem or divert the rush of people from the countryside to the city. This interest has been labeled counterurbanization: "a process of population deconcentration; it implies a movement from a state of more concentration to a state of less concentration" (Berry, 1976, 17).

Sri Lankan urban scholars also have developed an extensive literature describing and explaining the evolution of the country's urbanization forces (Panditharatna, 1964; Jones and Selvaratnam, 1970; Abeysekera, 1980; Silva, 1979; and Mendis, 1982).

Development in Sri Lanka

Sri Lanka's United National Party came to power in the 1977 elections. The new government adopted a series of economic liberalization measures that were designed to stimulate private-sector initiatives and to reduce the society's dependence on government (Stern, 1984). As part of many actions intended to promote development and employment, and to strengthen the country's balance of payments, the government of President J.R. Jayewardene implemented several "lead projects" including: (1) the Accelerated Mahaweli Programme; (2) the Urban Development Authority; (3) the Greater Colombo Economic Commission, and (4) the Integrated Rural Development Programme.

The Democratic Socialist Republic of Sri Lanka. (formerly Ceylon) is a small (25,332 square miles or 65,610 square kilometers) island state just off the southeast tip of India (Fig. 3.1). The Island is 278 miles (447 km) long and 136 miles (219 km) wide. The northern and eastern portion of the island is referred to as the Dry Zone (it receives less than 75 inches of rain annually); the southwestern portion of the island is the Wet Zone (it receives about 75-200 inches of rain annually). The island's largest river, the Mahaweli Gaga, has its headwaters in the central highlands, and it flows northeastwards through the Dry Zone and empties into the Indian Ocean near the large natural harbor and town of Trincomalee.

Just under 2,000 years ago, the Sri Lankans developed an hydraulic paddy-culture civilization in the Dry Zone. This development was possible in large part because of the valve pit (bisokotuva) which was invented by Sinhalese engineers by the 3rd century BC. This device controlled water pressure and flow of water from a reservoir or tank into canals and irrigation channels (de Silva, 1981, 28). Thus, a highly developed irrigation system gave rise to cities, architecture, and social systems that were comparable in sophistication to the ancient Egyptians and Chinese. Early in the 16th century the European colonial era began in Sri Lanka with the arrival of the Portuguese. The Dutch and the British followed. European colonization produced an urban pattern concentrated in the southwestern Wet Zone area of the island punctuated by port towns in the maritime littoral. Urban development then was focused on sea ports, through which passed such commodities as cinnamon, spices, elephants, gems and precious stones, and during the British colonial period, tea, rubber, and coconut estate products. Rice then had to be imported to meet the country's total demand.

In 1981, the Sinhalese were Sri Lanka's majority at 74% of the population; Buddhism is the dominant faith of the Sinhalese. Sri Lankan Tamils (12.6%) and Indian Tamils (5.6%), both mostly Hindu, combine to form the largest ethnic minority. Moors (7.1%), Burghers and Eurasians (0.3%), Malays (0.3%), and others (0.2%) comprise the remaining ethnic groups at 7.9%. As regards the other religions, Christians form 7.4% and Muslims

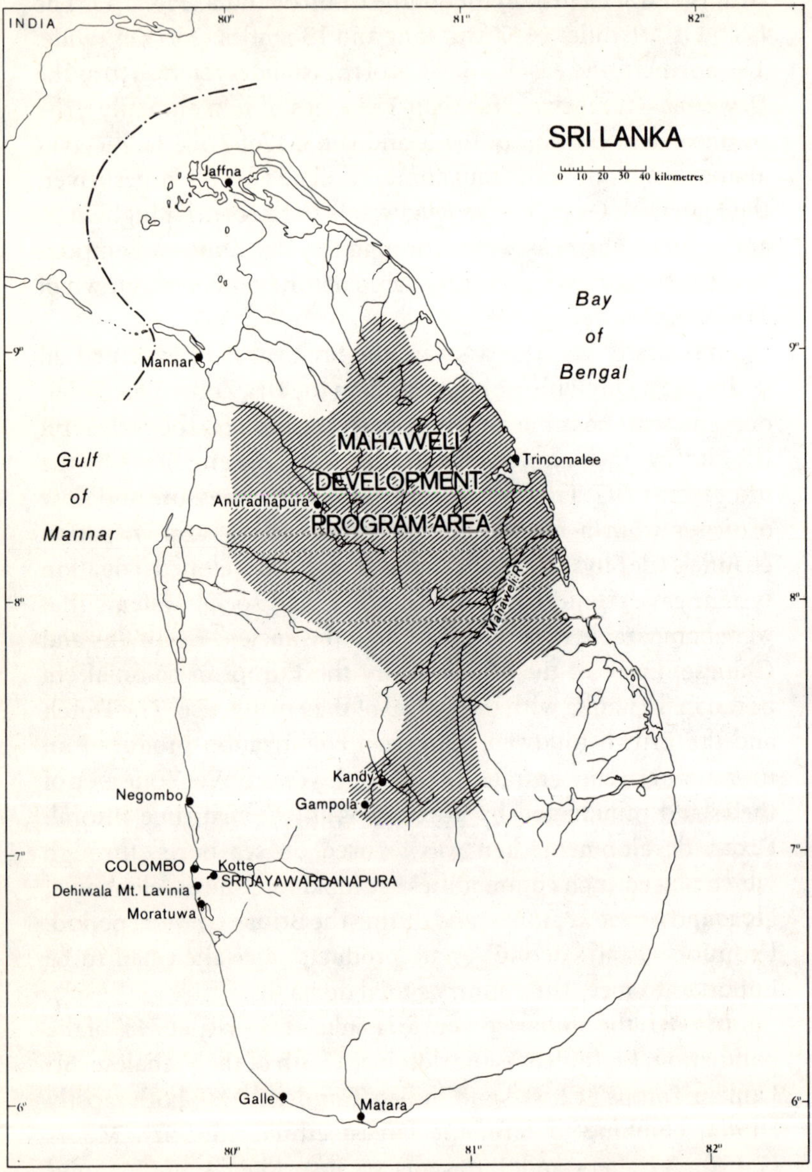

Fig. 3.1 Major Urban Centers and the Mahaveli Development Programme Area

form 7.6% of the Sri Lankan population.

In 1981 the population of Sri Lanka was nearly 15 million. Approximately 3.2 million (21.5%) of these were urban; approximately 11.7 million (78.5%) of these were rural, including the estate sector, i.e., plantations. Sri Lanka is a nation of villagers; there are about 20,000 villages in the country. Most of the population lives in the southwestern Wet Zone districts. This concentration of population is a consequence of past colonial-era trade and commerce (Abeysekera, 1980, 30-33) channeled through the port of Colombo to the outside world.

The Sri Lankan economy is predominantly agricultural. Of the 4,737,000 employed population in 1981, 45.8% (2,172000) were classified as "agriculture, hunting, forestry and fishing" (Department of Census and Statistics, 1983b, 30-32). Paddy is the staple of the subsistence-farmer economy. Today, the plantation sector, with its colonial origins, is based on the estate export crops of tea, rubber, and coconut.

The development of the country has long traditions in democracy and social welfare. The roots of these traditions can be found, in part, in Buddhism, Hinduism, British colonial administration, and the early introduction of the universal franchise. Recently, Sri Lanka is noteworthy for the high loadings that it has attained on many social indicators and physical quality-of-life indicators (The World Bank, 1984; Sumanasekera, 1981). For example, Sri Lanka's infant-mortality rate at 37.4 in 1979 is low; its life expectancy at birth is over 67 years for females and 64 years for males (1971); the literacy rate in 1981 was 86.5%; and the population growth rate was down to 1.5% in 1980 (Department of Census and Statistics, 1983 a, ix). The country also ranks well in educational attainment, number of years of school attended, and various measures of health service and nutrition (Richards and Gooneratne, 1980; and Ministry of Plan Implementation, 1981, 112-113).

METHOD

The overall goal of this research was to explore the linkages between Sri Lanka's development policies, planning, and urbanization. The specific objectives were: (1) to examine the role that government policy has played in producing Sri Lanka's modern pattern of urbanization and (2) to learn about the way development planning is practiced in Sri Lanka and to assess Sri Lanka as a counterurbanization model for other developing countries.

By means of a series of nominations and referrals, 16 key informants were identified and interviewed. They were selected for their direct knowledge of urbanization, policy formulation, development and planning in Sri Lanka. The respondents included mostly central government officials; they ranged from a cabinet-level minister to division heads and from middle program managers to project-level managers; five academic development researchers also were interviewed. Each respondent was questioned by means of an open-ended depth interview; each interview lasted at least an hour, and most approached two hours in length. One respondent was interviewed twice. The "lead projects" were represented by several respondents for each project. Agencies represented included: Central Bank of Ceylon, Urban Development Authority, Mahaweli Programme, Ministry of Finance and Planning, Integrated Rural Development Programme, several units within the Ministry of Plan Implementation, Ceylon Electricity Board, and Greater Colombo Economic Commission.

Although some nongovernment respondents were interviewed, the intent of the research was to probe the results of public policy; therefore it was considered appropriate to permit the findings to be dominated by the observations of various government officials.

The interviews were conducted over a five-week period from mid-June through the third week of July, 1983. It should be noted that all interviews were completed immediately prior to the time of the watershed Sinhalese -Tamil communal violence; these disturbances broke out in Colombo on Monday, July 25, 1983.

The principal questions cited above were posed to each respondent. All responses referred to the period between 1978 and 1983; many responses included statements about the post-independence period as well. The procedure of the open-ended interview was flexible. Interviewees were encouraged to develop their responses in depth. The researcher captured the response in nearly word-for-word detail by means of note-taking. In order to elicit full and free responses to the questions, the assurance of anonymity was provided to each interviewee.

The large volume of responses was subjected to a modified content analysis (Bailey, 1982, 312-324). The procedure involved several passes at sorting individual responses by their subject matter in order to classify the answers, first generally and then in detail. In the end, the primary classes of responses that were used to write up the findings were: (1) past and current urbanization and concentration; (2) past and current counterurbanization and deconcentration; (3) interrelationships between policy, planning, coordination, and management; (4) future urbanization and concentration; and (5) future counterurbanization and deconcentration. Only data from categories (1), (2), and (3) are used in the analysis that follows.

The stages of Delbecq's Program Planning Model (PPM) were used as the analytic framework (Delbecq, 1978). The PPM stages made possible an ordering of the content-analysis results (Van de Van and Koenig, Jr., 1976). For an elaboration of this approach to policy analysis, see Corey, 1984b.

Some terms used in this study require elaboration. In Sri Lanka, urban is defined by the census as composed of all population living in Municipal Urban, and Town Council areas.

> Urban status is conferred on an area by the Minister in charge of Local Government purely for local administrative purposes. However, Ministrial discretion seems to be based on "the nature of the development. . .(of the locality). . .or its amenities and urban character" (Mendis, 1982, 1).

The definition of urban in Sri Lanka has changed over the years. Considerable discussion of the research problems associated with the changing definition of urban in Sri Lanka is well documented in the literature (Abeysekera, 1980, 2-3; Jones and Selvaratnam, 1970, 200). Further discussion of this issue is outside the scope of this presentation (cf. Moore, 1984). The various definitions of urban are accepted here as being interchangeable enough for the objectives of this study.

Colombo is referred to in several distinct ways. Colombo City is the Colombo Municipal Council, the 1981 population of which was 585,776. The District of Colombo has a 1981 population of 1,698,322; 1,262,998 of these were urban. Metropolitan Colombo and the Colombo region are composed of the Colombo and Grampha Districts. The 1981 population of the Colombo region was 3,087,812 (Department of Census and Statistics, 1981); this was approximately 20% of the country's population.

Planning is used here to mean the generic process of forward programming a sequence of activites, the outcome of which is innovation, i.e., a new policy, program, or project. The content of the innovation can be physical or social. In area terms, planning may be "town, urban, regional, or country," and so on. This form of planning is a sociotechnical process, in that it recognizes that a rational-logical sequence of technical functions is most effective when particular roles, actors, and behavioral expectations are assigned appropriate to individual planning stages for execution (Van de Ven and Koening, Jr., 1976).

The last major concept that permeates this presentation is development. It has been defined as

> a widely participatory process of social change in a society intended to bring about both social and material advancement (including greater equality, freedom, and other valued qualities) for the majority of the people through their gaining greater control over their environment (Rogers, 1976, 225).

This definition of development is used throughout this research.

ANALYSIS

The following section includes the answers of the key informants to the principal research questions posed during the interviews. Care was taken to minimize substantive reinterpretation in the analysis and to capture the content and the spirit of the actual statements, as well as the context of the interviewee answers. Occasional direct quotations are used to accent key points. Except for these few quotes, the analysis consists entirely of the paraphrased words of the respondents. Any misstatement is the responsibility of the researcher, not the respondents.

THE ROLE OF POLICY IN SRI LANKA'S URBANIZATION PATTERN

The interviewees addressed two major questions about the policies of the goverment and the extent to which policy seemed to have produced the country's relatively low level of urbanization. One question asked was "what intentional *urbanization* policy or program produced Sri Lanka's pattern of deconcentrated settlement?" The other question asked was "what recent intentional *counterurbanization* policy or programs produced Sri Lanka's pattern of deconcentrated settlement?" Each question is treated in turn.

Urbanization Policies?

The key informants identified the following influences on urbanization. Distinctions were made between nationwide urbanization influences and Colombo-region urbanization influences.

Urban in the Colombo region. The Colombo region is the focal area for Sri Lanka's urbanization. Any population increase in the Colombo region is seen as having been due principally to natural population increase rather than to migration. People are said to prefer Colombo City for both residences and businesses. As part of its liberal economic policy, the government has invited foreign investors to Sri Lanka. Interviewees remarked that the underemployed labor pool in and around Colombo offers a virtually unlimited resource for further foreign investment.

Historically, Colombo's deteriorated core-area infrastructure has not tended to attract people. But recently, it has begun to be seen as possible to refurbish the city's existing infrastructure, thus making metropolitan Colombo more attractive to investors and residents. Nationally, the most sophisticated and developed infrastructure is in the Colombo region. Trincomalee was perceived to be the only other location to have significant attraction to foreign investors. Galle was seen as relatively underdeveloped; "it does not have the infrastructure."

The Greater Colombo Economic Commission (GCEC), with its Free Trade Zone adjacent to the Katunayake International Airport to the north of metropolitan Colombo, is interested in the creation of employment by means of promoting foreign investment (Ramanayake, 1982). The GCEC wants the new industrial firms it attracts to be concentrated so that it can monitor their operations to insure that they are performing according to their investment agreements with the Commission. The difficulty of monitoring firms scattered around the island is seen as a factor reinforcing Colombo-region urbanization.

A related recent development trend in Colombo City is the construction of new banks and hotels, primarily for the sake of tourists, international enterprises, and joint ventures. These enterprises want to locate in the center of Colombo City; most of the business services and facilities are there already.

The Minister of Local Government, Housing and Construction and then Prime Minister, Ranasinghe Premadasa, was seen by interviewees to be actively interested in modernizing Colombo by: (1) improving the quality of housing; (2) providing working-class flats in central Colombo; and (3) upgrading the city's functional effectiveness (e.g., flyovers have been built over busy arteries to improve traffic flow and to provide safety for pedestrians).

Counterurbanization Policies?

What intentional counterurbanization policies and programs over the last generation have produced Sri Lanka's settlement pattern? The responses to that question were diverse, but they may be grouped according to several themes and influences.

Quality of life. In simplest terms, respondents generally agreed that the Sri Lankan villager does not have to go to the largest cities in order to take advantage of society's opportunities (cf. Sumanasekera, 1981). Since the 1930s, successive governments have decided that major public investments would be in the countryside. Social-welfare opportunities and services are available, at comparable levels of quality, to rural and urban residents alike. Children receive formal education in the villages and small towns. Higher education quotas operate in favor of students from rural areas. In admission to universities, rural youths are given priority, i.e., they are given a lower pass. Colombo residents complain about this. One interviewee said,

> The small-village schools are somewhat comparable to Colombo schools; even well-to-do-parents keep their children in the village. Rural hospitals are free; if you are really sick, then you go to Colombo. People simply do not need to be near big cities.

Respondents supported the statement that the countryside is stable by saying that "unlike other areas in South Asia, Sri Lanka did not have a refugee problem," where large numbers of rural refugees might stream into the relative safety of cities. (Again, it should be noted that these interviews were conducted literally days before the late July 1983 communal violence that erupted throughout Sri Lanka.)

Respondents observed that the natural population increase has been kept down in both urban and rural areas, especially in urban areas. It was said that the Ministry of Local Government, Housing and Construction is charged with providing housing in both urban and rural areas. The Prime Minister, who also holds this ministry's portfolio, has been instrumental in providing basic infrastructures; village people can complete the erection of shelter for themselves. These self-help approaches are part of the Village Re-Awakening Scheme. One-hundred thousand new housing units were said to have been planned and built from 1978 to 1983, and one million housing units were planned for construction by 1990.

Similarly, health services, life expectancies, and nutritional standards for the rural poor have been maintained. In addition, the quality and accessibility of roads, irrigation, and agricultural systems (e.g. larger sugar projects) were said to be helpful to the rural population. There were many complaints that the non-rural sectors are being starved.

Politics and tradition. Interviewees described the District Development Councils as mechanisms whereby local ministers of parliament can see that set amounts of funds are spent in their districts. It was said that getting the politicians re-elected motivates the system of District Development Councils. This decentralized budget mechanism has been in place for a number of years and has operated to insure that a regular flow of public investment and development occurs in local areas throughout Sri Lanka. For example, under the decentralized budget process electricity was provided in rural areas. The Accelerated Mahaweli Programme and various other rural development programs have also administered major investments in certain rural areas.

The management of development takes place primarily at the district level. People express their views through ministers of parliament and rural development societies. With involvement at the village level, district officials prepare an outline of development action. According to interviewees, villagers' views are sought in some detail.

Some respondents mentioned the Integrated Rural Development Programme (Regional Development Division, 1981) areas wherein, at the request of foreign donors, a target-group approach has been adopted. This has not been done before. At the grass-roots level, people are said to be happier with this targeting approach, and some observed that this method is meeting the development objectives of the Prime Minister.

Rural economy. The countryside was described as dynamic. During the four-to five-year period to mid-1983, many jobs have been created in the Mahaweli Programme area. Laborers in Mahaweli were said to be rural and skilled workers, many of them masons and carpenters. Agricultural income has been good. An indication of this is that savings deposits in the rural banks were high at the time of the interviews.

Demand for land. The ownership of land is important in Sri Lanka. High land prices in Colombo have kept people out of the city. The major costs of living in Colombo were said to be housing and related costs. Additionally, residential development has been constrained by the lack of finance; people have not been able to get loans to purchase real property.

When Mahaweli colonization areas are opened, it was reported, there are often invasions of squatters who enter the areas to try to get land. Furthermore, many Sri Lankans who have taken jobs in the Middle East use money earned there to buy land in rural Sri Lanka when they return.

Connectivity and commuting. The small island-country is compact and well connected. Even for residents of Colombo, roots to the villages were described as strong and active. Many residents are first generation Colombians. The fact that points on the island are well connected and the high cost of housing in Colombo combine to produce a great deal of daily commuting. Because Colombo house rents are so high, many public servants and others cannot afford to live in the city. Many Colombo workers reside 20 miles or so outside the city. A large part of the working population commutes into Colombo by railway; public servants get cheap fare rates on the intercity trains. The railway fare reduction is said to be one of the few benefits received by the low-paid public servant. The coach (bus) fare is not comparably cheap. The recent addition of private coach service island-wide and in the metropolitan area has given the widely dispersed population improved transportation and access. Respondents observed that since Colombo can be reached within eight to nine hours from anywhere in the country, people can live outside Colombo and come to the city whenever they want to.

Deficiencies of Colombo. Colombo has had little attraction and dynamism. Respondents perceived Colombo to be not large enough and not attractive enough. Colombo was seen to have been inadequately maintained and to have become run-down over the last 50 years. For example, one respondent compared Colombo to Kuala Lumpur; "40 to 50 years ago it was one-third the size of Colombo. Now, Kuala Lumpur is larger and more prosperous. Similar comparisons can be made between Colombo and Bangkok and Manila. However, in those places, the gap between the urban and rural areas has increased." Colombo was not seen to have a parasitic relationship to the rest of Sri Lanka. Instead it was observed that perhaps Colombo has "run down too much." For example, interviewees said that in Colombo, sewage treatment facilities and the water supply have not kept pace with development. These systems were seen as barely meeting the requirements of the existing population. There are few private systems such as septic tanks. Consequently, there is little treatment of sewage; much is simply dumped into the river (e.g., Kelani Ganga) and the sea.

Deconcentration in Colombo. As is the case with the island as a whole, Colombo is relatively small in area; its development has been relatively compact, as well as low in density. For example, it was said that six km. might be the longest distance from any major shanty area to the heart of the city. In the past, equal distribution of schools and good public transportation within the Colombo region have served to minimize the spread of Colombo's population. In recent years, however, a number of centrifugal forces seem to have been operating to deconcentrate Colombo's development. There has been a policy of deconcentrating industry. Because of high land prices, residential infill has been possible but principally by the affluent. Instead, most people have formed households in metropolitan Colombo, but outside

Colombo City. They have been aided in this by the good services provided by railway and public coach transport and the recently added private coach service. As a consequence, there has not been an overconcentration of population within Colombo region. Also, relative to the rest of the country and the region, Colombo's primacy has been moderate. Colombo region accounts for only 20% of the country's population.

Respondents noted that the actions of the Urban Development Authority (UDA) have operated to spread out Colombo's development. The UDA has the legal authority to control development in the Kotte area of Sri Lanka's new capital, Sri Jayawardanapura, just to the east of Colombo City. However, it was observed that UDA's regulations and requirements have not had the effect of muting demand for residential development in the new-capital area. It was said that by motor car Sri Jayawardanapura is "minutes from the Pettah and the Fort" (in the center of Colombo City). Thus this residential development has urbanized an heretofore underdeveloped peripheral part of the metropolis.

Greater Colombo Economic Commission (GCEC) officials said that in developing the Free Trade Zone in the northern part of the metropolitan area, they have been trying to minimize the urbanization likely to result from the foreign investments. The GCEC stated that it has drawn employees into the factories of the Free Trade Zone from the immediately surrounding areas. Respondents said that there has been little displacement and little uprooting of new employees from their present home surroundings. However, the Free Trade Zone was said to have drawn employees from as far as 15 to 20 miles away.

Colombo's shanties and slums. It was perceived that, unlike shanty areas in much of the rest of South and Southeast Asia, Colombo's shanty areas are stable. These shanties generally have not served as a transition stage for people to filter up to other, higher-quality housing. It was observed that Colombo's shanties are repaired or improved both in situations when security of tenure is granted and when there is no security of tenure

(Weerasinghe and Fernando, 1982). It was noted that many of the recently built shanties are more solidly constructed than has been the norm for Colombo-area shanties in the past.

Most shanties and slums in Colorado did not result from a rapid, recent influx of population from rural areas. UDA surveys show that most families have lived in such areas for 10 years and more. Among shanty residents there is much informal and casual labor (Marga Institute, 1979); among slum residents there is more formal employment. Almost 90% of the shanty and slum population was said to be employed - somehow. Much of this employment is with local government. Also, children from shanties and slums go to school; this was cited as yet another indicator of the stability of these areas.

Summary

To sum up the interview results on the role that government policy has played in producing Sri Lanka's recent pattern of urbanization, all respondents opined that there has been no single policy of urbanization or counterurbanization *per se*. They observed that there has been a series of sectoral policies and programs over the years that has produced Sri Lanka's rural-urban distribution of 80% or so rural population and 20% or so urban population. Amenities and essential services were widely seen as accessible to all of Sri Lanka's population. Rural/urban disparities therefore have been slight.

SRI LANKA'S POLICY AND PLANNING AS A MODEL FOR OTHER COUNTRIES

The second purpose of the survey was to extract from the above urbanization policy analysis some policy and planning lessons for other developing countries. Therefore, in the examination of the interviewees' responses particular attention was given to identifying the institutional and procedural relationships surrounding urban development policy and planning in Sri Lanka. This section: (1) reviews the roles and principal actor agencies in Sri Lankan planning, (2) draws some conclusions about urban development planning as it has been practiced recently in Sri Lanka, and (3) assesses Sri Lanka as a counterurbanization model for other developing countries.

Capital Planning

Besides municipal planning agencies and the Ministry of Local Government, Housing and Construction, the primary planning and program evaluation organizations in Sri Lanka include the Ministry of Finance and Planning, the Mahaweli Programme, the Greater Colombo Economic Commission, and the Urban Development Authority.

The Ministry of Finance and Planning, responsible for national planning, is charged with looking five years ahead. It plans how public capital investment should be allocated. The Ministry's plans are documented in the Public Investment Report (National Planning Division, 1983).

The Mahaweli Programme does the operational planning for its area in the Dry Zone. Its planners indicated that until recently detailed operational spatial planning had not been done in the field. Rather, it had occurred in Colombo. However, with the formation of the new System C, the practice of centralized planning has apparently been changed by decentralizing recent sub-system planning in the Mahaweli Programme area.

The Greater Colombo Economic Commission is charged with administering the investment and employment activities of Sri Lanka's Free Trade Zones. It also is charged with doing the planning for those areas. The GCEC's managers said that "part of what we are about is tinkering and seeing which way to go. There is little awareness of the problem that we create."

The Urban Development Authority is reported to have the majority of the planning staff in Sri Lanka. It's principal responsibility is to plan the country's major urban sector projects. These have included: the new capital, Sri Jayawardanapura; hotel and bank projects in central Colombo; commercial development projects in other cities and towns across the island; and other urban-sector activities. Some UDA planners observed that planning the urban sector is not organized to take into account the whole development process. Coordination between UDA and GCEC planning was seen to need improvement. It was said that fundamental information on the urban condition is not available. The primary base for recent town planning in Colombo has been the United Nations master plan (The Republic of Sri Lanka, n.d.). This document has been relied upon in relating planning to the urban development needs of the government. Respondents said that spatial planning should be emphasized in the next phases of planning in Colombo.

Urban Development Planning

One major conclusion that can be drawn about development planning in Sri Lanka is that experimentation, personality, and politics play important, interdependent roles. For example, the Prime Minister and Minister of Local Government, Housing and Construction, Ranasinghe Premadasa, was perceived by many respondents as a project-oriented activist; he was seen as a decisive implementor of project-level plans. State President of Sri Lanka, J.R. Jayewardene, has stated:

> Our government is a practical government. We see the world as evolutionary since we became free and we, as a national organization, must change to remain viable. This is not the time to quarrel about ideology. We have to concentrate on finding out what works and how it works to help us in our development program (Jayewardene, 1978, 7).

The interviews revealed that if a deductively initiated project (e.g., in housing) was regarded as successful by Local Government Minister Premadasa, then he would have the project replicated elsewhere in the country. Policy, therefore, seems to have been the response to, not the stimulus of, this kind of experimental decision-making. In Colombo, planning often has taken place after development. "Let's see what happens, then we'll take action." At the Greater Colombo Economic Commission they said that they have been given the task of attracting investment and creating jobs; "we have not reflected on our activities" .Time and again, respondents describe the operation of this learn-by-doing approach in various programs of the country's development planning and management.

Politics and planning seem to have worked together in Sri Lanka. According to respondent, the polticians determine the policies, and the planners help them. Planning cannot be separated from politics.

Bearing in mind the incremental nature of these experimental planning tactics, respondents suggested a number of ways to improve planning in Sri Lanka. Some planners saw the need for the governmemt to develop national planning policy and a national spatial strategy. Increasingly, policymakers seemed to be becoming more aware of the need for spatial plans.

> We plan nationally, but by sector, not spatially. Things are not coordinated and brought into a whole as such. There is no overall physical plan.

Respondents also noted that regional planning needs attention: It was said that such a planning approach should be encouraged in the Dry Zone in place of the existing system-by-system approach. For example, the Mahaweli command planning approach was perceived to have ignored the infrastructure in a town just outside one planning area while it was developing another town inside an adjacent planning area. In the urban sector it was suggested that regional planning can come only formally, such as by an amendment to the UDA Act.

Coordination and Planning

The planning need that emerged most frequently from the interviews was for more effective coordination among the many roles and actors engaged in the various levels of Sri Lankan policy and planning. For example, an interviewee observed that there is little coordination between Integrated Rural Development (IRD) programs and Urban Development Authority schemes.

Mainly, IRD was said to provide additional funds for line agencies. It was stated that the IRD Division did have a monitoring unit with which to liase.

It was observed that the urban sector should not be considered only from a microplanning, project-level approach; it also should involve planning policy for urban areas. Some respondents said that Sri Lanka's planning should be more concerned with locational strategies. Individual development projects were identified with the particular ministries involved. For Colombo, there was perceived to be a need to coordinate economic, social, and physical planning, and to coordinate it all into a spatial plan. "The bottlenecks in my country are administrative. To do a major physical facility project, we have to deal with seven or eight agencies. How to coordinate?"

It was perceived that the centralizing forces associated with coordination are resisted, perhaps because the policiticians deal with the people who have the vote; consequently various personal appeals and other relationships exist.

From 1977 onwards there was said to have been operating in the government a high-level committee of development secretaries. The purpose of the committee is to coordinate all development-policy matters - including policies at the national level. The committee also monitors progress on development projects. "This mechanism seems to work"; it is a collegial, peer style of coordination.

Also discussed in the interviews was the need for information in Sri Lankan development policy, planning, coordination, and management. For example, it was said that the Integrated Rural

Development Programme does not have baseline data. Fundamental information on the urban situation is not available. No centralized data retrieval seems to exist among the various planning agencies. UDA however, has been developing an urban information system (Robinson, 1982). Migration has been monitored by the Ministry of Plan Implementation, but primarily through the approximately decennial census. There was seen to be no formal attempt to define or measure urbanization other than by means of the census.

In sum, from the interviews, urban development policy and planning activities in Sri Lankan would seem to have a number of notable characteristics and needs. In the rush of the then-new government in 1977 to develop the nation, the dominant approach to planning seemed to be that a policy initiative was first conceived at the highest level of government, then assigned to or conceived by a lead project or sector ministry. The project, when it had developed some political attractiveness, was executed. It was through such a trial-and-error experience in planning and implementing programs and projects that development policy seemed to have emerged.

In turn, this top-down ministry and lead-project approach has spawned the need for program planning that is more spatial and holistic at national, regional, and urban scales. Program and project planning and implementation coordination that cut across sectors and ministries at both regional and urban levels seem to be particularly needed. A suitable goal would be to have programs coordinated in a way that improves the effectiveness of planning and therefore the quality of resulting projects, but also accommodates the needs of the political process for flexibility and responsiveness. Finally, as Sri Lanka's development planning capacity continues to evolve and mature, the need for improved information and the measurement of both pre-and post-planning conditions will have to be satisfied.

Sri Lanka as a Counterurbanization Model for Other Developing Countries

Are urban development patterns in Sri Lanka transferable to other developing countries, particularly ones that need to counter their own high rates of urbanization? Sri Lanka's overall experience in policy and development (as it appears in the interviews cited here) probably is not a generally transferable planning model or method. The current government and other development organizations in Sri Lanka seem to be drawing on the country's unique cultural and historical traditions as they pursue their development goals (Goulet, 1983, 19-20). Since Sri Lanka's cultural evolution and process of urbanization are more idiosyncratic than universal, it seems unlikely that other countries could simply transplant Sri Lanka's approach to urban development (Berry, 1981).

However, while the history and *means* of Sri Lanka's urbanization may not be replicable or even desirable for others, the *ends,* or results, may be worth emulating. For example, some of Sri Lanka's urban-rural conditions might well serve as urban development goals for another country.

Sri Lanka's planning process as model. From the analysis above it may be assumed that there is a need in Sri Lanka to achieve more effective coordination between sectoral (Herbert, 1979, 190-196) and lead-project planning, especially at the program and project levels of planning; some cross-ministry policy planning does occur. Another need is to make plans before forming policy. Forward program planning and project planning that flow directly from policy plans would seem to strengthen development policy and make policy-driven actions a more informed and anticipatory outcome of planning. By continuing to employ experimental tactics, such planning need not necessarily be less responsive to the demands of the political environment. Another planning procedural need that emerged from the interviews was for urban-sector planning to complement the now-dominant physical planning approach with an interrelated policy, national, regional, and spatial planning set of approaches. Spatial impact assessment might be considered (Lim, 1984).

An experiment approach is one of the aspects of the planning process in Sri Lanka that should be considered for transferability by policy and planning officials in other developing countries. Some contemporary planning theory (Delbecq, 1978; Van de Ven and Koenig, Jr., 1976) advocates such an approach. However, such learning-by-doing (Cohen, 1983) as a systematic planning tactic does not seem to be used widely around the world.

Another element of Sri Lanka's planning practice worth some emulation by planners elsewhere is the pragmatic linking of politics and planning. It is the view of this researcher that such a relationship is appropriate, but in Sri Lanka the existing relationship might be made more effective if the politicians and policymakers used their staff planners more for program and project planning before the decision to implement a development policy. Not only would a policy likely benefit from being selected from a set of thoroughly researched alternatives, but also it would be useful to have a system for incorporating what has been learned from past experiments into new policy (Corey, 1984b). Recently other planning-procedure needs have been identified: (1) strengthening UDA's financial analysis and investment planning approaches for urban development project planning (Prakash and Huddleston, 1984) and (2) using appropriate information and data-management systems technology in Sri Lankan urban planning (Robinson, 1982).

Sri Lanka's settlement pattern as model. Other developing countries could do worse than to look to the resulting settlement pattern in Sri Lanka as an end-state goal to pursue in their own efforts to counter rapid urbanization. It would seem that the following conditions that have been attained in Sri Lanka might be worth seeking: (1) a low level of primacy; (2) a long-term pattern of low-level urbanization; (3) low rates of natural population increase; (4) minimal urban-rural disparities in terms of income, quality-of-life measures and social indicators; (5) new, previously landless settlers being granted land; (6) jobs being created for the unemployed; (7) progress being made toward near-term self-sufficiency in electricity generation; (8) self-sufficiency in a food staple (i.e., paddy) is nearly attained; (9) a primate city that has operational and maintenance problems but is not a behavioral sink; and (10) the support of a majority of its electorate (as demonstrated in recent elections and referenda).

However, all is not ideal, even with this idealized synthesized "counterurbanization model of Sri Lanka." While people have not clogged the cities in Sri Lanka, there is some emerging evidence that rural areas and villages have been experiencing some of the problems normally associated with cities. Recent rural-to-rural migration has produced complaints from long-term resident villagers that social organization and community safety have deteriorated (Obeysekere, 1983, 18-19; Morrison, Moore, and Lebbe, 1979). Suicide rates in Sri Lanka's rural districts are rising; they even exceed those in the Colombo District (Kearney and Miller, 1984, 27). A distinction has been made between "rural development" and "development of or in rural areas" (Dias and Silva, 1981, 104). Those who make this distinction see the need for a less passive reception of government-decided investments by rural Sri Lankans, with the people themselves making the decisions that relate to their own development and self-reliance (Rogers, 1976).

In macroeconomic terms, any concern over urbanization in Sri Lanka is likely to be merely academic unless the country is able to increase dramatically its exports and come to grips with tariffs, exchange rates, and balance-of-trade deficits. In the process, its policymakers must address the basic structural problems of the economy and create a dynamic economy that systematically decreases reliance on foreign donors and borrowing from abroad (Stern, 1984). In short, there will be little urbanization without a growing economy in Sri Lanka.

Finally, the communal problems between the majority Sinhalese and the minority Tamils must be addressed and resolved or again, concern over urbanization in Sri Lanka becomes a relatively insignificant issue by comparison. Given the political and electoral effectiveness of the current government prior to mid-1983, and given the ancient philosophical precepts that underpin the espoused beliefs of most Sinhalese and the Tamils, it seems reasonable to hope that the needs and grievances of these two communities can be negotiated and reduced so that the country can get on with its development. The lesson here for other countries is that development is retarded by ethnic and other violent conflict.

CONCLUSIONS

The answer to the question about the role of government in producing Sri Lanka's recent pattern of urbanization essentially is twofold. First, a succession of recent governments has pursued a bundle of largely disparate sectoral policies and lead-project programs. In the aggregate, these actions have maintained the country's long-term low level of urbanization. Second, from the findings of this research it is concluded also that Sri Lanka's urban-rural settlement pattern has not been the result of an integrated and unified policy of counterurbanization or of an explicit attempt to restrain concentrated development or urbanization. Rather, it seems that the existing settlement pattern has been produced over the decades by the relatively uncoordinated implementation of diverse sectoral programs and projects in support of agricultural and rural-area investment. It is concluded therefore that Sri Lanka's pattern of long-term deconcentrated urbanization is more a case of "policy serendipity" than an outcome of an intentional, planned, coordinated, and unified counterurbanization policy (Corey, 1984a). (It should be noted parenthetically that the seafarers of old Arabia called Sri Lanka "Serendib," "a word that has since evolved into the soothing state of mind known as serendipity" (Keuneman, 1983, 25). Serendipity has come to be understood as "an assumed gift for finding valuable or agreeable things not sought for" (Gove, 1966, 2072).

The answer to the second question on Sri Lanka as a counterurbanization model for other countries also is twofold.

First, as regards planning means, other developing countries probably should avoid a process of development planning that is uncoordinated across sectors and ministries. Rather, they should seek to address urbanization problem by using planning procedures that explore experimentally alernative policies with attention to both their technical and their political effectiveness. Second, as regards planning outcomes, other developing countries are well advised to seek Sri Lanka's resultant long-term low level of urbanization and a rural sector that has provided employment and amenities sufficient to keep the villages and countryside populated. In addition, contemporary urban and rural settlement patterns that are congruent with a country's cultures and traditions probably represent essential ingredients for stable development results. Rather than a model, Sri Lanka has served more as a treasure trove of development lessons for the urban scholar and official alike.

REFERENCES

Abeysekera, Dayalal. 1980. *Urbanization and the growth of small towns in Sri Lanka, 1901-71*. Paper No. 67 of the East-West Population Institute. Honolulu: East-West Population Institute.

Bailey, Kenneth D. 1982. *Methods of Social Research*. Second Edition. New York: The Free Press.

Berry, Brian J.L. (ed.) 1976. *Urbanization and Counterurbanization*. Beverly Hills, California: Sage Publications.

Berry, Brian J.L. 1981. *Comparative Urbanization: Divergent Paths in the Twentieth Century*. Revised and enlarged second edition. New York: St. Martin's Press.

Champion, A.G. 1989. Counterurbanization in Europe. *The Geographical Journal* 125: 52-80.

Cohen, Michael A. 1983. *Learning By Doing: World Bank Lending for Urban Development, 1972-82*. Washington, D.C.: The World Bank.

Corey, Kenneth E. 1984. Qualitative Planning Methodology: An Application to Two Cases in Development Planning in *Focus on Quality: The International Conference on Research Methodology in the Social Sciences*. Durban: University of Durban-Weatville.

Corey, Kenneth E. 1984b. Qualitative Planning Methodology: An application to South Korea and Sri Lanka. *Development Planning Review* (Sri Lanka) 3: 1-14.

Delbecq, Andre L. 1978. Relating Need Assessment to Implementation Strategies: An Organizational Perspective. Paper presented at the Second National Conference on Need Assessment in Health and Human Services, Louisville, KY.

de Silva, K.M. 1981. *A History of Sri Lanka.* London: C. Hurst and Company.

Dias, Hiran D., and Silva, W.P.T. 1981. *Strategy Without Ideology: Experience of Rural Development in Sri Lanka.* Bangkok: Division of Human Settlements Development, Asian Institute of Technology.

Duncan, J.S. 1990. *The City as Text: The Politics of Landscape Interpretation in the Kandyan Kingdom.* Cambridge: Cambridge University Press.

Goulet, Denis. 1983. *Mexico: Development Strategies for the Future.* Notre Dame, Indiana: University of Notre Dame Press.

Gove, Philip Babcock. *1966. Webster's Third New International Dictionary of the English Language Unabridged.* Springfield, Massachusetts: G. & C. Merriam Company Publishers.

Herbert, John D. 1979. *Urban Development in the Third World: Policy Guidelines.* New York: Praeger Publishers.

Jayewardene, J.R. 1978. Role of Scientists in a Developing Society. Address at the inauguration of the 34th Annual Session of the Sri Lanka Association of the Advancement of Science, Colombo.

Jones, Gavin W., and Selvaratnam, S. 1970. Urbanization in Ceylon, 1946-63. *Modern Ceylon Studies* 1: 199-212

Kearney, Robert N., and Miller Barbara D. 1984. Social Change and the Spiralling Rise in Suicides in Sri Lanka. Paper presented at the 1984 Meeting of the Association for Asian Studies, Washington, D.C., 29 pp.

Kelley, Allen C., and Williamson, Jeffrey G. 1984. *What Drives Third World City Growth: A Dynamic General Equilibrium Approach.* Princeton, New Jersey: Princeton University Press.

Keuneman, Herbert, *et. al.* 1983. *Sri Lanka.* Hong Kong: Apa Productions.

Lim, Gill-Chin. 1984. Urban Agglomeration and Spatial Policies in Developing Countries. Paper presented at the 1984 Meeting of the Association of American Geographers, Washington, D.C.

Linn, Johannes F. 1983. *Cities in the Developing World: Policies for Their Equitable and Efficient Growth.* New York: Oxford University

Press.

Marga Institute. 1979. *The Informal Sector of Colombo City (Sri Lanka).* Colombo: Marga Institute.

Mendis, M.W.J.G. 1982. *Urbanization and Urban Development in Sri Lanka.* Colombo: Office of Housing and Urban Development USAID.

Miller, E. Willard and Miller, Ruby M. 1989. *The Third World: India, Sri Lanka, and Nepal, A Bibliography.* Monticello, Illinois: Vance Bibliographies, Public Administration Series: Bibliography 2654.

Ministry of Plan Implementation. 1981. *Development 1931-1981. Sri Lanka.* Colombo: Ministry of Plan Implementation.

Moore, Mick. 1984. Categorizing Space: Urban-Rural or Core-Periphery in Sri Lanka. *The Journal of Development Studies* 20: 102-122.

Morrison, Barrie M., Moore, M.P., and Lebbe, M.U. Ishak. 1979. *The Disintegrating Village: Social Change in Rural Sri Lanka.* Colombo: Lake House Investments, Ltd.

Obeysekere, Gananath. 1983. *The Goddess Pattini and the Parable on Justice.* Punitham Tiruchelvam Memorial Lecture, Tamil Womens Union, Kalalaya.

Pandítharatna, B.L. 1964. Trends of Urbanization in Ceylon 1901-1953. *The Ceylon Journal of Historical and Social Studies* 7: 203-217.

Prakash, Ved, and Huddleston, Jack R. 1984. *Approaches to Financial Analyses and Investment Planning for Urban Development Projects.* Nairobi, Kenya: United Nation Center for Human Settlements (HABITAT).

Ram, Mohan. 1989. *Sri Lanka: The Fractured Island.* New Delhi: Penguin Books India.

Ramanayake, Dennis, 1982. *The Katunayake Investment Promotion Zone: A Case Study.* Colombo: Ministry of Plan Implementation.

Regional Development Division. 1981. *District Integrated Rural Development Programme.* Colombo: Ministry of Plan Implementation.

Renaud, Bertrand. 1979. *National Urbanization Policies in Developing Countries.* Staff Working Paper No. 347. Washington, D.C.: The World Bank.

Richards, Peter and Gooneratne, Wilbert. 1980. *Basic Needs, Poverty and Government Policies in Sri Lanka.* Geneva: International Labour Office.

Robinson, Vincent B. 1982. Development of a Microcomputer Urban

Infomation System Unit in Colombo, Sri Lanka. Paper presented before the Annual Conference of the Urban & Regional Information Systems Association, Minneapolis, Minnesota.

Rogers, Everett M. 1976. Communication and Development: The Passing of the Dominant Paradigm. *Communication Research* 3: 213-240.

Silva, P.T. 1979. Land Settlement and Urban Development in the Dry Zone. *Sri Lanka Journal of Social Sciences* 2: 55-76.

Sri Lanka, Department of Census and Statistics. 1981. *Census of Population and Housing, 1981.* Colombo: Ministry of Plan Implementation.

Sri Lanka, Department of Census and Statistics. 1983a. *Socio-Economic Development and Fertility Decline in Sri Lanka: Case Study Background Paper.* Colombo: Ministry of Plan Implementation in collaboration with United Nations Population Division.

Sri Lanka, Department of Census and Statistics. 1983b. *Statistical Pocket Book of the Democratic Socialist Republic of Sri Lanka 1983.* Colombo: Ministry of Plan Implementation.

Stern, Joseph J. 1984. Liberalization in Sri Lanka; A Preliminary Assessment. Paper presented at the 1984 Meeting of the Association for Asian Studies, Washington, D.C.

Sumanasekera, H.D. 1981. Measuring the Regional Variation of the Quality of Life in Sri Lanka. *Sri Lanka Journal of Agrarian Studies* 2: 27-40.

Tambiah, Stanley *et al.* 1990. Sri Lanka Introduction. *The Journal of Asian Studies* 49: 26-96.

The Republic of Sri Lanka. n.d. *Colombo Synthesis Report, Colombo Master Plan Project,* Vol. 4. Colombo: Ministry of Local Government, Housing and Construction, Department of Town and Country Planning in co-operation with the United Nations Development Programme (Project SRL/71/528).

Van de Ven, Andrew H., and Koenig, Jr., Richard. 1976. A Process Model for Program Planning and Evaluation. *Journal of Economics and Business* 28: 161-170.

Weerasinghe, A.S., and Fernando, R.C.A. 1982. Settlement Up-Grading Programs as an Alternative to Slum Clearance. Paper presented to the Fourth Annual International Shelter Workshop, Washington, D.C.

The World Bank. 1984. *World Development Report 1984.* New York: Oxford University Press.

PART TWO

AGRICULTURE IN SRI LANKA'S DEVELOPMENT

Chapter IV

AGRARIAN CHANGE AND AGRICULTURAL DEVELOPMENT IN SRI LANKA

G.H. Peiris
University of Peradeniya, Sri Lanka

The island of Sri Lanka, 25,000 square miles in extent, lies off the southern tip of peninsular India from which it is separated by a narrow strip of sea. Occupying the south-central parts of the island is a rugged mountainous area which in its innermost parts reaches elevations of over 8,000'. These "central highlands" are circumscribed by a plain, the general elevation of which ranges from sea level to about 1,000'. The plain is narrow and dissected in the south and southwest but is relatively flat and featureless elsewhere.

The tropical location of the island ensures perennially high temperatures, the monthly means of which range between 78^0 and 85^{0}F in the lowlands. In rainfall there is greater diversity. Though most parts of the island have an average annual rainfall of over 50", spatial differences relating to the amount of rain and to its seasonality, reliability and effectiveness have formed the basis of the perception of Sri Lanka as comprising a Wet Zone and a Dry Zone (Farmer, 1957, 22-28). In the former, which extends over the southwest quadrant of the island, the rainfall is heavy, seasonally well distributed, reliable and agroecologically effective throughout the year. Over the rest of the island-the Dry Zone - rainfall is largely restricted to the period from October to January, deviates markedly from the recorded averages, and is less effective in terms of defined criteria than in the Wet Zone.

Certain other diversities of the physical environment within Sri Lanka exhibit a rough correspondence with the foregoing climatic zonation. For instance, while Red-Yellow Podzolic Soils cover an estimated 82% of the Wet Zone, Reddish Brown Earths form the dominant soil group of the Dry Zone (Moorman & Panabokke, 1961). Again, while the climax vegetation in most parts of the West Zone is Tropical Evergreen Forest, that of the Dry Zone is Semi-Evergreen Monsoon Forest (Holmes, 1956; Mueller-Dombois, 1968). In agricultural land use, the former area has nearly 75% of its surface under permanent agriculture, whereas about 55% of the latter area remains unused or only periodically used for shifting agriculture.

The northern Dry Zone plains - the *Rajarata* of the ancient chronicles - were the principal venue of the early history of Sri Lanka the historiographic traditions of which date back to about the 6th century B.C.. The pioneer agricultural settlements of the *Rajarata* were located among some of its riverine tracts and were based on rice growing with simple techniques of irrigation. With the growth of population and the emergence of monarchical forms of government in the centuries that followed, the area under permanent agriculture expanded and the techniques of irrigation became more refined. Thus, by the early years of the Christian era, large storage reservoirs with extensive networks of canals had been constructed in certain favored localities close to the centers of political power. They were the forerunners of still larger hydraulic works of later times. By the 12th century - the highnoon of the *Rajarata* civilization - when irrigation technology in Sri Lanka had reached its zenith, two massive hydraulic systems designed for transbasin conveyance of water from the wetter parts of the country spanned much of the northern Dry Zone plains (Gunawardena, 1971). This according to some historians (Murphy, 1957; Paranavithana, 1956, 69-74; 1960, 703-720), was the product of a highly centralized system of government and an elaborate and hierarchically arranged administrative apparatus which had evolved by that time.

The *Rajarata* civilization began to disintegrate by about the 13th century. Concurrently, there occurred a gradual shift of population and centers of political power to the southwestern parts of the country. Thereafter, except for a brief interlude during the 15th century, Sri Lanka remained politically fragmented and weakened by foreign invasion and internecine conflict until, at the end of the 16th century, the Portuguese who had arrived on the scene a hundred years earlier established their hegemony over the island's littoral, confining local political power to the "Kandyan Kingdom" of the mountainous interior. The Portuguese were followed by the Dutch who in turn were displaced by the British in the closing years of the 18th century. Meanwhile, most parts of the Dry Zone fell into desolation and decay.

The emergence of the Wet Zone as the main venue of political and economic activity in the "late-medieval" period meant that rice production (still the mainstay of the economy) became localized in an area where rain is both abundant and near perennial. Thus, the cultivation of paddy had no longer to depend on elaborate irrigation which, in turn, meant that the construction and maintenance of hydraulic works became relatively unimportant as a function of government. This, as well as the fact that other public works of monumental scale which characterized the *Rajarata* days were conspicuously absent in late-medieval times, suggests that agriculture had no longer to depend on or to sustain an elaborate and centralized government infrastructure. The upkeep of the relatively modest royal and religious establishments and the defense of the realm - the main functions of the government - came to be based on a complex system of service tenures operating within the framework of feudalistic societal relations which, from an agrarian point of view, is likely to have been different from what prevailed in earlier times. Apart from this, the emergence of the Wet Zone was also accompanied by increased maritime contact and, consequently, enhanced importance of producing commodities in agriculture and forest extraction for export trade.

The "modern period" of the history of Sri Lanka is conventionally regarded as commencing with the establishment of British power over the entire island in the early decades of the

19th century. In 1833, the country was brought under a unified system of administration the apex of which was occupied by the governor directly responsible to the Colonial Office in London. In the period which followed, the composition of the Legislative Council (which in its early existence served the governor in a purely advisory capacity) was gradually changed, paving the way for the evolution of representative forms of government. Constitutional reforms that were introduced from time to time during the early decades of the 20th century enlarged the legislature, increased its power and functions, made it more representative of the interests of the local people, and, in 1948, culminated in the grant of independence.

In economic change, the British Period was featured by the increasing importance of systematic and large-scale production of crops geared to export trade. Plantation agriculture which, even as late as the third decade of the 19th century, was confined to a few hundred acres of coffee, soon became the leading sector of the island's economy. When coffee plantations were destroyed by a fungal disease in the 1880s, coffee was promptly replaced by other plantation crops. By the end of the British Period, plantation agriculture in Sri Lanka had expanded to cover an aggregate extent of over 2 million acres.

Throughout the greater part of the British regime in Sri Lanka, the agrarian policies pursued by the government were generally oriented towards the promotion of the "modern sector" of the economy which consisted of plantation agriculture and related secondary and tertiary activities. Land legislation promulgated from time to time (for example, the Crown Land Encroachment Ordinances of 1840 and 1841, the Temple Lands Ordinance of 1856, the Partition Ordinance of 1863 and the Waste Lands Ordinance of 1896) and various other fiscal measures such as those that related to agricultural taxation were designed mainly to facilitate the release of land for plantation agriculture and/or to induce the spread of the concept of private property in land and thus stimulate commercialized economic activity among the peasantry. In many parts of the country these policies and practices are known to have had adverse effects on the peasant economy leading to the gradual pauperization of a large segment of the peasantry (Peiris, 1981).

The new era ushered in by the rise of plantation enterprise witnessed the construction of a modern network of communications; the development of services in transport, commerce, health-care and education; and a proliferation of trade, commerce and activities of government. Concurrently, with lowered mortality, the country's population increased to over 6 million at the time of independence. The development of capitalist modes of production and the emergence of entrepreneurial and professional groups and an urban and plantation proletariat resulted in far reaching changes not only in the pre-modern property relations but also in the traditional class structure of Sri Lankan society.

Many changes that have occurred in Sri Lanka since the attainment of independence four decades ago may be seen as continuations of earlier trends. The population which has increased persistently now stands at about 16 million. The economy, despite some diversification of production and a lowered dependence on foreign sources for the supply of certain essentials of consumption, still retains elements of the sectoral dichotomy which characterized it in the colonial era and still leans heavily on the income generated by the plantation sector. Further, regardless of the ideological differences among the political parties that have held the reins of government since independence, development effort has always been imbued with a concern for social, welfare; and welfare measures such as food subsidies, free education, and free health services have received high priority from successive governments, as in fact they did during the closing decades of the British regime. In politics, the representative form of government inherited from the British has survived in many of its essential elements, despite stresses and strains which relate invariably to the slow growth of the economy and the ethnic plurality of the population.

In terms of average per capita incomes and levels of consumption, Sri Lanka ranks among the "Low Income Developing

Countries", with a lower GNP per capita than some of its Asian neighbors, but a comparatively higher level of food consumption and life expectancy and better standards in the provision of "basic needs" services in education, health-care and housing (Table 4.1). In international comparisons of "Physical Quality of Life", the status of Sri Lanka appears distinctly superior to that of most low-income countries of the Third World.

TABLE 4.1
Selected Indicators of Development:
South Asian Countries and U.S.A.

	Sri Lanka	India	Pakistan	Nepal	Bangladesh	U.S.A.
GNP per capita 1985, US $ equivalent	380	270	380	150	160	16,690
Share of agriculture in the GDP, 1985 (%)	27	31	25	50	62	2
Life expectancy at birth, 1985, (yrs.)	70	56	51	51	47	76
Infant mortality rate, 1985 (per 1000)	36	89	115	123	133	11
Daily calorie supply 1985 (per capita)	2,385	2,189	2,159	1,899	2,034	3,633
Primary school enrollment, 1984 (% of age group)	103	90	42	62	77	101
Secondary school enrollment, 1984 (% of age group)	61	34	15	19	23	95
Urban population as % of total population, 1985	21	25	29	18	7	74

Source: World Bank, *World Devēlopment Report*, 1987

With an average density of population of 640 persons per square mile, Sri Lanka is one of world's most densely populated countries. Within the country, excessively high rural population densities (of over 1,500 per sq. mile) are encountered in the Wet Zone and in certain coastal areas of the northern and eastern parts of the island. Per capita availability of farm land is less than 1/2 acre. The acute "land hunger" prevalent in many parts of the country manifests itself in unemployment and underemployment in the agricultural sector, a rapidly expanding rural proletariat, and other agrarian features such as the widespread occurence of share-tenancy, minuscular frangmentation of farm units and general poverty in the countryside. A recent estimate (Edirisinghe, 1987) relating to Sri Lanka's "ultra poor" (Table 4.2) suggests that, despite the economic advances made during the past decade, a large segment of the rural population still live in conditions of dire poverty.

The "Dual Economy" model has been used as a framework of analysis of the economy which evolved in Sri Lanka under colonial dominance (Snodgrass, 1966), as it has in the case of many other ex-colonial dependent economies (Bocke, 1953; Allen and Donnithorne, 1957; Pelzer, 1957; Van Gelderen, 1961). This model in its application to Sri Lanka perceives a continuing structural dichotomy within the economy in the coexistence of an export-oriented modern sector dominated by plantation agriculture and a traditional sector made up largely of subsistence agriculture.

Plantation agriculture (mainly tea, rubber, and coconut) contributes about 14% of the Gross Domestic Product and accounts for approximately 10% of the country's gainfully employed workforce. The value of plantation exports is equivalent to about 45% of Sri Lanka's total export earnings. The plantation crops cover in aggregate almost 2 million acres, which represents about 40% of the area under permanent agriculture in the country. Typically, the units of production in the plantation sector are large and prior to the land reforms of the 1970s were owned by private investors, both foreign and local.

TABLE 4.2
Share of Agricultural Households in the Category of "Ultra-Poor", 1978/79 and 1981/82

Household Category	Percent of 'ultra-poor' in the total of households			
	all households		poorest 20% of households	
	1978/79	1981/82	1978/79	1981/82
General farmers (mostly, those self-employed in agriculture)	3.0	3.2	15.8	17.8
Plantation workers (laborer grades)	3.2	6.3	14.0	23.8
Agricultural workers (wage earners in subsistence agriculture)	10.8	15.4	23.8	36.7

Note: 'Ultra-poor' are those in households consuming less than 80% of the recommended calorie intake though spending more than 80% of their income on food (Lipton, 1975).
Source: Edirisinghe, 1987

Subsistence agriculture in Sri Lanka is largely focused on the production of rice, the staple food crop. Paddy is grown over about 1.4 million acres and has recorded a gross harvested acreage of 2.1 million acres each year during the recent past. In contrast to plantation agriculture, subsistence farming is characterized by small units of production and low levels of productivity per unit of labour input. For an estimated 18% of the gainfully employed workforce in Sri Lanka, subsistence farming is the main source of livelihood.

EVOLUTION OF AGRARIAN POLICY

Concern on the part of the ruling elite in British Sri Lanka about the plight of the more depressed segments of the peasantry and the stagnancy of "native" agriculture is a phenomenon that can be traced back at least to the regimes of the more benevolent British governors like Henry Ward (1855-60) and Hercules Robinson (1865-72) who gave expression to this concern through sporadic welfare measures such as the restoration of village irrigation works (Keane, 1905). Since about the turn of the century, for various reasons both internal and external (for example, the influence of welfarism-a dominant strand of political ideology in contemporary Britain - and, in Sri Lanka, the problems caused by the dependence on foreign sources for internal food requirements) the peasant economy began to receive enhanced government attention.

During the early decades of the 20th century, the overall official policy towards agrarian affairs of the country was remarkable free of ambiguity. It rested on the belief that, while the prosperity of the colony depended largely on the fortunes and prospects of the plantation sector, and that policy must hence continue to be geared to the promotion of plantation enterprise, for reasons of economic stability and general welfare the agrarian needs of the peasantry must also be satisfied.

By the early 1920s, however, it is possible to discern the emergence of certain new trends in agrarian thought. The nationalist movement was by this time far more articulate than before, the Legislative Council had been enlarged to include more elected representatives, the franchise had been widened, and local members of the legislature were bolder in their claim to represent the people. Further, the acute scarcity of food during World War I and the market slump which adversely affected the plantation industries in the post-war years brought into sharp focus the fundamental weaknesses of Sri Lanka's dependent economy. Thus, the idea that the economic stability of the country and the well-being of the local people would rest upon the creation of a dynamic peasant sector rather than on the perpetuation of the plantation system rapidly gained ground.

On the need to strengthen the peasantry as a remedial measure for the country's ills, there was consensus among the elite, both local and foreign. But on the causes for the prevailing ills, there developed sharp differences of opinion, in the sense that the notion that the plantation system itself was the prime cause for the country's poverty and instability was gaining currency among a segment of the local leadership. The main element of this new wave of thought and its exact time perspective are caught in the following remarks which Governor Hugh Clifford made in 1927:

> I have noted with great regret since my return to Ceylon after an absence of nearly a decade and a half, that a school of thought has, in the interval, grown up in the Island which teaches with persistent reiteration the doctrine that tea and rubber are a parasitic growth, which is battening upon the Colony's lifeblood; that they have evoked no appreciable benefit to the indigenous inhabitants of the country; and that they owe their existence to a systematic series of acts of expropriation and spoilation. (Clifford, 1927, 289).

The "parasitic theory" on plantation agriculture, as the antiplantation notions came to be referred to, was, of course, summarily rejected by the British. Nor did the "conservatives" among the Nationalist vanguard support such notions with fervor. Nevertheless, throughout the decades that followed, this "theory" continued to have a powerful impact upon popular agrarian perceptions in the country. It was, in fact, a prominent theme in the campaigns that heralded the radical land reforms in Sri Lanka during the 1970s (Peiris, 1975: 78-80).

A further new dimension to agrarian perceptions in Sri Lanka emerged with the origin of the Left movement in the early 1930s. The doctrinaire opposition of the Marxist's to private ownership of the means of production and to exploitation of labor meant that they stood firmly against not only large-scale capitalist enterprise epitomized in the country by plantation agriculture, but also the feudal elements of tenurial relations within the peasant sector. In the Marxist's scheme of thinking, it is only radical agrarian reform which constitutes a part of a general socialist transformation of society that could solve the problems of the peasantry in Sri Lanka. Thus, from the inception of their movement, they urged the nationalization of plantations, the liquidation of service tenures, the regulation of share tenancy, the formation of peasant unions, and the promotion of communal modes of agricultural production.

To generalize, then, by the closing years of the British Period, it is possible to recognize four overlapping shades in the prevailing spectrum of agrarian perception among the country's political elite. (For a cross-section of this spectrum, see the contributions of E.B.I Alexander, D.S. Senanayake and E.W. Perera to the Legislative Council debate on the "Land Law of Ceylon", *Hansard*, 1927, 419-523; Corea, 1925; Clifford, 1927; Perera, 1932; Bandaranaike, 1933; Brayne, 1934; Senanayake, 1935; and the contributions of D.P.R. Gunawardena to the debate on the Annual Appropriation Bill in *Hansard*, 1938, 2312-2316.)

First, there were the attitudes and notions of officialdom - at the apex still almost exclusively British - which by this time were less authoritarian and more accommodating than before and more sensitive to the aspirations of the local people. Though generally stringent in the allocation of funds for the development of peasant agriculture, they recognized the need to place priority on the requirements of the peasantry in Crown land alienation. They maintained a critical concern on what they believed to be the basic institutional weaknesses of peasant agriculture, exemplified in features as fragmentation of holdings, land disputes and litigation, insecurity of tenure in share-tenancy contracts, and rural indebtedness. They were also committed to the belief that the progress of the country would depend largely on the strength of plantation agriculture.

The second shade of the spectrum was represented by the viewpoints articulated by the more conservative segments of the national leadership. They shared in large measure the views of officialdom on the problems of peasant agriculture and the role of plantation agriculture. However, in their strong and persistent advocacy of a vigorous policy of State-aided land settlement and peasant colonization in the Dry Zone, they differed from officialdom. They believed that the Dry Zone had the potential to make Sri Lanka economically stable and independent and to create within the country "... a prosperous, self-supporting and self-respecting multitude of peasant proprietors".

Third, there was among the national political leadership of this time a group of persons who shared with the "conservatives" the ideas and ideals relating to Dry Zone development but differed from them in respect of attitudes towards plantation enterprise. Their notions were largely shaped by the perception that the emergence of plantation agriculture in Sri Lanka was facilitated by iniquitous land policies imposed under alien rule. They thus stood for remedying the past injustices through the adoption of policies that involve the redistribution of plantation land among the peasantry at least in those parts of the Wet Zone where the problems associated with land hunger are acute.

The stance of the Marxists was altogether different. While they were unopposed to relief measures directed at the poor, they had little faith in the millennial visions of the others among the local political elite on Dry Zone colonization. In their ideological antipathy towards private property, they saw the strategy of settlement development in the Dry Zone within the framework of individual peasant proprietorship as an attempt to promote the latent *petit bourgeois* tendencies of the peasantry. For plantation agricultural, their unequivocal demand was for total nationalization.

These different perceptions have outlasted the British Period and have continued to figure (albeit at varying degrees of clarity) in government agrarian policy of the past four decades, providing the basis for what may be referred to as a "conservative" approach and a "reformist" approach to agricultural development in Sri Lanka. The former approach is one which does not envisage fundamental changes in the structure and production relations of the economy. On the contrary it strengthens the agrarian pattern inherited from colonial times. It accords high priority to government intervention in the extension of the frontiers of agriculture in the Dry Zone through the establishment of peasant colonies. It stands for the preservation of the plantation system and for strengthening the plantation sector through government assistance to private initiatives in its rehabilitation. The second approach has been one which places emphasis on institutional reform as a strategy of agricultural development. It has been featured by attempts to extend State control over plantation agriculture, reduce inequalities in the ownership of agricultural land, eliminate exploitative production relations in peasant agriculture, and establish rural institutions to facilitate the direct involvement of the people in development activities.

The two approaches identified above have not always been mutually exclusive. In fact, what one can identify from the records of the past 40 years is that, at most times, there has been a blend of the two approaches, with periodic shifts of emphasis from one to the other depending largely on the professed persuasions of those in political authority.

For instance, the approach of the United National Party (UNP) which ruled the country during the first eight years after the withdrawal of the British, was basically conservative towards agrarian affairs. The leadership of the party was then in the hands of those who had been in effective control of internal affairs of the country during the closing years of the British regime. In peasant agriculture, their main preoccupation continued to be the establishment of agricultural colonies in the Dry Zone. Although their land policy gave token accommodation to demands for government purchase of private plantations for distributive alienation among landless peasants, their strategy for development of peasant agriculture had no place for radical agrarian reform.

Following the defeat of the UNP at the general elections of 1956 by a coalition of political parties the leadership of which included some prominent Marxists, radical reformist perceptions became strongly evident in agrarian policy. Tenurial reform was attempted in the peasant sector. Provision was made to set up a network of "Cultivation Committees" througout the country consisting of elected representatives of the farmers, vested with a wide range of powers and functions relating to paddy cultivation. The scope of the cooperative movement of Sri Lanka was extended into aspects of production and input supply in agriculture. The government, for the first time, became an entrepreneur in plantation agriculture. Direct and indirect taxes imposed on plantation agriculture were increased. And, the implications of nationalization of plantations were publicly made the subject of an official study and its findings were incorporated in an Agricultural Development Plan.

In overall terms, the 1960s were, once again, a period of lull in the radical strategies of agricultural development. The failure of the reforms initiated in the late 1950s was itself the principal reason for discarding further attempts at reform. Within the governments in office, there were many shades of political ideology resulting in a general lack of commitment to any specific direction of change. From 1965, when the UNP was in office for a 5-year spell, the government's preoccupation with a drive towards agricultural intensification through new technology was also a cause for the move away from the path of reform.

At the general elections of 1970 a "United Front" of political parties (which included two of the main Marxist groups in the country) was returned to office with a massive parliamentary majority. This change marked yet another pronounced swing of the policy pendulum towards radicalism. The approach adopted in agricultural development was mainly one of reform which aimed at eliminating foreign ownership of plantations, reducing the prevailing inequalities in the ownership of agricultural land in the country, promoting cooperative and communal modes of production in agriculture, facilitating popular participation in agricultural decision- making, stimulating production by creating a protected local market, and, in general, increasing State control over the economy as a whole. While these reforms were being implemented during the 7-year tenure of the United Front government, there was a distinct downgrading of the earlier strategies such as expanding the area under agriculture through settlement development in the Dry Zone and increasing crop yields by facilitating the adoption of new technology. To some extent, this eclipse of growth-oriented strategies was caused by the prevailing capital scarcities, which itself can be attributed partly to the effects of the radical policies which were in vogue.

The change of government in 1977 which brought the UNP once again into office marked another turning point in agrarian policy. The new leadership, being advocates of an "open economy". adopted a policy package intended to encourage capital accumulation, increase export earnings, attract foreign investment, curtail government intervention in the economy, and accelerate economic growth. In the agricultural sector, this change of policy was marked by the adoption of measures such as a massive infusion of capital into the development of irrigated agriculture in the Dry Zone, denationalizing some of the land brought under State control during the previous regime, encouraging large-scale private investment in certain spheres of agriculture, and enhancing the scale of government assistance to farmers for the adoption of yield-increasing technology. In plantation agriculture, although the organizational structure brought into being by the reforms of the 1970s has been retained more or less intact, investment has been increased and private sector participation has been encouraged.

In the sections of this chapter that follow, three specific strategies of agricultural development which have been prominent at various times since Sri Lanka gained independence are taken up for discussion with the objective of comparing what has been achieved with initial expectations. When placed against the earlier discussions of agrarian policy, it will be evident that these strategies are distinguished from one another by the varying blends of perceptions they represent. It will also be seen that they differ distinctly from one another in terms of the nature of their impact.

PEASANT COLONIZATION IN THE DRY ZONE

Since the early successes achieved in the establishment of several small peasant settlements under restored irrigation works in the drier parts of the country about 60 years ago, for most of the time, "colonization" of the Dry Zone has remained in the forefront of the development strategies pursued in Sri Lanka. The main objectives of this strategy were those of increasing the country's food production and providing relief to the acute "land hunger" prevailing among the peasantry in the densely populated areas. The former was to be achieved by harnessing the under-utilized physical resources (land and water) to expand the area under agriculture. The latter was expected to result from the movement of "surplus" population from overcrowded areas of the Wet Zone into the sparsely populated Dry Zone interior.

On closer scrutiny, it appears, there were several factors that shaped the specific elements of the strategy forged in the 1930s for agricultural and settlement development in the Dry Zone. Perhaps the foremost among them was that the extent of land available in the Dry Zone for irrigated agriculture was unknown. To the pioneers of this strategy, the myriad remnants of ancient hydraulic works suggested a boundless potential which, if utilized, could not only result in a substantial redistribution of the country's population and make the country self-sufficient in its food requirements, but also enable the large majority of peasants to each own an extent of land which could generate an income adequate for a "reasonable standard of living" (Senenayake, 1935, 36-37).

The ideals of egalitarianism and social welfare were also made fundamental ingredients of the Dry Zone colonization strategy as reflected in features such as the emphasis it placed on "landlessness". as a criterion in the selection of colonists, the careful maintenance of uniformity in the size of the individual allotments alienated, and the statutory safeguards adopted against "involutionary" agrarian processes found to be endemic to unregulated peasant agriculture. Above all, there was the lavish package of direct assistance made available by the government to those selected as colonists. In the majority of colonization schemes, apart from the fact that the establishment of irrigation facilities, the development of land for agriculture, and the institution of economic and social infrastructure were all done entirely by the government, the colonists were also provided government subsidies for house construction, purchase of agricultural implements, and living expenses for several months after initial settlement in the colony.

The main features of the Dry Zone colonization strategy outlined above have remained more or less intact up to the present time. The only significant modification of the original design has been the progressive reduction of land alienated to each settler family (from 5 acres of irrigable land and 3 acres of non-irrigable homestead land in the schemes established up to the mid-1950s to 3 acres of irrigable and 2 acres of non-irrigable land in the 1960s and to 2.5 acres and 0.5 acres, respectively, in the two categories of land in those of the recent past).

This was aimed both at reducing the cost per settler family by maximizing their number accommodated in the colonies as well as at inducing more intensive utilization of the alienated land. A system of "advanced alienation", another cost-reduction deviation from the original model (under which the selected colonists were required to participate collectively in aspects of initial land development), attempted in the colonies opened up in the 1960s was abandoned at the end of that decade largely because of its failure to reduce costs.

Most colonization schemes of the Dry Zone are based on restorations of ancient storage reservoirs and channel systems. The only significant exceptions in this regard up to the launching of the current Mahaveli Development Programme were the river basin development project of Gal-Oya in the eastern lowlands and Walave in the southeast. The colonies vary widely in size and migration impact from those with a few hundred settlers drawn from their immediate vicinity to those that have attracted thousands of migrants from the densely populated areas of the country. By the early 1980s, there were about 100 colonization schemes scattered throughout the Dry Zone in which an overall aggregate of some 100,000 peasant families had been settled (Table 4.3 and Fig. 4.1).

From several viewpoints, the Mahaveli Development Programme marks a new stage in the processes of settlement development in the Dry Zone. Its novelty lies mainly in its unprecedented scale. Based as it is on the physical resources not only of the Mahaveli River but also of several adjacent river catchments, its hydraulic matrix extends over a large part of the northern Dry Zone plains, supplying water to several complexes of new peasant settlements and improving the existing irrigation in many of the older colonies (Table 4.4 and Table 4.2). Moreover, the Mahaveli Programme is also more genuinely multi-purpose in its objectives than any of the previous colonization schemes.

TABLE 4.3
Settlement and Land Development in
Major Colonization Schemes
(as at the end of 1980)

District	Number of Schemes	Number of Allottees	Extent of Land Developed	
			Paddy	Highland
Kandy	1	1,982	5,425	3,454
Matale	4	3,785	7,992	5,290
Nuwara Eliya	1	152	152	152
Hambantota[1]	3	2,127	4,631	1,922
Uda Walave Scheme	1	10,835	n.a.	n.a.
Kurunegala[2]	9	6,610	15,172	9,631
Puttalam	10	2,358	6,276	7,282
Anuradhapura[3]	9	20,381	52,038	23,806
Polonnaruwa	7	14,687	52,287	24,089
Badulla	9	4,128	9,566	4,996
Monaragala	9	2,114	5,365	2,158
Ratnapura	1	552	1,318	378
Mannar	3	587	1,761	1,174
Vavuniya	4	1,439	4,257	2,510
Mullaitivu	9	5,286	8,812	11,482
Jaffna	9	3,054	8,548	6,134

Trincomalee	6	6,325	18,105	8,938
Batticaloa[4]	8	3,394	11,763	4,819
Amparai[5]	1	10,815	32,643	11,798
ALL DISTRICTS [6]	104	100,611	247,111	135,007

Notes: 1. Hambantota data exclude those on Uda Walave Scheme
2. Kurunegala data include the Left Bank unit of the Rajangane Scheme which has been reckoned as 1 scheme.
3. Anuradhapura data include the Right Bank unit of the Ranjagane Scheme which has been reckoned as 1 scheme (distinct from the LB unit)
4. Parts of the Gal-Oya Scheme located in Batticaloa District has been regarded as constituting I scheme and added to the district total.
5. Amparai data refer to those portions of the Gal-Oya Scheme located in their district.
6. There are no 'Major Colonization Schemes' in the Districts of Colombo, Gampaha, Kalutara, Galle, Matara and Kegalle.

Sources: Land Commisioner's Department
Uda Walave Scheme data, from the Agricultural Research Station at Angunukolapelessa

Given the detailed attention which many scholars have devoted over several decades to the study of peasant colonization in the Dry Zone, it is not possible to engage in a comprehensive evaluation of the impact of this strategy on agricultural development and agrarian change in Sri Lanka. However, the research literature available on this subject forms the basis of an assessment of the extent to which Dry Zone colonization has achieved, or failed to achieve, its main objectives of increasing food production, alleviating the scarcity of agricultural land and raising the standards of living among the peasantry.

The colonization schemes of the Dry Zone are today the main surplus areas of rice production in Sri Lanka having in aggregate about 30% of the country's total extent of land devoted to paddy and contributing an estimated 40% to the total output of rice in the country. In this context, a recent publication [Ministry of Plan Implementation (MPI), 1983] has pointed out that about

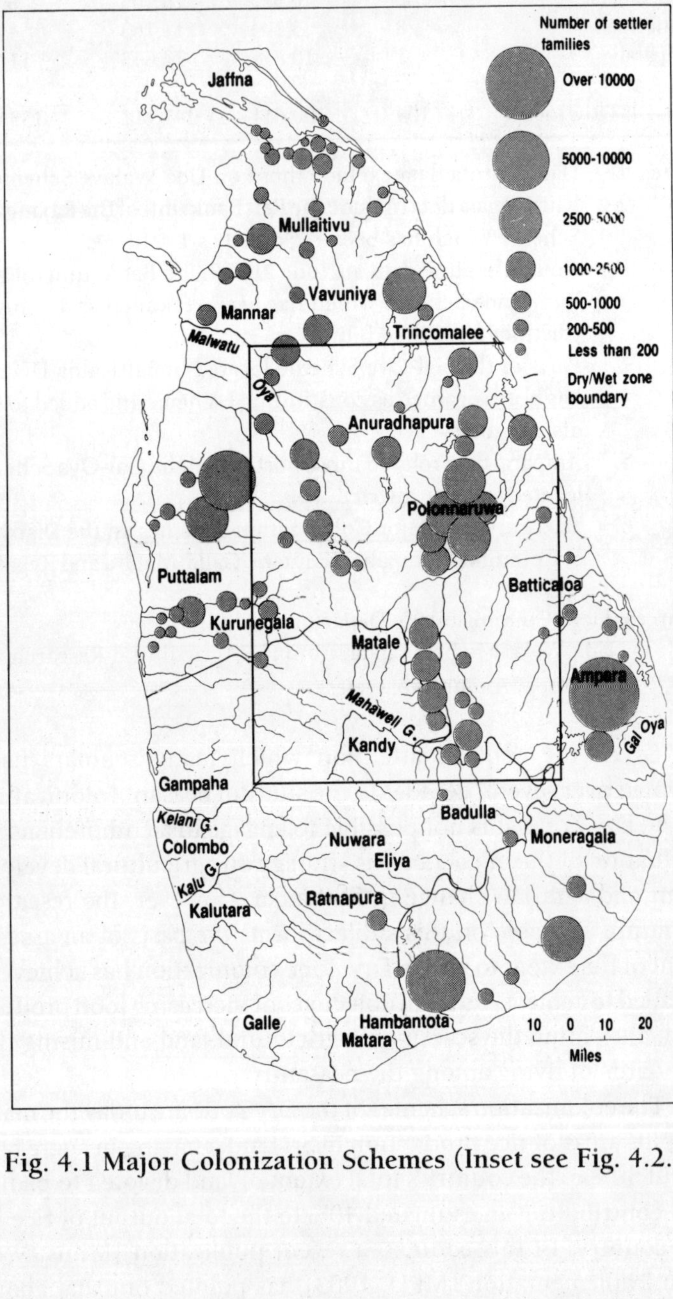

Fig. 4.1 Major Colonization Schemes (Inset see Fig. 4.2.)

65% of the additional rice output in Sri Lanka in the 1974-82 period was derived from the settlement areas fed by the major irrigation schemes. Yet another study (Wijetunga, 1985) has shown that in the recent past the major colonies of the Dry Zone have recorded an average paddy yield over 30% higher than other paddy growing areas of the country. It has also been noted (Gooneratne and Gunawardena, 1984, 26) that the paddy cropping intensity in the irrigated settlement schemes is substantially higher than in other areas. This latter has been attributed (Wanigaratne, 1987, 26) to the more stable conditions of water supply and the better organised systems of input supplies which characterize agricultural conditions in the majority of these settlement schemes. The foregoing observations, taken together with the fact that the establishment of colonization schemes has entailed an extension of the area under paddy cultivation of about 400,000 acres, point to the conclusion that, when measured against the objective of increasing Sri Lanka's food production, this strategy has achieved an appreciable measure of success.

TABLE 4.4

Land Development and Peasant Settlement under the Mahaveli Development Programme, 1987

Spatial Component*	Up to the end of 1987 Number of families settled	Extent under irrigation (ac.)	Total Irrigable Extent (estimated acreage)
System H	28,997	72,492	73,000
System C	13,826	34,565	50,500
System B	9,403	23,508	86,500
System G	2,260	5,650	12,750
Total	54,486	136,215	227,750

*See Fig. 4.2 for location

Source: Mahaveli Development Authority

The impact of the Dry Zone colonization schemes on the scarcity of agricultural land in the country and the phenomenon of "landlessness" among the peasantry is somewhat more intractable. Demographic records of the past few decades show that the

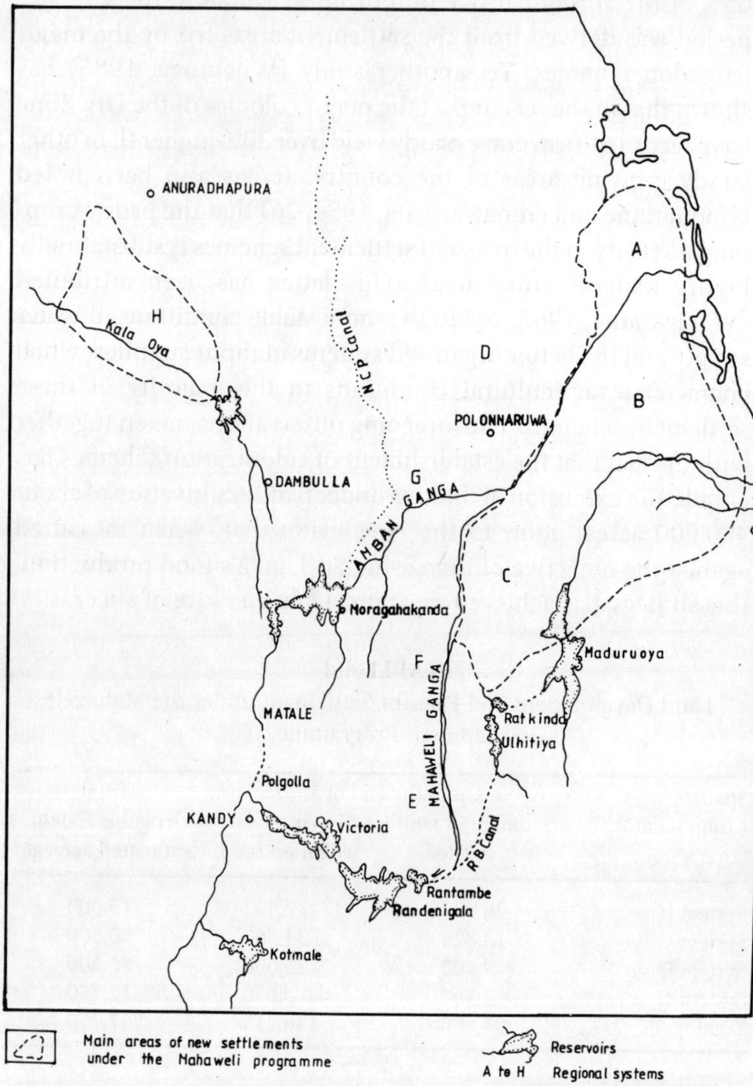

Fig. 4.2 Physical Layout of the Mahaveli Development Area

movement of people into the colonies of the Dry Zone and the related expanision of secondary and tertiary activities in the areas concerned have contributed to a rearrangement of the pattern of population distribution in the country. As a rough estimate, the share of Sri Lanka's total population accounted for by the present colonization areas has increased from about 8% in 1931 to 17% by 1981. Furthermore, over a period which spans about 60 years, the colonization schemes have enabled the settlement of approximately 160,000 peasant families on some 580,000 acres of land most of which was unoccupied and uncultivated in earlier times (Table 4.5). To place these figures in perspective, the total population now living in the colonies (migrants and their "natural increase" after settlement) can be estimated at around 1.3 million (8% of the country's total population) and the amount of land they occupy represents approximately 12% of the total area under permanent agriculture in Sri Lanka.

TABLE 4.5
Progress of Peasant Colonization in the Dry Zone
(up to the end of 1987)

Period	Number of families settled			Extent alienated (acres) total for period	
	average per year	total for period	cumulative total at end of period	irrigable land	non-irrigable land
up to the end of 1938	—	5,596	5,596	21,248	11,552
1939-48	526	5,258	10,854	23,123	15,354
1949-58	4,617	46,165	57,019	130,445	63,478
1959-68	2,747	27,474	84,498	60,491	40,955
1969-78	2,293	22,399	106,892	48,248	12,454
1979-87	6,035	54,313	161,205	128,283	25,657

Note : These estimates are based on data furnished by the Land Commissioner's Department and the Mahaveli Development Authority. They include data on the Mahaveli Settlement Systems of H, C, B and G and on the settlement schemes of Lunugamvehera and Inginimitiya opened up in the 1980s. The estimates are liable to contain a small margin of error.

The proportion of the present colony population accounted for by migrants from the densely populated areas of the country cannot be ascertained with the data currently available. However, the records of the Census of 1981 indicate that only about 30% of the population in the rural areas of the main colonization districts (Hambantota, Amparai, Batticaloa, Trincomalee, Polonnaruwa, Anuradhapura, Vavuniya and Mullaituvu) were migrants from other districts, which points to the likelihood that the transfers of population from the areas of high population density into the Dry Zone induced by colonization were not particularly large. Moreover, even on the assumption that the entire colony population consists of those who have moved in from the densely populated rural areas of the country, and given the rates of population increase which have prevailed in the past few decades in these latter areas, it appears obvious that Dry Zone colonization could not have made a significant dent in the phenomenon of peasant landlessness in such areas.

What has been hitherto achieved through the strategy of Dry Zone colonization by way of increasing food production and alleviating the agrarian pressures in the densely populated rural areas of the country has also to be considered in the light of two observations that have been repeatedly made in the writings on agrarian affairs of Sri Lanka. They pertain to the cost of colonization and to the living conditions of the colonists and are based on empirical data drawn from many related investigations.

The average expenditure incurred in settling a family in a Dry Zone colony up to 1953 was estimated to have been about Rs. 8,000 (Farmer, 1957, 316-324). When this estimate was made it was also noted that if the trend of increasing costs witnessed since the inception of colonization continued into the future, the strategy of agricultural development itself would soon become uneconomical from the viewpoint of both returns to investment as well as opportunity costs of capital. In the mid-1960s, by which time the size of allotment per settler family had been reduced to 5 acres (from the earlier 8 acres) and the cost-reducing measure of "advanced alienation" had also been adopted, the average cost per settler family in the colonies that were then being opened up was estimated to be around Rs. 18,000 (Ministry of Agriculture and Food, 1966, 78-80). The costs of colonization continued to escalate. In the latter part of the 1970s when land alienation under the Mahaveli Programme commenced in System H, the average cost of settling a family on a land unit reduced by this time to 3 acres was estimated to be about Rs. 75,000 (Iriyagolle, 1978). The corresponding cost estimate made for Mahaveli Systems B and C where land alienation is currently under way ranges from Rs. 250,000 to 300,000. Making allowance for inflation, this persistent increase in the cost of settlement development should be attributed to the fact that the physical resources required for a continuing extension of the frontiers of the agriculture in the Dry Zone have been (and will continue to be) increasingly expensive to harness.

Cost considerations are, of course, especially germane to the choice of options available in Sri Lanka for generating employment. Studies of labor use in paddy cultivation in the colonies of the Dry Zone (Jogaratnam, 1971; Amarsinghe, 1973; Agrarian Research and Training Institute (ARTI), 1979; Perera and Gunawardena, 1980; ARTI, 1980a; ARTI, 1980b) indicate that, even under conditions of intensive labor application, an acre of paddy (cultivated over two crop seasons) seldom absorbs more than 110 man-days per year. Thus, given the prevailing rates of costs referred to above, this implies that the investment required for generating a single farm employment opportunity in a settlement scheme now averages out to well over Rs. 150,000, a figure which is substantially higher than that in other segments of the economy such as plantation agriculture and export-oriented manufacturing industry.

Several critics of the strategy of peasant colonization in the Dry Zone (Uswatte-Aratchi, 1967, 163; Gooneratne and Gunawardena, 1984, 269; Wanigarante, 1987, 6-8) have also argued that, despite the enormous resource outlay which the colonies represent, they have failed to alleviate rural poverty and that, in essence, Dry Zone colonization has been a process of transferring rural poverty from one part of the country to another. Several sets of data can, indeed, be cited in support of this contention. For instance, a recent study (MPI, 1983: 5-6) of nutritional conditions among children drawn from the different agro-ecological zones of Sri Lanka revealed that the second highest incidence of acute malnutrition was found in those districts where the colonization schemes are concentrated. In a similar inter-district comparison of the "Physical Quality of Life" (Morrison and Waxler, 1986) the lowest scores were recorded by the same districts referred to above. Again, using information generated by several case-studies of individual colonies, Wanigaratne (1987, 41) has compiled a set of data (Table 4.6) which suggest that poverty is both acute and widespread in the colonization schemes of the Dry Zone. The phenomenon of low incomes alongside the high productivity per acre (referred to earlier) may appear irreconcilable. However, it can be explained by the higher cost of production and the lower rates of return per unit of labor input which characterize paddy cultivation in these colonies.

In an evaluation of the strategy of peasant colonization in the Dry Zone, several other features that influence poverty levels need to be highlighed. Perhaps the most important among them is that the "family farm" has provided the basic structural arrangements within each colony since settlement development in the Dry Zone began. Each settler family is given a fixed amount of land the size of which has generally been determined on the basis of maximizing the total number of settler families rather than by the income-generating capacity of the land and the labor requirements of the particular agricultural type. The implication of this has been that, even if the allotment is large enough at initial settlement to provide the colonist's family an adequate income, when the family size increases over time, the income obtainable becomes progressively inadequate. This will persist unless technological improvements maintain an increase in income from the land at a pace commensurate with the increase in family population. Technological progress in peasant agriculture has, of course,

TABLE 4.6
Poverty Conditions in Selected Colonization Schemes of the Dry Zone

Colonization Scheme	Survey Period	Officially defined 'poverty line (Rs./month/household)	Percentage of settler households below 'poverty line'
Mahavilachchiya	1976-77	300	47
Minipe	1976-77	300	8
Mahakandarawa	1976-77	300	26
Mahaveli System H	1977-78	300	66
Pavatkulam	1977-78	300	31
Vavunkulam	1977-78	300	7
Padaviya	1979-80	300	7
Kirindi-Oya	1979-80	300	43
Mahaveli System H	1979-80	300	61
Kaltota	1982-83	440	42
Mahareli System	1983-84	440	29
Kirindi-Oya (Old)	1985-86	800	5.5

Source: Wanigaratne, 1987 (cited with permission of the author)
Note that the 'poverty line' remaining constant from 1976 to '80 detracts from its usefulness as an indicator, in the context of inflation which is known to have occurred at the time.

seldom been a continuing process. What past experience shows is that increases of income induced by technology occur (if they do) in periodic spurts and that, in any event, within a particular system of agricultural production (external and internal production relations remaining unchanged) there is a threshold beyond which application of new technology cannot bring about improvements in income. What this means in the present context is that in the older colonization schemes of the Dry Zone - some of which have a third generation of settlers (Samarasinghe and Samarasinghe, 1984) - there appears to have been, in the long run, a general process of pauperization. This has been only partly mitigated by two counteracting processes - one, the periodic, infusion of new technology as witnessed during the "green revolution", and the other, the absorption of a part of the surplus population from the older colonies by those that have been established later. In the context of this latter feature, it is of interest to note that of some 55,000 families accommodated in the Mahaveli Settlement Systems up to the end of 1987, about 32,000 have been drawn from the very same areas over which the Mahaveli Programme extends (unpublished data furnished by the Mahaveli Development Authority).

As observed in numerous Third World situations, where an impoverished peasantry is exposed to wider commercializing forces of "modern" economic activity, "intermediary" groups from outside, consisting typically of traders, money lenders and land speculators, find it possible to penetrate the peasant economy and, over time, gain control of its key aspects. This process can be (as it has been) looked at from different perspectives. On the one hand, it can be acknowledged that these "intermediaries" perform certain vital functions such as sharing risks with peasant farmers in credit and marketing transactions, spearheading the diffusion of new technology in peasant agriculture, and linking the economic activities of the peasantry with the national economy. From such a viewpoint, the ascendancy of the "intermediary" is an evolutionary product of the interplay of the free market forces. On the other hand, the "intermediary" is seen as a crude exploiter of an improvident and guileless peasantry, whose function is to extract the maximum possible surplus from the peasant economy. In the context of the Dry Zone colony environs, empirical evidence can be cited in support of either of these viewpoints, the acceptance or the rejection of which would ultimately depend on one's ideological paradigms. As a frequently observed phenomenon, however, it may be noted that in the colonies of the Dry Zone these "intermediary" groups invariably perform an important role in a variety of activities such as the supply of credit to the colonists, primary marketing of agricultural produce, and retail trade in "imported" subsistence goods and farm inputs. Many writers (for example, Amunugama, 1965; Abeyratne, 1972, Amarasinghe, 1973, Wanigaratne, 1979; Perera and Gunawardena,

1980; Silva, 1982; Siriwardena, 1982; Weeramunde, 1982) have shown that these transactions enable the "intermediaries" to acquire control over substantial areas of colony land which often leads to the creation of a landless proletariat among the colony population. Such a process obviously negates one of the cardinal objectives of the strategy of Dry Zone Colonization - namely, the 'preservation of the peasantry'.

REGULATION OF SHARE-TENANCY: A REFORM IN PEASANT AGRICULTURE

Share-tenancy is a system of land tenure found in many rural areas of Sri Lanka, mainly in association with the cultivation of paddy. It is a tenurial arrangement which involves the payment of a fixed proportion of the gross product from the land by the tenant to the owner of the land as "land rent". It can, of course, be looked at from a different perspective as an arrangement under which the land owner pays a fixed proportion of the gross product to the tenant as a "wage". Share-tenancy is a remnant of pre-modern agrarian relations, the survival of which can be attributed largely to the continued presence of economic and social constraints on the substitution of cash for kind in wages and rent in peasant agriculture. Its presence also usually reflects the fact that some in the rural community own more land than they could themselves cultivate, alongside conditions of general scarcity of land in relation to the farm population. In certain instances, share-tenancy is associated with the phenomenon of absentee landlordism.

Where economic considerations alone determine land rent (or the tenants' wages) in share-tenancy agreements, the rent (or the wage) becomes a function of the supply and demand of land and labor. Thus, in those parts of Sri Lanka where there is a scarcity of agricultural land and an abundance of potential tenants, the land owner can claim a relatively large share of the gross produce as rent. In such situations, moreover, the land owner can also resort to the practice of periodically changing his tenants through a procedure which is tantamount to the auctioning of cultivation rights among competing tenants, and thus maximize his rent (or minimize the tenant's wage). In peasant communities there are various social constraints on such "free market" determinations of wages and rent.

There is considerable diversity of opinion on both the nature of share-tenancy as well as its implications for peasant agriculture in Sri Lanka. According to the "reformist" viewpoint, share-tenancy represents an exploitative and conflictual relationship between the land owner and the tenant; one in which the twin phenomena of rack renting and insecurity of tenure for the tenant are usually evident. From this viewpoint, there are several ways in which share-tenancy inhibits agricultural development. In the first place (it is claimed) the "expropriation" of a share of the product by the land owner depresses the tenant's income, curtails his capacity to invest, and perpetuates the "vicious circle of poverty" in the production efforts of the tenant. Again, since the land rent always constitutes a *constant* proportion of the product, the entire marginal additions to product which result from increases of input do not accrue to the tenant; and this, allegedly, inhibits input application on the part of the tenant. It has also been claimed that insecurity of tenure (held to be typical of share-tenancy contracts) constitutes yet another disincentive on the tenant's efforts at securing any long-term improvement of the land (see Lipton, 1974:276, for a summary of these "theoretical" arguments against share-tenancy).

This "reformist" viewpoint on share-tenancy has been challenged on both empirical and theoretical grounds. Evidence has been produced (Peiris, 1976) to show that share-tenancy does not necessarily involve an eploitative relationship between the land owner and the tenant but that, in many situations, there are various forms of mutual collateral help and risk-sharing in investment which promote congruence rather than conflict of interests. From a theoretical standpoint, it has been argued that, if the tenant's share of the value of marginal additions to product that results from additions of input is greater than the cost of the latter, land rent being a constant share of the product would not inhibit increases in the levels of input application. The absence of an appreciable difference in levels of input between land under share-tenancy and land operated under other types of tenure (such as "owner cultivation") in Sri Lanka seems to support this theoretical assertion.

In 1958, a program of tenurial reform aimed at regulating land owner-tenant relations was launched in Sri Lanka, with the Paddy Lands Act of that year providing its statutory base. This represented one of the foremost expressions of the radical approach to the development of peasant agriculture since Sri Lanka gained independence.

The main provisions of the Paddy Lands Act were designed to restrict land rent to one-quarter of the gross product from the land (subject to an absolute ceiling) and to make tenancy rights in all existing and future share-tenancy agreements permanent and heritable. The act prohibited any demands by the land owner for additional payments or unrenumerated services from the tenant and restricted the interest recoverable on inputs (seed, fertilizer) supplied by the owner. It also prohibited unilateral tenant eviction. These provisions, it may be noted were in many respects similar to those that had been incorporated in tenurial reform legislation in other countries like India, Egypt and Taiwan at this time.

An important innovation of the Paddy Lands Act was the provision made for setting up a network of "Cultivation Committees" in the country. Such committees consisted of elected representatives of farmers and served as the village-level organization for implementing reforms. The wide range of powers and functions vested in these committees encompassed activities such as irrigation and water management, supply of farm inputs, arbitration in land disputes and promoting mutual cooperation among farmers. The architects of the reform, it was reported, expected the Cultivation Committees to "... eventually blossom out as collective farms."

An evaluation of this reform attempt rests primarily on a

review of the operation of those provisions of the Paddy Lands Act that were intended to reduce share-tenancy rents and prevent tenant evictions. The general conclusion drawn from evaluations undertaken since the introduction of the Act (Jayasinghe, 1966; Raza, 1970; Sanderatne, 1972; Lipton, 1974; Weerawardena, 1975) is that the reform had failed to achieve its objective of imposing a uniform set of controls on share-tenancy as it operates in all parts of Sri Lanka. On the degree of failure, however, there has been some diversity of opinion. Weerawardena (1975, 47), citing data from a comprehensive survey conducted in the mid-1960s, contends that while the rent restricting provisions of the Act have achieved an appreciable measure of success in certain parts of the country, its provisions relating to security of tenure have generally been ineffective. Jayasinghe (1966), Raza (1970) and Sanderatne (1972) are among those who have argued that the overall impact of the reform on land rents and tenant evictions has been minimal. Lipton (1974) has claimed that the Act was followed by higher rents and more evictions.

Weerawardena's assertion that the Act brought about a reduction of rents in certain parts of the country (southern and southwestern coastal districts) is to some extent substantiated by the relatively lower rents that seem to prevail in those areas. Data from an all-island survey (Central Bank, 1967: 18) showed that in the districts of Kalutara, Galle, Matara and Hambantota (areas referred to by Weerawardena) and also in Trincomalee and Vavuniya, the land owners share of the crop in all categories of "leased" land averaged out to about 25%. A more recent survey (ARTI, 1974, 34) of Hambantota District revealed that 86% of tenants were paying the land rent stipulated by the Act. In contrast, in most other parts of the country, many investigations (cited by Peiris, 1976, 42) indicate that the overwhelming majority of tenants pay substantially more than the legally specified rent. It must be stated, however, that in the absence of specific information on rents in pre-reform times, any conclusion drawn about the impact of the reform on rents on the basis of data on post-reform rent levels has to remain conjectural.

As for the provisions of the Paddy Lands Act concerning security of tenure, there is little doubt of the failure of the reform to prevent tenant eviction; and Lipton's assertion that the Act was followed by more evictions (though not based on a comparison of pre-reform and post-reform data) may well be correct, It is, indeed, likely that the complaints of eviction (in excess of 40,000 by the end of 1971) which flooded the Department of Agrarian Services (the government agency in overall charge of implementing the reform) after the introduction of the Act represented only a fraction of the evictions that actually occurred. These recorded evictions also exclude tenants who were affected by the conversion of former share-tenancies to nominal "owner cultivation" (or "concealed share-tenancy") to which Gold and Clifford (undated) have referred.

There are several other negative features of the reform. For example, as Weerawardena (1975, 14) has shown, 13 years after the promulgation of the Paddy Lands Act, in less than 25% of the evictions formally reported had the rights of evicted tenants been restored. Furthermore, the provisions of the Act dealing with those land owners who had violated the rent restriction provisions of the Act or those entitling evicted tenants compensation from their land owners had never been exercised.

The Cultivation Committees that were established under the Paddy Lands Act were intended to occupy a key position in the reform strategy. In fact, during the early stages of implementation of the Act, it was envisaged that these committees would not only ensure the effective operation of the tenurial provisions of the Act but would also mobilize the support of the peasantry and spearhead a movement towards communal forms of agriculture in the rural areas.

A lucid account of the problems that confronted the Cultivation Committees during their early existence is found in Weerawardena's monograph (1975, 24-25) on the Paddy Land Act. Among them were the cumbersome and dilatory procedures that had to be followed at their elections, the questions that arose about the legality of those committees that had been constituted without the full and proportionate representation of land owners and tenants as specified by the Act (land owners were able to sabotage the setting up of the committees simply by non-participation at elections until the introduction of amendments to the Act), the non-recognition of the committees by other government agencies, and the inadequacy of funds and other resources made available to the committees. Only some of these initial difficulties were overcome through administrative adjustments and statutory changes.

Some of the problems and shortcomings of the Cultivation Committees could be regarded as characteristics of gestation rather than problems basic to the concept of an elected village-level institution serving as the instrument for agrarian reform. While they would undoubtedly have influenced the molding of peasant attitudes towards this new institution, corrective and supportive action *could* over time have strengthened the Cultivation Committee system.

The problem that did affect the role of the Cultivation Committees in a more fundamental sense was that they did not become genuinely representative of those sections of the peasantry which were regarded by the architects of the reform as the underprivileged. Like many other village-level institutional systems in Sri Lanka and contrary to the expectations of the reformers, the Cultivation Committees often became the domain of the more affluent groups in the rural areas and were frequently used as instruments of subversion and retaliatory action by those who would have been adversely affected by the reform (for specific evidence, see, Ministry of Agriculture and Food, 1966, 111-112; Bansil, 1971, 135: 7; Dias and Wickremanayake, 1974, 13). One of the main consequences of this was that the Cultivation Committees failed to evoke an enthusiastic response from those for whose benefit the reform was primarily meant.

Among the other problems which were encountered in the implementation of the Paddy Lands Act were those that arose from loopholes and ambiguities in the Act itself. Such legal defects detracted from the effectiveness of the Act, not only by creating at the crucial early stages of the reform much administrative confusion but also by providing opportunity for evasion and sabotage.

Certain legalistic defects of the Act were essentially those of weak formulation and could have been avoided if greater precision and foresight were exercised and the relevant lessons drawn from other countries like India at the stage of drafting the legislation. Some of these defects were, in fact, rectified through later amendments to the Act and had no fundamental significance except that the ensuing delays in the proper implementation of the Act created among the prospective beneficiaries of the reform considerable loss of confidence.

There was, however, a more important and conceptually more basic set of legal problems that arose out of the complexity and varied nature of the phenomena to which the legislation was intended to apply. Practicalities associated with certain key concepts like "eviction", "tenancy" and "cultivation" did not readily lend themselves to precise legal definition; and, when disputes arose, the law courts were called upon to clarify issues such as "who is a tenant", "what constitutes an act of eviction" and "what is cultivation". Several such clarifications by the judiciary, though useful as examples of legal thinking, did not help the implementation of the reform.

For example, in an appellate judgement of the Supreme Court in 1966, it was held that:

> The ordinary meaning of 'evict' ... (implies) the dispossession by due process of law or else by force. In the present case... there had neither been eviction by force nor eviction by judicial process. The former tenant had merely stated in evidence that he was asked not to cultivate for a further season and that he did not cultivate. Section 3(2) (of the Act) does not in our opinion apply to a case where the tenant either gives up possession or else does not take steps to resume possession after his contract or agreement is terminated.
>
> (*New Law Reports*, LXVIII, pp. 470-471).

In another decision made in 1967, the Supreme Court pronounced that:

> ....the Act in defining the expression "tenant cultivator" only clarifies the ordinary meaning of the expression. The protection conferred by the Act to an individual is enjoyed only by a person who actually by his own labour and that of members of his family cultivates a paddy land. The definition contemplates three different kinds of work (ploughing, sowing and reaping) for which actual labour is necessary, and if hired labour is in fact employed for two of these kinds of work, then the cultivator is not a tenant cultivator, and in regard to watching and tending the crop, this must be done only by the tenant himself or members of his family.
>
> (*New Law Reports*, LXX, pp. 83-84)

The first of these decisions implied that, in the absence of proof of the tenant making a physical attempt to resume possession (or proof of the use of force in the removal of the tenant) such removal is not tantamount to eviction as defined by the Paddy Lands Act. Hence, when an owner of a share-cropped plot of land issues oral instructions to his tenant not to cultivate and the tenant makes no attempt physically to recover his cultivation rights, the tenant has no redress under the Paddy Lands Act.

For the implementation of the reform, the latter decision created a paradoxical situation in that a tenant who employs hired labor for two of the three main cultivation activities (plowing, sowing and reaping) could not qualify as a "tenant cultivator" in the statutory meaning of the term, whereas a land owner who employs hired labor for any or all such work could maintain the legal status of "owner cultivator". Further speculation on this issue suggests that even if the law stipulated that an individual's physical participation in plowing, sowing and reaping is a mandatory requirement to qualify as "cultivator", since these are usually group activities, it is possible for a non-cultivating land owner to claim the status of land owner himself if he wishes to retain or assume the status of "cultivator". This type of evasion could have been minimized if the power of final arbitration on claims and counterclaims to status of "cultivator" was vested in impartial institutions at the "grass roots". The architects of the Paddy Lands Act expected the Cultivation Committees to perform this role. But, as the implementation of the Act proceeded, it became evident that the committees had neither the impartiality nor the statutory competence required to do so.

In the wider context of tenancy reform in post-colonial South Asia, the problems which were encountered in the implementation of the Paddy Lands Act of 1958 were not experiences without precedent and parallel. The difficulties of formulating uniform sets of law which, in their practical application, could encompass the manifold remifications of a traditional tenurial system, the contractual arrangements within which are invariably oral and informal; the failure of newly established rural institutions to withstand the pressures of societal inequity and provide leadership and direction to processes of socio-economic transformation; and, more specifically, the meager success achieved in attempts to safeguard the rights of tenant cultivators through legislative devices; have all been observed and documented in detail in many parts of South Asia.

Similarly, as in other areas where share-tenancy prevails, in Sri Lanka the case for introducing legislation to regulate tenancy relations rested on a weak empirical foundation. The data available on paddy cultivation in Sri Lanka sustain neither the assumption that high rents and insecurity are features universally inherent to unregulated share-tenancy nor the assumption that they make unregulated share-tenancy an intrinsically inefficient system of land tenure. Nor do such data support the corollary that reducing land rents and ensuring security of tenure result in increased efficiency.

EXTENSION OF STATE CONTROL OVER PLANTATION AGRICULTURE

"Leading the country towards socialism" was the declared goal of the United Front government which assumed office after the general parliamentary elections of 1970. Among the strategies that were adopted by the government in pursuance of this goal was a program of land reform designed mainly for the purpose of extending state control over the plantation sector. The reform was also expected to facilitate an increase in agricultural production and a diversification of agriculture, expand farm employment, release some land from plantation agriculture for redistribution among the landless peasantry, reduce the prevailing inequalities in income and wealth, and change the external and internal production relations in plantation agriculture.

The reform program commenced with the enactment of the Land Reform Law, No. 1 of 1972 which stipulated that the maximum extent of land which could be owned by an individual in Sri Lanka shall be 25 acres if the land is devoted to paddy or 50 acres in respect of all other categories of land (those of over 18 years of age in land owning families were each allowed to retain an extent equivalent to these "ceilings"). The Land Reform Law also provided for the setting up of a Land Reform Commission (LRC) vested with powers to acquire privately held land in excess of the ceilings and to facilitate the development of the land so acquired in accordance with the economic and social policies of the government.

Three years later, the scope of the reform was extended to the estates held by public companies through the enactment of the Land Reform (Amendment) Law, No. 39 of 1975. This amending legislation provided for the immediate nationalization of the land and all related assets belonging to such companies on the basis of a negotiated system of compensation.

The legislative package that formed the basis of the reform program included several other enactments. The Estates Control and Transfers Act of 1972 which imposed government controls over land transfers from properties of over 100 acres in extent and the State Agricultural Corporations Act of 1972 which provided for the formation of public corporations for the management of plantations, were laws enacted in anticipation of the reform. The Agricultural Lands Law of 1973 extended the provisions of the Paddy Lands Act to all share-cropped land in the country.

Throughout the reform period, the government also invoked the provisions of the Land Acquisition Act of 1950 for the purchase of private land "required for public purposes."

The Land Reform Law made it mandatory for all family units owning areas of land above the stipulated ceilings to declare their assets to the LRC and placed the onus of claiming the land retainable by them, on the owners themselves. When these latter areas of land were finally determined and released to their owners, the total extent of land brought under the ownership of the government was around 560,000 acres (Table 4.7).

The process of land acquisition under the Land Reform Law was remarkably free from the type of problems and delays which characterized the implementation of land ceiling legislation in many other countries (Doner, 1972, 29-37). Among the reasons for this were that, since the architects of the reform programs were able to draw from a range of international experiences, the drafted legislation was relatively devoid of confusion. The basic data and documentation on existing patterns of land ownership were readily available, providing the reformers an advantage which their counterparts in other countries engaged in similar reforms did not possess. Moreover, the Land Reform Law vested wide powers in the Land Reform Commission, thereby avoiding many of the legalistic obstacles that retarded the progress of agrarian reform attempts in the past. The fact that the "Emergency Regulations" (of the Public Security Act) were in force throughout the reform period also contributed to the rapid execution of take-overs since these regulations enhanced the normal powers of the executive branch of government and dispossessed land owners remained wary of litigation against executive action.

The nationalization of company-owned estates under the provisions of the Land Reform (Amendment) Law of 1975 was equally free of difficulties and delays. In the past, whenever nationalization of company-owned estates was contemplated two considerations persistently weighed the scales against such a move. First, the widely held notion that company management presented was that its disruption would have adverse affects on the productivity of plantations. More significantly, there was a fear that a government takeover of company estates, many of which were British owned, might result in reprisals against Sri Lanka in the British tea market. In 1975, neither of these considerations appear to have carried much weight. Detailed investigations (not necessarily with a great deal of objectivity) had persuaded the government that, contrary to popular belief, most company-owned estates were being mismanaged and that this was decidedly against the economic interests of the nation (Commission on Agency Houses and Brokerage Firms, 1974). Second, in the context of the prevailing low profitability of tea and rubber plantations and provisions made in the reform for negotiated compensation, the company owners showed little resistance to the nationalization of their assets.

TABLE 4.7
Government Land Acquisitions during the Land Reform Period

	Acquired through the ceiling legislation of 1972	Acquired through 'amending legislation' of 1975	Purchased Under the Land Acquisition Act of 1950	Total
Tea	139,354	237,592	34,240	411,186
Rubber	82,563	94,835	6,676	184,074
Coconut	112,523	6,406	—	118,929
Other (including uncultivated)	228,971	79,124	13,315	321,410
Total	563,411	417,957	54,231	1,035,599

Source: Land Reform Commission

The Land Reform Law laid down, in general terms, the purposes for which the land acquired by the government may be used. The LRC was empowered both to develop the land under its own management as well as alienate the land in large blocks to other public sector agencies and cooperative organizations or in small allotments to individuals for agricultural and residential use. It seems clear that a measure of flexibility was deliberately retained in the choice of form and purpose of redistribution and development of the acquired land so that different strategies might be pursued under varying conditions of demand for land and farm employment, crop technology and infrastructure availability. Among the factors taken into consideration in the redistribution of the acquired land was that the acquisitions consisted of about 60% of the total tea acreage, 30% of the rubber acreage and 10% of the coconut acreage in the entire country. As it turned out, the system of land redistribution followed by the LRC was such that it vested the control of the large plantations that had been acquired in several public corporations, leased units of varying size (usually within the range of 50 to 300 acres) to government-sponsored organizations for setting up cooperative farms, and allocated a relatively small percentage of the acquired land for distribution among peasants in small allotments. Land alienation by the LRC as it stood four years after the initiation of the reform program is shown in Table 4.8.

The public sector agencies that were entrusted the management and control of the plantations brought under government ownership were the State Plantation Corporation (which had been in existence since 1958) and two other newly established institutions - namely, the People's Estate Development Board and the Up-Country Cooperative Estates Development Board. These institutions, together with the Tea and Rubber Research Institutes were vested the control of about 50% of the total acreage acquired under the reform.

In their organizational structure, scope and functions, the State Plantation Corporation and the People's Estate Development Board have been similar to one another. The plantations that were brought under their control retained the same system of management which they have always had and, in the large majority of cases, the same managerial and supervisory person-

TABLE 4.8
Principal Recipients of Land from the Land Reform Commission (up to October 1976)

	Approximate extent alienated (acres)
Public Sector Agencies	
State Plantation Corporation	261,500
People's Estate Development Board	234,100
Cooperative Estates Development Board	73,100
Cooperative Organization	
Land Reform Cooperatives	48,000
Electoral Cooperatives	175,000
Special Cooperatives and others	40,000
Peasant Smallholders	115,000
Others (including land under the control of LRC)	88,500

Source: Land Reform Commission

nel. The only change in their organizational structure brought about by the reform was, of course, the replacement of the former multiplicity of owners with government ownership.

The Up-Country Cooperative Estates Development Board at its inception attempted a cooperative system of estate management which was intended to be in tune with the social objectives of the reform program. With the passage of time, however, this new system was abandoned, due allegedly to its unworkability, and all its estates reverted to the former wage-labor system of operation conventional to plantation agriculture.

The promotion of cooperative forms of agricultural production was one of the most important objectives of the reform program. Soon after the commencement of the reform, new cooperative farming complexes were hurriedly set up, existing cooperatives were strengthened, and a large extent of acquired land (265,000 acres by late 1976) was entrusted to their control.

Distributing land among landless peasants remained unimportant in the overall pattern of alienation of the reform program. According to a statement released by the LRC at the end of 1976, since the commencement of the reform some 350,000 peasant families had received from the LRC about 115,000 acres.

Assessed in the context of the principal objectives of the Land Reform Programme, each of the above types of alienation was seen as possessing certain advantages. In tea and rubber, from the viewpoint of maximizing production, opinion has always favored the preservation of the integrity of economically viable large units and has stood firmly against distributive reform (Peiris, 1978, 621-622). The claim made repeatedly during the past few decades is that in plantation agriculture the conversion of large units of production to smallholdings adversely affects productivity. Hence, particularly in the case of tea and rubber plantations located in the physically well endowed areas, the LRC avoiding both fragmentation as well as disruption of their former managerial infrastructure.

Counterbalancing the higher productivity claimed through the preservation of large units were certain advantages claimed for cooperative farming and for the proliferation of small peasant farms. Among them were that the conversion of estates into cooperative farms and peasant smallholdings could alleviate the prevailing land hunger among the peasantry, eliminate the sectoral dichotomy within the economy, enable the mobilization of mass support for the reform and, in some instances, facilitate the intensification and diversification of agriculture and thus increase both production and employment. It was also claimed that low cost production which characterizes peasant farming could be extended to plantation crop production by converting estates into smallholdings.

In molding the alienation policy of the land reform program, no less important than the economic claims and counterclaims for the different options, were certain socio-political considerations. Although the reform was not a "land-to-the-tiller" restructuring of agriculture, one of its most frequently publicized propaganda themes was the need to "restore the ownership of agriculture land to the peasantry". There was also the populists' demand by politicians for land to be made available for distribution among their voters. Similarly, cooperative farming had to be made available especially among those political groups for which the development of cooperative forms of production meant the disintegration of older property relations. The manner in which the LRC alienated the land placed under its control indicate that these "realities" were also taken into account.

Certain modifications were introduced to the pattern of land ownership during the land reform period by the new government which assumed office in 1977. These took the form of the liquidation of one of the plantation managing corporations and most of the cooperative organizations referred to above and the transfer of their land either to the two other corporations or to the newly established National Agricultural Diversification and Settlement Authority, or, in a few instances, to peasant smallholdings. An estimated 50,000 acres of acquired land were also restored to former owners in settlement of grievances relating to acquisition. Despite new policies adopted by the government in many areas of the economy there have been no significant moves towards re-privatization of plantation agriculture and the control by the government of a large segment of the plantation sector has continued unchanged into present times (Table 4.9).

The manner in which the foregoing reforms affected the plantation industries of Sri Lanka has received considerable scholarly attention for, apart from all else, the reform created an exceptional situation of extensive State ownership and control in an avenue of production which in most "mixed economies" is left largely or entirely in private hands. If plantation agriculture in its classical form epitomizes private transnational capitalist enterprise, the post-reform plantations of Sri Lanka certainly represents a mutation of the classical model.

On certain aspects of the reform's impact, there is considerable consensus among the critics. For instance, there is general agreement that the impact of the land reform program on the external structural relations of the plantation system in Sri Lanka

Table 4.9.
Changes in the Ownership of Land under the Main Plantation Crops

	approximate extent in acres with (% in parentheses)		
	at the commencement of the reform	at the end of 1976	at the end of 1980
Sterling & Rupee companies	470,500 (20.7)	0* (0)	?**
All public sector agencies	36,500 (2.0)	782,700 (35.1)	790,500 (34.7)
Cooperatives	900 (<1.0)	82,000 (3.7)	0 (0)
Private Sector (including small holdings)	1,760,000 (77.3)	1,366,200 (61.2)	1,490,000 (65.3)

*excludes an unverifiable extent under disputed ownership
**information not available

was slight (Gooneratne, 1980; Fernando, 1984, Peiris, 1984; Rote, 1986). The only change brought about by the reform from this particular perspective was that direct profit transfers from the "center to the periphery" have been reduced considerably by the elimination of foreign ownership of plantations. With respect to external relations, a land reform implemented within the framework of a dependent mixed economy cannot, in fact, be expected to make a major change. That it did not is of little relevance except to a critique of global economic arrangements.

Even with respect to the internal production relations of the plantation system, most critics agree that the reform had little tangible impact. What the reform meant, particularly from the viewpoint of the wage-earning workers in the plantation sector, was a partial replacement of private ownership and management by those of the State. As a criticism of the reform, the main thrust of the argument is that the same exploitative production relations that characterized plantation agriculture in pre-reform times have persisted after the reform. This viewpoint, however, needs some clarification. That the reform did not bring about a total elimination of worker exploitation (i.e. the expropriation of the surplus value of labor) can be readily admitted. Yet, the post-reform experiences also indicate that, for the workers absorbed into State sector employment as a result of the reform, their changed status has meant a strengthened bargaining position and simplified bargaining procedure in wage and other demands with an employer whose response to worker demands cannot be guided entirely by considerations of commercial profit.

One of the major objectives of the land reform program, as noted earlier, was that of increasing production and employment. The extent to which this objective has been achieved is a controversial issue which does not lend itself to simple quantitative verification. There is hardly any doubt that while the reform was in progress and in its immediate aftermath there was a decline in the production levels of the main plantation industries (Table 4.10) It has also been widely acknowledged that some of the reasons for this decline were related to the reform. Among them were the lag effects of the neglect of plantations by their former owners in anticipation of the reform, the organizational dislocations that accompanied the reform, and the incompetence of some of the managerial systems brought into being by the reform. The decline in the effective area under plantation crops due to the diversion of land into other forms of use and/or other types of farm management which occurred during the reform was also responsible for the drop in production.

TABLE 4.10
Decennial Change in the Output of Tea, Rubber and Coconut, 1951-1980

	Cumulative annual change for the 10-year period		
	Tea	Rubber	Coconut
1951-60	+36.8	-13.5	+6.1
1961-70	+8.0	+46.7	+14.2
1971-80	-8.0	-12.7	-15.0

This decline in production, however, cannot be used to either substantiate or refute a contention that State-controlled plantation agriculture is intrinsically less efficient than plantation agriculture in private hands. There are several reasons for this. In the first place, productivity of plantations is prone to short-term fluctuations that are caused by many factors including those relating to the physical environment, cost of inputs and price levels. In this context, it is important to note that the reform coincided with a sharp escalation of the cost of inputs such as fertilizer and agro-chemicals caused by global increases in the price of petroleum products. Second, a restructuring of ownership and control of the scale which occurred during the reform could be expected to involve an "abnormal" period of gestation and uncertainty with adverse affects on production. Third, the plantations that were brought under the control of the State sector agencies by the reform did increase their productivity levels after a lapse of time and that, since then, they have maintained relatively higher levels of productivity than those that remained under private ownership (Table 4.11).

TABLE 4.11.
Average Yield on Estates (kg/ha), 1977-1985

	Tea			Rubber		
	SPC[1] Estates	JEDB[2] Estates	National Average	SPC[1] Estates	JEDB[2] Estates	National Average
1977	1,123	1,266	979	1,006	846	773
1978	927	1,066	958	865	1,032	845
1979	1,069	1,266	993	883	1,013	820
1980	1,103	1,105	922	985	918	718
1981	n.a.	n.a.	857	n.a.	n.a.	705
1982	n.a.	n.a.	989	n.a.	n.a.	729

1983	962	1,131	n.a.	937	1,107	818
1984	1,062	1,298	n.a.	993	1,179	840
1985	1,125	1,284	n.a.	879	1,079	838

Notes: 1. State Plantations Corporaton (SPC)
2. Janata Estate Development Board (JEDB)

Among the criticisms that have been levelled at the Land Reform Programme is that it has had adverse effects on employment and earnings of the workers in the plantation sector (Wanigaratne & Samad, 1980; Gooneratne, 1980; Kurian, 1981, Fernando, 1984). The main causes which have been adduced for such losses are:

(a) the decline in the effective area under the main plantation crops due to the diversion of some land for other uses,
(b) the decline in the productivity of plantations (discussed above), and,
(c) the displacement of a segment of the plantation workforce as a result of forced eviction and discriminatory recruitment.

The claimed reduction in the extent of productive plantation land can be substantiated with a solid body of evidence. During the first phase of the reform (which involved the imposition of ceilings on private ownership of land) the 563,000 acres acquired by the government consisted of 16,732 units, mostly in the form of small blocks of land carved out of pre-reform properties. In many instances, it was uneconomical to retain the plantation form of management for this type of acquired land. They were used, therefore, for distributive alienation for residential and homestead use. Second, by the end of 1976 approximately 35% of the total extent of land acquired by the government had either been leased to cooperatives or been distributed among peasants. Third, there is evidence that since the late1970s, the two plantation-managing State corporations have tended to concentrate effort on the more productive land under their control (as a measure of maximizing profits in the face of increasing costs) thus "pruning" away some land from the plantation sector.

The reform-induced productivity recession referred to earlier also brought about some losses in employment in the plantation sector. For those segments of the plantation workforce employed on the basis of daily wages, prolonged spells of low productivity invariably bring about curtailments in the number of work-days offered by the employer. In the early stages of the reform, such curtailments were so intense that some wage-earners in the plantation sector were pushed out to seek their livelihood in other parts of the country. This was one of the reasons for the 21% decline of the "estate population" recorded during the inter-censal period 1971-81.

The employment effects of the land reform program also had certain discriminatory features. At the initial take-over of private land in 1972, for example, there were several instances of simulated (Sinhalese) "peasant revolts" reported from certain plantation areas where Tamil workers were forcibly evicted from estates. Probably a much larger number of Tamil workers lost their employment when 13 estates were vested in the Cooperative Estates Development Board which, at its inception, was expected to promote cooperative forms of plantation management. Employment in the cooperative farms that were established in the wake of the reform was also largely confined to Sinhalese workers.

The post-reform experiences of plantation enterprise in Sri Lanka brought into sharp focus a fundamental contradiction in the strategy of extending State controls over plantations for the purpose of bringing about a socialist transformation of society. This contradiction arose from the very nature of the plantation system which, for maximizing production and profits, relies on a high degree of regimentation of a numerically large and low paid workforce, and lavish incentives in the form of high salaries, bonuses and other fringe benefits for its managerial and supervisory cadres. In tea and rubber produced on plantations, labor wages account for about two-thirds of the cost of production by unit weight. In Sri Lanka, these two plantation industries employ a workforce of over 500,000. This implies that even a small increase in labor wages involves a substantial addition to the supply price of the final product. Given the small margins of profit (per unit weight) which these commodities can fetch, the plantation industries can maintain their competitive position in the world market mainly by minimizing labor costs, which unavoidably entails efforts to keep labor wages at the lowest possible levels. On the other hand, the management and supervision of plantations can never be effectively reduced to a routine administrative function. It requires initiative, decision-making ability, personalized accountability and hard work from those entrusted with such tasks. Because the managerial and supervisory cadres are numerically small, the incentives they receive, though lavish and ostentatious, have but little effect on the costs of production. Maintaining this disparity between the workers and their masters obviously runs counter to the socio-political objective of the reform. Yet, any attempt to reduce the disparity results either in the conversion of the managerial and supervisory infrastructure to a lethargic bureaucracy or in enormous additional costs being burdened on the plantation industries. This has continued to remain a fundamental dilemma of the nationalized plantations of Sri Lanka.

In Sri Lanka, propagating socialism through an extension of State control over plantation agriculture was made even more elusive by the presence within the plantation sector of a minority ethnic group (the so-called "Indian Tamils") which is still considered "alien" and which has no community of interest with the impoverished sections of the peasantry living in the plantation and peasant economies in these areas. Given the sharp duality which persists between the plantation and peasant economies an improvement in living conditions among plantation workers invariably results in a reduction of what could by syphoned off from the plantation sector and channelled to other sectors of the economy. At the same time, an attempt to break down the barriers that exist between the plantation sector and the peasant sector (by providing more employment on estates to the peasantry, for example) intensifies poverty among the existing plantation workforce. Since the implementation of the land reform program, this irreconcilability of interests and what it implies have become increasingly pronounced, producing a potentially volatile socio-political situation in the main plantation areas of Sri Lanka.

REFERENCES

Abeyratne, G.M. 1972. *Economic Aspects of some Peasant Colonizations of Ceylon*, unpublished Ph. D. thesis, University of Oxford.

Agrarian Research and Training Institute (ARTI). 1974. *Agrarian Situation Relating to' Paddy Cultivation: Hambantota District.* Colombo: ARTI.

Agrarian Research and Training Institute (ARTI). 1979. *Mahakandarawa Scheme.* Colombo: ARTI.

Agrarian Research and Training Institute (ARTI). 1980. *Vaunikulam Scheme.* Colombo: ARTI.

Agrarian Research and Training Institute (ARTI). 1980. *Pavatkulam Scheme.* Colombo: ARTI.

Allen, G.C. and Donnithorne, A.G. 1957. *Western Enterprise in Indonesia and Malaya.* London: Macmillan.

Amarasinghe, N. 1973. *A Study of Economic Resource Use and Production Possibilities on Settlement Schemes in Sri Lanka*, unpublished Ph. D. thesis, University of London.

Amunugama, S. 1965. Chandrika Weva: A Recent Attempt at Colonization on a Peasant Framework. *Ceylon Journal of Historical and Social Studies* 8: 1-2.

Bansil, P.C. 1971. *Ceylon Agriculture: A Perspective.* Delhi: Dhanpat Rai.

Bandaranaike, S.W. R.D. 1933. The Spinning Wheel and the Paddy Field in *Speeches and Writings.* Colombo: Department of Information.

Bocke, Jan H. 1953. *Economics and Economic Policies of Dual Societies* Amsterdam: Institute of Pacific Relations.

Brayne, C.V. 1934. The Problems of Peasant Agriculture in Ceylon. *Ceylon Economic Journal* 6: 34-46.

Clifford, Sir Hugh. 1927. Some Reflections on the Ceylon Land Question. *Tropical Agriculturist* LXVIII: 221-253.

Commission on Agency Houses and Brokering Firms. 1974. Report of Inquiry . . ., *Sessional Paper XII - 1974*. Colombo: Government Press.

Corea, C.E. 1925. A Dissenting Minute in Report of the Communal Pastures Committee. *Sessional Paper XXVII - 1925*. Colombo: Government Press.

Dias, Hiran and Wickremanayake, B.W. 1974. The Gambrayan System in Hambantota District in *Proceedings of the Conference on Agriculture in Sri Lanka*. University of Peradeniya: Ceylon Studies Seminar.

Doner, Peter. 1972. *Land Reform and Economic Development*. Harmondsworth: Penguin.

Edirisinghe, Neville. 1987. *The Food Stamp Scheme in Sri Lanka: Costs, Benefits and Options for Modification*. Washington, D.C.: International Food Research Institute.

Farmer, B.H. 1957. *Pioneer Peasant Colonization in Ceylon*. London: Oxford University Press.

Fernando, N.A. 1986. Land Reform in the Plantation Sector: Employment and Income Effects in *Plantation Agriculture in Sri Lanka - Issues in Employment and Development*, eds. Gooneratne W. and Wesumperuma D. Bangkok: ILO/ARTEP.

Ganewatta, P. *Fragmentation of Paddy Land: A Case Study of a Cluster of Five Villages in Anuradhapura District*. Colombo: ARTI.

Gold, Martin E. and Clifford, John. undated. *Traditional Agrarian Tenures and Reform Legislation in the North Central Province of Ceylon*. Library of the University of Peradeniya, Sri Lanka.

Gooneratne, H.M. 1980. *The Plantation Raj*. Colombo: Cave and Co.

Gooneratne, W. 1974. *The Role of Cultivation Committees in Agricultural Planning at Village Level*. Colombo: ARTI.

Gooneratne, W. and Gunawardena, P.L.J. 1984. Poverty and Inequality in Rural Sri Lanka in *Poverty and Inequality in Rural Asia*, Eds. Gooneratne and Gunawardena, Bangkok: ILO/ARTEP.

Gunawardena, R.A.H.L. 1971. Irrigation and Hydraulic Society in Early Medieval Ceylon. *Past and Presant* 53: 3-27.

Hansard. 1927. *Legislative Council of Ceylon*. Proceedings. 419-423. Colombo: Government Press.

Holmes, C.H. 1956. The Broad Pattern of Climatic and Vegetational Distribution of Ceylon. *Proceedings of the Symposium on the Study of Tropical Vegetation*. Paris: UNESCO.

Iriyagolle, G. 1978. *The Truth about the Mahaveli*. Nugegoda: Deepani

Press.

Jayasinghe, A.B. 1966. Paddy Lands Act. *Proceedings of Conference on Research and Production of Rice*. Peradeniya: Department of Agriculture.

Jogaratnam, T. 1971. *Survey on Nine Colonization Schemes in Ceylon: Summary Report*. Peradeniya: University of Ceylon (mimeographed).

Keane, John. 1905. Report on Irrigation in Ceylon. *Sessional Paper XLV-1905*. Colombo: Government Press.

Kurian, Rachael. 1981. *The Position of Women Workers in the Plantation Sector of Sri Lanka*, Geneva: ILO, WEP Working Paper.

Lipton, Michael. 1975. Towards a Theory of Land Reform in *Agrarian Reform and Agrarian Reformism*, ed. David Lehmann. London: Faber & Faber. 269-315.

Moormann, F.R. and Panabokke, C.R. 1961. Soils of Ceylon. *Tropical Agriculturist*. 117.

Morrison, B.M. and Waxler, N.E. 1986. Three Patterns of Basic Needs Distribution within Sri Lanka: 1971-73. *World Development* 14: 97-114.

Meuller-Dombois, D. 1968. Ecological Analysis of the Climatic Map of Ceylon. *Ceylon Forester* VII: 39-58.

Murphy, Rhoads. 1957. The Ruin of Ancient Ceylon. *Journal of Asian Studies* 16: 181-200.

Paranavithana, S. 1956. Glimpses of the Political and Social Conditions of Medieval Ceylon. *Sir Paul Peiris Felicitation Volume*. Colombo: 69-74.

Paranavithana, S. 1960. The Withdrawal of the Sinhalese from the Ancient Capitals. *University of Ceylon History of Ceylon* 713-720.

Peiris, G.H. 1975. Current Land Reforms and Peasant Agriculture in Sri Lanka. *South Asia* 5: 78-89.

Peiris, G.H. 1976. Share Tenancy and Tenurial Reform in Sri Lanka. *Ceylon Journal of Historical and Social Studies* VI: 24-54.

Peiris, G.H. 1978. Land Reform and Agrarian Change in Sri Lanka. *Modern Asian Studies* 12: 611-628.

Peiris, G.H. 1984. Structural Change in Plantation Agriculture in *Plantation Agriculture in Sri Lanka - Issues in Employment and Development*, eds. W. Gooneratne and D. Wesumperuma. Bangkok: ILO/ARTEP, 33-56.

Peiris, G.H. 1981. Agrarian Transformation in British Sri Lanka. *Sri*

Lanka Journal of Agrarian Studies 2: 1-26.

Pelzer, Karl J. 1957. *Pioneer Settlement in the Asiatic Tropics.* New York: American Geographical Society.

Perera, U.L.J. and Gunawardena, P.J. 1980. *Hired Labour in Peasant Agriculture in Sri Lanka.* Colombo: ARTI.

Perera, W.A. 1932. *Problems of Rural Ceylon.* Colombo: Associated Newspapers.

Raza, Ameer. 1970. *Report to the Government of Ceylon on Evaluation of the Paddy Lands Act.* Rome: FAO/UNDP.

Rote, Ron. 1986. *A Taste of Bitterness - The Political Economy of the Tea Plantations of Sri Lanka.* Amsterdam: Free University Press.

Samarasinghe, V. and Samarasinghe, S.W.R. de A. 1984. Income and Wealth Disparities in a Land Settlement in the Dry Zone in *Understanding Green Revolutions*, eds. T. Bayliss-Smith and S. Warmali. London: Cambridge University Press.

Sanderatne, Nimal. 1972. Tenancy in Ceylon's Paddy Lands: The 1958 Reform. *South Asian Review* 5: 117-136.

Senenayake, D.S. 1935. *Agriculture and Patriotism.* Colombo: Associated Newspapers.

Snodgrass, Donald R. 1966. *Ceylon: An Export Economy in Transition.* New Haven: Yale University Press.

Silva, Percy. 1982. Land Settlement and Regional Development in the Dry Zone of Sir Lanka in *Land Settlement Experiences of Sri Lanka,* ed. Kapila Wimaladharma. Colombo: Karunaratne and Sons.

Siriwardena, S.S.A.L. 1982. *Emerging Income Inequalities and Forms of Hidden Tenancy in the Mahaveli H Area.* Colombo: People's Bank Research Department (mimeographed).

Sri Lanka, Ministry of Agriculture and Food. 1966. *Agricultural Development Proposals, 1966-1970.* Colombo: Government Press.

Sri Lanka, Ministry of Plan Implementation. 1983. *Nutritional Strategy.* Colombo (mimeographed).

Uswatte-Aratchi, G. 1967. Some Questions Concerning Settlement Policy in *Development of Dry Zone Agriculture*, ed. O.S. Pieris. Colombo: Chemical Industries.

Van Gelderen, J. 1961. Economics of a Tropical Colony in *Indonesian Economics.* Amsterdam: Tropical Institute.

Wanigaratne, R.D. and Samad, M. 1980. *Land Alienation under Recent Land Reforms.* Colombo: ARTI.

Wanigaratne, R.D. 1987. *Intra-Regional disintegration effects of Frontier*

Land Settlement in Sri Lanka, Colombo: ARTI (unpublished manuscript).

Weeramunde, A.J. 1982. *Transforming Peasants: Social Change in Dry Zone Settlement Scheme*. University of Colombo: Department of Sociology.

Weerawardena, I.K. 1975. *Lessons of an Experiment*. Colombo: Ministry of Agriculture and Land.

Wijetunga, A.A. 1985. Results of the Land Development Ordinance. *Proceedings of the Seminar on the Land Development Ordinance, 1935-1985*. Colombo: Ministry of Mahaveli Development.

Chapter V

MEETING THE DEMAND FOR TRAINED AGRICULTURAL WORKERS IN SRI LANKA

James C. Hanson
University of Maryland, College Park

Sri Lanka's major industry is agriculture. Three manpower assessment studies have been conducted in the past ten years to insure that the country has a sufficient quality and quantity of trained manpower to meet their food and fiber needs. This chapter: a) describes the type of postsecondary agricultural training currently available in Sri Lanka, b) summarizes the three manpower studies, c) reviews other countries' experiences in manpower training, specifically focusing on the vocational versus academic debate, and d) makes suggestions to aid Sri Lanka in their manpower efforts.

POST SECONDARY AGRICULTURAL TRAINING IN SRI LANKA

The three primary types of postsecondary trained agricultural workers in Sri Lanka are: a) the practically trained graduates with one-year certificates or two-year diplomas, b) college graduates from the different Faculties of Agriculture, and c) the postgraduates with a Master's degree or Doctorate of Philosophy.

The Department of Agriculture's (DOA) Division of Extension and Training is the major source of practically trained agricultural workers in the country. The DOA operates schools at *Kundesale, Augunukolapalesse,* and *Palwehera.* Their training courses are two years in length and students graduate with a diploma. Kundesale is the largest facility, graduating approximately 200 students per year. The DOA reserves a portion of the openings in these schools for its own employees who are being upgraded in training. Many graduates of these programs find work with the Extension Division of DOA. Other schools that offer diplomas are the Hardy Institute under the Ministry of Higher Education at Amparai and the privately run Aquinas College in Colombo. Three new diploma programs, with their first graduating classes in the mid-1980s, are: a) Kuliyapitiva Technical Institute under the Ministry of Education, b) Schools of Animal Husbandry (Ragama) and Animal Health (Peradeniya) under the Ministry of Rural Industrial Development, and c) Irrigation Technology Institute under the Ministry of Land and Land Development at Galgamuwa. Most programs which had offered one-year certificates in agriculture have been discontinued (Jones, 1985). The only recent certificate holders are the few graduating in dairy technology and craft agriculture. The general sentiment among employers is that one year of training is inadequate.

The three Faculties of Agriculture in Sri Lanka are located at the Universities of *Peradeniya*, *Ruhuna* and *Batticaloa*. There is a fourth university and faculty planned for the Jaffna Peninsula. However, the ethnic tension in that area has delayed full establishment. All colleges were closed for approximately four years in the late 1980s. When in operation, Batticaloa graduates about 25 students per year. The largest Faculty of Agriculture is at Peradeniya which annually has graduated between 130 and 140 students with Bachelor of Science degrees. Ruhuna had its first graduating class in 1983 and its normal annual graduation rate is 40 students.

The Postgraduate Institute of Agriculture (PGIA) at Peradeniya, established in 1976, is the only agricultural graduate school in Sri Lanka. A student may specialize in agricultural engineering, agricultural economics and extension, animal science, agricultural chemistry, crop science, or agricultural biology. In 1985, the PGIA had 195 students (CIAED, 1985). Fifty-one of them were studying for a Master of Science (M.Sc.), 120 were completing a Master of Philosophy (M.Phil.), 18 were in a Doctor of Philosophy program (Ph.D.), and 16 were taking courses while provisionally awaiting acceptance into the program. Students must pay their own educational costs at the PGIA. Over 80% are sponsored by institutions in Sri Lanka to whom the students return for employment upon graduation. The PGIA was not closed during the ethnic tensions of the 1980s.

AGRICULTURAL MANPOWER ASSESSMENT STUDIES IN SRI LANKA

Three assessments of the supply and demand for agricultural manpower in Sri Lanka have been recently completed. The Consortium for International Agricultural Education Development (CIAED, 1977) conducted the first assessment in 1977. CIAED interviewed all major agricultural employers in the country. The employers were asked to project their demand for manpower by agricultural degree. The relevant degrees were Doctor of Philosophy (Ph. D.), Master of Philosophy (M.Phil.), Master of Science (M.Sc.), Bachelor of Science (B.Sc.), and diploma holders from two-year farm schools. The M.Phil. and M.Sc. degrees were differentiated by the former requiring a thesis. CIAED then compared these needs with the projected supply of new graduates from the technical schools, universities and graduate programs. The 1977 assessment was duplicated by Hanson and Jogaratnam in 1983. This second manpower study interviewed all employers contacted in 1977. The employers were asked to make projections of their manpower needs by agricultural degree for 1984, 1985, 1986, 1987, and 1988. Each study (1977 and 1983) could be more accurately described as a census rather than a statistical survey.

Results from both studies showed that the projected annual demand for diploma holders, Ph.D, and M. Phil. would be increased from the 1978- 82 period to the 1984-88 period. In contrast, the demand for B.Sc. and M.Sc. graduates decreased between these two periods. Hanson and Jogaratnam compared the demand for these degrees between 1983 and 1988 with the projected supply for that period. They found that there would be: a) too many B.Sc. graduates, b) too few diploma holders, and c) the appropriate number of M.Sc., M.Phil, and Ph.D. graduates. The reason for the latter is that these graduates usually obtain their education through the PGIA and are sponsored by future employers.

Jones (1985) completed a third assessment of manpower needs in Sri Lanka. It was expanded to include fisheries, forestry, and animal science in addition to the traditional agricultural analysis. For the agricultural assessment, which is of interest here, he found similar but less dramatic trends when compared to Hanson and Jogaratnam. He concluded that there would be an excess of B.Sc. graduates but not to the extent projected in the 1983 study. Jones concluded that the supply and demand for diploma holders would be in surplus as opposed to the shortage forecast by Hanson and Jogaratnam in 1983. One explanation is that Jones separated the demand for certificate holders from diploma holders while the 1983 study combined them. When these two classifications are viewed together the supply and demand for practically trained agriculturists are in balance.

Jones commented on the difficulty of correctly estimating the supply of these practically trained workers which might further explain differences between the 1983 and 1985 studies. He noted that duplication in training existed among Ministries and that many programs were sporadic in operation. These 1983 and 1985 studies do reaffirm, however, that the demand for practically trained agriculture workers is the largest of all other agricultural degrees in Sri Lanka. An evaluation of the diploma holder programs should be conducted to make sure the supply of practically trained agricultural workers, the largest numerical manpower need of Sri Lankan agriculture, is adequately and efficiently met.

All of these studies identify the essential bipolar nature of Sri Lanka's agriculture. At one end of the educational scale, there is a need for diploma holders who can, a) help farmers improve their productivity, b) work as field technicians monitoring research plots at the research institutes, or c) supervise other farm laborers in the production of sugarcane, tea, coconuts, milk, minor export crops, and other products important to the Sri Lankan economy. At the other end of the spectrum is a need for researchers with graduate training who can develop new technologies or adapt existing ones to increase potential production.

In contrast, there is a diminished need for those people trained in the middle of the educational scale (B.Sc. or M.Sc.). While many college graduates hope to go to graduate school to become researchers, few are chosen. In addition, college graduates receive little training for applied work. These two types of degrees are caught in the middle between the two primary needs of the Sri Lankan agricultural community (production and research) and produce trained personnel not specialized in either.

THE EDUCATIONAL CONTROVERSY: VOCATIONAL VS. ACADEMIC TRAINING

These supply and demand discrepancies in the agricultural labor market are important. First, Sri Lanka is expanding its agricultural base. For example, the Accelerated Mahaweli River Development Project is bringing 117,000 hectares of new land under irrigation and resettling 100,000 landless people on one-hectare plots. These people need instruction from trained agricultural workers (two-year diploma holders). Also, Sri Lanka with its expanding production of basic commodities needs workers to manage this acreage.

On the other hand, a study by the Marga Institute (1981) notes that the problems associated with the unemployment of educated youths is quite severe in Sri Lanka. Some have labeled this unemployment as a major contributing factor to the 1971 youth insurrection. Even if the thesis that unemployment leads to social unrest is not accepted, it still indicates a misallocation of educational funds. Sustained underemployment of college graduates (with specific reference here to agricultural B.Sc. graduates) is the market's way of saying that either the quantity or quality of this degree is unacceptable. These problems of manpower shortages and surpluses are too complex to simply advocate building more vocational schools and counsel that university enrollment be cut in half.

Providing vocational training for students in developing countries has always held a strong fascination for central planners. An economy based on agriculture needs workers trained in basic agricultural skills. However, Foster (1965) in a review of education in Ghana popularized the phrase "fallacy of vocational education" in which he challenges the traditional viewpoint. Foster's main points can be summarized as follows:

1) In a developing country where agriculture is dominant, there is a need for trained agriculture workers. That fact, in itself, is insufficient to justify a major investment in vocational institutes.
2) Before any investment in vocational training is made, an inventory of the institutional incentives that exist or do not exist should be completed. It is often the case that agricultural workers receive lower wages than their counterparts in other sectors. Land tenure schemes often discourage graduates from going into production unless they already come from a farm.
3) Often students attend vocational schools for the "wrong" reasons. Many students see a vocational institute as a stepping stone to an academic institution or have been rejected by alternative institutions. In either case, there is a strong likelihood that these students will not end up pursuing a career in agriculture.
4) The primary role of the academic schools should be training their students in the 3 "R's". Vocational training is greatly enhanced by those students who can read and write. Vocational training is best conducted at the job site after employment.

In a similar, more recent study, Urevbu reviewed Nigeria's

experience in vocational education (1984). In 1977, Nigeria had introduced a National Policy on Education. While this policy addressed a wide variety of educational needs in Nigeria, it specifically advocated vocational education in the countryside. It was felt that traditional academic education encouraged rural young people to migrate to the city. If they were taught vocational subjects, it was reasoned, the rural to urban movement would be slowed.

Urevbu concluded that progress in vocational education had been disappointing since 1977. He noted, not unlike Foster above, that those who do participate in vocational programs are often dropouts from the academic schools. Students unfortunately perceive (and perhaps correctly) that the path to success lies along the academic track. They pursue that goal initially, only to change to the vocational alternative after being rerouted. Urevbu reiterated the concept that vocational education does not promote economic development anymore than conventional schooling does. Students respond to job opportunities and anticipated high salaries. Also, given the lack of attendance in the vocational programs, the rural people seem to realize that, "when the elite, the top federal government officials, advocate vocational expansion it is often for other people's children rather than for their own" (Urevbu, 1984, 227).

Psacharopoulos (1986) reviewed the findings of many authors in several different countries concerning the debate between vocational and academic education. He concluded that vocational education costs more on a per student basis than academic. This is not unexpected given the expense of materials, equipment and laboratories needed to duplicate real world situations. In Colombia and Tanzania, Psacharopoulos found that the average vocational student has a longer period of initial unemployment before finding his first job than academic graduates. In Colombia, academic graduates also earn more after graduation than their vocational counterparts.

In another study, Psacharopoulos (1985) compared the social returns to secondary education by curriculum. In five countries, (Cyprus, France, Indonesia, Liberia, and Taiwan) the social returns to academic training exceeded that of vocational. He noted that the differences lay mainly on the cost side. The benefits from either vocational or academic curricula are basically equal, but vocational education costs more, lowering the returns.

This review of the literature seems to capture the essence of studies on this subject, that is, that vocational education while continuing to appeal to central planners cannot be economically justified. At the secondary school level, traditional academic training provides a better return for the educational dollar. While the weight of the literature supports academic training in the developing countries; is it possible to overinvest? For example, Sri Lanka has made a major commitment to academic training at all levels; but have they invested in education to the detriment of other basic needs, or beyond the economic ability of their society to assimilate these workers?

Isenman (1980) reviewed the results of Sri Lanka's investment in basic needs. Between 1965 and 1980, Sri Lanka spent one-half of its current expenditures on food subsidies, health, and education programs. This investment did not go unrewarded (World Bank Development Report, 1985). Among the 35 low-income countries (GNP per capita of less than $400), Sri Lanka had the highest life expectancy with 69 years, the second lowest fertility rate at 3.4, the lowest infant mortality rate (age less than 1) with 37 per 1,000 and tied with China for the lowest child mortality rate (age 1 to 4) at 2 per 1,000. In 1975 (World Development Report, 1980) among the same grouping of countries, Sri Lanka had the second highest literacy rate with 78% of the population able to read. In addition to the obvious advantages of a healthier more educated populace, Isenman noted the correlation between basic needs and productivity. He cited as an example the relationship between Sri Lanka's high rice yields and literacy, suggesting that people who can read are likelier to adopt new technologies in a quicker, more accurate fashion.

There have been negative aspects of this major commitment to basic needs. In general, the more money allocated to basic human needs, a longterm investment, the less available for short-term capital improvements. Sri Lanka, despite its literate population, is still a poor country as measured by GNP per capita. Isenman especially noted the problems associated with their education program which is geographically centralized with a relatively large proportion of the budget committed to those students proceeding beyond the secondary level.

One result is that Sri Lanka has a large number of highly educated unemployed workers. Because of food subsidies, other government benefits, and the support of parents; many highly educated young people can afford to wait for a good job. In 1973, the average waiting period for a job in the public sector was 3.5 years. In 1977, Sri Lanka's unemployment rate was 20%. The composition of this unemployment adds insight to the discussion of the educated unemployed. Of the total unemployed in Sri Lanka, 90% are under 30, 75% have a post-primary education, 85% are still supported by their parents, and 75% are looking for their first job. The type of unemployment seems more indicative of a mismatch between a student's education, his employment expectations, and the reality of the marketplace. In comparison, the poor of Sri Lanka are generally employed, receiving low wages in distant rural outposts.

In response to this problem of education and unemployment, Sri Lanka intoduced the Junior Secondary School Curriculum in 1972. This program was designed to take a more holistic approach to education, melding academic training with preparation for a job. The result would be a more vocationally oriented curriculum helping those who leave school before graduation become employed while not abandoning traditional academic goals. The program was discontinued in 1977.

Wanasinghe (1982) offered the following reasons for the failure of the Junior Secondary School Curriculum; a) teachers were not adequately prepared to teach the broader range of subject matter required by this curriculum, b) proper materials were not supplied, c) the public and the teaching profession lost faith in the program, and d) a student's vocational aspirations were unaffected by classroom instruction. This last reason forms a common thread from the previous experiences described in this chapter. While a country may need people to work with their hands in a vocational occupation, it is foolish to think education has the power to materially reorient people's attitudes in that direction.

MODIFYING SRI LANKA'S AGRICULTURAL EDUCATION SYSTEM

The price mechanism and its affect on shortages and surpluses is often ignored in assessments of manpower needs. For example, it has been established that there is a strong demand for diploma holders working in agriculture. Perhaps, this demand will be met if there are an adequate number of efficiently run training sites. However, if the wages paid diploma holders are too low then, no matter how many training sites are established, the demand will go unmet. Low wages could contribute to employers overstating their demand for this type of labor. Diploma holders might be a bargain when comparing paid wages with services rendered.

An evaluation should be made to determine the validity of this proposition. Since Sri Lanka needs trained agricultural workers, sufficient wages should be offered to entice workers. Sri Lanka has a unique opportunity to act quickly in this case because many of the trained workers will be hired by government or quasi-government agencies where wages can easily be increased. This type of analysis is equally valid for the surplus of B.Sc. graduates. An often overlooked economic principle is that continued subsidization causes a surplus. While there are many egalitarian reasons for providing free university education, an almost certain response will be too many college graduates.

It is helpful to delineate some differences between primary and secondary education, and university education in Sri Lanka. The former is oriented to educating a person in the rudiments of reading, writing, and mathematics; or making that student a "more productive" member of society. The latter guides a student into career specialization. If a society benefits from literacy, then society should subsidize that education. In deciding to attend primary or secondary school, a student (with ancouragement of his parents) is seeking to improve himself. He will be a better worker (vocationally or academically) because of his basic educational skills. This is a strong argument for Sri Lanka continuing its subsidization of primary and secondary education. At the university level, students are making definite career choices. By subsidizing this education, Sri Lanka is implying that jobs will be available in a student's chosen field of study, a difficult promise for any economy to deliver. If university students were made to pay a portion of their education, then they would be forced to assume more personal responsibility for evaluating the potential benefits from a particular career choice with its actual monetary costs. Sri Lanka could still offer student loans and scholarships to protect the right of all its citizens to pursue higher education.

The surplus of university educated laborers for the market place is further aggravated by Sri Lanka's subsidization of basic human needs. A graduate is able to wait a long time for a particular job because his food needs are being met. One conclusion from such a situation is that food subsidies, and the like, should only be offered to the truly needy. In addition, if the country judges that its citizens are seeking too many white-collar jobs, then the wages should be lowered. Sri Lanka is a free market economy, but a large portion of the jobs are found in the public sector where wages are sticky and not responsive to the market place. If the government takes the lead in lowering these wages, the private sector will follow.

People respond to economic incentives and disincentives. By lowering white-collar wages, raising blue-collar wages, and having students pay a portion of their university costs, Sri Lanka could make major strides in alleviating its current misallocation of labor. But, what if wages are raised for diploma holders, or if they were sufficient to begin with? Is it possible for Sri Lanka to expand and improve its training and still avoid the well documented problems of vocational education? The answer to that question is "yes" and it results from Sri Lanka's unique employment situation in agriculture.

Before proceeding to describe how this training might be conducted, let us consider what should not be done first. This training should not take place in the primary and secondary schools. Sri Lanka has a solid record of educating its students at that level and its success should not be tampered with. Given the documented failure of the Junior Secondary School Curriculum, that experience would doom any comparable program to at best an uphill battle.

Also, Sri Lanka should not make any investments in new schools like those that already exist. Interviews conducted by this author found that the Department of Agriculture had the best reputation in its training. In attending DOA's schools, however, it was visibly apparent and supported by conversation with teachers, that equipment and laboratories were lacking. This is not to fault the program but to illustrate that these schools should be brought up to par before new institutions are created..

Given the experiences in other countries, the most cost-effective way to educate the new diploma holders, in the view of this author, would be on the job site. The usual problem with job site training in most situations is that the number of employers hiring only small number of employees is large. This creates duplication of effort and increases the problem of monitoring quality. But the advantage of the Sri Lankan situation, as already alluded to, is that there are at present a few employers (primarily government or quasi-government) who hire a large portion of the diploma holders.

The major employers of diploma holders are the various research institutes, estates, plantations, and the Department of Agriculture's Extension Service. In 1983, a large portion of the demand for diploma holders came from such large agencies as the Extension Service, Sri Lanka Sugar Corporation, Coconut Research Institute, Coconut Cultivation Board, and Minor Export Crops Department (Hanson and Jogaratnam, unpublished data). This provides efficient opportunities for on the job site training.

For example, the Sri Lankan Sugar Corporation and the associated private sugar companies have projected a large demand for diploma holders. The government could establish a two-year program at the principal sugar plantation. The government could provide teachers to work with the sugar production students. In this way, the students are assured of an up-to-date education in sugar production technology. The plantation would benefit from surplus labor in the present and trained employees in the future, and the government would require less investment in duplicative machinery and laboratories at other locations.

This type of program reduces the government's expense, a common criticism of vocational education. It also helps to alleviate the problem of those people who attend school with no actual intention of pursuing that career. The plantations could require a period of payback service in exchange for the cost of the education. If a trainee really did not wish to make his permanent home in the hill country where the tea is grown, he would probably not agree to a two-year training program in that location either.

A common mistake made by central planners with minimal previous practical agricultural experience is to underestimate the difference in production technologies among crops. Vocational training is, by definition, specific and skill oriented. Growing tea and sugarcane are two entirely separate enterprises. To develop skills in tea production, a person should be trained in tea production and not the general principles of crop production alone. By developing training institutes specifically oriented to different types of crop cultures, this problem of an nonspecific education could be avoided.

This chapter has examined the supply and demand for agricultural workers in Sri Lanka within the larger context of vocational versus academic training. Several conclusions have been reached which are repeated here:

1) Because of the costs of laboratories and equipment, vocational education costs more on a per student basis than academic training.

2) Perceived wages and opportunities affect a student's career goals more than the type of education received.
3) Sri Lanka has made a major commitment to both academic and vocational training. In terms of agricultural workers, there has been a strong tendency to an oversupply of college graduates and an undersupply of practically trained workers.
4) Sri Lanka should evaluate its institutional and wage structure in order to give the most reliable signal possible to the labor markets.
5) If it is determined that Sri Lanka needs more practically trained workers in agriculture than are being currently supplied, strong consideration should be given to training at the job site. Job site training reduces the cost of vocational education, improves the quality of instruction, and insures participation by only those who are interested in pursuing that type of training.

REFERENCES

Consortium for International Agricultural Education Development (CIAED). 1977. *Postgraduate Institute of Agricultural University of Sri Lanka: A Preliminary Assessment.* Peradeniya: CIAE.

Consortium for International Agricultural Education Development (CIAED), 1985. *Agricultural Education Development Project, Quarterly Report.* Peradeniya: CIAED.

Foster, P.J. 1965. The Vocational School Fallacy in Development Planning in *Education and Economic Development*, eds. C.A. Anderson and M.J. Bowman. Chicago: Aldine.

Hanson, J.C. and T. Jogaratnam, 1985. Some Estimates of Future Demand for the Supply of Trained Manpower for Agricultural Development in Sri Lanka. *Sri Lankan Journal of Agricultural Sciences* 22: 128-156.

Isenman, Paul. 1980. Basic Needs: The Case of Sri Lanka. *World Development* 8: 237-258.

Jones, E. 1985. *The Supply of and Demand for Technical and University Personnel in Agriculture, Animal Sciences, Fisheries, and Forestry in Sri Lanka.* San Francisco: Development Associates, Inc.

Marga Institute. 1981. Review Workshop on the Study *University Education and Graduate Employment in Sri Lanka.* Colombo, 16-18 October, 1981.

Psacharopoulos, G. 1985. An Evaluation of Curriculum Diversification in Colombia and Tanzania. *Comparative Education Review* 29: 507-525.

Psacharopoulos, G. 1986. To Vocationalize or Not to Vocationalize? That is the Curriculm Question". Presented at the American Educational Research Association Annual Meeting, San Francisco, April, 1986.

Urevbu, A.O. 1984. Vocational Education in Nigeria: A Preliminary Appraisal. *International Journal of Educational Development* 4:223-229.

Wanasinghe, J. 1982. A Critical Examination of the Failure of the Junior Secondary School Curriculum and Pre-Vocational Studies in Sri Lanka. *International Journal of Educational Development* 2: 61-72.

World Bank. 1980. *World Development Report*, 1980. New York: Oxford University Press.

World Bank. 1985. *World Development Report*, 1985. New York: Oxford University Press.

Chapter VI

THE CONTRIBUTION OF AGRICULTURAL RESEARCH CENTERS TO SRI LANKAN AGRICULTURE

Kurt Finsterbusch
University of Maryland, College Park

THE ROLE OF AGRICULTURAL RESEARCH

Agricultural research is one of the most important development activities in which a Third World country can engage. The productivity of research and development (R & D) generally and its productivity in agriculture specifically generate high rates of return. The marginal rate of return on research and development is very high on average across all sectors of both agriculture and industry. Terleckyj (1974) studied 33 manufacturing and monmanufacturing industries in the U.S. and found that R and D expenditures greatly increased productivity within the industry and netted about a 30% rate of return. They also had a substantial indirect effect on the productivity of other industries so the social rate of return far exceeded 30%. Mansfield reviewed the research literature on returns to investment in R & D and while acknowledging the methodological problems and limitations, concluded that:

> In sum, practically all of the studies carried out to date.... indicate that the average social rate of return from investments in technology in both agriculture and industry has tended to be very high. Moreover, the marginal rate of return also seems high, generally at least 30 per cent. (Mansfield, 1983, 110)

It is important to note that the research payoff is not just in innovations but also in the development and utilization of innovations. Mansfield and his colleagues documented these benefits of research and indicated why such research is crucial to economic development.

> Nations that spend comparatively large amounts on R and D (in the relevant industry) tend to produce a new product relatively quickly, even if they are not the innovator. This finding is analogous to our finding in an earlier book that firms that spend relatively large amounts on R and D tend to be quick adopters of new technology developed by others. Both for entire nations and individual firms R and D enables the nation or firm to evaluate external developments and react more quickly to them. In some economic models, R and D is viewed as an invention-producing or innovation-producing activity. While minimally correct, this view misses a critical element of R and D, which is the quick response to rivals and the clever modification, adaptation, and improvement of their results. (Mansfield, 1982: 209).

Within the agricultural sector R and D produces high rates of economic return. Pinstrup-Anderson presented the annual rates of return for investments in agricultural research for fifty studies on a variety of crops in fifteen different countries and concluded that:

> Average annual rates of return for these programmes are slightly less than 50 per cent, only four showing returns of less than 20 per cent. Expected rates of return from investment of public funds in other activities are typically 10-20 per cent. Furthermore, interest rates in the international capital market have traditionally been below 10-15 per cent. Thus, public investment in agricultural research appears to be a very profitable undertaking. (Pinstrup-Anderson, 1982:102).

The average annual rate of return from investment in agricultural research for the twenty-three studies in Pinstrup-Andersen's set (which examine agriculture in developing countries) is 48%. Though Sri Lanka is not included in these studies, four involve India and might be comparable to Sri Lanka. Their average rate of return is also 48%.

Pinstrup-Andersen carefully analyzed various methodological issues and claims the overall results are not seriously biased. Ruttan (1982) reviewed many of the same studies and many additional studies and concluded that investment in agricultural research has very high rates of return. Evenson, Waggner and Ruttan (1979) demonstrated the tremendous impact research and extension has had on U.S. agricultural productivity from 1868-1971. The research results are clear and the major conclusion is obvious: Agricultural research has high levels of return and countries, especially Third World countries, should invest more heavily in agricultural research. Pinstrup-Andersen asserts "Therefore, from the point of view of effective utilization of public funds for economic growth, public investment in agricultural research should be increased, both in absolute terms and relative to investment in other publicly financed projects." (1982: 105). Ruttan adds "It is hard to imagine many investments in either private - or public - sector activities that would produce more favourable rates of return." (1982: 241).

Unfortunately, there are no studies which evaluate the rate of return for agricultural research in Sri Lanka. The assumption must be made, therefore, that the high rates of return found in other South Asian countries also apply to Sri Lanka. We conclude, therefore, that Sri Lanka underinvests in agricultural research as do her neighbors. Certainly those research center personnel interviewed felt that more funding was badly needed and could be used productively.

THE STATE OF SRI LANKAN AGRICULTURE

Sri Lanka is an agrarian country. About 50% of employed workers are in agriculture, forestry and fishing compared to about 10% in manufacturing and 10% in wholesale and retail trade. Income, however, is not so overwhelmingly distributed to the agricultural sector. The proportion of gross domestic product (GDP) accounted for by agriculture, forestry, and fishing in terms of factor costs in 1984 was only 25%, for manufacturing (including food and beverage industries) it was 15%, and for wholesale and retail trade it was 21%. In 1950, by comparison, agriculture, forestry and fishing accounted for 40% for GDP, manufacturing 16% and wholesale and retail trade 13% (*Annual Reports* of the Central Bank of Ceylon for various years and Peebles, 1982).

As in most agriculturally-based economies the agricultural sector is not keeping pace with the other sectors of the economy. The average annual rate of increase in GDP between 1965 and 1988 was 4.1% and for GDP in agriculture it was 2.7% (World Bank, 1990). However, slower growth of the agricultural sector is due largely to the stagnation in production of the three main export crops: tea, rubber and coconut products. The average annual rate of increase for these crops in the 1960s and 1970s was only 0.2% while it was 4.6% for paddy.

Sri Lankan agriculture is divided between the domestic sector (peasant agriculture) and the export sector (plantation agriculture) (Johnson and Scrivenor, 1981; Peiris, 1977; and Wikremeratne, 1977). Plantation agriculture usually encompasses large-scale commercial agriculture but in Sri Lanka it includes both large and small units devoted to tea, rubber and coconut and even some minor export crops such as cinnamon, cardamon, cacao, citronella, and peppers. The term "peasant agriculture" is also imprecise because there has been considerable, though sporadic, modernization and commercialization in certain sectors.

Plantation agriculture was well developed (except for the minor export crops) at the time of independence of the country in 1948 and largely controlled by the British. It dominated exports; 96% of the value of exports in 1948 was contributed by three crops - tea (63%), rubber (15%) and coconut products (18%). These plantation agriculture crops no longer dominate exports. In 1987, tea accounted for 26% of export earnings, rubber 7% and coconut products 5% for a total of 38%.

Plantation agriculture is experiencing difficulties. Tea production in millions of kilograms increased from 135 in 1948 to 197 in 1960 and has remained close to that figure to the present (211 in 1986 and 212 in 1987). Rubber was stagnant from 1948 to 1965 (97 and 105 millions of kilograms respectively), then increased to 159 in 1970 and declined to 138 in 1986 and 122 in 1987. Coconut production has barely increased since independence and has experienced a serious decline in the late 1980s due to droughts and declines in subsidies.

The two main reasons for the stagnation of plantation agriculture are the interrelated factors of increased international competition and worsening terms of trade. At independence, Sri Lanka supplied a little more than one-third of the world's tea exports, second only to India's control of one-half of the market. Currently Sri Lanka supplies about one-fifth of world tea exports as East African exports of this commodity have increased sixfold and now lead Sri Lanka in market share.

Agricultural output is the product of area planted times yields. The area in the major Sri Lanka export crops has remained quite constant since 1959. The area devoted to tea was 227,000 ha. in 1959-61 and 222,000 ha. in 1986-88, to rubber 168,000 ha. in 1959-61 and 202,000 ha. in 1986-88, and to coconut 400,000 ha. in 1959-61 and about 420,000 ha. from 1982 to 1987 (Department of Census and Statistics, 1989). In comparison, the area devoted to paddy has increased 54% over the same period from 576,000 to 887,000 ha. Plantation agriculture is also relatively stagnant in terms of yields. There has been some increase in average yields for rubber but yields have declined since the mid-1960s for tea and coconut. Tea yields were 970 kg./ha. in 1964-66 and 837 kg./ha. in 1982-84, rubber 666 kg./ha., and 796 kg./ha. respectively, and coconut 7601 kg./ha. and 5752 kg./ha. respectively. In comparison paddy yields have increase 78% in the same period from 1866 kg./ha. to 3315 kg./ha. The plantation and peasant agricultural sectors, therefore, have very different performance records since independence.

The structure of plantation agriculture has changed considerably because of two significant pieces of legislation. The Land Reform Act of 1972 limited an individual's holdings to 20 ha. but allowed corporations larger holdings. Within two years of passage, 225,000 ha. had been acquired for redistribution with 60% of the area in tea, rubber or coconut. the Land Reform Amendment Law of 1975 provided for government takeover of all lands owned by corporations. Under the two land reform acts 63% of land in tea, 32% of land in rubber and 10% of land in coconut was vested in the Land Reform Commission. Few plantation estates, however, were subdivided into smallholdings and distributed to the landless as occurred in the peasant agriculture sector. Rather, the majority was turned over to cooperatives or government enterprises. Nevertheless, these laws continued a trend since Independence of increasing smallholder shares of land under tea or rubber. For example, tea estates of over 100 acres declined from 81% of total acreage in 1950 to 69% in the early 1970s and the proportion of rubber estates with over 100 acres declined from 53 to 46% during the same period.

Performance in the plantation sector is mixed. By Asian standards tea production is relatively high, rubber production mixed and coconut production low. Sri Lanka is a leading tea exporter because it has climatic conditions which are favorable to producing quality tea throughout the year and it has a highly skilled and disciplined labor force. Performance in terms of maintenance, pest control, fertilizer, replanting, plant quality and agricultural practices is also comparatively high especially on the estates. Improved practices need further diffusion into the smallholder sector, however, and technological and institutional upgrading must continue for Sri Lanka to remain competitive on world markets.

Peasant agriculture is the dynamic agricultural sector in Sri Lanka. As indicated earlier the average annual rate of increase in GDP for tea, rubber and coconuts in the 1960s and 1970s was low (0.2%) while the rate for paddy was higher (4.6%) and equal to the rate of increase for the economy as a whole. This growth in paddy is the result of both a 54% expansion in cropped land between 1959-61 and 1982-84 and a 78% increase in yields per hectare over the same period. Behind these statistics are three success stories: irrigation, the green revolution and government policies. The result of these changes has made contemporary Sri Lanka almost self-sufficient in rice. In 1987 Sri Lanka produced 2128 thousand metric tons (TMT) of rice and imported only 102 TMT or 4.8% of domestic consumption. In 1969, however, Sri Lanka produced 934 TMT and imported 264 TMT or 22% of domestic consumption.

Irrigation is both an ancient and a modern achievement in Sri Lanka. Irrigation development has been emphasized by the government since independence and cultivated irrigation lands increased from 100,000 ha. in 1949/50 to 651,000 ha. in 1969/70. After 1970 irrigated lands did not increase substantially until the massive additions associated with the Mahaveli projects in the late 1980s. The biggest economic development project in Sri Lanka today is the Mahaweli Development Scheme, a major irrigation and hydroelectric project involving a series of dams on the Mahaweli River and irrigating an area of 337,000 ha. by 1991 (almost the area in paddy at independence). Its impacts on agriculture and the entire economy are substantial. For example, by the end of 1990, the Mahaveli area produced 17% of Sri Lanka's paddy production.

The *green revolution* is based on high yield varieties (HYV) but also involves water control, fertilizer, pest control and improved methods. Ultimately it is based on agricultural research, both foreign and domestic. The original rice HYV were developed abroad, principally in Japan, Thailand and the Philippines under the leadership, since 1959, of the International Rice Research Institute (IRRI). The HYV were adapted to Sri Lankan agriculture and crossed with local varieties by agricultural research centers in Sri Lanka. In the 1960s the rate of adaption of HYV in Sri Lanka was very high and HYV were utilized in 70% of paddy areas by 1970. In the 1970s new HTV (NHYV) were developed by the Sri Lankan agricultural research center system using genetic material developed at IRRI and crossed with local varieties. Now the NHYV are more prevalent than the old HYV.

The HTV require considerable changes in farming practices. They require good water management so they are particularly suited to irrigated areas. Second, since one variety is adapted over sizeable areas pest control becomes much more crucial. Third, they are responsive to fertilizer but farmers need to know the most effective amounts under various conditions. Thus the new technology requires more managment, more careful agricultural practices, and more inputs. The research centers have helped meet these needs by developing improvements in methods and new technologies for handling HYV.

Fertilizer is another factor in the green revolution. Its use in paddy cultivation has increased dramatically from 9.4 TMT in 1954 to 47.1 TMT in 1962-63, 128 TMT in 1973 and 204 TMT in 1988. The government played a major role in the expansion of fertilizer use by the founding in 1964 of the Sri Lanka Fertilizer Corporation to distribute and subsidize fertilizer.

The agricultural research system in Sri Lanka has made considerable progress but difficulties still remain. Farming involves many hard choices. transplanting increases yields over broadcasting seed but is more labor intensive. Tractors can cost-effectively increase production where labor is scarce during cultivation times as in the Dry Zone. Choice and amounts of pesticides, fertilizers, and seeds and selection of methods vary with climate, soils and farmers' resources. Research on these and other problems and the diffusion of results to farmers via the agricultural extension service are needed to further increase production.

National *government policies* have helped increase production in the peasant agriculture sector. For example, the Paddy Lands Act of 1958 gave sharecroppers secure tenure to make them interested in long-term productivity of the land and willing to invest in its improvement. Secure tenure also made it easier for sharecroppers to obtain credit. The Act also reduced the sharecroppers rent from one-half or more to one-quarter of the crop in many regions. The law thus attempted to correct some of the structural bases for low productivity on sharecrop lands. Landlords, however, largely circumvented the law so the problems were readdressed in the Land Reform Law of 1972 and the Land Reform Amendment Law of 1975. These acts have given land to many landless peasants and provided incentives to increase yields, but they have not significantly changed traditional relationships and patterns and the problem of fragmented holdings remains.

The government has also greatly increased croplands through land development and land settlement schemes. Much of the expansion of paddy lands is due to such schemes as the Mahaweli project which has continued land development and land settlement throughout the 1980s. By the end of 1990, 106,000 families had settled in the Mahaveli project area.

The other major government agricultural policies and programs for peasant agriculture are rice price supports, crop insurance, input subsidies and the provision of credit. The Guaranteed Price Scheme has assured a good price for paddy since independence and generally has been equal to or above inflation. It is a major reason, together with the use of HYV, for the large growth in paddy production and Sri Lanka's near self-sufficiency in rice. These price supports, however, do not allow Sri Lanka to export rice since world prices are lower. In crop insurance Sri Lanka is the leader in South Asia. In 1977-78, 40 percent of the maha crop was insured but this is largely attributable to compulsory insurance in some areas. Farmers are still unsure of the value of the insurance program. The subsidy programs, however, are appreciated by farmers because they reduce their costs for fertilizers, paddy seeds and other inputs. Finally, the government has a comprehensive Fund Credit scheme which utilizes cooperatives as dispersion and collection agencies. The credit may be short-term for seeds and fertilizer or medium-term for machinery. The cooperatives themselves use credit for investments in storage, transportation, milling and processing facilities. The credit program, however, has become a welfare program because the farmers feel only a modest obligation to pay it back except in good years so defaults are high, around 40% between 1967-68 and 1975-76 (Johnson and Scrivenor, 1981).

Since Sri Lanka is an agrarian country, dependent on agricultural exports for foreign exchange and on the agriculture sector of the economy for employment and food self-sufficiency, it is not surprising that it has a well developed system of agricultural research centers. It is a two-part system which closely aligns with the split between plantation and peasant agriculture. Each major plantation crop (tea, rubber, coconut) has a research center and substations exclusively devoted to it. These are the three oldest centers with more than a half century of continuous operation. They are relatively well financed from crop export levies and well staffed, equipped and organized. Administratively they are under the Ministry of Plantation Industries and Ministry of Coconut Industries rather than the Ministry of Agricultural Development and Research. The other centers serve the peasant agriculture sector and are grouped under the Department of Agriculture except for the Sugar Research Institute and the Minor Export Crops Research Center which are in separate departments and serve both estates and small farmers. The ten centers of the Department of Agriculture include eight multi-crop regional centers and two specialized centers: the Potato Research Center and the Rice Research Center. Most of the regional multi-crop centers, however, emphasize rice. The major center in the regional system is the Central Agricultural Research Institute at the University of Peradeniya. It is better equipped and staffed than the other regional centers and serves as a resource to the rest of the system.

The ten Department of Agriculture centers had 258 research officers in 1983 out of the system total of 393 for an average of 26 per center (Table 6.1). These centers, however, were below average in terms of technical worker support and expenditures. Nevertheless they performed equally well in their contribution to Sri Lankan agriculture as the average of the other five centers and somewhat better for on-farm adaption. A comparison of the production value of various corps to the research effort devoted to them shows that the scientist/production ratio is above average for paddy but that the research expenditure/production ratio is below average (Table 6.2) RRI is the center with above average ratios on both measures.

RESEARCH DESIGN FOR THE PERFORMANCE STUDY OF AGRICULTURAL RESEARCH CENTERS

Thirteen of the fifteen agricultural research centers for crops in Sri Lanka were visited in June and July of 1983 (not visited were Kilenochchi and Bandarawela) to study factors related to the performance of the centers. The director of the center (or his assistant if he was unavailable) and a research officer were interviewed and their judgements on the characteristics of the center were illicited through the use of a formal questionnaire (Table 6.3) Two respondents having different perspectives were interviewed in an attempt to reduce bias.

The informant was asked to compare his or her research center with the other research centers in Sri Lanka and indicate the degree and direction of its deviation, if any, from the average. Since this method is unsatisfactory for sensitive performance measures two outside experts judged the set of research centers on these variables. The scores for the two respondents were combined for the analysis reported below.

The data are analyzed in terms of the Pearson Product-Moment Correlation Coefficient. The analysis focuses on the factors which correlate with center performance. Since the 13 research centers constitute almost the entire population of research centers dealing with agricultural crops in Sri Lanka the results are descriptive of Sri Lankan agricultural research centers except for the effects of measurement error which are likely to weaken correlation coefficients.

TABLE 6.1
Staff and Expenditure Statistics for the Agriculture Research Centers in Sri Lanka, 1983

	DA*	SRI	MECRI	TRI	RRI	CRI	Total
Research Officers	258	11	23	31	31	37	391
Percent of Total	65%	3%	6%	8%	8%	9%	100%
Ratio Technicians to Scientists	1.1	2.7	1.0	1.8	2.4	1.7	—
Total Capital Expenditures (Rs '000)	16,891	3,045	5,777	3,466	965	11,492	41,636
Total Recurrent Expenditures (Rs '000)	31,979	9,455	3,177	21,399	11,962	21,833	99,805
Personal Emoluments (Rs'000)	22,044	3,881	1,921	6,748	5,271	10,720	50,585
Total Expenditures (Rs '000)	48,870	12,500	8,954	24,865	12,927	33,325	141,441
Total Expenditures (US $ '000)	2,036	521	373	1,036	539	1,388	5,893
Recurrent Costs per Scientist (Rs '000)	124	860	138	690	386	590	255
Recurrent Costs per Scientist (US $)	5,170	36,000	5,755	28,750	16,100	24,100	—

Note: The exchange rate in 1983: Rs. 24 = Us $1.
*Summed data for 10 research centers administered by the Department of Agriculture.
Symbols: DA = Department of Agriculture, SRI=Sugar Research Institute, MECRI = Minor Export Crops Research Institute, RRI = Rubber Research Institute, CRI = Coconut Research Institute.
Source: Central Bank of Ceylon, *Annual Report*. Colombo: Central Bank of Ceylon, 1984, 154, 157.

TABLE 6.2
Research Scientists and Recurrent Research Expenditures on Major Commodities in Relation to Production Value in Sri Lanka, 1982-83

Crops	Production Value		Scientists		Research Expenditure		Ratios	
	mill Rs 1	% 2	number 3	% 4	'000 Rs 5	% 6	Scientists/ Prod. Val. 3/1	Res. Expend./ Prod. Val. 5/1
Food Crops								
Paddy	5,482	31.4	306	69.7	26,547	27.3	38	4.84
Other food crops	2,409	13.8	—	—	3,032	3.1	—	1.26
Sugarcane	1,299	7.4	11	2.5	9,455	9.7	9	7.28
Total food crops	9,190	52.7	317	72.2	39,034	40.1	34	4.25
Export Crops								
Coconut	3,283	18.8	37	8.4	21,833	22.4	13	6.65
Tea	2,302	13.2	31	7.1	21,399	22.0	13	9.30
Rubber	1,024	5.9	31	7.1	11,962	12.3	30	11.68
Minor export crops	1,645	9.4	23	5.2	3,177	3.3	14	1.93
Total export crops	8,254	47.3	122	27.8	58,371	59.9	15	7.07
Total all crops	17,144	100.0	439	100.0	97,405	100.0	25	5.58

Source: Central Bank of Ceylon, *Annual Report*. Colombo: Central Bank of Ceylon, 1984, p.155.

TABLE 6.3
Evaluation Questionnaire for Agricultural Research Centers

Note: Most of the following questions ask you to evaluate the center in terms of a 7 point rating scale by circling the best answer. The center is to be compared to the average center of its size. Use the following scale:

exceptionally little or low			average		exceptionally much or high	
1	2	3	4	5	6	7

CHARACTERISTICS OF THE CENTER

	low av. high
1. Quality of the operation of the center: Overall	1 2 3 4 5 6 7
2. Skill, capabilities, and motivation of the staff	1 2 3 4 5 6 7
3. Degree of difficulty in obtaining and retaining qualified researchers	1 2 3 4 5 6 7
4. Degree of difficulty in obtaining and retaining skilled agricultural workers	1 2 3 4 5 6 7
5. Adequacy of facilities and equipment	1 2 3 4 5 6 7
6. Maintenance of Constructed Facilities	1 2 3 4 5 6 7
7. Adequacy of Financing	1 2 3 4 5 6 7
8. Degree of autonomy of the researchers in choice, design and execution of research	1 2 3 4 5 6 7
9. Power of the director in the center	1 2 3 4 5 6 7
10. Size of the administration relative to rest of organization	1 2 3 4 5 6 7
11. Degree of sophistication of research technologies	1 2 3 4 5 6 7
12. Prediction about future prospects for growth or decline; -3= much decline 0 = stable, +3 = much growth	-3-2-1 0 +1+2+3
13. Rate of growth in last 5 years: -3 = much decline 0 = stable, +3 = much growth	-3-2-1 0 +1+2+3
14. Extent of diffusion of center's technology to growers by extension agents	1 2 3 4 5 6 7
15. Incentives and motivation of beneficiaries to work with center	1 2 3 4 5 6 7
16. Desirability of the goods, services or benefits of the center	1 2 3 4 5 6 7
17. Commitment of the national government to the center	1 2 3 4 5 6 7

Note: For the following three questions use a scale ranging from -3 = exceptionally negative to +3 = exceptionally positive with 0 = neutral.

18. Effect of national government policies on the success of the center	-3-2-1 0 +1+2+3

19. Effect of market factors on the success of the center -3-2-1 0 +1+2+3
20. Effect of local values and social structures on the success of the center -3-2-1 0 +1+2+3
21. Extent center benefits from government planning/priorities 1 2 3 4 5 6 7
22. Extent of contacts of the director with other government organizations 1 2 3 4 5 6 7
23. Extent of contacts of the researchers with other government organizations 1 2 3 4 5 6 7
24. Degree of autonomy of the center vis-a-vis government ministry and funding agencies 1 2 3 4 5 6 7
25. Understanding and communication between involved agencies 1 2 3 4 5 6 7
26. Extent of publications per researcher 1 2 3 4 5 6 7
27. Success in developing new varieties per researcher 1 2 3 4 5 6 7
28. Success in developing new methods of farming per researcher 1 2 3 4 5 6 7
29. Extent of advancement of practical agricultural knowledge per researcher 1 2 3 4 5 6 7
30. Extent of contribution to Sri Lankan agriculture per researcher 1 2 3 4 5 6 7
31. Extent of on-farm implementation of center's technology per researcher 1 2 3 4 5 6 7

Six performance criteria for research centers were examined: publications, new varieties, new methods, contribution to agricultural knowledge, contribution to Sri Lankan agriculture, and extent of on-farm implementation of the center's technologies (the overall effectiveness of these research centers has been discussed elsewhere by Finsterbusch and Jogaratnam, (1983)). Some research centers are oriented towards contributions to science as represented by *publications*. Others are oriented toward serving the expressed needs of farmers as represented by the development of *new varieties* and *new methods*. The most general depiction of the outputs of agricultural research centers is the extent of *contributions to agricultural knowledge*. This measure applies to both basic and applied research. The last two performance measures overlap and depend on the utilization of the knowledge produced. The first is the *contribution to Sri Lankan agriculture*, and the second is the *extent of implementation of the center's technologies by farmers*. Many external factors are important to these last two measures of performance. The center's research might be highly successful but poor extension services, adverse market factors or lesser significance of the crop could minimize the effects of the research on *Sri Lankan agriculture*. Also on-farm adoption of the center's technologies can not be controlled by the research center since adoption is dependent on the actions of farmers.

FACTORS AFFECTING THE PERFORMANCE OF AGRICULTURAL RESEARCH CENTERS

Table 6.4 presents the Pearson Zero-Order correlations for 33 characteristics of the centers with the six performance variables discussed above. These correlations are based on thirteen cases and the subjective judgments of respondents. They cover 13 of the 15 agricultural research centers in Sri Lanka devoted to crops so they are descriptive of the Sri Lanka system. The findings can be summarized as follows.

—*The older established research centers have a better performance record than the newer centers.* The Karadiya Aru and Makandura centers were only three or four years old at the time of the study and not yet satisfactorilly equipped nor operating normally. Their performance measures were understandably very low. Nevertheless, the results suggest that research efforts may have high pay-offs in the long run but low pay-offs in the short run.

—*Size and resources contribute to high performance per researcher as expected but mostly in terms of basic research and publications and only modestly in terms of contribution to agricultural knowledge.* Contrary to expectations, size and resources do not determine overall contribution to Sri Lankan agriculture nor extent of on-farm adoption. Large/small size, number of researchers, number of employees, adequacy of financing, adequacy of facilities, and maintenance of facilities correlate highly with publication rate, moderately with new varieties and new methods, but only slightly with contribution to agricultural knowledge and not at all with contribution to Sri Lankan agriculture and on-farm adoption. Some small, poorly financed research centers made valuable contributions to Sri Lankan agriculture while some large well-financed centers contributed only moderately.

— *Distance from Colombo or Kandy is related to center performances.* Sri Lankans have strong preferences about geographic location and this creates considerable staffing problems for "remote" centers. Distance from Colombo or Kandy correlates negatively with the ratio of Ph. Ds at r=-.42, staff quality at r=-.62, and quality of operations at r=-.50. Distance correlates positively with researcher staffing difficulties at r= .43 and agricultural staffing difficulties at r= .59. Distance also makes good government connections difficult. It correlates with director's

TABLE 6.4·

Pearson Zero-Order Correlations of 33 Selected Center Characteristics with Six Performance Indicators for 13 Agricultural Research Centers in Sri Lanka based on Informant Interviews, 1983

	Center Performance Measures on a Per Researcher Basis					
Selected Characteristics	Publications	New Varieties	New Methods	Ag. Knowledge	Sri Lankan Ag.	On-Farm Adoption
Age of center	.47	.59	.42	.45	.26	-.26
Large Size	.75	.36	.59	.26	.06	.03
Number of researchers	.61	.08	.37	.09	-.20	-.15
Number of employees	.45	.39	.35	.10	.07	.09
Distance from Colombo or Kandy	-.56	-.44	-.41	-.57	-.53	-.71
Adequacy of facilities	.75	.32	.39	.45	.16	-.06
Adequacy of financing	.67	.40	.08	.12	.17	.21
Maintenance of facilities	.68	.33	.31	.28	.14	.43
Relative size of administration	.69	.47	.67	.59	.28	-.10
Overall quality of operation of the center	.56	.10	.64	.31	.28	.13
Skill and motivation of staff	.63	.22	.42	.29	.27	.13
Difficulty of obtaining and retaining ag. workers	-.46	-.38	-.40	-.50	-.78	-.42

Difficulty of obtaining and retaining researchers	-.66	-.54	-.65	-.56	-.71	-.49
Autonomy of researchers	.41	.53	.29	.54	.53	.40
Sophistication of research technology	.60	.27	.65	.56	.09	-.25
Researcher's government connections	.70	.39	.11	.25	.28	.13
Director's government connections	.49	.36	.20	.15	.17	.18
Power of the director	.14	-.24	-.80	-.24	-.01	-.25
Atonomy of the center	.32	.40	.01	-.01	.28	.21
Commitment of national government	.63	.34	.36	.35	.27	-.04
Effects of government policies	.42	.57	.36	.51	.75	.55
Conducive market factors	.43	.26	.49	.32	.21	.39
Conductive local values	.40	.19	-.17	.07	.40	.17
Benefits from government priorities	.60	.12	.38	.44	.45	.04
Extent of diffusion by extension services	-.18	.14	-.06	.06	.06	.58
Understanding with relevant agencies	-.17	-.32	.12	-.13	-.22	.42
Incentives and motivation of beneficiaries	.57	.44	.26	.49	.75	.76
Desirability of services for users	.42	.40	.03	.39	.41	.47
Rate of growth in the last 5 years	-.38	-.09	-.47	-.33	-.05	.30
Predicted future prospects	-.63	-.56	-.52	-.47	-.26	-.17
Tea, rubber, coconut	.33	.42	.35	.23	-.03	-.32
Rice, strong emphasis on	.58	.22	.02	.23	.49	.47
Variety of crops	-.56	-.65	-.43	-.74	-.60	-.31

government connections at r=-.58 and researchers' government connections at r=-.57. In sum, geographic location is a great asset or liability for agricultural research centers in Sri Lanka depending on whether they are at the center or the periphery.

—*The relative size of the administration is a positive rather than negative factor in the performance of Sri Lankan agricultural research centers.* While administration may be viewed as slowing work down, stifling creativity and "getting in the way," it can also obtain resources and facilitate operations. It is the latter positive effect which seems to prevail in Sri Lankan agricultural research centers. In fact, a high administration ratio correlates with overall quality of the operation of the center at r=.54 and adequacy of financing at r=.45. In addition, it correlates with the skill and motivation of the staff at r=.70, researcher autonomy at r=.26 and relative power of the director in the center at only r=.16, so it would appear to facilitate research in Sri Lankan research centers rather than stiffle or control it. These positive benefits of large administration ratios do not apply as strongly to the "contribution to Sri Lankan agriculture" and the effect is negative for on-farm adoption.

— *The overall quality of the operation of the center and the skill and motivation of staff are associated with several of the performance measures as expected but seem to be practically unrelated with on-farm adoption.* Caution is necessary in interpretating any findings for quality of operation because it is the characteristic most vulnerable to bias. The subjective variables are based on the combined judgements of the director and researcher. The directors probably had a great deal of difficulty remaining objective while scoring this variable. In fact, the correspondence of the directors' scorings and researchers' scorings on this variable are lower than on other variables. Nevertheless, if this measure does reflect differences in the quality of the operation of the centers, quality operation along with quality of staff have practically no relationship to on-farm adoption and only a weak relationship to "contribution to Sri Lankan agriculture." External factors are more important to these performance measures than internal factors such as quality operation, quality staff, and administration ratio.

—*Three variables involving staff-the degree of difficulty in obtaining and retaining researchers, of obtaining agricultural workers, and the autonomy of researchers — are significant for on-farm adoption as well as for the other performance variables.* These variables are very important to the performance of Sri Lanka agricultural centers for they have some of the highest average correlations across the six performance variables. Only crop variety has a higher average correlation than staffing agricultural workers and, after these two, only beneficiary motivation, distance and government policies have higher average correlations with the performance measures than staffing researchers and researcher autonomy. More importantly, the two staffing variables have very high correlations with contribution to Sri Lankan agriculture which is the important criterion for performance evaluation as far as the country as a whole is concerned. These findings suggest that staffing problems may have been the most critical problem affecting the performance of Sri Lankan research centers in 1983. They also suggest that staff turnover is a major problem in the translation of research findings into farmer practices and benefits.

Staffing is an important problem that demands further comment. Our respondents talked about the many qualified researchers who go to the Middle East to work at much higher salaries than Sri Lanka can afford, and others who are hired away by businesses in Sri Lanka. These problems, however, would afflict all research centers fairly equally, especially since pay scales are roughly similar across centers. The lead in salaries previously held by the tea, rubber and coconut centers has diminished over the years.

We conclude that location is the critical variable affecting the degree of staffing difficulties. The respondents in remote centers mentioned losing researchers to centers which are closer to Colombo and its (perceived) more attractive life style, including better educational opportunities and health care. In fact, some researchers keep their families in or near Colombo and travel to Colombo on the weekends. Most researchers interviewed in remote areas complained about the living conditions and often admitted that they were seeking employment in a better location. This explanation is supported by the fairly high correlations of distance from Colombo or Kandy with researcher and worker staffing difficulties as indicated earlier.

Staffing difficulties not only lowered performance directly

but also indirectly by affecting the quality of operation and the skill and motivation of the staff. Researcher staffing difficulties correlated with quality of operation at r=-.60 and with skill and motivation of the staff at r=-.42 (the correlations for agricultural worker staffing difficulties were r=-.73 and r=-.55 respectively). In sum, staffing problems appear to be a major explanation for differential performance among the centers.

The importance of researcher autonomy for high performance of research centers is no surprise because high discretion and autonomy of professionals is essential to high innovativeness in organizations according to organizational theory (Hage, 1980). Bureaucratic and hierarchical organizational structures with little staff discretionary powers can contribute to efficiency and quantity of production but hinder innovation and the quality of production. Researchers must be granted considerable autonomy for research centers to innovate and develop quality technologies. If researchers have little training or experience, however, then they must be more closely supervised and directed by senior researchers. Thus researcher autonomy is correlated with the ratio of Ph. Ds at r=.43. Researcher autonomy also tends to be greater in the better financed centers (r=.35) and the better equipped centers (r=.48).

There are two features of researcher autonomy in Sri Lanka which are special. First, researchers' autonomy is positively correlated with administration ratio at r=.26. As indicated earlier, administration in Sri Lankan research centers does not seem to hinder research performance. A strong administration seem to facilitate research performance by, for example, supporting researcher autonomy. Second, researcher autonomy does not translate into ivory tower research, an emphasis on publications, or the pursuit of basic science. Rather many researchers use their autonomy to serve farmers. Researcher autonomy is fairly strongly correlated with contribution to Sri Lankan agriculture (r=. 53), on-farm adoption (r=.40) and the incentives and motives obeneficiaries to work with the center's technologies (r=.51).

— *The sophistication of research technology is perhaps the best indicator of the relative emphasis on basic research and is strongly related to publication, new methods, and contributions to agricultural knowledge.* However, it is negatively related to on-farm adoption and unrelated to contribution to Sri Lankan agriculture. The sophistication of research technology is related to many resource measures: age of center (r=.52), size (.74), number of researchers (.63), ratio of Ph. Ds. (.38), adequacy of facilities (.74), administration ratio (.86) and quality of staff (.40). Nevertheless, some relatively unsophisticated research, mainly in rice, has recently had substantial pay-offs for Sri Lankan agriculture and on-farm adoption and has matched the benefits for Sri Lanka of more sophisticated research by more advanced and well equipped researchers.

— *The government connections of directors and researchers contribute only modestly to most measures of center performance.* It was expected that political connections would be an important factor in center success but our measures of political connections had lower correlations with the performance measures, except publications, than expected. What inputs do political connections have? The extent to which directors or researchers are connected with relevant government officials is correlated with the following characteristics of the centers: with age (r=.57 and .49 respectively), size (.29 and .33), Ph. Ds (.33 and .69), distance to Colombo or Kandy (-.57 and -.58), adequacy of facilities (.45 and .24), adequacy of financing (.60 and .59), administration ratio (.64 and .40), quality of staff (.57 and .52), center autonomy (.38 and .62), and tea/rubber/coconut crops (.57 and .58). Thus political connections are associated with established, resource rich centers and the influence is presumably two directional. Strong research centers, therefore, facilitate political connections and political connections gain resources for the centers. Nevertheless, political connections are not a key factor in success as indicated by their modest correlations with performance variables. Also political connections have generally low or negative correlations, with several variables which one would expect would result from good connections, namely, commitment of the national government to the center (.41 and .03), effects of government policies on the center (.08 and -.05), benefits from government priorities (.20 and .11), center growth rate (-.11 and -.15) and expected future growth rate (- .37 and -.68).

—Environmental factors are very important to the performance of the research centers. Six variables measure various aspects of the relation of the centers to their political and cultural context and each performance variable has a relatively high correlation with one or more of them. Center autonomy and "conduciveness of local values" had the lowest average correlations of these six variables while the six performance variables and the effects of government policies had the highest. The latter includes price support policies and is especially important to contribution to Sri Lankan agriculture and on-farm adoption. The other important contextual factor for on-farm adoption is conducive market factors. The other important contextual factors for contribution to Sri Lankan agriculture are conducive local values and beneficial government priorities.

Several of these contextual variables are interrelated. Beneficial policies is the most central variable in this group and it correlates with the others as follows: center autonomy (.21), government commitment (.41), market factors (.42), local values (.59), and beneficial priorities (.32). These contextual variables are also highly correlated with the quality of staff variables and quantity of resource variables. Finally, the centers which are the most favored by these contextual factors are the ones concentrating on rice. Rice concentration correlates with beneficial policies at r=.56, with beneficial markets at r=.23 and with conducive local values at r-.67.

—Beneficiary motivation and the desirability of the center's technologies are related to the center's performance but the extent of diffusion by the extension service and agency linkages were not related to the center's performances except for on-farm adoption. The research centers which provide services most desired by farmers and which have the interest and cooperation of farmers are the most effective. Normally research centers must work

smoothly with other organizations to be effective. In Sri Lanka, however, the quality of the links to other organizations does not seem to be essential for most measures of success. The only performance which seems to be related to the extent of diffusion by the center's or the government's extension service is on-farm adoption (r-.58). Understanding with relevant agencies displays a pattern of correlation with performance measures similar to extension diffusion. This is not surprising since extension would count as one of the relevant agencies (they correlate at r=.64).

Extension diffusion is related to on-farm adoption because it is highly related to beneficiary motivation (r=.56) and the desirability of center's technologies to farmers (r=.69). These factors probably were mutually interdependent. Desirable technologies made extension diffusion successful and successful extention diffusion made the technologies desirable. We also note that extension diffusion was also related to the external factors of conducive government policies (r=.51) and favorable local values (r=.43).

— *The high performance centers are not the fast growing centers nor the centers which are expected to grow in the future.* The performance variables correlate negatively with these two variables except on-farm adoption correlated positively with recent growth rate. The Sri Lankan system of agricultural research centers is undergoing growth and development. All centers claim to have grown in the past five years and the fastest growth is claimed for the more recent centers (r=-.46 for growth and age). The system also is being transformed into a regional system with a regional research center in each of eight regions which are defined largely by climatic zones. In the previous five years, however, growth has been unrelated to distance from Colombo or Kandy (r = - .05). Not so with predicted future growth. The periphery centers are expecting the highest growth rates (r = .50 for distance with future growth).

The recent and future growth variables are not only negatively related to the performance variables but also to most of the other variables in Table 6.3. Both are negatively related to size and resources. Further growth especially is negatively related to number of researchers (-.76), Ph. Ds. (-.88), adequacy of finances (-.72) and adequacy of facilities (-.66.). The expectation within the system, therefore, is for reductions in the size and resource inequalities between the various research centers.

What is surprising about future growth expectations is that they are negatively related to government commitment to the center (-.37), government policies (-.25), government priorities (-.22) and market factors (-.49). The Department of Agriculture is committed to building a regional system of centers but may not have articulated a coherent plan for the system of centers much beyond this.

— *Finally, the centers concentrating on rice have the highest performance scores,* the major export crop research centers (tea/rubber/coconut) perform well on research and innovations but not well at the implementation stage, and the multi-crop centers have the worst performance record. The export crops and rice are the economic life blood of Sri Lanka so they are appropriately emphasized in the system. The centers devoted to the export crops are particularly strong in research but weak on diffusion and on-farm adoption. The centers which emphasize rice are strong on on-farm adoption and contribution to Sri Lanka agriculture.

SOME LESSONS FOR SRI LANKAN AGRICULTURE

The agricultural research system and Sri Lankan agriculture are currently undergoing considerable change. World markets for tea, rubber and coconut products are becoming more competitive, the Mahaweli project has increased water availability over a wide area and involves substantial land development and resettlement, domestic agriculture is becoming more productive as indicated by increasing rice yields, regional agricultural research centers are becoming better established, and labor markets for research scientists are volatile. The one constant amongst all these changes is the need for agricultural research to make Sri

Lankan export crops more competitive, to adapt domestic agriculture to new conditions, and to expand domestic agriculture to keep up with population growth. Sri Lanka, therefore, should strengthen its agricultural research system. While this study did not attempt to determine the best methods for improving the agricultural research system, a few suggestions have emerged from the data and the comments of the respondents.

The research system has devolved into a regional system which has made it more effective in influencing farmers' practices and improving Sri Lankan agriculture. Now Sri Lanka must upgrade the facilities at the regional centers and improve the incentives for researchers to remain at these centers. The respondents called for greater decentralization of administrative powers. More budget decisions should be made at the centers instead of at the ministry level to improve the quality of the operation of the centers and to allow the centers to adjust their research programs to changing needs.

There is some evidence that the older, better equipped, and better staffed research centers need to improve the transmission of their knowledge to the farmers. They are generally more successful than the newer and poorer centers but their on-farm adoption rate is lower than average. Perhaps the incentive systems at these centers should be modified to encourage closer work with farmers. On the other hand, the present system concentrates more basic research at the more established centers and more applied research at regional centers where closer contact with farmers can be maintained. National agricultural research policy must reaffirm the existing basic/applied division or move to reduce it. Furthermore, the division which exists between basic and applied research may be more the result of past traditions than of a rational policy and there may be inadequate linkages between the specialized centres. Many informants commented on the inadequate coordination of the agricultural research system but this problem has been recognized and is being evaluated at high levels in the national government and by foreign lending institutions.

It is clear that manpower problems must be addressed because they have a profound impact on center performance. This is widely understood within the system but effective efforts to address the manpower problems are not yet apparent. A major problem is the insufficient number of agricultural workers in some centers which significantly hinders performance. A first step, therefore, might be to greatly increase support staff per scientist.

Agricultural research is only one factor contributing to increased agricultural production. The direct policies of the government in the form of generous price supports for paddy and other crops and subsidies for inputs have provided incentives for farmers to which they have responded. Agricultural policy, therefore, is a major way that Sri Lankan government is directing the economy. Some agricultural policies have been criticized as not being cost effective but, overall, government policies seem to have benefited Sri Lankan agriculture.

REFERENCES

Central Bank of Ceylon. *Annual Reports* (various years). Colombo: Central Bank of Ceylon.

Evenson, Robert E., Waggoner, Paul E. and Ruttan, Vernon W. 1979. Economic Benefits from Research: An Example from Agriculture. *Science* 205: 1101-1107.

Finsterbusch, Kurt and Jogaratnam T. 1983. Factors Related to the Success of Agricultural Research Centers. *Sri Lanka Journal of Agrarian Studies* 4: 65-79.

Hage, Jerald. 1980. *Theory of Organizations: Form, Process, and Transformation.* New York: Wiley-Interscience.

Johnson, R.L.C. and Scrivenor M. Le M. 1981. *Sri Lanka: Land, People and Economy*. London: Hinemann.

Mansfield, Edwin W. et al. 1982. *Technology Transfer, Productivity, and Economic Policy*. New York: w.w. Norton.

Mansfield, Edwin W. 1983. Economic Effects of Research and Development, the Diffusion Process and Public Policy in *Planning for National Technology Policy*, eds. R. A. Goodman and J. Pavon. New York: Praeger.

Peebles, Patrick. 1982. *Sri Lanka: A Handbook of Historical Statistics.* Boston: G.K. Hall.

Peiris, Gerald. 1977. Plantation Agriculture in *Sri Lanka: A Survey*, ed. K. M. De Silva. Honolulu: University Press of Hawaii.

Pinstrup-Andersen, Per. 1982. *Agricultural Research and Technology in Economic Development.* London: Longman.

Ruttan, Vernon W. 1982. *Agricultural Research Policy.* Minneapolis: University of Minnesota Press.

Sri Lanka, Department of Census and Statistics. 1989. *Statistical Pocket Book of the Democratic Socialist Republic of Sri Lanka.* Colombo: Ministry of Plan Implementation.

Terleckyj, Nester. 1974. *Effects of R and D on the Productivity Growth of Industries,* Washington, D.C.: National Planning Association.

Wickremeratne, L. A. 1977. Peasant Agriculture in *Sri Lanka: A Survey*, ed. K.M. De Silva. Honolulu: University Press of Hawaii.

World Bank. 1990. *World Development Report.* New York: Oxford University Press.

PART THREE

COMMUNAL CONFLICT
AND
SRI LANKA'S DEVELOPMENT

Chapter VII

THE TYRANNY OF SPACE: A SOCIO-ECONOMIC ANALYSIS OF THE SPATIAL DIMENSION OF THE ETHNIC CONFLICT IN SRI LANKA

Vidyamali Samarasinghe
The American University, Washington D.C.

Solidarity within an ethnic group is based on bonds of common language, beliefs and notions of common descent, common religion and segregation in geographic space. In a pluralistic society where many such groups coexist, competition for resources usually leads to conflict. Indeed, many researchers claim that ethnicity is the most prominent factor in what Dahl identified as "conflictive pluralism" (Despres, 1975). In Sri Lanka the separate ethnic identity between the two groups in conflict, i.e. the majority Sinhala group and the minority Sri Lanka Tamil group which is language-based is further strengthened by a religious difference.

The geographic dimension of the ethnic conflict in Sri Lanka is of singular importance since the demand for separation by the Sri Lanka Tamil group explicitly threatens the unity of the multi-ethnic state and calls for a permanent cleavage on essentially geographic lines. The spatial dimension in any ethnic conflict is rooted in the phenomenon of geographic concentration of distinct ethnic groups. There is an increasing tendency for such groups to cling to common neighborhoods, cities, rural areas or regions. Saul B. Cohen has in fact argued that race, religion and culture are more important operational forces in the politics of space at all geographic scales than economic and that they form an essential basis for linking people with territory (Cohen, 1983).

This ethno-spatial aspect brings into focus a new dimension in the study of spatial inequalities resulting from an unequal distribution of resources especially in the Less Developed Countries (LDCs) where resources are more limited. Equity issues both in terms of income classes and spatial manifestation have become increasingly important in formulating plans and strategies for resource allocation. The introduction of an ethno-spatial dimension in the political economy of a country may lead to two alternative situations. Assuming that there is a distinct ethno-spatial pattern of population distribution in the country, if the dominant group allocates the resources at its command persistently in favor of its own ethnic group then indeed spatial inequalities are bound to occur coincident upon ethnicity. Alternatively, if the priorities in spatial resource allocation are geared specifically to redress existing spatial imbalances, dissatisfaction may occur among those ethno- spatial units which are left out of the major resource allocations since the limited quantum of resources are used for the uplift of less developed areas.

The main objective of this chapter is to identify the spatial manifestations of resource distribution in Sri Lanka in an attempt to understand its impact on the ethnic conflict. The study will identify the different components of economic and social well-being of the population of Sri Lanka and seek to understand the mechanisms and processes that have led to the present pattern of resource allocation. The study will focus mainly on the period after 1977 since the ethnic crisis in Sri Lanka sharpened only towards the latter half of the 1970's. However, since an analysis of this nature cannot be compartmentalized into distinct time periods, general reference will be made to the preceding period since independence in 1948. The units of observation of the study are the 24 administrative districts of Sri Lanka which fall within 9 provincial units (Fig. 7.1).[1]

Ethno-Spatial Population Clusters

Sri Lanka has a multi-ethnic society where 74% of the population

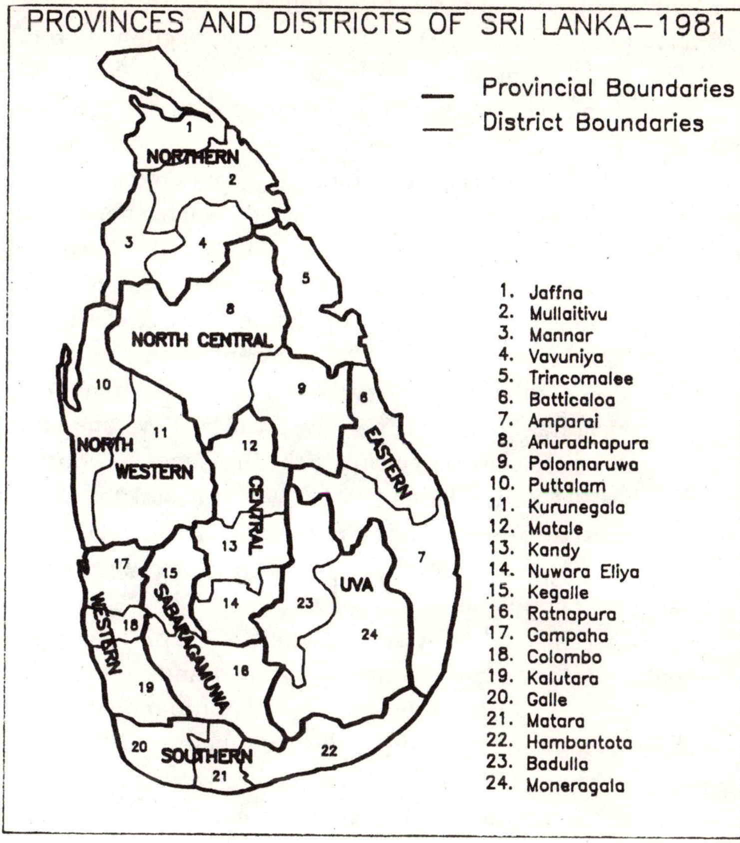

Fig. 7.1 Provinces and Districts: Sri Lanka , 1981.

are Sinhalese, 12.6% are Sri Lankan Tamils, 7.1% are Moors and 5.5% are Indian Tamils. Nearly 78% of the population are rural and agrarian. Its economy is essentially agricultural.

The ethnic concentration among population clusters is mapped in Figure 7.2. Three levels of clusters are identified in relation to the degree of concentration of any one ethnic group in a particular district. At *level one* more than 80% of the population of a district belongs to one ethnic group. Fourteen of the twenty-four districts in Sri Lanka fall into this category. Among them thirteen districts have Sinhalese population concentrations and one has a Sri Lankan Tamil population concentration. Among the Sinhalese dominant districts of level one, seven fall into the agro-climatological area of the Wet Zone, five are in the Dry Zone while Kurunegala District has a larger area in the Dry Zone and a smaller area in the Wet Zone.[2] Jaffna District which is situated at the northern most tip of Sri Lanka is also in the Dry Zone and belongs to level one of ethno-spatial clusters with a predominant Sri Lankan Tamil population concentration.

At the *second level* of ethnic clusters 60-79% of the population belong to one ethnic group. Sri Lanka Tamils account for three districts, while the Sinhalese account for four districts. At the *third (bottom) level* of ethnic clusters where 40-59% of the population belong to one ethnic group there are two Sri Lankan Tamil districts, none among the Sinhalese, and one Indian Tamil district.

Nearly 72% of the Sinhalese population is distributed in level one ethno-spatial clusters. Forty-three per cent of the Sri Lankan Tamils are also concentrated in the level one ethno-spatial district i.e. Jaffna. When the top two levels are taken together almost 96% of the total Sinhala population is concentrated in a total of sixteen districts. Among the Sri Lankan Tamils 58% of the total population is concentrated among the first and second levels (60% and above) of ethno-spatial clusters (Fig. 7.2). Sixty-four per cent of the Sri Lankan Tamils live in the five districts of Sri Lanka where more than 40% of the population belong to the Sri Lankan Tamil ethnic group.

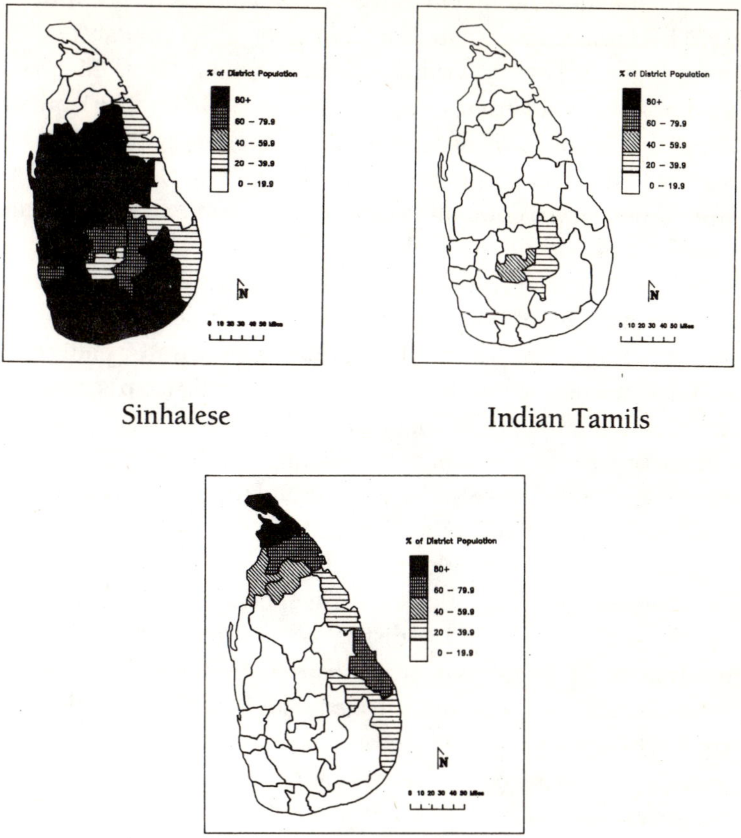

Sinhalese

Indian Tamils

Sri Lankan Tamils

Fig. 7.2 Distribution of Ethnic Groups by District: Sri Lanka, 1981

All Sinhalese dominant ethno-spatial clusters have contiguity. There is a distinct spatial concentration of Sri Lankan Tamils in the four contiguous Northern districts, namely Jaffna, Mannar, Vavuniya and Mullaitivu. However, the predominantly Sri Lankan Tamil district of Batticaloa in the East is not contiguous with the Northern cluster. It is bordered by the district of Trincomalee which has a mixed population of Sinhalese, Moors and Sri Lankan Tamils, and the districts of Anuradhapura and Polonnaruwa which are level one Sinhalese ethno-spatial clusters. The population distribution of the majority Sinhalese ethnic group and the minority Sri Lankan Tamil ethnic group demonstrate a pattern of regional clustering. [3] While the Sri Lankan Tamil group is concentrated in the northern sector and a strip along the east coast, the Sinhalese are predominant in the remaining territory. The major ethno-spatial clusters of the Sinhalese and the Sri Lankan Tamils remained virtually unchanged from 1963 to 1981.

Among the other ethnic groups in Sri Lanka the spatial concentration of the group defined as Indian Tamils is predominantly in the tea plantation district of Nuwara Eliya. Forty-five per cent of the population of the district are Indian Tamils. The Indian Tamil group is concentrated mainly in the central highlands where the plantation sector is located. They were originally brought to the island by the British colonial rulers to work as laborers in the coffee/tea/rubber plantations. Nearly 78% of this group reside in the contiguous central plantation districts of Matale, Kandy, Nuwara Eliya, Badulla and Kegalle. However, their share of the total population in these districts ranges from 45% in Nuwara Eliya and 21% in Badulla to 6.4% in Kegalle (Fig.7.2).

An examination of the density of population of Sri Lanka indicates a distinct spatial variation. Among the districts with a density of population of less than 100 per sq. km., three (Mannar, Vavuniya and Mullaitivu) belong to the Sri Lankan Tamil ethno-spatial clusters of level two. Three districts belong to the Sinhalese ethno-spatial districts of level one i.e. Anuradhapura, Polonnaruwa and Monaragala. Two districts in the East i.e. Trincomalee and Amparai also have densities below 100 per square km. They both have mixed population distributions of

Sinhalese, Sri Lankan Tamils and Moors. The six districts with high densities of over 600 per sq. km. are Colombo, Gampaha, Kalutara, Galle, Matara and Kandy. They belong to the first and second level Sinhalese ethno-spatial clusters and are located in the Wet Zone.

MEASURES OF SPATIAL INEQUALITY

Spatial inequalities may be defined as the incidence of varying levels of social and economic well-being of the population at a regional level. They reflect the differential impact of socio-economic activities over time on geographic space - which in turn is a manifestation of resource generation and allocation. Studies have shown that such spatial inequalities do exist in the island (Samarasinghe, 1980, Moore, 1984). In Sri Lanka, with a political system based on electoral representation, the dilemma of successive governments has been how best to allocate the limited quantum of resources so as to achieve a balance between growth and equity, the latter possessing dimensions of income, class and region. The task before us is to examine the ethnic dimension of such inequalities and the rationale for the allocation of resources.

The point of departure of this study is the understanding of the nature of the pattern as it exists today and the mechanisms and the processes that led to it. Socio-economic development has two basic components. The economic component which is manifested in *income levels* and the social component reflecting the *volume and nature of social welfare facilities*. These two components certainly are not mutually exclusive and in fact the historical experience of socio-economic development in the Advanced Countries of the West (ACs) suggests that social welfare normally follows upon economic growth. However, in most LDCs, where interventionist public policy operates at a much earlier stage of economic development to stimulate both social and economic development, resource allocations are meant to achieve simultaneously both growth and welfare as different aspects of the same package. Hence, for the purpose of the present analysis, the impact of social and economic resource allocations will be treated separately. The measures of spatial inequality used here are regionally derived income levels, unemployment levels and the Physical Quality of Life Index (PQLI).

Income Distribution

In the *Consumer Finance and Socio Economic Survey* conducted periodically by the Central Bank of Sri Lanka, the spatial distribution of income for Sri Lanka is recorded within a framework of five geographical zones. The boundaries of the districts in each of the zones coincide with the district administrative boundaries (Fig. 7.3).[4] Zone I which consists of five districts borders the Western and Southern coast of Sri Lanka. Zone II which claims six districts is mainly confined to the Dry Zone. Apart from the district of Amparai in the east which has an ethnically mixed population, the population of Zone II is predominantly Sinhalese. Among its six districts, three (Anuradhapura, Polonnaruwa and Amparai) are the major beneficiaries of the Dry Zone irrigated agricultural colonization projects of Sri Lanka. Zone III accounts for six districts, four of which are in the north (Mannar, Vavuniya, Mullaitivu and Jaffna) and two are in the east (Trincomalee and Batticaloa). Except for Trincomalee, which has an ethnically mixed population distribution, the other five districts of Zone III are predominantly peopled by Sri Lanka Tamils. Zone IV is located in the central highlands and is generally identified with the plantation agricultural sector. It consists of seven districts. The Sinhalese population accounts for 77% of the total population of this zone, and the Indian Tamil population about 13%. However, among the Indian Tamil group, nearly 79% are resident in Zone IV. Zone V is a small spatial unit which encompasses the Colombo metropolitan area. Its population consists of 50% Sinhalese, 22.2% Sri Lankan Tamils, 20.9% Moors and 1.9% Indian Tamils.

An examination of income data reveals that in general inequality levels have increased since 1973. A clear decrease in income inequality levels is recorded between 1963 and 1973 (*Central Bank*, 1974; Karunatilaka, 1974; Jayawardene, 1974). Although the absolute real incomes of each income-receiving

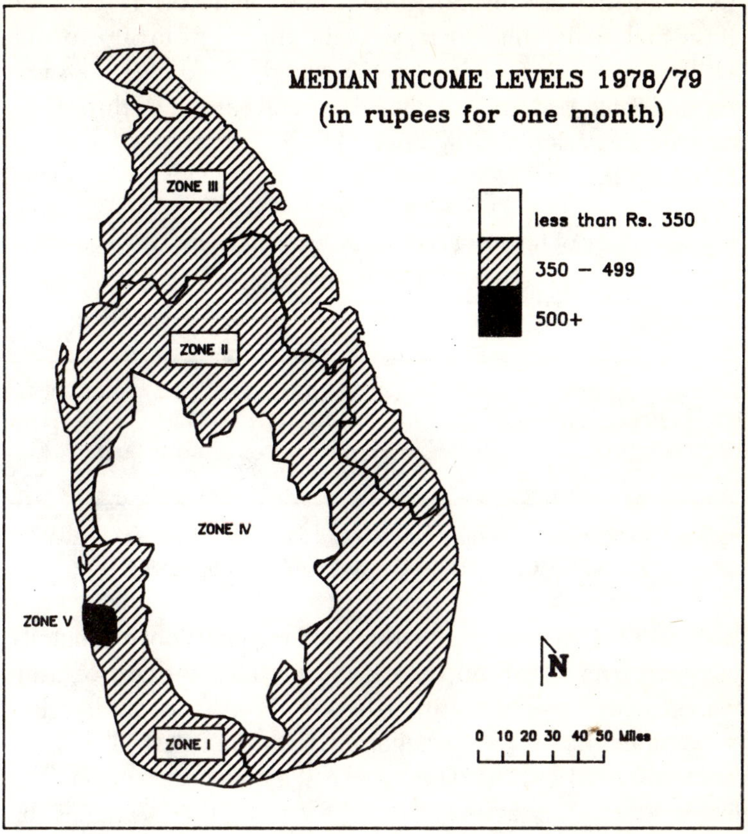

Fig. 7.3 Median Income Levels by Zone: Sri Lanka, 1978/79

group had increased by 1978/79, the share of the total real income of the highest 40% had increased substantially from 30% to 39% while the share of the lowest 40% had declined over the same period (Table 7.1). Indeed, the same trend continued during the subsequent period leading up to 1981/82.

TABLE 7.1
Percentage of Income Received by Ranked Income Receivers, 1963-1981/82

	1963	1973	1978/79	1981/82
Lowest 10 per cent	1.2	1.8	1.2	1.2
Lowest 40 per cent	12.0	16.1	12.1	11.8
Highest 40 per cent	39.2	30.0	39.0	41.7
Gini coefficient	0.49	0.41	0.49	0.52

Source: *Reports on Consumer Finance and Socio-Economic Survey*, 1973, 1978/79 and 1981/82. Central Bank, 1976, 1983, 1984.

Although real income of all groups and regional zones generally increased over the period, there is a steady fall in the ratio of mean to median incomes indicating a deterioration of income distribution among the different categories (Jayantha Dilesh, 1985).

From 1973 to 1981/82 median real income per recipient has increased in every zone (Table 7.2). Among the five zones the highest median income and the sharpest increases are seen for Zone V (Metropolitan Colombo). The lowest median income is in Zone IV (Central Plantation districts). The base level of incomes in Zone IV in 1973 was very low (Rs. 137) but its rate of overall increase from 1973 to 1982 has been second only to Zone V. It is noteworthy that Zone II representing the Dry Zone colonization districts records the lowest overall increase over the period. The Wet Zone, Southern and Western coastal districts of Zone I, which has predominantly Sinhalese population and the Northern and Eastern districts of Zone III, which are predominantly Sri Lankan Tamil, have increased their lead over Zone II (Figs. 7.3 and 7.4) between 1973 and 1981/82. Zone III (Northern and Eastern districts) which had an identical income level

(Rs. 451) as Zone I in 1978/79 increased its level of median real income by 1981/82 and occupied the second position on the median income real income by 1981/82 and occupied the second position on the median income scale for all zones in 1981/82.

TABLE 7.2
Median Income (one month) in Rupees (at current prices) by Zone, 1973-1981/82

	1973	1978/79	% increase 1973-79	1981/82	% increase 1979-82	% increase 1973-82
Zone I (Western, Southern coastal districts mainly Sinhalese) Wet Zone	202	451	123	721	60	256
Zone II (Dry Zone Colonization districts, mainly Sinhalese)	223	401	79	641	60	187
Zone III (Northern and Eastern districts, mainly Sri Lankan Tamils)	236	451	91	752	67	218
Zone IV (Central High-land Plantation districts Sinhalese and Indian Tamils)	137	301	119	534	77	289
Zone V (Colombo Metropolitan)	224	501	123	966	93	331

Source: Computed from *Reports on Consumer Finance and Socio-Economic Surveys, Central Bank*, 1973, 1978/79, 1981/82.

The income zones do not fall neatly into the already defined ethno-spatial population clusters. However, it is evident that the major ethno-spatial clusters are clearly identifiable and distinct among the income zones. The main urban area of Sri Lanka, Metropolitan Colombo (Zone V) has the highest income levels and, at the other end of the scale, the central plantation districts (Zone IV) show the lowest income levels. A distinct feature of the latter zone is the high concentration of Indian Tamil plantation workers. Zone III, which has a Sri Lankan Tamil population concentration, records a median real income level which is second only to Metropolitan Colombo. Both Zones I and II have predominant Sinhalese ethno-spatial population concentration. They occupy positions three and four respectively in the hierarchy of incomes zones next to Metropolitan Colombo and the Northern and Eastern district category of Zone III.

Regional levels of unemployment

The spatial distribution of unemployment levels throws some light on the incidence of spatial inequalities. A comparison of the unemployment data in the *Reports of Consumer Finance and Socio-economic Surveys* suggests that unemployment rates declined among all communities in Sri Lanka between 1978/79 and 1981/82 (Table 7.3). Data on unemployed persons as a percentage of

TABLE 7.3

Unemployed Persons by Community, 1978/79-1981/82

Community	as a % of the Labor Force 1978/79	1981/82
Kandyan Sinhalese	13.9	11.3
Low Country Sinhala	18.5	14.6
Sri Lanka Tamils	10.5	6.7
Indian Tamil	5.6	4.9

Source: *Report on Consumer Finance and Socio-Economic Survey*, 1981/82. Central Bank of Ceylon, 1984.

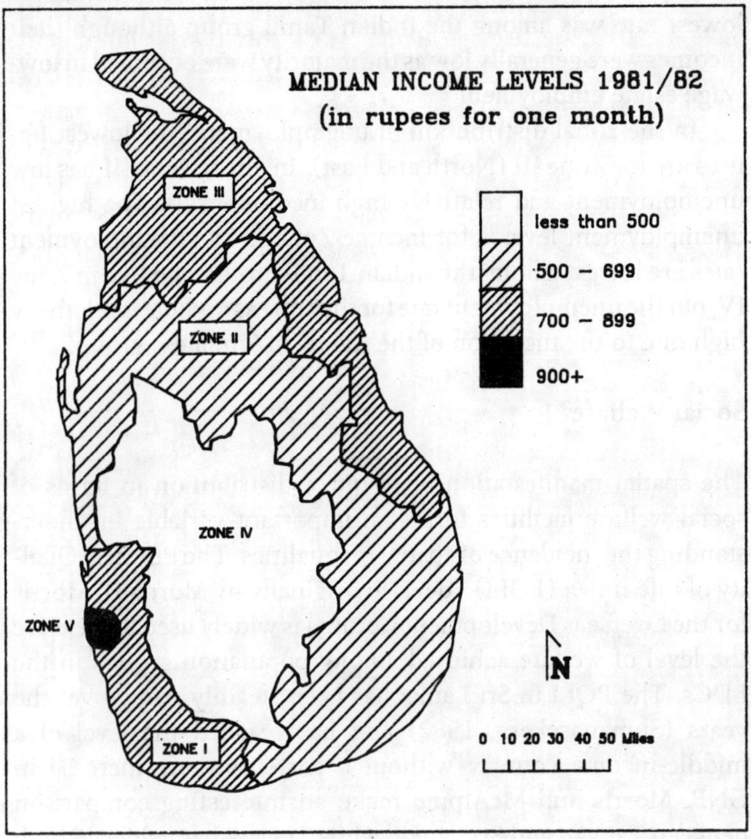

Fig. 7.4 Median Income Levels by Zone: Sri Lanka, 1981/82

the population in the labor force by community disclose that the lowest rate was among the Indian Tamil group although their incomes were generally low as the majority were occupied in low-wage estate employment.

In the zonal distribution of unemployment, the lowest figures are for Zone III (North and East). In effect Zone III has low unemployment and relatively high income levels. The highest unemployment level is for income Zone I. The unemployment rates are lowest among the Indian Tamil group who live in Zone IV, but the unemployment rate for the zone as a whole is relatively high due to the inclusion of the Kandyan Sinhalese group.

Social Welfare

The spatial manifestation of resource distribution in terms of social welfare facilities forms an important variable in understanding the incidence of spatial inequalities. The Physical Quality of Life Index (PQLI) [5] devised originally by Morris D. Morris for the Overseas Development Council is widely used to measure the level of welfare achieved among population groups in the LDCs. The PQLI in Sri Lanka has been steadily rising over the years (Sumanasekera, 1982) and has reached the level of a middle-income country without a corresponding increase in GNP. Morris and McAlpine make an interesting comparison between Taiwan and Sri Lanka; while Taiwan has achieved high rates of economic growth with an accompanying increase in the PQLI, a pattern which corresponds well with the historical experience of the ACs, in Sri Lanka the increase in PQLI has not been a result of such economic growth (Morris and McAlpine, 1982). Thus the relatively high levels of the PQLI in Sri Lanka have to be explained not in terms of high income per capita but in terms of *inter alia* the establishment of a relatively sophisticated social infrastructure and an effective delivery system of welfare benefits to all income groups and regions.

TABLE 7.4
Unemployment by Zones, 1978/79-1981-82

	1978/79	1981/82
Zone I (Western and Southern coastal districts mainly Sinhalese)	6.8	5.6
Zone II (Dry Zone colonization districts mainly Sinhalese)	3.3	2.4
Zone III (Northern and Eastern districts mainly Sri Lanka Tamil)	2.6	1.7
Zone IV (Central Highland Plantations Sinhalese and Indian Tamil)	5.8	4.0
Zone V (Colombo Metropolitan)	7.2	4.0

Source: *Computed from Report on Consumer Finance and Socio-Economic Survey*, 1981/82. Central Bank of Ceylon 1984.

It is evident that there is a distinct inter-regional variation in social welfare levels reflecting the differential impact of resource distribution. A comparison of the PQLI scores for Sri Lanka between 1971 and 1978-1981 shows that there has been a further inprovement: however, the regional variation seems to persist (Table 7.5, Figs. 7.5, 7.6).

In 1971, the PQLI scores range from 64 in Nuwara Eliya to 88 in Jaffna. Only three districts recorded PQLI scores below 75. They were Nuwara Eliya, Batticaloa and Badulla. While Nuwara Eliya and Badulla are in the central highlands and identified with plantation agriculture, Batticaloa is in the east and has a predominantly Sri Lankan Tamil population. During the subsequent period, 1979/81, the individual scores for each district had improved and the minima had increased from 64 to 71. However,

TABLE 7.5
Districtwise Distribution of PQLI Scores, 1971-1979/81

Districts	1971	1979/81
Colombo	85.3	86.0
Gampaha	—	n.d.
Kalutara	87.3	88.4
Kandy	75.1	78.2
Nuwara Eliya	64.0	71.6
Matale	78.0	83.0
Galle	86.6	86.8
Matara	85.6	85.6
Hambantota	84.6	87.4
Jaffna	88.1	91.2
Mannar	79.8	86.7
Vavuniya	84.2	86.3
Mullaitivu	—	89.3
Batticaloa	68.1	72.5
Amparai	79.1	78.5
Trincomalee	79.0	85.1
Kurunegala	85.4	86.8
Puttalam	85.6	88.4
Anuradhapura	80.2	86.4
Polonnaruwa	86.2	89.6
Badulla	72.4	75.4
Monaragala	80.4	86.2
Ratnapura	76.6	79.5
Kegalle	81.6	87.3
Sri Lanka	78.9	84.2

Source: *Literacy, Infant Mortality Data* 1971, 1981 - *Census of Population*, 1971, 1981 - Department of Census and Population, 1973, 1984.
Life expectancy data, 1971 *Bulletin of Vital Statistics* 1979, Registrar General's Office, Department of Census and Statistics, 1981.
Life expectancy data 1979 - unpublished data. Department of Census and Statistics, 1985.

the hierarchy of levels remains more or less constant.

Nuwara Eliya, the main plantation district in the central highlands, with a high Indian Tamil population had the lowest scores in both periods. Generally scores are relatively low for

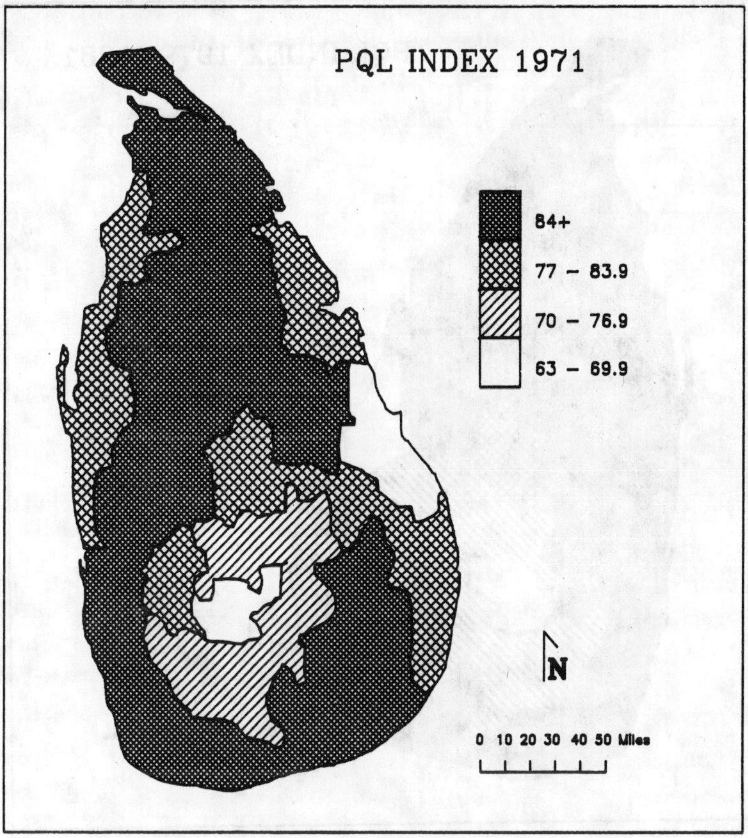

Fig. 7.5 Physical Quality of Life Index by District: Sri Lanka, 1971

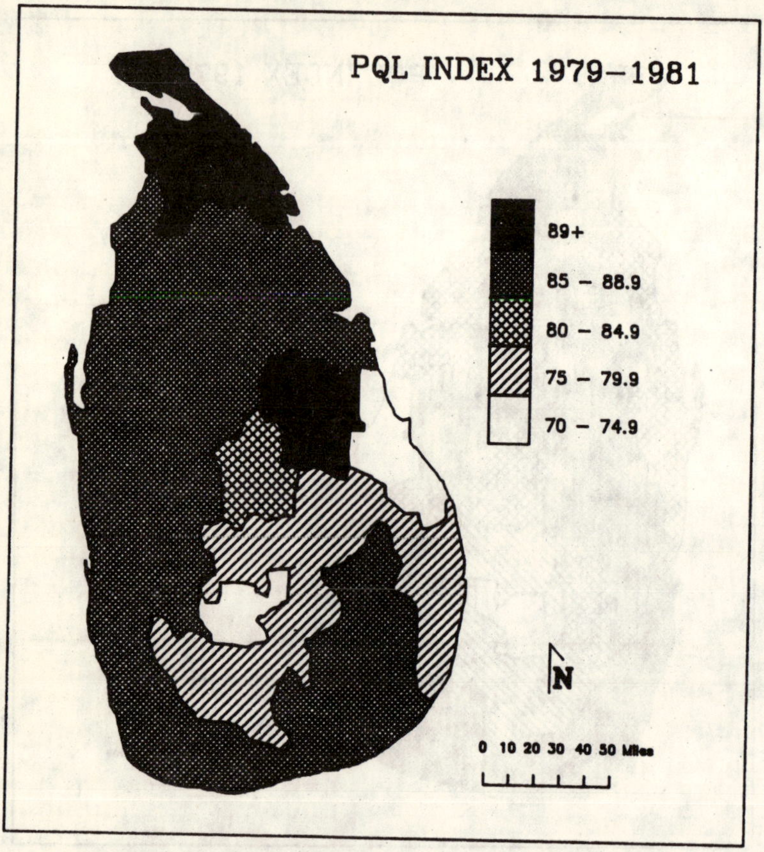

Fig. 7.6 Physical Quality of Life Index by District: Sri Lanka 1979-1981

most plantation districts in the central highlands, most of which fall into Zone IV of the income zones, where the median real incomes were the lowest for all income zones. At the other end of the scale Jaffna District in the North had the highest PQLI scores for both 1971 and 1979/81.

In 1971, the top cluster of PQLI scores is occupied by Jaffna, Kalutara (Wet Zone western coastal district) and Polonnaruwa (Dry Zone colonization district). In the 1979/81 period the top cluster is formed by Jaffna, Mullaitivu and Polonnaruwa. Mullaitivu which has a predominantly Sri Lankan Tamil population lies adjacent to Jaffna District and was a part of Vavuniya District until 1978. (It is possible that Gampaha, which was separated from Colombo in 1978 also would show a high PQLI score, since its literacy rate is high and infant mortality rate is low. But life expectancy data were available only for the two districts together and it was not possible to compute a separate index for Gampaha). Polonnaruwa, a major agricultural colonization district situated in the Dry Zone continues to have a high PQLI score.

When regional clusters are identified, the districts with highest scores are in the Dry Zone, i.e., Jaffna and Mullaitivu (predominantly Sri Lankan Tamil) and Polonnaruwa (predominantly Sinhalese). It is significant that all three have very low infant mortality rates (18 per 1000) and high literacy rates (above 86%). The predominantly Sri Lankan Tamil ethno-spatial cluster in the North consisting of Jaffna, Mannar, Vavuniya and Mullaitivu has average scores above 86 per district. However, Batticaloa in the East which also has a predominantly Sri Lankan Tamil population has very low PQLI scores. Batticaloa District has consistently been in the low score group. Its literacy and life expectancy rates are below the national average. Apart from the fact that Sri Lankan Tamils in Batticaloa have not received the same level of educational opportunities as in the Northern districts, its sizeable Muslim population (24% of the total for the district) with its high rate of illiteracy (21% versus the national average of 9.5%) also has contributed towards the overall poor performance of Batticaloa District. In terms of ethno-spatial population distribution the clusters with the lowest PQLIs are concentrated in the central plantation regions. As a region, although it has a predominantly Sinhala population, the PQLI scores are depressed largely due to the relatively high concentration of Indian Tamil population which has very high infant mortality rates and low life expectancy and literacy levels.

The western and southern coastal districts have high PQLI scores and so has the Dry Zone colonization area - both have mainly Sinhala population distributions and correspond roughly to income Zones I and II. In general the PQLI scores have a direct relation to income zones. The exception is the correspondence of Zone II to the Dry Zone colonization areas where the income levels are comparatively low but PQLI comparatively high. The delivery system of government sponsored welfare facilities may have been more efficient in these districts particularly since the irrigated colonization scheme package included the diffusion of better health and educational facilities over the region.

PROCESSES AND MECHANISMS

During the British period of Sri Lankan history the main concentrations of population were in Colombo, the western and southern coastal areas and Jaffna in the North. Colombo's development was due mainly to its commercial and administrative functions. While eventually both the western and the northern areas would benefit from better educational and welfare facilities, the fact that the two areas could continue with subsistence agricultural practices unhampered by a major health hazard such as malaria contributed towards their population concentrations. The neglect and low level of development of the vast Dry Zone area was intensified by the widespread prevalence of malaria and by the emphasis on the part of the colonial power on commercial agriculture. The central hilly plantation area was merely the "factory" that produced the goods (mainly tea for export) and the resident population - both native Sinhalese and Indian Tamils - was on the margins of poverty. However, the need to produce rice locally set in motion a massive transfer of resources to the Dry Zone which culminated in a restructuring of the spatial order. By eradicating malaria, a new area hitherto neglected and underdeveloped was opened up for food cultivation, mainly paddy (Samarasinghe, 1980).

The central plantations were used more for resource generation than for resource allocation. While its Sinhala population remained at the margins of poverty (Goonatilake, 1978) its Indian Tamil population fared no better. Devoid of political power, having been disenfranchised in 1948, the Indian Tamil group had little bargaining power in relation to resource allocation. Although they were in wage employment, their incomes and standards of living were among the lowest in the country. As part of the repatriation program made effective in the 1970s, those who were allowed to remain in the country were given citizenship rights. Indeed wage incomes improved considerably after nationalization in 1975. However, the obvious low levels of income and welfare in the central region are linked to the relatively low level of early resource allocation.

In 1972 the government introduced a regional development strategy named the Divisional Development Council (DDC) Programme. Its purpose was to encourage the grass-root level participation of the population in small-scale regional economic development programs initiated with state funds. However this strategy failed and was abandoned by 1978 (Karunatilake 1978).

The Sri Lankan economy came under increasing state control over the period 1956-1977. The spatial manifestation of this was evident in planned settlement in agriculture, location of state-owned industry and the continued policy of spatial diffusion of welfare facilities. However, resource distribution in terms of economic activity was severely hampered between 1971 and 1977 due to a variety of reasons ranging from internal factors such as the 1971 insurrection to external factors such as low levels of foreign aid and the oil crisis. Overall growth suffered but spatial inequality levels were reduced.

Post-1977 Trends

In 1977 the government liberalized the economy and reduced state control. Market forces were given greater play to induce growth which has led to an acceleration of growth itself. The growth rate of the GDP has been maintained at a steady 5%. Let us now examine public policy on productivity-oriented activities since 1977 and its ethno-spatial impact.

State policy on agriculture had two distinct dimensions. The main focus of attention was in the disbursement of funds for the development of the physical structure for irrigated agricultural colonization schemes. In this sphere the Accelerated Mahaweli Development Programme (AMDP) constituted the biggest investment decision of the government. Second, the government adopted a policy of lifting controls on import trade so that protected markets for local agricultural products were no longer guaranteed.

On a spatial basis the main beneficiaries of irrigation and the settlement scheme harnessing the waters of the largest river in Sri Lanka (the Mahaweli) are the predominantly Sinhalese districts of Anuradhapura and Polonnaruwa in the North-Central region of the country and Trincomalee in the east. These three districts belong to Income Zone II which has one of the lowest median real incomes among all income zones.

The Accelerated Mahaweli Development Project seeks to transform an existing natural setting in a particular geographic space into a viable resource. It is geared towards achieving self-sufficiency in the staple food crops, an effort started in the 1930s. Sri Lanka depends on the foreign exchange earned mainly from the sale of cash crops (tea, rubber and coconut) to purchase rice to feed her population. Hence, achieving self-sufficiency in rice has been a major target for every government in independent Sri Lanka. The strategy is to rechannel the excess river water from the Wet Zone into water scarce regions of the Dry Zone where land is available and also provide the infrastructure for the settlement of farmers in small family farms. The AMDP constitutes the biggest single investment program of the government since 1977. Apart from agricultural development, the major benefit of the AMDP is the generation of hydroelectric power which would be used to extend rural electrification and for industrial purposes islandwide.

The full impact of the AMDP is yet to be felt since the program has not been fully completed. However, decades of effort in developing irrigated paddy agriculture in the Dry Zone districts have resulted in some of these districts becoming major paddy surplus areas. In 1984, the districts of Anuradhapura, Amparai, Batticaloa, Polonnaruwa and Trincomalee belonged to this category (Department of Census and Statistics, 1985). While Anuradhapura and Polonnaruwa belong to the ethno-spatial population clusters of the Sinhalese, Batticaloa has a predominantly Sri Lankan Tamil population. Trincomalee and Amparai have mixed population distributions of Sinhalese, Sri Lankan Tamils and Moors. Although the government in 1977 lifted price controls on most locally grown agricultural produce, it retained a guaranteed price scheme for the purchase of paddy. This stood at Rs. 62.50 per hushel in 1983. The open market price was Rs. 78.00 per bushel.

Price controls, protected internal markets and a drastic reduction in the importation of wheat flour during the period 1970-77 saw an expansion of agricultural land devoted to subsidiary food crops. An analysis of the acreage under subsidiary food crops during the period 1972-76 reveals that the highest acreages were devoted to manioc (cassava), maize, kurakkan, sweet potatoes, chilies and red onions (Department of Census and Statistic, 1972, 1977). While manioc, maize, kurakkan and sweet potatoes are basically substitutes for rice and wheat flour, red onions and chilies constitute two essential items of Sri Lankan cooked food.

Approximately 40% of the cultivated land in red onions and 15% of the land in chilies is in the Northern districts of Jaffna, Vavuniya and Mullaitivu. The overwhelming proportion of land under the other major subsidiary crops is in the predominantly Sinhalese districts (Department of Census and Statistics, 1978). After 1977 with the lifting of price controls and protected markets on most locally produced agricultural products, and with increased imports of wheat flour, subsidiary food crop cultivation in manioc (cassava), maize, kurakkan and sweet potatoes virtually collapsed. Hence the acreage devoted to these crops, which was mainly in the south, fell sharply (Department of Census and Statistics, 1978, 1983). The Northern districts of Jaffna, Vavuniya and Mullaituvu relied more on the cultivation of red onions and chilies and to a lesser degree on potatoes and gingelly. These crops are not substitutes for imported food items. While under the liberalization policies of 1977 protective markets for red onion, chilies and potatoes were abolished, locally- produced crops continued to be competitive.

Red onion cultivation has the highest percentage of land in the Northern districts of Jaffna, Vavuniya and Mullaitivu. Production increased from 66,300 metric tons in 1977 to 92,200 metric tons in 1981. The three Northern districts increased their percentage share of the national acreage of red onion cultivation from 40% in 1972/73 to 55% in 1980/81 (Department of Census and Statistics, 1976, 1982). However, chili production in the three Northern districts has dropped slightly since 1977. It should be noted that the Northern districts claimed less than 15% of the cultivated acreage in chili during the 1970s.

TABLE 7.6

Percentage of National Acreage Devoted to Red Onion (RO) and Chilies (C) by Northern Districts, 1971-1983

1972/73		1973/74		1974/75		1975/76		1979/80		1980/81	
RO.	C.	RO.	C.	RO.	C.	RO.	C.	RO.	C.	RO.	C.
39.8	13.9	42.9	14.0	41.5	10.1	42.7	13.3	56.6	25.7	55.5	22.1

Source: Computed from *Statistical Abstracts*, 1976-1982. Department of Census and Statistics, 1977, 1983.

Investment in manufacturing industries in Sri Lanka has been consistently less than for agricultural development (Samarasinghe, 1973). A limited program of industrialization was launched in 1956 which had a distinct import-substitution orientation. The spatial location pattern revealed a dispersal of government-owned industries away from the metropolitan district of Colombo, while the smaller- scale, privately-owned, light consumer industries were allowed to make use of the locational advantages offered by Colombo (Samarasinghe, 1982). The dispersal of public industry meant an implied acceptance by the state of the need for regional locations. In general, the manufactured goods produced locally, both by the public and private sector, were assured of a protected market. Imports of goods of similar nature were either totally banned or very high tariffs were imposed. Private sector industrialists had to follow state guidelines prescribing those industrial plants that could be established. A limited quota of foreign exchange needed to import machinery and raw materials was allocated on an individual basis to industrial entrepreneurs by the Ministry of Industries.

The government of 1977 lifted most of the controls. Thus many small-scale industries had to face competition from foreign manufacturers. Nearly 85% of small-scale light industries were located in Colombo and it is likely that a majority of them were owned by the Sinhalese. Gunasinghe argues that small industrialists who were managing light industrial production for the domestic market, among whom Sinhalese were predominant, were adversely affected by liberal trade policies adopted in 1977 (Gunasinghe, 1984).

In 1978 the Greater Colombo Economic Commission (GCEC) was established to promote industrialization. This amounted to a state decision to encourage the location of industries in the Colombo and Gampaha districts. The main component of the GCEC is the Investment Promotion Zones (IPZ), the first of which is in operation in Katunayake 20 miles north of the city of Colombo. The second is in Biyagama, 12 miles northeast of Colombo, where infrastructural facilities are now being built.

The IPZs are planned to develop an export-oriented structure of manufacturing industries largely, but not exclusively, relying on foreign owned capital. The government industrial policy of phasing out uneconomic public industrial ventures, eliminating local private industry that cannot face foreign competition and introducing a scheme of incentives for foreign capital in industrialization is a strategy oriented primarily towards growth. Resources were provided not in terms of achieving spatial equity but of inducing growth. As such, with better banking, transport, port facilities and labor availability, Colombo provided the optimum locational facilities. In relation to public policy since independence in Sri Lanka, Colombo stood to gain only when market forces were allowed a free play. Now the IPZs, though inspired by the need to expand industrial growth, have provided Colombo with a "new avenue" of development. It is clear that public policy on industry is specifically growth-oriented. Manufacturing industry has a distinct urban bias. The strategy of the government is quite obviously geared towards achieving industrial growth, accumulating foreign exchange and in the process transferring technology, skills and management knowhow to the local population. Achieving spatial equity in relation to the location of industries is not a major component of this strategy. Indeed, it could be argued that by establishing a relatively fast growing economic activity in an area such as Colombo, which already occupies the highest socio-economic development level of the country, there could be a sharpening of spatial inequality (Samarasinghe, 1982).

The open economic policy has given a new buoyancy to trade especially in relation to imports and exports. Liberal import policy has facilitated a major import trade centered in Metropolitan Colombo. Gunasinghe argues that vast numbers of small-and middle-level traders stood to gain by the accumulation of substantial profits from trade and services and that Tamils and Muslims were over-represented in relation to their proportion in the population (Gunasinghe, 1984). Metropolitan Colombo, where most of the commercial activity is centered, has the highest median personal income for any zone. Ethnically it consists of 50% Sinhalese (24% points below the national average) 22% Sri Lankan Tamils (10% points above the national average) and 21% Moors (14% points above the national average). As in all ethno-spatial units, Metropolitan Colombo has its share of poor ethnic areas but the probability remains that a sizeable proportion of population from among the main minority groups benefits from the lucrative commercial sector.

A sector in which the ethno-spatial units of the North dominate is fisheries (Table 7.7). A decline in the fish catch has been recorded since 1983. This is attributed almost entirely to the drop in production in the Northern and Eastern districts where civil disturbances disrupted fisheries activities (Central Bank, 1985). The security surveillance zone operated by the Sri Lankan Navy in the fishing areas of the North has severely restricted the fisheries activity of the area. The districts of the North and the East which engage in fishing are Jaffna, Mannar, Mullaitivu, Batticaloa and Trincomalee. The first four districts belong to the predominantly Sri Lankan Tamil ethno-spatial units. In terms of the number of fishing boats that were issued by the government under a subsidy scheme the fishermen of the North and the East received only 39% of the total number of boats issued. However the fishermen of the Northern and Eastern districts received 58% of the total bank loan given by the state banks to fishermen (Ministry of Plan Implementation, 1985). Among the four fishery development projects undertaken by the government since 1977 with some foreign funding, two (the East Coast Fisheries Development Project and the North West Fisheries Development Project) will benefit Batticaloa and Mannar respectively. The *Central Bank Report* of 1984 states that most of the people in the fishing industry remain in the category of absolutely poor and indeed a sizeable proportion are in the Northern and the Eastern districts where Sri Lankan Tamils predominate. The report adds that since neither the producers nor consumers have been able to reap the benefits of government investment, a complete reorganization of the institutional structure and a reorientation of the investment program is necessary (Central Bank, 1984). The fisheries sector of the Northern and Eastern districts has the potential for further development and there is an assured market among the population of the country. Fishermen of the Northern and Eastern districts possess the necessary skills. There is no lack of resources in the seas surrounding the districts.

TABLE 7.7

Production of Fresh Fish (in metric tons) and Percentage of Production in the North and the East, 1978-1981

	1978		1979		1980		1981	
	Prod.	% of S.Lanka Production	Prod	% of S.Lanka Production	Prod.	% of S.Lanka production	Prod.	% of S.Lanka Production
Northern and Eastern districts (Jaffna, Mannar, Mullaitivu, Trincomalee, Batticaloa)	73,546	53.7	81,788	54.9	93,394	56.5	99,543	56.8
Northern districts (Jaffna, Mannar, Mullaitivu)	49,743	36.4	56,472	37.9	66,315	40.1	68,178	38.9

Source: Computed from the *Statistical Abstract*, 1982, Department of Census and Statistics, 1983.

Resource allocation in the tertiary economic activities has been mainly in the tourist trade. The locations of activity are predetermined by the "whims" and "choices" of the tourists who are mainly drawn from Europe and North America. In graded hotels Colombo has the highest capacity, followed by the beach resorts of the western and southern coastal areas, the east coast, and historic cities. The ethno-spatial units in the North have not attracted the tourist trade and as such the main beneficiaries of the attractive incentives offered by the government are in the South. However, tourism as an industry is more vulnerable to external forces like recession and ethno-political conflicts. This was evidenced by the slump in the tourist trade after the civil disturbances of July 1983 which resulted in major dislocations in employment and reductions in tourist-generated income in the South.

An explicit spatial component of rural development forms the basis of the Integrated Rural Development Programme (IRDP) inaugurated in 1978. A sizeable land area of the country running from the northwest to the south-east that does not fall within any of the lead projects is included in the IRDP which is already being implemented in 12 of the 24 districts. Programs for Killinochchi, Mallaitivu and Trincomalee are in the planning stage (Ministry of Plan Implementation, 1984). Six of the seven districts in income Zone IV, which records the lowest median personal income levels, are included in this program. A major study undertaken to evaluate the IDRP in Sri Lanka states that the selection of districts for the program is based mainly on the relative level of underdevelopment compared to other districts and that the selected districts receive little or no direct benefits from other lead projects undertaken by the state. They receive a low proportion of government expenditure and the per capita investment remains low (Rao, Tilakaratne, Peiris, 1983). Five of the districts, namely Vavunia, Mannar, Matale, Puttalam and Kurunegala, have World Bank sponsored programs and their investment levels are relatively high compared with the country-sponsored programs (Sweden, Netherland, Norway) implemented in the other districts. The northern districts with a low density of population get a higher investment per capita (Table 7.8).

TABLE 7.8
Investment Pattern—IRD Program

District		Total Investment (in Rs. Million)	Investment Per Capita (in Rs.)
Vavuniya	(1984)	379.4	4221
Mannar	(1981)	337.9	3371
Matale	(1981)	337	962
Puttalam	(1984)	397.7	810
Badulla	(1983)	370	578
Kurunegala	(1979)	465	384
Hambantota	(1979)	260	619
Monaragala	(1984)	150	555
Nuwara Eliya	(1980)	150	288
Ratnapura	(1984)	150	190
Matara	(1979)	100	156

Source: *Performance*, Ministry of Plan Implemetation, 1984.

The government also has a Decentralized Budget (Ministry of Plan Implementation, 1985A) whereby a annual grant of Rs. 2.5 million is allocated to each member of Parliament for a variety of infrastructural projects such as village level irrigation works, road construction, education, land and agrarian services, health and electricity. In 1983, a total of Rs. 293 million was allocated for new projects and an additional Rs. 8 million for the continuation of old projects; of the total investment of Rs. 373 million set aside only about 9.7% had been used by the end of the year. The main item of expenditure from the funds of the Decentralized Budget in the Northern districts of Jaffna, Mannar and Mullaitivu was in the sphere of education (Ministry of Plan Implementation, 1985A).

Resource Allocation on Social Welfare

Government expenditure on social welfare is mainly on education, health and food subsidies. Sri Lanka as noted earlier has reached a remarkably high level in the diffusion of welfare measures compared to most other Third World countries. This is reflected in the PQLI scores.

The four Northern districts of Jaffna, Mallaitivu, Mannar and Vavuniya which belong to the Sri Lankan Tamil ethno-spatial cluster showed high PQLI scores. It has been argued that in the sphere of education (which forms a component of the PQLI) historically the Jaffna District had many advantages. However, this historical momentum alone cannot be expected to sustain a high level of education unless fresh resource allocation is made continuously. With the nationalization of the schools in 1960, the state took over the financial burden of assisted schools[6] of which Jaffna District had many. While Jaffna District has high literacy rates and facilities for technical and scientific studies, high school enrollment figures are also high (Ministry of Education, 1983). On the other hand, in the adjacent districts of Mullaitivu, Vavuniya and Mannar, educational facilities are relatively poor. In fact, the school enrollment numbers are the lowest for the country. Furthermore, in terms of expenditure per student the two northern districts of Mannar and Mullaitivu again have the lowest levels in the nation. Vavuniya and Mallaitivu are net immigration districts (Samarasinghe, 1985) and the demand for educational facilities will certainly increase in the future.

A scrutiny of state expenditure on students indicates that in general those districts which have a higher density of population have high per capita expenditure on students. The high density areas of Colombo, Gampaha and Kandy received high per capita expenditure per student. On the other hand, eight districts with densities below 100 per square kilometer had less than the national average of expenditure per student (Ministry of Education, 1983).

Educational attainment is generally low for the Indian Tamil group who are concentrated in the districts within the central highlands. An index of educational attainment by ethnic group computed in the *Consumer Finance and Socioeconomic Surveys* of the Central Bank shows that the index for the Indian Tamil group was only 1.89 in 1973 but rose to 2.10 in 1978/79 and 2.28 in 1981/82. The Kandyan Sinhalese group who reside in the same central highland area had higher scores ranging from 3.72 in 1973 to 4.60 in 1981 (Central Bank, 1984). The estate sector with which the Indian Tamil group is identified is noted for very poor educational facilities. In the estate sector, estate management was responsible for the educational program. Facilities for education in the estates were available only through the primary levels. Expansion of educational opportunities in the estate sector by bringing it into the mainstream of the Sri Lankan educational system is only now being undertaken.

Nutrition Levels

It is generally acknowledged that nutritional levels of the population improve with increasing incomes. Income support schemes such as food subsidies are implemented in order to upgrade the nutritional levels of the vulnerable groups. The food and kerosene stamp scheme was introduced by the government in September 1979 to replace the rice ration scheme which spanned four decades. The food stamp program is a means-tested scheme where the mean income of the food and kerosene stamp recipient household was estimated to be less than Rs. 300 per month in 1982. The average value of food stamps when all 24 districts were considered amounted to Rs. 90 per household per month. It has been acknowleded by policy makers that there are weaknesses in the food stamp program due to the decline in the purchasing power of the stamps and poor targeting (Ministry of Plan Implementation, 1982). The highest state priority in implementing a nutrition strategy to enhance the levels of nutrition is given to the Central region districts of Matale and Badulla. The lowest to the four Northern districts of Jaffna, Mannar, Mullaitivu and Vavuniya, and the Western maritime districts of Colombo, Gampaha and Kalutara (Table 7.9).

Health

There are five main sectors of the health care system in Sri Lanka. They are the government western sector: the government "Ayurveda" or indigenous sector: the private western sector: the private "Ayurveda" sector, and the private "other" sector - mainly homeopathy. Although it is estimated that the private "Ayurveda" sector is well patronized by the population of Sri Lanka (Simeonov, 1967) it accounts for only 8% of the capital stock of the whole health care system of the country. Moreover in terms of annual recurrent budget allocations, expenditure on the "Ayurveda" was only 1.6% of the total budget for health care in 1985 (Central Bank, 1986).

TABLE 7.9

A Composite Index and Ranking of Nutritional Status by Regions

Region	(a)	(b)	(c)	(d)
1. Colombo (Urban)	22.8	24	10	7.5
2. Colombo, Gampaha, Kalutara	19.5	27	11	7.7
3. Jaffna, Vavuniya, Mannar, Mullaitivu	10.5	41	11	7.7
4. Kandy, Nuwara Eliya	24.1	55	12	3.5
5. Kegalle, Ratnapura	21.6	40	12	5.3
6. Matale, Badulla	33.0	47	12	2.2
7. Galle, Matara	29.5	31	11	5.5
8. Kurunegala, Puttalam	16.7	33	16	6.0
9. Monaragala, Hambantota	31.5	37	14	3.1
10. Anuradhapura, Polonnaruwa, Trincomalee, Batticaloa, Amparai	16.3	40	14	6.2

Notes(a) Percent of households with less than 30% calorie adequacy.

(b) Percent of households with children under 60 months with evident stunting. Stunting reflects the long-term effect of improper nutrition.

(c) Percent of households with children under 60 months with evident wasting.

(d) Score based on the status of each region on calorie adequacy, stunting, and wasting. Priority in state investment is given to those regions with low scores.

Source: Computed from (Ministry of Plan Implementation) *Nutrition Strategy*, 1983.

Free state-sponsored health services have been an essential part of the welfare package initiated by the British Colonial administrators and continued by each successive government since independence. The total health expenditure by the government has increased over the years. However, the government health expenditure as a percentage of total government expenditure decreased from 5.1% in 1973 to 3.1% in 1983 but rebounded to 4.6% in 1984 (Ministry of Health, 1985). The government sector provides almost all of the public health services and in-patient treatment and about 40% of outpatient medical services (Simeonov, 1976).

One of the most important services offered free by the state is hospital facilities. In terms of beds per 1000 population the mean for Sri Lanka in 1983 was 2.4 (Ministry of Health, 1984). The mean for the Northern districts of Jaffna and Mannar with predominantly Sri Lankan Tamil populations was 3.1 beds per 100 population which is above the national mean. Vavuniya and Mullaitivu which also belong to the Sri Lankan Tamil ethno-spatial cluster had 2.0 beds per 100 population which was below the national mean. The lowest rate in terms of beds per 1000 population among all the districts of Sri Lanka was recorded for Amparai (1.6 per 1000) followed by Trincomalee (1.7 per 1000). Both of these districts are in the eastern sector of the country and have an ethnically mixed population distribution. Kandy District recorded the highest rate (3.5 per 1000) followed by Jaffna and Mannar (Ministry of Health 1984).

Sri Lanka recorded an average rate of 11.4 medical officers (Western medicine) for 100,000 population in 1983. The majority of medical officers are in the government sector and employed in state hospitals while the others are in the private sector mainly in urban areas and particularly in Colombo District. On a regional basis Colombo District had the highest rate of 81 per 100,000. The districts of Mannar, Vavuniya and Mullaitivu which form one State Health Service Unit (SHS division)[7] had a rate of 8.4 per 100,000 while Batticaloa had a rate of 8.2 per 100,000 (Ministry of Health, 1984). Only two other districts, namely Jaffna (16.8 per 100,000) and Kandy (13.6 per 100,000) record marginally higher than average rates of doctors per 100,000 population. The Ministry of Health also employs a group of health personnel trained by the western medical sector as intermediate level medical officers mainly on curative medical care. They are known as Registered Medical Practitioners (RMP's). Their main function is to man government dispensaries located regionally. The average rate of RMPs per 100,000 population for Sri Lanka is 6.0. Thirteen of the 20 SHS divisions had an above average rate of RMPs. Colombo District had a below average rate of 2.7 per 100,000, obviously compensated for by the better distribution of doctors. Vavuniya and Mullaitivu had the highest rate of RMPs at 16.2 per 100,000. Jaffna and Batticaloa districts had 8.2 and 8.5 per 100,000 respectively (Ministry of Health 1984).

In general, resource allocations on social welfare by successive governments since 1948 have been on an island-wide basis. The major exception was in the allocation of resources to the Dry Zone during the pre-independent era in order to eradicate malaria. These districts have also benefited from the Social Welfare Component of the irrigation and settlement development program which started during the mid-1930s.

An analysis of the spatial distribution of social welfare suggests that its volume and intensity is generally related to density of population. Moore suggests that in Sri Lanka it is the population density and its aggregate need and demand for service per square kilometer that has contributed significantly towards the high PQLI (Moore, 1984). Indeed, population density is associated with Sri Lanka's political process whereby regions with higher densities of population have larger numbers of members in Parliament. The delimitation of electorates, however, ensures that regions with smaller populations but which encompass large land areas are also well represented in Parliament. Hence, in a system where each member of Parliament strives to deliver a reasonable flow of welfare to his constituents in order to maintain his popularity, social welfare resource distribution cannot be too heavy biased in favor of more densely populated areas at the expense of those less densely populated.

CONCLUSIONS

The ethnic conflict in Sri Lanka is an issue between the majority Sinhalese community and the minority Sri Lankan Tamil community. Thus, the present analysis was mainly focused on the spatial dimension of resource distribution between the two communities. The foundation of the analysis was the ethno-spatial units identified on the basis of the distribution of ethnic groups in Sri Lanka. An attempt was made to identify ethno-spatial inequalities in terms of both economic and social indicators which are known to reflect the volume and nature of resource distribution over time. It is often claimed that "the four basic issues that fuel conflict between the Sinhalese and the Sri Lanka Tamils are, (1) Language and Employment (2) Regional Autonomy (3) Land Settlement; and (4) Access to higher education." (de Silva, 1984). All four aspects are clearly linked to patterns of resource allocation. This chapter deals with the wider aspect of the spatial distribution of resources in the economic and soical welfare spheres.

It is contended that the economic strategies of successive governments in Sri Lanka since independence were directed mainly towards the implementation of programs capable of generating much needed economic growth in general. They have succeeded in some and failed in others. For instance, Sri Lanka was able to reach near self-sufficiency levels in rice production (the staple food item) despite increases in population mainly due to concerted efforts by successive governments to develop that sector. In addition, the island-wide diffusion of social welfare facilities is reflected in relatively high PQLI scores. On the other hand, the public sector industrial program initiated in 1956 did not bring about the desired result of regional growth.

The assertation that in economic development "the government has discriminated against Tamil areas and neglected them completely" (A. Amirthalingam, quoted in Tiruchelvam, 1984) clearly reveals the ethno-spatial dimension of competition for resources among spatially separated ethnic groups. The levels of socio-economic attainment betwen the ethno-spatial clusters do not support the contention of Mr. Amirthalingam. However, it should not be implied that the ethno-spatial clusters of the Sri Lankan Tamil group were well looked after in all respects. The underdevelopment of the fisheries sector is a case in point. It should be noted that certain policy measures adversely affected the mainly Sinhala employment in the south. For instance the collapse of the handloom industry after 1977 brought a certain degree of dislocation to the employment structure of that area. The argument here is that all these different aspects are part of a whole - the whole being the economic system. Constant adjustments and restructuring occur in relation to the parts (which certainly have regional manifestations) in response to changes in the system. Such restructuring and readjustments in the context of Sri Lanka cannot be interpreted as discriminatory practices perpetrated on the ethno-spatial clusters of the Sri Lankan Tamil group.

Social welfare resource distribution has been generally related to the density of population and momentum derived from the early development of specific regions. The general exception has been where Indian Tamil people predominate. A lack of political accountability has contributed to this situation.

Weiner considers ethnic inequality more offensive than class inequality. He views the distinctions between ethnic groups as an indication of differences of opportunity, proof that the dominant group has allocated crucial resources in order to restrict others mobility. Hence, the presumption is made that the results may have been "fixed". The same contentions are not necessarily made in relation to class inequalities (Weiner, 1984). In Sri Lanka, the two groups are separated not only by language, culture, religion and notions of common descent but also by their separate identity in geographic space. As a result, polarization becomes even sharper and hence the constant tug-of-war over resources, based on actual or perceived notions, inevitably leads to conflict.

NOTES

1. This analysis uses administrative districts as the basic spatial units. There were 22 districts in 1971 which were increased to 24 in 1981. In 1981 Gampaha District was carved out of the original Colombo District while Mullaitivu District was carved out of the original Vavuniya District.
2. The country is divided into two main agro-climatological areas, i.e., the Wet Zone and the Dry Zone. The Wet Zone is limited to approximately one quarter of the land area in the southwestern quarter of the country, and includes the lowland coastal area and the western section of the central hilly region. The Dry Zone which is mainly lowland encompasses the north, north-central, eastern and parts of the northwestern, central and southern regions of the country and accounts for nearly three-quarters of the land area.
3. A publication titled "Sri Lanka: the Ethnic Conflict, Myths, Realities and Perspectives" by the Committee for Rational Development (CRD, 1984) indicated that Sri Lankan Tamils accounted for 65.1% of the total population of the Northern (Districts of Jaffna, Mannar, Vavuniya and Mullaitivu) and Eastern Provinces (Districts of Trincomalee, Batticaloa and Amparai). If spatial contiguity is used as a criterion for amalgamation of districts on ethnic lines, then the two districts of Trincomalee and Amparai when joined with the districts of Anuradhapura and Polonnaruwa will have a Sinhalese population amounting to 67% of the total population. However, it should be noted that the districts of the Eastern Province (Amparai, Trincomalee and Batticaloa) are mainly Tamil-speaking regions.
4. The 24 Administrative Districts excluding the area covered by the Colombo Municipality are divided into 4 zones.

Zone I: (Western Coastal)	Colombo (excluding the municipality), Gampaha, Kalutara, Galle and Matara
Zone II: (Dry Zone)	Hambantota, Monaragala, Amparai, Polonnaruwa, Anuradhapura and Puttalam
Zone III: (Northern and Eastern)	Jaffna, Mannar, Vavuniya, Mullaitivu, Trincomalee and Batticaloa

Zone IV: (Central Estate)	Kandy, Matale, Nuwaraeliya, Badulla, Ratnapura, Kegalle and Kurunegala
Zone V:	Colombo Municipality

5. The PQLI developed at the Overseas Development Council, Washington, D.C. under the direction of Morris D. Morris is a composite index of 3 simple indicators (equally weighted): life expectancy at age one, infant mortality, and literacy.
6. Assisted schools are secondary schools for which financial assistance by way of teachers salaries is paid by the state. The administration of such schools is the responsibility of independent school boards.
7. The Health Ministry has been adopting regional units for administration known as State Health Service (SHS) divisions. There are 20 such units in the country. In most cases, the boundaries of these units are the same as district units.

REFERENCES

Central Bank of Ceylon. 1964. *Report of Consumer Finance and Socioeconomic Surveys* Colombo: Central Bank of Ceylon (see also reports for 1973, 1974, 1978/79, 1981/82 and 1984).

Central Bank of Ceylon. 1985. *Annual Report 1984*. Colombo: Central Bank of Ceylon (see also report for 1985).

Committee for Rational Development (CRD). 1984. *Sri Lanka: The Ethnic Conflict, Myths, Realities and Perspectives*. New Delhi: Navrang.

Cohen, Saul B. 1985. Theory and Traditional Political Geography in *Pluralism and Political Geography: People, Territory, State*. eds. Nurit Khot and Stanley Waterman. London: Croom Helm.

Despres, Leo. A (ed.). 1975. *Ethnicity and Resource Competition in Plural Societies*. Hague: Mouton.

Goonatilake, Godfrey. 1978. *Participatory Development and Dependence - The Case of Sri Lanka*. Colombo: Marga Institute.

Gunasinghe, N. 1984. The Open Economy and Its Impact on Ethnic Relations in Sri Lanka in *Sri Lanka: The Ethnic Conflict, Myths, Realities and Perspectives*. New Delhi: Navrang.

Jayanth Dilesh. 1985. Poverty in Sri Lanka: An Assessment of Some Trends in the Period 1953 to 1981/82. *Economic Review* 11: 23-28.

Jaywardena, L. 1974. Case Study of Sri Lanka in *Redistribution With*

Growth eds. H. B. Cheney, J. Montek, S. Ahluwalia, H. Duloy and R. Jolly. Oxford: Oxford University Press.

Karunatilake, H.N.S. 1974. Changes in Income Distribution in Sri Lanka, *Central Bank Staff Studies* 4: 87-109.

Karunatilake, H.N.S. 1978. An Evaluation of the Development Programme under Divisional District Councils on Sri Lanka. *Sri Lanka Jounal of Social Science* 1: 1-26.

Moore, M. 1984. Categorizing Space: Urban-Rural or Core-Periphery in Sri Lanka, *The Journal of Development Studies* 20: 102-123.

Morris, M.D. 1979. *Measuring the Condition of the World's Poor. The Physical Quality of Life Index.* New York: Pergammon.

Morris, M.D. and McAlpine, M.B. 1982. *Measuring the Condition of India's Poor.* New Delhi: Promilla.

Rao, V.K., Tilakaratene and Peiris, G.H. 1983. *Planning for Rural Development. A Study of District Integrated Rural Development Programme of Sri Lanka.* Bangkok: ARTEP.

Samarasinghe, V. 1973. *Polarization of Colombo in the Economic Geography of Sri Lanka.* Ph.D. dissertation, Department of Geography, Cambridge University, England.

Samarsinghe, V. 1980. The Impact of Government Policy on Regional Development. Peradeniya: Ceylon Studies Seminar.

Samarasinghe, V. 1982. Spatial Polarization of Colombo: A Study of Regional Inequality. *Sri Lanka Journal of Social Sciences* 5: 75-95.

Samarasinghe, V. 1985. An Evaluation of the Differential Impact of Public Policy on Spatial Inequalities in Sri Lanka since 1977. Paper presented at the *Workshop on Spatial Inequalities in the Developing World*, Commonwealth Geographical Bureau, Kano, Nigeria.

Simeonov, L.A. 1975. Better Health for Sri Lanka. *Report on a Health Manpower Study*. New Delhi: WHO.

Sri Lanka, Department of Census and Statistics. 1976. *Census of Population, 1971*. Colombo: Government Printing Office.

Sri Lanka, Department of Census and Statistics. 1984. *Census of Population, 1981*. Colombo: Ministry of Plan Implementation.

Sri Lanka, Ministry of Education. 1983. *School Census 1982*. Colombo: Ministry of Education.

Sri Lanka, Ministry of Health. 1984. *Annual Development Plan 1984*. Colombo: Ministry of Health.

Sri Lanka, Ministry of Health. 1985. *Health Development Plan 1984*.

Colombo: Ministry of Health.

Sri Lanka, Ministry of Plan Implementation. 1982. *Evaluation Report on the Food Stamp Scheme.* Colombo: Ministry of Plan Implementation.

Sri Lanka, Ministry of Plan Implementation. 1984. *Performance 1983.* Colombo: Ministry of Plan Implementation (see also report for 1984).

Sri Lanka, Ministry of Plan Implementation. 1984. *Nutrition Strategy 1983.* Colombo: Ministry of Plan Implementation.

Sri Lanka, Ministry of Plan Implementation. 1985A. *Public Investment, 1985-1989.* Colombo: Ministry of Plan Implementation.

Sri Lanka, Ministry of Plan Implementation. 1985B. *Patterns of Investment.* Colombo: Ministry of Plan Implementation.

Sumanasekera, H.D. 1983. Measuring the Regional Variation of Quality of Life in Sri Lanka. *Sri Lankan Journal of Agrarian Studies* 2: 27-37.

Tiruchelvam, N. 1984. Ethnicity and Resource Allocation in *From Independence to Statehood* eds. R.B. Goldman and A.J. Wilson. London: Frances Pinter.

Weiner, Myron. 1984. The Pursuit of Ethnic Equality through Preferential Policies: A Comparative Public Policy Perspective in *From Independence to Statehood* eds. R.B. Goldman and A.J. Wilson. London: Frances Pinter.

Chapter VIII

ETHNIC CONFLICT AND ECONOMIC DEVELOPMENT IN SRI LANKA

S.W.R. de A. Samarasinghe
International Centre for Ethnic Studies, Kandy, Sri Lanka

In Sri Lanka, Tamil separatists have been fighting a violent battle against the predominantly Buddhist Sinhalese majority who form 74% of the 16.5 million (end 1987) population in the island. The separatists, who want to establish an independent state of Tamil *Eelam* in the north and east of the country, come from the predominantly Hindu Sri Lankan Tamil group (13%). The other two principal minority groups, the "Indian" Tamil plantation workers (6%) whose leader is in President J.R. Jayewardene's cabinet and the Muslim's (7%) do not support the separatist demand. In the above context, the main objective of this chapter is to analyze the inter-relationship between the current ethnic conflict and the economic development of the country in the last three decades.

The analysis is based on a theoretical framework focussed on the concept of economic equity. It is argued that in multi-ethnic societies such as Sri Lanka ethnicity adds an extra dimension to the development process through the issue of *ethnic* economic equity that must be taken into account in development programs. Ethnic economic equity is essential to achieve successful economic integration in a multi-ethnic society. The notion of ethnic economic equity must be understood in relation to the relative economic circumstances of the different ethnic groups at a given moment in time. It must also be considered in relation to the rate at which those circumstances change over time. The concept of ethnic economic equity also has a psychological dimension related to group perceptions of how and to what extent they benefit from economic development relative to others and the time lags involved in the adjustments of those perceptions to changing economic realities. Indeed, Sri Lanka's experience after Independence (1948) illustrates the manner in which the ethnic economic equity factor relates to the development process in a multi-ethnic society and the substantial long-term economic costs that its negligence by development planners might entail.

Ethnic consciousness and ethnic identity of groups have a strong socio-cultural and psychological dimension to them that to some extent are independent of political and economic factors and are based on shared language, culture and history. For example, the simmering language row in Belgium between those who are French-speaking and those who are Dutch-speaking is largely an identity conflict. The strong sense of ethnic identity shown by the French-speaking Canadian minority that almost led to the separation of Quebec from the rest of Canada in the late seventies can only be partly attributed to the sense of relative political and economic deprivation that they felt vis-a-vis the English-speaking Canadian majority (Jacobs 1980). However, there is no doubt that economic grievances entertained by ethnic groups generally hope to sharpen ethnic differences and, more often than not, precipitate ethnic violence.

Some modernization theorists such as Pye (1966) and Apter (1972) expected ethnic sentiments, considered by them to be a feature of traditional society, to fade away due to modernization and development. Experience proves that this generally has not happened. This has led Deutsch (1961) and others to theorize that ethnic divisions can be sharpened during economic development by the competition that it encourages between the different ethnic groups, particularly between the respective elites. Similar views are expressed in Marxist models of ethnicity which stress the class character of such competition either between ethnic elities (e.g. Prabhakar, 1971) or ethnic working-class groups (Bonacich, 1972)

Unequal competition between different ethnic groups for

scarce economic resources has persuaded countries such as the USA, Malaysia and India with widely different economic conditions to adopt affirmative action programs to help the weaker groups. Such policies implicitly recognize that in order to ensure the successful integration of the different ethnic groups into the economy it is necessary to combine economic growth with relative equality of economic opportunity (Stavenhagen, 1981) in economic development.

Economic inequality between ethnic groups in a static sense relates to differences in wealth, incomes, employment levels and so forth. In a dynamic sense economic inequality relates to differences at the rate at which the different groups improve their respective living standards. The point of interest is to analytically examine the circumstances under which ethnic stratification is strengthened (or weakened) by the development process and the economic factors that could help to precipitate or avoid ethnic conflict.

ETHNIC AND SOCIAL STRATIFICATION AND ETHNIC CONFLICT

Ethnicity is an ascriptive characteristic. It is possible to imagine a multi-ethnic society with each ethnic group occupying a given social class defined to mean a group that shares much the same economic conditions and prospects in life based on their occupational roles and/or their inherited wealth. The position of whites and blacks in the US South before emancipation and that of whites and blacks in South Africa today roughly approximate such a situation. In Sri Lanka, however, there is no sharp overlap of class and ethnic divisions. The only qualified exception to this is the plantation Tamils who are overwhelmingly unskilled and semi-skilled laborers in the plantation sector. However, this is not a strictly exclusive group as a social class because approximately 25% of plantation laborers are Sinhalese.

In Sri Lanka, caste is a form of social stratification but it has lost its importance due to the modernization process and has, to some extent, been replaced by class. The majority Sinhalese as well as the minority Sri Lankan Tamils and Muslims are differentiated in terms of social class. All have strong elite groups consisting of rich businessmen and big landowners, professionals, higher level bureaucrats and business managers. All these ethnic groups also have middle and lower-middle classes, urban working classes and rural peasant components. However, there is no compelling evidence to suggest that modernization has helped to develop strong class solidarity cutting across ethnic barriers. The trend in fact has been in the opposite direction. For example, Moore (1985) has pointed out that the Sri Lankan peasantry has failed to develop a class consciousness to act as a cohesive group to articulate their special economic interests on the national agenda. The division of electoral support along ethnic lines is another obvious example.

It is my contention that a fundamental economic factor which strengthens ethnic solidarity is economic inequality along ethnic lines. In a competitive free-market economic model such as the one that Sri Lanka has adopted since 1977 under the liberalized policies of President J.R. Jayewardene, economic inequalities are considered to be socially acceptable because of the positive contribution to economic growth via promotion of savings and, more importantly, the incentive offered to work and higher productivity. In principle, private savings can be replaced by public savings by collecting more taxes. However, higher remuneration offered as an incentive to work can cause inequality in wealth and incomes and cannot be done away with because there is no viable collective substitute for it as in the case of savings. This, it appears, is what China under Deng Xiaoping and the Soviet Union under Mikhail Gorbachev have admitted in effecting radical reforms in their respective socialist economies. However, if differential rewards are to receive social sanction then such a system must fulfil two conditions. First, the differentials must be within limits that are considered reasonable by the community at large. Second, the higher rewards must be accessible to the members of that community at large. The non-fulfillment of either can lead to social conflict which can be analyzed within the framework of a general theory of stratification and conflict.

The presence of the ethnic factor in a situation where the conditions outlined remain unfulfilled, however, leads to the addition of a new dimension to ordinary social conflict. An ethnic group which perceives itself to be economically discriminated against generally has a common language and cultural affinity which makes it easier to build a sense of solidarity sparked off by economic grievance. Sometimes the concentration of the minority population in a clearly definable geographic space makes such group solidarity even stronger. The Sri Lankan Tamils in Jaffna are an example. Second, in a society where social classes are vertically cleavaged by ethnic division, an ethnic group which perceives itself to be discriminated against has the advantage of having an elite segment within its ranks that is capable of quickly organizing itself to provide leadership in a conflict situation. Here too, the Sri Lankan Tamils who have had ethnic political parties with an educated leadership are an example. Third, it is a moot point whether the threshold of tolerance of economic inequality based on ethnicity is lower than in the case of such inequality based on social class. Theoretically, this may well be the case because of the first two points, group solidarity that exists due to cultural and other factors and the leadership potential that can be mobilized.

ETHNO-ECONOMIC INEQUALITIES

There are three conditions under which ethno-economic inequalities can arise. First, in situations where one ethnic group occupies a region which is relatively poor in natural resources compared to other parts of the country, economic inequalities with ethnic undertones develop over time. For example, in the Sri Lankan Tamil district of Jaffna the average agricultural "small" holding in 1982 was 1.07 acres, which was only 55% of the all-island average of 1.94 acres.[1] Migration is the normal way in which an ethnic group overcomes such disadvantages, a practice which has been common among the Sri Lankan Tamil community in the north. Large numbers have always come to the south, especially to Colombo, for employment. Many have also emigrated. During the British colonial administration Malaya was a favorite destination. In more recent times large numbers have gone to western countries and to the Middle East. Second, immigrant communities such as the plantation Tamils who are assigned to or traditionally occupy a specific occupation or set of occupations may also be subject to economic differentiation that brings relative disadvantages or deprivation. This will be particularly true of groups working in industries subject to secular decline. Third, structural restrictions on socio-economic mobility - e.g. language disabilities, caste-related occupations, etc, - may also result in ethno-economic disparities.

Generally, state intervention can either help or hinder the reduction or removal of such differences. The actual state policy in a given situation depends on political power relations between the different ethnic groups and the overall macro-economic environment. Broadly speaking, given the political conditions, the experience in some plural societies, especially in newly independent nations, has been one of the dominant ethnic group using its political power to secure for itself a share of the economic resources which the minority groups find unjustified and unacceptable. Sometimes, this may simply be a situation where a minority was in a privileged position and, following independence, the majority claiming for itself their legitimate share denied to them for historical reasons. Black African countries such as Zimbabwe where minority white regimes existed in colonial times are an obvious example. The bloody conflict that occurred between the "privileged" Ibos and the rest of Nigeria in the late 1960s is another. However, the fact is that as Skinner (1975) shows, groups which have enjoyed certain advantages historically find it difficult to quickly adjust to a new situation. The adjustment becomes even more painful when it takes place in a stagnant economic environment and, in most Third World countries, it is further aggravated by demographic pressure and a hostile world economic environment. Indeed as the Chinese case in Malaysia demonstrates, an ethnic group may well tolerate some measure of even open discrimination provided the economy is expanding at a rate sufficient to meet what they consider to be their legitimate economic demands.[2]

However, there are conditions under which "enlightened self-interest" can prevail to persuade the dominant group to work towards lessening ethno-economic differences. One is a belief in a set of moral principles that favour equity. A second is one where the eradication of poverty that may exist in a particular ethnic group is helpful to economic growth. Third is a situation where the economic and social costs of policies that aggravate ethnic conflict exceed the gains accruing to the dominant group from such policies.

DEMOGRAPHY

In the context of our theme it is most important to have a clear understanding of the demographic pressures under which the Sri Lankan economy and policy functioned after independence in 1948. Table 8.1 presents some relevant data. The first point to note is that Sri Lanka's population doubled between 1946-77. A successful program to eradicate malaria with the use of DDT coupled with a general improvement in mass nutrition and social welfare standards reduced the crude death rate from 21 per 1000 in the mid-1940s to 10 per 1000 in the mid-1950s (while the crude birth rate remained unchanged in the 35-39 per 1000 range) was responsible for this growth. Second, the impact of this on the labor force was evident after 1963. Thus between 1946 and 1963 the labor force increased by about 750,000 over a seventeen year period or annually by an average of a little less than 50,000. The situation radically changed after 1963 when the labor force began to grow rapidly as a result of the rapid population growth experienced after 1946. Between 1963 and 1970 over a period of only seven years the labor force expanded by another 700,000 (100,000 annually) which was double the absolute expansion experienced in the previous decade. After 1970 the absolute growth increased still further especially in the late 1970s to reach over 150,000 per year.

TABLE 8.1
Population and Labor Force, 1946-84

	1946	1963	1970	1977	1986	Average growth rate % 1971-77	Average growth rate % 1977-86
Population ('000)	6657	10582	12514	13942	16117	1.6	1.7
Labor force ('000)	2846	3589	4296	5139	6396	2.6	2.7
Employed ('000)	2646	3199	3550	3854	5284	1.2	4.1
Unemployed ('000)	200*	390	747	1284	1113	8.0	-1.5
Unemployment rate (%)	7.0	10.9	17.4	25.0	17.4	-	-

* Estimate

Source: Population data from the Department of Census and Statistics, *Statistical Abstracts*, Annual; Central Bank, *Annual Report*
Employment data for 1946 and 1953, Central Bank, *Economic Review 1979*, p. 955
Labor Force and employment data for 1986, Korale (1988) p.60
Remainder from Ministry of Finance and Planning, *Public Investment 1985-1989*, Colombo 1985, p.9

The economic implications of these demographic changes are self-evident. The growth in population exerted tremendous pressure on food supplies and social welfare facilities most notably on health and education. The labor force figures are indicative of the intense competition that developed in the job market. However, to be properly understood, these changes must be related to the broader macroeconomy.

THE MACROECONOMY

In the 1960s Sri Lanka's GDP grew by about 4.5% annually. Matched against an annual increase in the population of 2.5% the per capita output growth was a modest 2.0%. In the 1971-77 period (Table 8.2) the GDP growth rate dropped to 2.9% and per capita income increased by a mere 1.3% per annum. It was this relative stagnation of the economy that helps explain the 25% unemployment rate recorded by 1977.

TABLE 8.2
Macroeconomic Indicators: 1970-86

	1970	1977	1986	Average rate of growth % 1971-77	1978-86
GDP (Rs ml)	13187	16078	25761	2.9	5.4
GDP per capita (Rs)	1054	1153	1590	1.3	3.6
	% of GDP 1970	1977	1986	Annual Average % 1971-77	1978-86
Gross domestic investment	18.9	14.4	23.2	16.0	24.0
Private investment	10.7	7.2	9.3	8.3	9.5
Public investment	8.2	7.2	13.9	7.7	14.5
National savings	14.1	18.0	13.9	12.7	14.3
Foreign savings	4.8	-3.6	9.3	3.3	9.6
Terms of trade	106	102	50*	-	-

Note: GDP figures in constant 1970 prices.

* In the terms of trade index (1978 = 100) the figure 50 refers to the 1984 value. In 1985 and 1986 Sri Lanka's commodity terms of trade declined by 20% and 5% respectively.

Source: Ministry of Finance and Planning, *Public Investment 1987-1991*, Colombo 1987.
Central Bank of Ceylon, *Annual Report*, 1984.

The growth performance improved after 1977 although international trading conditions and commodity prices were generally not favorable to Sri Lanka. The higher growth rate was the outcome of a 75% increase in the investment ratio after 1977. This increment was largely financed by foreign savings made available by western countries and multi-lateral aid agencies. The significant impact that the higher growth rate made on the employment situation is seen in the creation of about 1.6 million new jobs and the consequent decline in the rate of unemployment from 25% in 1977 to 14% in 1984.

The above story important though it may be for Sri Lanka is nothing special. There are a large number of countries in the Third World which have experienced slow economic growth and rising unemployment rates and there are quite a few countries - the so-called newly industrializing countries (NICS) - which have shown far more impressive growth rates. What is special about Sri Lanka's recent development history is the manner in which it has improved the social welfare standards of the general population notwithstanding the comparatively low per capita income and slow growth. For instance, for a nation with a per capita GNP of US $380 in 1985, Sri Lanka had a life expectancy at birth of 68 years for males and 72 years for females and an infant mortality rate of 36 per 1000 (World Bank, 1987). These measurements place Sri Lanka on a par with countries with a per capita GNP of US $2000 or more. Those countries in Sri Lanka's per capita GNP range have on average a life expectancy of about 50 to 55 years and an infant mortality rate of well over 100 per 1000 live births.[3]

The above analysis of Sri Lanka's economic performance raises the crucial issue that we set out to investigate. That is whether there was an ethnic bias to the sharing of the burdens of Sri Lanka's economic failures and the enjoyment of the fruits of economic successes. An ethnically integrated economy should show no evidence of discrimination on either count.

INCOME

Wealth and income are two indicators that are normally used to measure economic disparities between individuals and between households. Wealth data for Sri Lanka does not exist but income data by community is available (Table 8.3). As suggested by Arthur Lewis (1985) the median and the lower and upper quartile (Q1 and Q3) values of income for each community are used as a resonable measure of economic inequality. Four points are worth noting. First, in 1963 the median and quartile values of income of the Sri Lankan Tamils was on a par with that of the low-country coastal Sinhalese who account for 60% of the total Sinhalese population. Moreover the income level of both these groups was at least one-third more than that of the Kandyan (highlander) Sinhalese. Second, by 1973 the low-country Sinhalese had incomes which were about 10-15% higher than that of the Sri Lankan Tamils. The Kandyan Sinhalese had caught up with the Sri Lankan Tamils along the bottom half of the income scale but not at higher levels. Third, in 1981-82 the position had again changed. In the bottom quarter of the income scale the Sri Lankan Tamils were not far behind the low-country Sinhalese but were significantly ahead of the Kandyan Sinhalese. At the middle range the low-country Sinhalese maintained their superiority over the other two groups who were more of less on par with each other. In the higher income bracket the Sri Lankan Tamils had fallen behind the low-country Sinhalese but were marginally ahead of the Kandyan Sinhalese. Fourth, these data do not suggest that the Sri Lankan Tamils have, on average, enjoyed an appreciably lower level of income than the Sinhalese during the period under review. At least in comparison to the Kandyan Sinhalese the opposite appears to be true. However, Table 8.4 reveals that between 1963-73 the incomes of Sri Lankan Tamils in the lower- and middle-income ranges grew more slowly than that of the Sinhalese. However, in the upper range they did better than the Low Country Sinhalese. Between 1973-81/82 the Sri Lankan Tamil incomes had risen faster than that of the Sinhalese at the

TABLE 8.3

Distribution of Income (Rupees) per Income Receiver for One Month by Community, 1963-1981/2

		1963				1973				1981/2			
		Urban	Rural	Estate	All Island	Urban	Rural	Estate	All Island	Urban	Rural	Estate	All Island
Kandyan Sinhalese	Q1	56	40	38	40	183	114	70	114	551	371	251	376
	Median	130	78	55	73	283	188	100	189	934	726	433	726
	Q3	225	141	61	136	419	270	135	275	1735	1131	684	1156
Low Country Sinhalese	Q1	73	51	49	54	158	111	75	121	549	422	313	451
	Median	136	97	58	99	272	199	130	211	934	752	476	782
	Q3	243	164	77	198	394	303	175	282	1685	1226	601	1319
Sri Lankan Tamils	Q1	92	53	41	53	127	136	67	104	538	454	293	440
	Median	167	106	56	99	243	212	86	193	916	705	382	721
	Q3	268	189	73	192	300	288	146	329	1518	1109	534	1185
Indian Tamils	Q1	63	35	42	43	128	63	66	66	371	254	270	271
	Median	157	97	59	60	208	104	87	96	583	469	368	378
	Q3	225	213	75	80	225	213	145	137	967	720	499	476

Moors*	Q1	83	71	25	64	140	180	56	149	554	513	601	527
(Muslims)	Median	159	99	52	110	224	254	75	236	989	890	886	920
	Q3	311	196	71	202	316	363	138	327	2030	1418	901	1540
Others	Q1	119	63	-	73	125	125	-	147	589	451	-	679
	Q3	470	156	-	288	550	900	-	763	1501	1834	-	1876
All#	Q1	79	47	80	59	147	127	65	102	538	354	273	383
	Median	148	91	57	83	256	198	88	181	925	720	375	686
	Q3	347	159	96	162	384	359	132	290	1668	1096	518	1186

Notes: 1. The author has calculated the above values from the raw data in the original source.
2. * Not all 'Muslims' are Moors in Sri Lanka. There are small communities of Malays and Borahs who belong to the Islamic faith.
3. # Includes Burghers, Malays, and other 'micro' minorities.

Source: Central Bank of Ceylon, *Consumer Finance and Socio Economic Survey, 1963, 1973, 1982/83*, Part II.

lower level. In the middle level both communities had experienced similar increases. But at the higher level the Sinhalese had done better. During the same two periods consumer prices increased by 52% and 139% respectively (Annual Reports, Central Bank of Ceylon). Even if an allowance is made for the underestimation of inflation in this index, the figures suggest that the real incomes of all three groups increased by some margin during the period 1963-81. In sum, this analysis does not reveal any sharp disparities in incomes with respect to level and trend that are unfavorable to the Sri Lankan Tamils vis-a-vis the Sinhalese,

TABLE 8.4

Percentage Changes (Increase) in Nominal Monthly Incomes of Income Receivers, 1963-73 and 1973-81/82

	1963-73			1973-81/82		
	Q1	Median	Q2	Q1	Median	Q2
Kandyan Sinhalese	185	158	102	230	184	320
Low Country Sinhalese	124	113	42	272	271	282
Sri Lankan Tamils	96	94	71	323	274	260

Source: Table 8.3.

The other two minority groups, the Muslims and the Indian Tamils occupy the two extreme ends of the income scale (Table 8.3). As a group the Muslims have enjoyed an income level higher than the other communities. This is associated with the relative concentration of their population in urban areas where, on average, incomes are higher than in the rural and estate areas.[4]

Indian Tamils have remained at the bottom of the income ladder throughout the period under review. In fact their relative position worsened between 1963-73 when their median income dropped from 71.6% of the all-island level to 50.1%, but improved slightly between 1973- 81/2 when the ratio improved to 54.8%. These figures suggest that the Indian Tamil community remained unintegrated to the overall economy in terms of income earning opportunities, a factor associated with their overwhelming reliance on unskilled and semi-skilled work in the plantation economy. However, one important caveat must be noted. Compared to those living elsewhere people living on estates have always had more income earners per family. Nearly 79% of the females above the age of fourteen living on the estates are in the labor force whereas in the rest of the country it is only about 25%[5] (Central Bank of Ceylon, 1984) and children on estates also have traditionally worked. Therefore, the crude activity rate on the estates is also about 50 to 60% more than elsewhere. Thus, in 1963 there was little difference between the average family income on the estates and that of the rural sector. This parity persisted in 1973. After the mid-1970s a gap has opened up. By the early 1980s estate family income was around 70-75% of rural family income. However, the 1984 rate increases mentioned earlier and the guarantee of twenty-six days of work per month to all estate workers have probably helped to close this gap.

EMPLOYMENT

Data on unemployment by community is provided in Table 8.5. In every year covered (1953-81) the Sri Lankan Tamils have had a lower unemployment rate than either of the Sinhalese groups. Moreover, with the exception of 1953 the Indian Tamils also had lower unemployment rates than the Sinhalese.

However, this is one area where aggregates mask important details. First, the higher unemployment rates of all groups other than the Indian Tamils may partly reflect an underestimate of the actual number productively employed. Among the "educated" unemployed-of which the relative numbers are very much smaller in the Indian Tamil community-it is believed that there is a tendency to claim to be unemployed unless occupying a job that

TABLE 8.5
Unemployment as a Percentage of the Labor Force in the Community, 1953-1981/2

	1953	1963	1973	1978/79	1981/82
Kandyan Sinhalese	15.6	12.7	23.0	13.9	11.3
Low-Country Sinhalese	18.9	17.5	30.0	18.5	14.6
Sri Lankan Tamils	8.4	11.6	17.7	10.9	6.7
Indian Tamils	17.8	6.7	12.3	5.6	4.9
Moors	15.9*	14.9	21.3	13.8	10.4
All ethnic groups#	16.6	13.8	24.0	14.8	11.7

*includes the Malays
#Includes other small ethnic groups not shown here
Source: Central Bank of Ceylon, *Surveys of Ceylon's Consumer Finances* (year as shown)

fits their own idea of appropriate employment. This usually means employment in the formal sector. Second, if there is ethnic discrimination in formal employment the discriminated groups might prefer more self-employment. This may well result in lower unemployment rates among the discriminated groups. However, underemployment may be higher among the self-employed. Third, the repatriation of almost 350,000 Indian Tamils after 1967 would have contributed to the reduction in their unemployment rate after 1973. It is arguable that emigration of young men from the Sri Lankan Tamil community would also have had a similar impact on the 1981/82 figure but no reliable data exist to verify such an assertation.

However, the real dispute between the Sinhalese and Tamil communities relates to employment in the state sector. Here the evidence substantiates neither of the extreme positions often taken by the protagonists. For example, in 1980 Tamils (Sri

Lankan plus Indian) accounted for 24,000 (10%) out of a total of 229,000 state corporation employees (excluding state plantation workers) and 43,000 (12%) of a total of 368,000 central and local government employees. In 1985 the share of the Tamils remained practically unchanged at 10% in the corporation sector. In central and local government employment the Tamil share dropped to 10% by 1985 (Department of Census and Statistics, 1986). Very few of the Tamils here belong to the Indian Tamil community. For example in 1985 only 1.5% of the 40,846 Tamil employees in central and local government were Indian Tamils. In the corporation sector 11.7% of the 34,285 Tamil employees were of Indian origin. Thus the share of employment claimed by the Sri Lankan Tamils roughly approximates their proportion in the general population. Therefore, the popular Sinhalese perception that Sri Lankan Tamils dominate state employment is not supported by the facts. Indeed Wriggins (1960) using the 1951 Census of Government and Local Government Employees estimated that in 1951 Tamils probably accounted for about 22% of the total. Thus it is not correct to assert that the Tamils dominated overall employment in the state sector. However, it is true that they did account for a relatively large share of certain high-status jobs. For example in 1948 Tamils accounted for 40% of the irrigation engineers, 32% of government doctors and 47% of government accountants (Samarasinghe, 1984). Even in 1980 they had 29% of the administrative, professional and technical cadre in central government and 18% of equivalent positions in the state corporations. (Department of Census and Statistics, 1982). However, it is also important to appreciate the factors and processes that lay behind these figures. The privileged position of Jaffna with respect to secondary education facilities was one (de Silva 1984). The relative dearth of employment avenues in the Jaffna peninsula in agriculture and industry was another. Thus, it is a fact that people in Jaffna, especially those of the lower-and upper-middle class, looked to government service for employment. It is this situation which largely made Jaffna a major out-migration district after 1946 (Samarasinghe, 1973).

The other important point is that over the last three decades the share of the Tamils in state employment dropped by about half from 22% in 1951 to about 12% by 1980 (Department of Census and Statistics, 1982). This in itself is not evidence of discrimination. With the expansion of educational facilities for the Sinhalese equipping them to compete more effectively for these jobs, and given the unemployment situation among the Sinhalese, such a change becomes somewhat inevitable.[6]

However, the dispute is not so much about the total relative number in service as much as about new recruitment. Here too the argument is complex. In certain categories (teacher, stenographer, etc.) language proficiency is a key factor and the recruitment has to more of less conform to the linguistic population ratios. In other categories too, given the right of Sinhalese-speaking and Tamil-speaking people to transact business with the state in one's own mother tongue, the same argument holds to a greater or lesser degree. Nonetheless, there is evidence to suggest that recent recruitment to the state sector has had bias against Tamils. For example, from 1978 to 1981 only 279 (5.4%) of the 4870 clerks recruited by the central government were Tamils and from 1977 to 1979 out of 22,399 school teachers recruited only 6.1% were Tamils (Samarasinghe, 1984). In more recent times, given the peculiar circumstances, no Tamils have joined the armed forces. However, the instrument of discrimination, if such a thing exists, was not so much the language policy which is often cited as the culprit. All public service entrance examinations are conducted in Sinhala as well as Tamil. Although Tamil entrants may eventually be required to gain proficiency in the Sinhala language, there is no evidence to suggest that this has been a major barrier. It is the politicization of the recruitment process that has been mainly responsible for any discrimination that may exist. Here one must hasten to add that even those Sinhalese who are not in favor with the party in power, whichever that may be, suffer a similar fate.

LAND DISTRIBUTION

State land grants made to small farmers have also been a prominent issue of dispute between the Sinhalese and the Sri Lankan Tamils. The Tamils have alleged that the government has discriminated against them in granting such land. According to figures compiled by Peiris, the Sinhalese represent 76% of the families settled outside of the Mahaweli and Uda Walawe schemes and 81% if the Uda Walawe scheme in included (Peiris, 1985). This figure is higher than the proportion of Sinhalese in the population. However, Peiris also noted that these figures must be qualified with several observations. First, the Sinhalese have traditionally accounted for a larger proportion of the small farmers in the country who therefore, *ceteris paribus*, benefited more from land grants made to landless villagers. Second, the Indian Tamils have been largely by-passed in land grants because a large percentage of them were not Sri Lankan citizens until recently and non-citizens were not entitled to land grants. Thus the other communities have had the opportunity to acquire shares that exceeded their respective population percentages. Third, when youth settlement schemes are included the Sinhalese share falls to 78% of the total.

In the Accelerated Mahaweli Development Scheme, 39,622 settlers had been given land through June, 1985 (Department of Information 1986). Of this number 38,208 (96% were Sinhalese, 364 (0.9%) Tamils and 1,050 (3%) Muslims. Of the total number settled, 8,684 (22%) were those displaced by the construction of dams in the upper reaches of the Mahaweli outside the settlement area. Another 21,754 (55%) were "resettlers" selected from within the project area. The balance, 9,184 (23%) were migrants from outside the project area. The Mahaweli settlement program has been criticized for this apparent ethnic bias towards the Sinhalese.[7] While the figures strongly support such an argument the following points must also be noted. First, the vast majority of the 8,684 persons displaced by the headworks were Sinhalese. Second, systems B,C, and H of the Mahaweli where the settlements have already been developed are predominantly traditional Sinhalese areas. Third, as of July 1985, 45,766 allotments were yet to be made. Of this a large percentage falls within the Batticoloa District which is predominantly Tamil. The government anticipates allocating Tamil settlers their due share of Mahaweli land from this area based on national ethnic ratios (Department of Information, 1986).

The alienation of state land is one issue on which there is some agreement now between the Sri Lankan government and some Tamil groups. The formula agreed upon allows alienation in "national" land development schemes to take place according to national ethnic ratios. Land in "local" schemes will be given entirely to local residents. The formula also permits an ethnic group to refuse their quota in an area where they may feel uncomfortable, say, because of their minority status and get that quota reallocated from a more desirable area (Department of Information, 1986).

WELFARE

The standard indicators of social welfare in Sri Lanka reveal two important disparities in welfare levels. First, and most importantly, the Indian Tamil estate workers as a community are more backward and deprived than the others. For example, according to the Central Bank *Consumer Finance Surveys 1981/82* the illiteracy rate among the Indian Tamils was estimated to be 45% compared to 23% for other communities. However, according to the same source illiteracy on the estates declined by about 16% between 1953-73 and by another 14% between 1973-81. It is also generally acknowledged that the district of Nuwara Eliya records a maternal death rate and an infant mortality rate well above the respective national average because of the poor health and living conditions among the estate Tamil population. Second, in so far as general welfare indices such as literacy and infant mortality rates are concerned there is no evidence to suggest that the Sri Lankan Tamils are at a relative disadvantage.

GROUP PERCEPTIONS, ANXIETIES AND ETHNIC VIOLENCE

The above analysis suggests that at least with respect to some basic economic issues there is more myth than reality in the rhetoric and propaganda that guides the behavior of both the Sinhalese as well as the Tamils in the present conflict. In brief, the perception held by many Sinhalese that the Sri Lankan Tamils are an economically privileged minority is not borne out by the available evidence. The privileged position that they undoubtedly enjoyed in some limited areas of national economic life, most notably in government employment, has all but disappeared. By the same token, the Sri Lankan Tamil perception that they are an economically underprivileged minority is also not borne out by the evidence. Undoubtedly, they have lost some advantages in university education and professional and govenment employment that they enjoyed two or three decades ago but such changes have generally been the results of complex demographic, economic and socio-political changes that should be understood in proper perspective. Nevertheless it has to be conceded that Tamil behavior and Tamil responses to these changes have been driven by what Horowitz (1985) calls "group anxieties" and "mass psychology" of the fear of domination of the minority by the majority. The beginnings of this element of ethnic distrust can be traced back to the mid-1920s well before any of the economic issues discussed here appeared on the ethnic agenda. However, certain post-Independence economic policies only served to aggravate this mutual distrust and more particularly encourage the feeling among the Tamils of fear of domination by the majority. For example, as Peiris (1985) and de Silva (1986) show the Tamil claim to the Eastern Province as an exclusive Tamil "homeland" is a very weak one. Nevertheless, it is also true that the settlement of Sinhalese that changed the ethnic composition of the population in the area has weakened Tamil political strength in terms of their ability to elect MPs to parliament. In a country where voting is influenced by ethnic considerations this is a genuine fear that must be taken into account in land settlement policy. Similarly, the decline in the recruitment of Tamils for government jobs and the sharp decline of Tamil representation in certain key areas such as the military has given rise to frustration among Tamils that they were gradually losing or have already lost their fair share in these. Even with respect to income levels Tamils may entertain the fear that parity may give way to a second rank position.

Some observers (Gunasinghe, 1984) have expressed the view that ethnic perceptions and anxieties were aggravated by certain economic changes caused by President Jayewardene's liberal economic program initiated in 1978. This interpretation of events attributes the July 1983 ethnic violence to economic motivations. The argument is normally presented in terms of two social classes. One class, Sinhalese businessmen, who, it is suggested, enjoyed political patronage to secure business licenses and other privileges under the pre-1978, controlled economy, had to face competition from Tamil rivals under the new open economic system. Thus, it is asserted that the former instigated and at times even led and participated in mob violence against Tamil businesses to eliminate competition. The other class identified are the urban and semi-urban poor who, it is argued, have become poorer since 1978 as a result of inflation and a reduction in food and other consumer subsidies. These people, it is suggested, participated in acts of violence aganist Tamils to give vent to their class anger and frustration against the privileged class (both Sinhalese and Tamil).

As regards the Sinhalese business community, it is correct that certain acts of violence in the towns in July 1983 involved the participation of some Sinhalese businessmen and they may well have been motivated by considerations of business rivalry. However, there is no conclusive proof that economic liberalization resulted in a significant change in ethnic balance in business in favor of the minorities, especially the Tamils. Selective evidence can be marshalled to support such an argument. However, systematic and general studies are necessary before one can arrive at a firm conclusion. One such study by Gunawarena and Nelson (1986) of the business community in Kandy Town - Sri Lanka's second largest city and one where Tamil businessmen were attacked in July 1983 - shows that the Sinhalese strengthened their relative position in business after 1977.

Second, the assertion that the urban and semi-urban poor have been further impoverished as a result of the open economy is a debatable point. However, even if it were true, that does not necessarily mean that they were engaged in displaced class welfare. As is normally the case, the motives for mob violence are complex but would include a combination of several factors including resentment against relative deprivation, the desire to loot, the urge for violence for its own sake, the emotional need to do "something" in revenge for terrorist violence against the Sinhalese, and the attempt to embarrass the government by creating an unstable situation.

Third, July 1983 was not the first occasion when ethnic violence was seen in urban Sri Lanka. It occurred in 1977 before economic liberalization. Therefore, one must be cautious in assessing the impact of the open economy on ethnic relations and ethnic violence.

IMPACT ON DEVELOPMENT

The impact of the ethnic conflict on Sri Lanka's development effort can be analyzed in terms of short-term and medium to long-term perspectives. The first point to note is that despite the violence the economy has sustained an annual real growth rate of about 5% since 1982. However, it must also be noted that the growth rate declined in 1986 (4.3%) and 1987 (3%). The major short-term cost is the sharp increase in government spending on the military. Among Third World countries Sri Lanka was noted, especially before 1971, for its comparatively low military budget. For example in fiscal 1969-70 it was only US $14 million (0.8% of GNP and US $1.13 per capita). The armed youth insurrection of 1971 which caught the government militarily unprepared led to an increase in such spending which in 1978 totalled US $ 40 million (1.5% of GNP and US $2.81 per capita). Military spending escalated very rapidly following the intensification of separatist fighting in the north after 1982. In 1985 government military spending totalled US $220 million (3.6% of GNP or US $ 14.10

per capita and by 1987 reached an estimated US $525 million (8.3 % of GNP or US $33 per capita).[8] The implied diversion of resources for military spending can be gauged by the fact that in 1969-70 such spending amounted to 12% of total government spending on education and health whereas in 1986 it amounted to 106%. In fact, the actual expenditure on security-related activity is even higher than these figures indicate because almost every public and private establishment spends considerable sums on security.

There are other important short-term direct budgetary costs to the government. One is the money that it spends on refugees affected by ethnic rioting such as the one in July 1983 and by the fighting in the north and east. It is officially estimated that at its peak there were 100,00 refugees, almost all Tamils, who were displaced by the July riots and living in camps. As of the end of 1986 there were about 100,000 refugees belonging to all communities who had been displaced by the fighting. For the most part the government has to foot the bill of these camps and the cost has been estimated at Rs. 700 per family at 1986 prices. The Ministry of Rehabilitation which is only one among several government agencies involved in refugee work, reported that between August 1983 and September 1985 it had spent Rs. 131 million on refugees. During the same period the Ministry had also paid out Rs. 48 million as compensation to the victims of the July riots and loaned Rs. 81 million on easy terms to those who had to repair or reconstruct buildings demaged by those events.

Another short-term budgetary cost to the government is the loss of public property destroyed by acts of terrorism. It is difficult to accurately estimate such costs but reports suggest that it must be at least several hundred million rupees. For example, the government-owned railway which was attacked by separatists as many as 74 times between January and November 1985 had by then lost Rs. 90 million worth of property. In May 1986 it lost an entire passenger train worth Rs. 100 million when it was set on fire in Jaffna. Similarly, the state-owned airline Air Lanka lost two aircraft to terrorist bombing.

Then there are indirect or hidden budgetary costs of the conflict. One is the administrative cost of managing the conflict. This ranges from administrative effort at the district level to the efforts expended at the highest levels of government. Another hidden cost is the loss of tax revenue from economic activities such as tourism, transport services and so forth which have been adversely affected by the conflict.

The loss of output due to the present conflict is most evident in the tourist industry which in 1986 had only 230,000 visitors from abroad against 404,230 in 1983, a drop of 43%. This has cost an estimated 30,000 jobs in the industry. Official sources estimate that the disturbances reduced the 1984-85 national rice output by 150,000 metric tons, which is about 8% of the total. The north and the east are major fish producing areas in Sri Lanka and again mainly due to the troubles the national fish catch dropped from 221,000 metric tons in 1983 to 168,000 metric tons in 1985.

The adverse short-term effect of the conflict on business is partly due to the damage caused by violence. For instance, the July 1983 riots caused at least US $100 million worth of damage to private industry and left 22,000 people unemployed. Regular reports are received from the north of private businesses being destroyed or disrupted by acts of terrorism. The conflict also increases operational costs and reduces profits. For example, a spate of bank robberies in the north and east have cost the two state-owned commercial banks Rs. 500 million. They also report that largely to meet this threat they spend on security a combined sum of Rs. 200 million annually which is close to half of their combined annual pre-tax profits in recent years.

The medium to long-term economic impact of the conflict has to be assessed in terms of the liberal economic strategy of the Jayewardene administration that relies heavily on private investment and foreign aid. First, the present conflict has damaged the confidence of private investors, both local and foreign. A recent survey among businessmen in Kandy revealed that the Tamil businessmen in particular were reluctant to make new investments (Gunawardena and Nelson, 1986). Private foreign capital inflows which stood at Rs. 31 million in 1978 increased to Rs. 5370 million in 1982 but dropped back to Rs. 750 million in 1984 and recovered partially to Rs. 1400 million in 1985.

Second, the conflict could have had an adverse effect on foreign aid flows. In 1985, for example, Sri Lanka received US $480 million in aid from the Western aid consortium. Before the Indo-Lanka peace accord was signed in July 1987 a major campaign was mounted by the Tamil separatist groups to persuade western donors to suspend assistance to Sri Lanka as a means of pressuring the government. However, for a variety of reasons this effort did not yield any appreciable results. One probable reason is the sympathy that many western governments have had for the right-of-center Jayewardene government. Another was the reluctance of these governments to be seen supporting a separatist movement that resorts to terrorism.

Third, the reduction in the level of economic activity has again resulted in a rising level of unemployment. The unemployment rate which declined by half to 12% between 1977 and 1982 is estimated to have risen to 17% (1.3 million) by the end of 1987 (Korale, 1988). Many believe that the current youth unrest and southern terrorism is partly explained by the frustration among the unemployed youth.

The adverse economic consequences of the conflict cannot but make the task of achieving economic equity that much more difficult. First, this will be so because in general, given the deceleration in economic growth, the competition will be greater for the limited resources and jobs and that competition can easily run along ethnic lines. Second, the government will not be able to roll back military spending to the pre-conflict level. The commitment made to men and material in the last few years cannot be withdrawn quickly. Moreover, given the terror tactics used by the Tamil separatists, the Sinhalese believe that they have to be prepared for any future military eventuality. Thus resources that would otherwise have been available for development will be absorbed by the military. Third, the devastation caused to the north and east by the war will take a long time to repair even if peace is fully restored. In this respect the rehabilitation of the physical assets may be a comparatively easy task. Far more difficult will be the rehabilitation of the people, especially the youth, many of whom have lost several years of schooling and therefore are less able to compete in the job market.

ECONOMIC DIMENSION OF THE SOLUTION

On the positive side the current conflict may result in the establishment of political institutions, administrative mechanisms and practices in resource allocation that promote ethnic economic equity.

First, the devolution of power to the regions which is now considered to be an indispensable part of any solution will have major economic implications. The questions that have to be answered include the sharing of tax revenue between the center and regions and the division of responsibility between the two with respect to land, social and economic infrastructure. Assuming that these problems are resolved, devolution may help to redress geographical economic imbalances (Morrison and Waxler 1986) and promote more ethnic equity provided the center is left with sufficient powers to mobilize resources from the more prosperous areas to be channelled to the less prosperous.

Second, ethnic quotas in disputed areas such as state land distribution and government jobs are likely to be a part of the solution. As a short-term measure it is attractive because of its apparent precision and simplicity. However, as the experience of other countries demonstrates (Puthcheary 1984) a quota system also has serious shortcomings. It accepts the principle that population ratios are a valid basis for sharing opportunities irrespective of individual needs and talents, a notion that can be questioned on grounds of individual freedom and economic efficiency. It also encourages division of society along ethnic lines and sometimes, by encouraging new groups to demand their own quotas, promotes social fragmentation. There is also evidence (Puthcheary 1984) to suggest that quotas generally favor privileged individuals within groups but often fail to help the genuinely underprivileged. It is also noticed that quotas, once introduced, get entrenched and are hard to remove even if they have outlived their usefulness.

Third, in the final analysis the more important economic requirement for ethnic peace is rapid economic growth which alone can ensure that the economy will be capable of meeting the growing demands made on it by everybody in society.

Fourth, the post-1977 experience has shown that rapid economic growth is a necessary but not sufficient condition to promote ethnic economic equity and ethnic harmony. Thus, to ensure lasting ethnic peace it is not only necessary to have a rapidly growing economic pie but also to devise a set of institutions and rules that will ensure its equitable distribution.

NOTES

1. Department of Census and Statistics, *Sri Lanka Census of Agriculture 1982 - Small Holding Sector*, Colombo 1984.
2. Over 1965-85 Malaysia's GNP per capita in real terms grew at an average annual rate of 4.4% and that of Sri Lanka by 2.9% (World Bank, 1987).
3. As shown by Morris and McAlpine (1982), Sri Lanka's PQLI, which is considered to be a reasonable indicator of mass welfare, increased from 42 in 1946 to 79 in 1971 which implied an annual Disparity Reduction Rate (DRR or improvement rate in PQLI) of 3.0% over 1953-71. However, even more striking is the fact that by the early 1970s Sri Lanka had a PQLI of 82 which was the highest score in the lower income (per capita income less than US $300) country group (the group weighted average PQLI was only 40). Indeed Sri Lanka's PQLI was higher than the weighted average of 67 for the upper middle-income countries (per capita GNP US $700-1999) and was just two points below the mean (84) and 8 points below the weighted average for the high-income (per capita GNP US $2000 and over) countries.
4. This does not mean that there are no "poor" Muslims. There are sharp income disparities within the community and, broadly speaking, the Eastern Province Muslims (30.1% of the total Muslim

population) who are primarily either small farmers or agricultural laborers have comparatively low incomes (Samarsinghe and Davood, 1985).

5. The figure of 25% may be an underestimate because in the rural sector women often are unpaid family workers who are not counted as workers in either labor force surveys or the census.
6. For example, in April 1983 in an open competitive examination among 1760 graduates largely in the social sciences for recruitment as bank executives none of the Tamil candidates (165) made it to the final 100 to qualify for an interview. The examination was conducted in Sinhala, Tamil and English.
7. The Candian Government suspended aid to the Mahaweli Project for this reason (Source: Talk at the International Centre of Ethnic Studies, Kandy in July 1987 by Professor Alan Anderson of Saskatchewan University and Advisor to the Canadian Federal Government on Immigration).
8. In contrast India spent US $8 per capita and Pakistan US $24 per capita (World Bank, 1987).

REFERENCES

Apter, David E. 1971. *Ghana in Transition.* Princeton: Princeton University Press.

Bonacich, Edna. 1972. A Theory of Ethnic Antagonism: The Split Labor Market, *American Sociological Review* 37: 547-559.

Central Bank of Ceylon. 1984. *Report on Consumer Finances and Socio Economic Survey 1981/82 Sri Lanka - Part I.* Colombo: Central Bank of Ceylon.

de Silva, Chandra Richard. 1984. Sinhala-Tamil Relations and Education in Sri Lanka: The University Admission Issue - The First Phase, 1971-7 in *Ethnic Conflict in Five African and Asian States*, eds. Robert B. Goldman and A. Jeyaratnam. London: Frances Pinter.

de Silva, K.M. 1986. *The "Traditional Homelands" of the Tamils of Sri Lanka: A Historical Appraisal.* Kandy: International Centre for Ethnic Studies.

Deutsch, Karl. 1961. Social Mobilization and Political Development. *American Political Science Review* 55: 493-514.

Gunasinghe, Newton. 1984. The Open Economy and its Impact on Ethnic Relations in Sri Lanka. *Lanka Guardian* 6, 17: 6-8+15 and 6, 18:7+11.

Gunawardena, R.S. and Nelson, M.D. 1987. *Trade Activities in Kandy with Special Reference to Aspects of Ethnic Participation*. Kandy: International Center for Ethnic Research.

Horowitz, Robert. 1985. *Ethnic Groups in Conflict*. Berkeley: University of California Press.

Jacobs, Jane. 1980. *The Question of Separatism - Quebec and the Struggle over Sovereignty*. New York: Random House.

Korale, R.B.M. 1988. *A Statistical Overview of Employment and Unemployment Trends*. Colombo: Ministry of Finance and Planning.

Lewis, Arthur. 1985. *Racial Conflict and Economic Development*. Cambridge: Harvard University Press.

Moore, M. 1985. *The State and Peasant Politics in Sri Lanka*. Cambridge: Cambridge University Press.

Morris, M.D. and McAlpine, M.B. 1982. *Measuring the Conditions of India's Poor*. New Delhi: Promilla.

Morrison, Barrie and Waxler, Nancy E. 1986. Three Patterns of Basic Needs Distribution within Sri Lanka: 1971-73. *World Development* 14: 97-114.

Peiris, G.H. 1985. *An Appraisal of the Concept of a Traditional Tamil Homeland in Sri Lanka*. Kandy: International Centre for Ethnic Studies.

Prabhakar, M.S. 1971. The 'Bongal' Bogey. *Economic and Political Weekly*, October 21: 2140-2142.

Puthcheary, Mavis. 1984. Public Policies Relating to Business and Land and Their Impact on Ethnic Relations in Peninsular Malaysia in *From Independence to Statehood*, eds. Robert B. Goldman and A. Jeyaratnam Wilson. London: France Pinter.

Pye, Lucian W. 1966. *Aspects of Political Development*. Boston: Little Brown Press.

Samarasinghe, L.K.V. 1973. *Polarization of Colombo in the Economic Geography of Ceylon*. Ph. D. dissertation, Department of Geography, Cambridge University, England.

Samarasinghe, S.W.R. de A. 1984. Ethnic Representation in Central Government Employment and Sinhala-Tamil Relations in Sri Lanka, 1948-81 in *From Independence to Statehood* eds. Robert B. Goldman and A. Jeyaratnam Wilson. London: Frances Pintner.

Samarasinghe, S.W.R. de A. and Davood, Fazel. 1986. The Muslim Minority of Sri Lanka: A Business Community in Transition in

Muslims of Sri Lanka, ed. Shukri, M.A.M. Sri Lanka: Naleemia Institute.

Skinner, Elliot P. 1975. Competition within Ethnic Systems in Affrica in *Ethnicity and Resource Competition in Plural Societies*. ed. Despres, Leo A. The Hague: Monton.

Sri Lanka, Department of Census and Statistics. 1982. *Census of Public Sector and Corporation Sector Employment 1985*. Colombo: Department of Census and Statistics.

Sri Lanka, Department of Census and Statistics. 1986. *Census of Public Sector and Corporation Sector Employment 1980*. Colombo: Department of Census and Statistics.

Sri Lanka, Department of Information. 1986. *Draft Proposals*. Colombo: Government Press.

Stavenhagen, Rodolfo. 1981. Seven Falacies About Latin America in *Between Underdevelopment and Revolution*. New Delhi: Abhinav.

World Bank. 1987. *World Development Report*. New York: Oxford University Press.

Wriggins, W.H. 1960. *Ceylon: Dilemmas of a New Nation*. Princeton: Princeton University Press.

Chapter IX

DECENTRALIZATION AND REGIONALISM IN THE MANAGEMENT OF SRI LANKA'S ETHNIC CONFLICT

K.M. de Silva
University of Peradeniya, Sri Lanka

At the core of the current ethnic conflict in Sri Lanka, and of all the recent negotiations on a political settlement of that conflict, lies the issue of decentralization of administration and devolution of power.[1] The processes of centralization encouraged and deliberately pursued by the British in the nineteenth century have proved to be a formidably enduring legacy. The years 1815-18 during which the British established control over the whole island were a decisive turning point in the history of Sri Lanka. It was the first such attempt since the early and mid-fifteenth century when a Sri Lankan (Sinhalese) ruler last had effective control over the whole island for any considerable period of time. One had to go further back in history, to the 11th century in fact, for a period of political control from the national capital comparable to the period of British rule (1796-1947) in Sri Lanka in length of time and in the consistent pursuit of centripetalism as a desirable objective of state policy.

However, it was not until 1832 that a unified adminstrative system for the whole island was set up, eliminating the existing regional and subregional administrative divisions and replacing them with a new system, dividing the island into five zones of administration in the form of provinces.[2] The avowed objective in all this was a political one: to hasten the break-up of the Kandyan kingdom - the last independent Sinhalese kingdom, and one which had successfully resisted western invaders since the mid-sixteenth century - and to weaken "national" feeling there by attaching its lowlying and littoral regions to parts of the maritime regions conquered by the British from the Dutch who were in control there. In all except one of the new provinces the administrative capital was located on the coast.

When changes in these boundaries came in the course of time, and four such changes were made between 1845 and 1889 with the demarcation of the North-Western, North-Central, Uva and Sabaragamuva provinces, they signified a belated recognition of some traditional regional boundaries. By 1889 there were nine provinces. [3] With only minor adjustments to their boundaries introduced largely for administrative convenience, this structure has survived to the present day. From the 1950s the district (a smaller administrative division) replaced the province as the largest unit of administration. Even so provinces survived, bereft of all administrative energy and purpose, a remnant of a British system that did not fade away. As we shall see, they received a new lease of life in 1987-88.

In the first half of the nineteenth century aspirations to centralization were thwarted by the peculiarities of the island's physical features and the inadequacies in the means of communication. As a result, provincial administrators and those at the district level in the more isolated parts of the country enjoyed a great degree of independence and enormous scope for individual initiative in administration. But Colombo's control over the provinces became far more effective by the last quarter of the nineteenth century because of rapid improvements in communications by road and sea, and through the introduction of the railway and the telegraph.

By the beginning of the twentieth century the island's administrative system was, if anything, over-centralized. Critics of the system, especially Sri Lankan politicians, sought changes that would make it more responsive to popular opinion. Decentralization in some form was regarded as essential for this purpose. Nevertheless there was no noticeable shift of emphasis in the administrative structure in response to these criticisms, this is to say no deliberate policy of decentralization even at the end of the 1920s when the Donoughmore Commissioners arrived in the island from London to examine the island's constitution and administrative system. In its path-breaking report on the island's affairs that Commission proposed an expansion and democratization of the island's local government institutions as a remedy for over-centralization, a recommendation that was entirely in keeping with the British experience and political tradition.

In the last two decades of British rule in the island the Donoughmore Commission's report became the point of departure for some attempts, ineffective though they proved to be, to give some formal shape to decentralization and democratization at the provincial or district level. During this period (1931-47) and the first years (1947-51) of the post-independence phase the most prominent political figure associated with these attempts was S.W.R.D. Bandaranaike as the Minister in charge of Local Government affairs before independence (1936-47) and as Cabinet Minister and aspirant to the Prime Ministership (1947-51). He was the principal advocate of a system of provincial councils (modeled on the British County Councils) as the apex of the island's modern local government system. Indeed, in 1940, the national legislature of this period - the State Council as it was called - gave its formal approval to the principle of establishing provincial councils. Nevertheless the legislation required for this purpose was never presented for the legislators' consideration; indeed it was never prepared.

Although interest in the scheme of provincial councils revived after independence, the consensus that had existed in the 1940s in regard to this had evaporated in the face of new and more urgent concerns, and in any case the first cabinet of post-independence Sri Lanka gave it very low priority. The establishment of these provincial councils inevitably called for a reduction of the powers of Ministries under the control of Bandaranaike's cabinet colleagues, none of whom showed much willingness to accept diminution of their own political and administrative authority. Besides, Bandaranaike was seen to have established a solid political base through the expansion and revitalization of local government institutions and the extension of this system through powerful regional councils was perceived as a calculated attempt to strengthen his position further. These provincial councils came to be viewed as institutions which could confer an overwhelming political advantage on him, as the Prime Minister's main political rival within the government, in the coming struggle for the succession.

More important, once the Federal Party emerged on the political scene in 1949 as an important "ethnic" political party and a vocal Tamil pressure group and made the establishment of a federal system the main plank of its political platform, decentralization, which up to then had been viewed as a matter of administrative efficiency and therefore non-controversial, became acutely controversial. This was partly, at least, because of the deliberate ambiguity in which the Federal Party's demands and objectives were couched: these objectives could be interpreted and were interpreted both by its supporters and critics as a claim for a separate Tamil state. Thus federalism was soon linked with the issue of separatism. Thereafter, proponents of any scheme of regional, provincial or district councils have confronted an almost impregnable barrier of suspicion. The inevitable weakening of the unified political structure bequeathed by the British, inherent in any scheme of devolution of power, was viewed as a positive encouragement to separatist sentiment among the Tamils. Even so the issue of decentralization of administration could not be ignored. In the first two decades after independence one sees a strengthening and expansion of local government institutions as a third tier of an administrative structure, in which the second tier, provincial and district councils, had yet to be constructed. Successive governments sought to fill that void by other devices: they began to encourage and stimulate local initiatives in the provincial and district units of the government's administrative structure, through a process of "deconcentration", that is, granting greater responsibility to local units of government departments whose headquarters were, with a single exception, in

Colombo. In 1955 a Commission of inquiry appointed by the government to report on decentralization of administration recommended that the provincial secretariats (*Kachcheries* as they were called from British times) should be reconstituted to form regional committees in which the majority of members should be democratically elected. The next step was to be the transformation of these secretariats into regional councils. But before the recommendations could be considered, much less implemented, a change of government occurred at the general elections of 1956 which brought Bandaranaike to power at the head of a center-left coalition.

DECENTRALIZATION AND DEVOLUTION OF POWER 1957 AND 1968, TWO ABORTIVE ATTEMPTS

The salience of decentralization as a divisive issue in Sri Lanka's contemporary politics begins with the landmark general election of 1956. For one thing Bandaranaike, one of the early proponents of decentralization, was now Prime Minister. He had advocated a form of federalism for Sri Lanka in 1926, based on the nine provinces then in existence; and later on, in the 1940s and early 1950s, provincial councils as the apex of the island's local government system. In retrospect it would appear that one of the few points of consistency in his political career has been this commitment to decentralization and provincial or regional autonomy. In 1956 he was at last able to take the initiative in introducing his provincial councils scheme. But he did so at a time when the Sinhalese, and his own supporters in particular, viewed any reduction of the authority of the central government as both unwarranted and inherently threatening to the island's territorial integrity.

After independence the main, if not the sole, demand for devolution of power through federalism or a regional councils scheme came from the Federal Party and once they emerged as the principal political party of the Tamils, after the general election of 1956, devolution of power to regional units of administration became one of the key issues in negotiations between themselves and successive Sri Lankan governments. Two attempts were made, one in 1957 and one in 1968, to reach an agreement on this; through a revival of a scheme of provincial councils in 1957; and through the establishment of councils at the district rather than provincial level in 1968. Both attempts failed. They provoked strong opposition from the Sinhalese within the mainstream political parties, as well as from pressure groups representing Sinhalese-Buddhist interests: all of them viewed the Tamils' demand for a federal state as nothing less than the thin end of the wedge of a separatist movement.

Bandaranaike's Regional Councils Bill of which a draft was published in mid-1957 was intended to be a gesture of conciliation to the Tamils after the change in language policy - for which he had campaigned since 1955 - had caused grievous harm to relations between the Sinhalese and the Tamils especially with the eruption of communal riots in mid and late 1956. Early in 1957 he began negotiations with the Federal Party for an accommodation on, if not settlement of, the main issues that separated the two parties as representatives of Sinhalese and Tamil interests respectively. An agreement was reached in July 1957 and, as one of the key elements in it, Bandaranaike sought to modify his Regional Councils Bill to accommodate the Federal Party's demands on devolution of power. His original proposal envisaged the establishment of provincial councils based on the existing provincial boundaries. Now, in response to the Federal Party's pressure and especially the importance it attached to the so-called "traditional homelands" of the Tamils encompassing but not restricted to the Northern and Eastern Provinces,[4] far-reaching changes were proposed. The Federal Party urged that while the Northern Province should remain a single administrative unit in the new structure envisaged by Bandaranaike, the Eastern Province should be divided into two or more "regional" areas each of which could be a distinct unit. The Northern Province had an overwhelming Tamil majority; the Eastern Province had a mixed population. If Bandaranaike's acceptance of the Federal Party's proposals could have been regarded as an acceptance of demographic realities, other features of this new scheme of devolution proved to be even more controversial and none more so than the concept of a "region" introduced for the first time to the national debate on devolution of power. The concept of a region lacked clarity because it was at once larger than a province and smaller than a province. Provision was to be made to permit two or more regions to amalgamate within a province but also beyond provincial boundaries. Again, subject to ratification by Parliament, a region could divide itself into two or presumably more regions and collaboration for specified purposes of common interest between two or more regions was to be permitted.

When the terms of the settlement were made public, they provoked vehement opposition chiefly, but not only, from the diehard language loyalists in Bandaranaike's own party. The latter were mainly concerned with the concessions made to the Tamils on language rights. The United National Party (UNP) looking for a means of staging a comeback after its demoralizing rout at the general election of 1956 was provided with an ideal opportunity to embarrass the Prime Minister on a sensitive issue. To critics and opponents of the proposed settlement, the amendments to the Regional Councils Bill conjured up visions of a calculated but surreptitious attempt to concede the demand for a federal state with menacing potential for eventual division of the country into two separate states. The Federal Party's political rhetoric, and in particular pronouncements by its leadership that their pact with Bandaranaike was the first step in their quest for a federal political system, in combination with Bandaranaike's known ambivalence on the question of a unitary political structure for Sri Lanka, seem to lend credence to these fears and forebodings, and accounted for the vigor and passion with which the pact was attacked.

The arguments used by the UNP against proposed amendments to the Regional Council Bill on this occasion have a vitally important contemporary significance in Sri Lanka because the UNP's principal spokesman on that occasion was none other than

President J.R. Jayewardene himself, then in the political wilderness having lost his parliamentary seat in 1956, perhaps the most notable and most distinguished victim of that electoral debacle. It was grimly ironical that in the period 1977-88 the same debate was revived in the course of negotiations between the government of President Jayewardene and representatives of Tamil opinion, a theme to which we shall return later in this survey.

In retrospect it would seem that Banaranaike's pact with the Federal Party was doomed from the moment its contents were revealed. Confronted with mounting opposition to it, the Prime Minister played for time but the pressures against it proved too strong for him to resist. Led by a group of bhikkhus (members of the Buddhist order) who staged a "sit-in" or *satyagraha* on the lawn of the Prime Minister's private residence in Colombo, the extremists in his own party compelled him to abrogate the pact. Once again the tensions generated by these pressures and counter-pressures erupted in race riots in May 1958. The Regional Councils Bill was abandoned in the wake of these communal disturbances along with the pact with which it came to be associated.

Despite its abrogation in 1958 the principal elements in Bandaranaike's abortive pact with the Federal Party and in particular his proposals for devolution of power have continued to be the point of departure in all future discussions on this latter theme. The first occasion was in 1965 when the UNP formed a coalition government in which the Federal Party was a component element. The basis for securing the support of the Federal Party was an agreement reached between it and the UNP in which a version of the Regional Councils outlined in the draft bill of 1957 formed a key feature.

Dudley Senanayake, the UNP Prime Minister of that period, was all too aware that Bandaranaike's Regional Councils had lost their political viability because of suspicions and fears about the Federal Party's real objectives and he sought to reassure potential critics by reducing the territorial limits of the unit of devolution to the district rather than the province; and, more important, by emphasizing the point that these District Councils (22 in all) would "function under the control and direction of the Central Government." Over the next three years he expanded on these themes hoping that he could thereby allay the fears of the Sinhalese about the potentially divisive effects of such Councils.

Opposition parties and other critics of the UNP government's proposed District Councils Bill proceeded to exploit the well-entrenched suspicion among the Sinhalese that devolution of authority through any scheme of decentralization of power involving the creation of popularly elected councils at a district or provincial level would inevitably pave the way for a full-fledged federal structure which in turn would be the precursor of a separation of the Tamil units of such a federation from the Sri Lanka polity. Nor were these suspicions and fears confined to the Sinhalese. Muslim opinion was firmly opposed to these councils. Indeed Muslim suspicion of schemes of devolution of authority has remained since the mid-1960s as one of the critically important aspects of the national debate on this theme.

The opposition to this new initiative in decentralization was unusual in its range: it brought together a formidable combination of the SLFP in its traditional alliance with the Sinhalese Buddhist pressure groups but linked now with the Marxist left and a significant section of Muslim opinion. (From the 1960s onwards to the present day the SLFP under Mrs. Bandaranaike has consistently opposed all schemes of devolution of power proposed by the UNP). This combination of hostile forces proved to be altogether too powerful for the government and the proposed District Councils scheme suffered a fate similar to that of its predecessor of 1957. It was withdrawn by the government in mid-1969 but on this occasion there was not even the publication of a bill in draft form.

The failure of these efforts at institutionalizing decentralization gave added impetus to resort to more informal methods of achieving the same ends. In the period 1965-70 the government undertook the implementation of a major agricultural program aimed at self-sufficiency in rice and subsidiary food crops. Under this program the Government Agent, the head of the bureaucracy at the district level, was appointed coordinator of the activities of all government departments involved in its implementation and was vested with powers for administration of funds and control of expenditure. Coordinating Committees were set up as the lowest rungs of an administrative structure which had as its apex a Cabinet Committee chaired by the Prime Minister himself. The visible results of the vigorous implementation of this agricultural program in the late 1960s-in the form of a phenomenal increase in rice production-tended to overshadow the significance of the innovations in administrative machinery which sustained it: a very effective mechanism for the delegation of authority through a clear chain of command from the center to the localities, and an unusually successful coordination of developmental activities at the district level and lower down at sub-divisional units.

During the early 1970s under Mrs. Sirimavo Bandaranaike's center-left coalition two innovative programs designed to decentralize responsibility for formulating and implementing district and village development plans and also for obtaining popular participation in the preparation and implementation of such plans were introduced. These programs were the Divisional Development Councils (DDC) and the Decentralized Budget (DCB). A third innovation, the District Political Authority (DPA), came later in 1973.

With the institution of District Political Authorities and introduction of the decentralized budgetary system the district was at last provided with its allocation of funds and the political head of the district was given the authority to decide on local priorities. The Divisional Council's organization was expected to serve as part of the planning process and in the implementation of programs. Nevertheless, the Divisional Development Councils failed in almost all their objectives: in planning, implementation and monitoring of programs, no less than ensuring genuine popular participation in such planning as they indulged in. Political considerations distorted the choice of projects and allocation of resources.

There were also some conflicts and gaps in communication between the Political Authority and the bureaucracy, and in particular the Government Agent, owing to the lack of a proper demarcation of functions and authority. This was rectified to a large extent by the system of District Ministers created after 1978 (and which lasted until the end of 1988).

DEVOLUTION OF POWER —DISTRICT DEVELOPMENT COUNCILS, 1979-88

The third phase in our brief survey begins with the general election of 1977, the second landmark election of post-independence Sri Lanka. All the prominent politicians who had been swept to power in the victories of the Bandaranaikes in 1956 lost their seats, with the exception of Mrs. Bandaranaike and her deputy. Every candidate of the Marxist left was defeated, many of them quite decisively.

In its election manifesto, the UNP had spelled out its policy in regard to the Tamils. There were three items: first, a reference to minority rights in the section on constitutional reforms; second, a reference to decentralization of administration down to the village level, to "make the people partners in the planning, organization and implementation of policy". There was reference also to the administrative machinery to be established for this purpose with District Development Councils headed by a District Minister at the apex and consisting of Members of Parliament of the District, elected heads of local bodies, and government officials; and third, a whole section of the manifesto was devoted to "Problems of the Tamil-Speaking People."

In its Statement of Policy at the first session of the new Parliament on 4 August, 1977, these pledges to the Tamils were renewed. But an outbreak of communal violence in August 1977 proved to be a setback to the implementation of this program. While the riots brought the problem of relations between the two main ethnic groups in the island to the attention of the politicians, the communal violence delayed the implementation of the initiatives planned by the government on the basis of its election manifesto and its Statement of Policy on 4 August, 1977.

It was only in the middle of 1979 that the government turned its attention to the problem of decentralization of administration which the Tamil leadership had long-regarded as an essential ingredient in any political settlement which they could support. On 10 August, 1979 the ten member Presidential Commission was appointed to report on decentralization of administration through the device of District Development Councils. There were hopes that the composition of the Commission would reflect the truly plural nature of Sri Lanka's political system but it was eventually narrowed down to a membership of ten persons of whom only two were directly representatives of party interests, the UNP and the Tamil United Liberation Front (TULF) the successor to the Federal Party as the main Tamil political party. The SLFP declined the government's request that it should nominate a member of serve on the Commission.

Perhaps the most notable feature of this Commission's work was the limited nature of its assignment. Its terms of reference limited it to filling in the details of a policy that had already been laid down and which stemmed from the UNP's election platform of 1977. It was expected that this Commission would complete its work within three months of its appointment and considering its terms of reference this was not as unrealistic as it may sound. But it was mid-February 1980 by the time its report was ready.

The core of its recommendations was contained in the seventh chapter of its report, a chapter entitled "District Ministers and Development Council." The two objectives of its scheme of Development Councils the Commission explained were:

> ...First, the decentralization of the administration by placing an Executive Minister, in each District, who is charged with the development of the District, and the co-ordination of central Government activity there. Secondly, the scheme has the objective of enabling the participation of the local people in the planning and implementation of the development

projects in each District through Development Councils.

"...In our View," the report continued:

> a Development Council composed as it would normally be by persons holding a variety of political opinions and drawn from a diversity of social groups within a district will be the collective voice of the District, and ensure that due heed is paid to the needs and aspirations of the local people in the planning and implementation of the local development projects. The District Minister system will be strengthened by this institution of a Development Council for it makes it possible to ensure popular participation in the development of each District.

The brevity of the Commission's recommendations on some of the crucially important features of these Councils and on the relationship of Council and District Minister reflected sharp differences of opinion within the Commission. These differences were distinctly "ethnic," with most Sinhalese members reluctant to endow the Councils with as much power as Tamil members wished these bodies to have, and above all there was the strong opposition of the majority of the Muslim members to the very principle of the creation of such Councils, an opposition which they outlined at great length in a dissent to the Commission's report. The burden of the Muslim's argument was that the concessions made to the Tamils in the 1978 constitution were generous enough on there own and were adequate to meet all their (i.e. the Tamils) reasonable demands. The report, in fact, turned out to be a majority report and not a consensus of the Commissioners' opinions. The TULF representative also presented a dissent arguing in favor of greater powers to these Councils.

These sharp divisions within the Commission delayed presentation of its report by several months. Once that report was presented the government moved swiftly to give flesh and blood to the skeletal recommendations of the Commission. In a remarkable reversal of normal practice where legislation is often less comprehensive and far-reaching in scope than recommendations of a Commission on which it is based, the *Development Councils Act* which Parliament approved on 21 August, 1980 went well beyond the recommendations of the Commission's report. It incorporated many of the principles in the TULF member's dissenting report. In fact, while the Commission was proceeding with its deliberations, the government by the last quarter of 1979 had prepared the outlines of legislation on these Councils in anticipation of the report and once the report was published this draft ordinance was used as the basis of the bill presented to Parliament. If this procedure seemed unusual, the fact is that the Commission's terms of reference limited it to filling out the details of a scheme whose outlines had already been decided upon between the government and the TULF whose leadership was consulted at every stage in the preparation of the *Development Councils Act*.

In retrospect it would appear that the swift passage of the bill through Parliament and the unanimous support it received within the UNP constituted a major political achievement. Twice before, once in 1957-58 and again in 1966-68, political initiatives for devolution of power had been abandoned in the face of extra-parliamentary agitation and internal bickering within the ranks of the ruling party. On this present occasion the political will to persist with this bill to its eventual enactment was altogether greater and - more important - the opposition was also altogether weaker and less organized. The SLFP opposed the bill but walked out of Parliament before the vote on the bill was taken. As for the left-wing opposition, in all its diversity, the commitment to devolution of power was much more thoroughgoing so far as one could judge from public pronouncements than anything proposed by the government.

These elected councils were established in 1981. In the initial stages the councils did very well in the areas that mattered: in Jaffna and the other Tamil regions. They appeared to have blunted the edges of the separatist agitation and, indeed, helped to give the restive Jaffna peninsula a brief period of peace. The council at Trincomalee, in the Eastern Province, one of the critical areas in the interaction betwen the island's main ethnic groups was a pronounced success. In other parts of the country there was a noticeable lack of enthusiasm for the councils but the abler chairmen and executive committees did convert these bodies into effective instruments of local level development. From the outset, however, there were complaints about the inadequacy of finances for the work the councils were expected to undertake. The other main complaint was that even where the money was available the councils lacked the power to embark on any important development projects on their own initiative. Needless to say most of the criticisms came from the TULF, especially from Jaffna and the Northern Province, where expectations about these councils were greatest and where naturally the sense of disappointment was also very great when the aspirations of those who agitated for them seemed far away from speedy fulfillment.

These were teething troubles of a new institutional framework, not unmistakable evidence that the councils were doomed to failure from the outset. While the TULF critics of the system had some support from others in the rest of the system - i.e., in the Sinhalese areas - in regard to inadequacy of funds for these councils, there was none at all in regard to pressure for expansion of the powers of the councils. Nevertheless, in the early part of 1983 a committee of senior officials was appointed by President Jayewardene to examine the working of this system and to determine what measures should be taken to make the councils more effective. The committee identified three "constraints that inhibited the proper implementation of the Development Councils scheme...." namely the delegation of power to the districts, inadequacies in the budgetary process and the development fund, and in the district administrative service.

The delegation of powers, duties and functions to District Ministers by Cabinet Ministers had taken over a year and was formally made only in late September 1982, but as late as May 1983 it was still ineffective at a practical level because district officials of line Ministers and departments had "not yet been informed as to the manner in which they should carry out their duties in respect of the delegated functions." These delays were compounded by legal and constitutional difficulties. Thus, although the District Ministers had "in turn delegated the functions which had been delegated to them by the Ministers, to the Executive Committee of the Development Councils... the Attorney-General [had] questioned the legality of this further delegation..."

Besides, the funds appurtenant to the functions delegated to the District Ministers had not been passed down to the district. Also, the Development Fund of the districts had not been provided with monies envisaged under Section 19 of the Act. As for the district administrative service, no schemes of recruitment of qualified personnel for the district service were yet ready.

Many of these delays were inherent in the introduction of a new institutional framework and its administrative structure. The fact that 1982 became, quite unexpectedly, an election year when the Presidential election due in 1983 was advanced by fourteen months or so also aggravated the problem: political and administrative energies were concentrated on the presidential election to the neglect of other issues. Thus, the delegation of power to District Ministers by Cabinet Ministers was made on 23 September, 1982, only a month before the Presidential election and the second phase, the delegation in turn of these powers by the District Ministers to Executive Committees of Development Councils took place only on 27 December, 1982, two months after the Presidential election. Besides, general budget cuts and other financial restraints imposed by the Treasury in 1982-83 to keep inflation in check also adversely affected the financial position of the new Councils. Nevertheless, the problems identified by the Committee were not insuperable ones and remedies for these, also identified by it, presented few difficulties in adoption and implementation.

The ethnic disturbances of July 1983 which erupted with unparalleled virulence and shook the country's political system to its foundations gave the TULF the opportunity to revive the debate on the devolution of power on an altogether more comprehensive basis; on the lines, in fact, of the abortive agreement of 1957-58 between the then government and the Federal Party. In the negotiations begun in the last quarter of 1983 and continued into and through 1984 between the Sri Lanka government and the TULF, with an Indian government emissary often acting as a mediator, the TULF formally withdrew their support for the District Development Councils arguing that these were inadequate in meeting the needs of a genuine devolution of power as they perceived it in the changed situation brought about by the riots of July 1983 and resserting their commitment to the concept of the "traditional homelands" of the Tamils. They argued instead for a system of Provincial Councils, on the lines of those proposed by Bandaranaike in 1957, with over-arching regional councils linking these Provincial Councils. Their main objective now as in 1957 was in the creation of a supraprovincial entity encompassing the Northern and Eastern Provinces, in which the Tamils would be a dominant if not overwhelming majority. This proposal had the support of the Indian government through its intermediary and President Jayewardene was persuaded to consider accepting it as part of a package of concessions to the Tamils. But there was no support for this from the Sri Lankan Cabinet and governing party. The government nevertheless placed it for discussion at an All-Party Conference at which the TULF itself was represented. There it attracted vigorous and trenchant criticism from practically every political group and organization, both mainstream and fringe. Among those most strongly opposed were the Muslims who saw little advantage - on the contrary, very great disadvantage - in an enlarged regional council linking the Northern and Eastern Provinces in which they would face a dominant Tamil majority. And, of course, Buddhist opinion, lay and *sangha* (the Buddhist order), represented at the Conference reiterated their traditional opposition to schemes of devolution of authority to regional units of administration. The *sangha* representatives did show some flexibility and realism when they came out, at last, in support of the existing system of District Development Councils, and even agreed to a widening of their powers and a strengthening of their financial resources. But they would not go beyond that. When a draft ordinance incorporating a system of revitalized district councils empowered to link together, where necessary, on a wider provincial basis was tabled for discussion at the All-Party Conference on 30 September, 1984, critics focussed their opposition on this latter feature and declined to support the draft bill. The TULF itself declared its opposition to it, as did the SLFP (which had refused to participate in the discussions of the conference); the one because it did not go far enough in the direction of autonomy, the other because it seemed to go too far in eroding the country's unitary structure.

Despite this setback, discussions continued within the All-Party Conference, and outside it, on the framework of a political settlement which would incorporate an effective system of decentralization of power. To accommodate the wishes of the TULF two draft bills were placed before the Conference in December 1984, one of which was a draft district and provincial councils bill. This too was rejected by the TULF and with that the government itself withdrew its support of the proposal, relieved no doubt to jettison a scheme which has had so little political support in the country and which, on the contrary, had such ominous potential for arousing fear and suspicion among the Sinhalese as well as the Muslim minority.

FROM DISTRICT COUNCILS TO PROVINCIAL ASSEMBLIES—1985 ONWARDS

The District Development Councils were doomed to obsolescence as a necessary consequence of the ethnic riots of 1983. It was not merely that the TULF used the opportunity to pitch its demands higher and to return to its traditional objective of provincial or regional assemblies (if not a federal structure) but also that Tamil separatist organizations, of whom the most prominent were the Liberation Tigers of Tamil Elam (LTTE), who had never shown much enthusiasm for the District Development Councils, now had much greater influence in the shaping of Tamil opinion. There was also a second factor, India's mediatory role (to which we shall presently return), its support of the Tamil cause in Sri Lanka and its consistent pressure for a more thoroughgoing scheme of decentralization and devolution of power than that envisaged in the District Development Councils' scheme.

The collapse of the All-Party Conference had led within a few months to more formal diplomatic negotiations between the governments of India and Sri Lanka. Indeed, one of the immediate consequences of the political turmoil that followed upon the riots of 1983 had been the application of diplomatic and political pressure on behalf of the Tamils of Sri Lanka by India. While the main source of this latter pressure was the state government of Tamilnadu, Prime Minister Indira Gandhi's government also made public expressions of support for the Tamil demands in Sri Lanka. With her assassination in October 1984 and the succession of her son Rajiv there was a more balanced approach to India's policies on the management of ethnic tensions in Sri Lanka but even he was unable to dispel suspicions that India relished its self-imposed role of the champion of the Tamils of Sri Lanka more than it did the role of honest broker in the mediation of the dispute. That perception was to change to some extent after July 1987.

Within a few months of the breakdown of the negotiations at the All-Party Conference, however, diplomatic negotiations between the governments of Sri Lanka and India began. These eventually led to a meeting between President Jayewardene and Prime Minister Rajiv Gandhi in June 1985. As a direct result of these talks a three month cessation of hostilities was established in Sri Lanka and for the first time discussions were held between an official Sri Lanka delegation and the leaders of Tamil separatist organizations. The TULF was also a participant but overshadowed by the other Tamil groups. These talks held in Thimpu, Bhutan in July and August 1985, with India playing the role of mediator, eventually and inevitably ended in deadlock. In an attempt to continue the negotiating process the Indian government persuaded the Sri Lankan government to extend the cessation of hostilities to October, pending further discussions between the Sri Lankan government and the Tamils' leadership conducted once more through the mediation of Indian officials.

The eventual result of discussions was the presentation by the Sri Lankan government in June 1986 of proposals for a radical restructuring of the Sri Lanka polity. The essential feature of the plan was a system of provincial councils, with many of the powers of the states in the Indian Union, but with the essential difference that the Sri Lankan provincial councils would operate within the framework of the country's constitutionally-entreched unitary system.

The TULF and some of the Tamil separatist groups continued to press for a regional unit encompassing the Northern and Eastern Provinces as a Tamil ethno-region, a political manifestation of the concept of the "traditional homelands" of the Tamils in Sri Lanka. But the government of Sri Lanka held out against a merger of these two provinces as did the SLFP and representatives of Sinhalese-Buddhist opinion as well as the Muslims, especially representatives of the Muslims resident in the Eastern Province. The critical stumbling block was the demographic profile of the Eastern Province where the Tamils were a minority of only 40% of the population. The LTTE, the main Tamil separatist group, would accept nothing short of a separate Tamil state.

In a continous effort to break this deadlock, Indian negotiators came up with a number of proposals, one of which was to break up the Eastern Province into three units with the constituent elements of the Tamil majority unit being linked to the Northern Province by a narrow land corridor. But this had no support, least of all among the Tamils. Next, Indian negotiators prevailed upon the Sri Lanka government to agree to the excision of the Sinhalese parliamentary electorate (Amparai) of the

Batticaloa District of the Eastern Province so that the Tamil component of the latter would reach a level of parity with other ethnic groups there. This proposal formed part of the 19 December, 1986 formula which the Indian government treated as the basis for further negotiations between the Sri Lanka government and the Tamils. The LTTE rejected this formula as totally unacceptable.

Under continued pressure from India and in the hope that some concession on this would provide a breakthrough to a political settlement of Sri Lanka's ethnic conflict, the Sri Lanka government agreed, as part of the Indo-Sri Lanka peace accord signed on 29 July, 1987, to permit a temporary joinder of the Northern and Eastern Provinces into one unit in a system of provincial councils. The people of the Eastern Province were promised that within a year of the joinder, or at any appropriate later date, a referendum would be held in the Eastern Province to determine whether they would wish to continue the association with the Northern Province or to return to the *status quo ante.*

The offer of a referendum did not make the merger more palatable, much less acceptable, to the Sinhalese and Muslims living in the Eastern Province. The widespread civil unrest that erupted against the Indo-Sri Lanka accord in many parts of the country - the most serious anti-government riots in the country for over 30 years, with the exception of the people's Liberation Front (JVP) insurrection of 1971-was, in part at least, a reaction against the decision to create a North Eastern Province by a merger of the two provinces. Despite this opposition the North Eastern Province was created in 1988 but the referendum scheduled to be held in 1989 to determine its fate has been postponed. Each announcement of a date for the referendum has been followed by another in which a fresh date was set.

Once the Provincial Councils Bill and the Thirteenth Amendment to the Constitution were approved by Parliament on 12 November, 1987, the moribund provincial structure bequeathed by the British got a fresh lease of life. When these provincial councils were established in 1988 the second tier of government proposed by Bandaranaike came into existence fifty years after he first mooted them in the national legislature in the late 1930s, but without the national consensus in support of them which existed then. Equally significant, the party he founded, led by his wife and son, has been in the forefront of opposition to their establishment.

RETROSPECT

Efforts on the part of the Sri Lankan government in the 1980s to extend the scope of creative political initiatives on the devolution of power, which had hitherto been limited by a lack of political will, still confronted a major constraint in the form of conflicting perceptions on the value of devolution of power as a political and administrative device. This is quite apart from the parallel but subsidiary debate on the politically acceptable or viable size of the unit of devolution, whether it should be district or provincial units. The pressures that emerge from these contentious issues stretch the limits of political action available to Sri Lankan politicians in power perilously close to the breaking point, where the alternatives that loom ahead are either electoral defeat for themselves,[5] or major outbursts of violent opposition such as those of late July and early August 1987.

The current debate on devolution of power in Sri Lanka, and the passions that discussions on regionalism and regional autonomy arouse, illustrate two vital themes. The first is the dilemma that confronts the political establishment in the recently independent nations of the Third World in conceding legitimacy to regional loyalties. The political establishment in these nations, as legaties of departing imperial powers, passionately protects this inheritance in the shape of the state bequeathed to them at the transfer of power, and regards centralized authority as an essential political and administrative instrument at their disposal. They often justify this by arguing that centralization is essential for the introduction and management of processes of social change designed to eliminate poverty. In that situation anything likely to encourage, if not lead to, communal or ethnic fragmentation is regarded with the utmost suspicion. More important, once the threat of separatism appears as an objective fact of political life the choice is between the tolerance of cultural traditions and ethnic identity falling well short of secession - in fact, permitting the full expression of such cultural traditions - and the suppression of secessionist demands by armed force, where necessary, if there are signs that secessionist aspirations are striving for fulfilment. Of this, India's treatment of the Sikh agitation for autonomy and Sri Lanka's responses to Tamil separatist activity provide excellent examples. However, regionalism divorced from separatism is recognized as having advantages, if not positive value, in generating political participation in decision-making at the grass-roots level, a principle immanent in the two abortive attempts at establishing Provincial and District level councils, in 1957 and 1968 respectively, and in the more productive but equally controversial exercises which led to the *District Development Councils Act of 1980* and the *Provincial Councils Act of 1987*.

Secondly, and more specific to Sri Lanka, there is the close proximity of the Jaffna region in the north of Sri Lanka to Tamilnadu in Southern India, a great reservoir of Tamil separatist sentiments in India, which has encouraged, nurtured and protected Tamil separatist groups from Sri Lanka. Thus devolution of power to provincial councils is opposed because of fears that they could serve as a spur to separatist pressures rather than acting as an effective check on these in the north and east of the island. Large sections of the Sinhalese view the Tamils' pressure for devolution of power as the first step in an inevitable progression to separation of the Tamil majority areas of the country from the Sri Lankan polity. The fact is that the Sinhalese, although an overwhelming majority of the population of the island, nevertheless have a minority complex *vis-a-vis* the Tamils. They feel threatened by the more than fifty million Tamil-speaking people in present day Tamilnadu in Southern India. For although the Sinhalese outnumber the Tamils by more than five to one within

Sri Lanka, they in turn are outnumbered nearly six to one by the Tamil-speaking people of South Asia. The burden of history contributes greatly to the disquiet and apprehensiveness the Sinhalese feel about South India: the popular perception of events of centuries past and the abiding historical memory (with a recorded history stretching back over two thousand years) of South India as the single most powerful and persistent threat confronting Sri Lanka and the Sinhalese over the centuries.

In the early years of independence the Tamils of the north and east of the island had showed little inclination to identify themselves with the Tamils of Tamilnadu. Nevertheless the Sinhalese feared this possibility and the campaign for a federal structure for the island served to aggravate these fears. Those in the forefront of the Tamils' agitation for devolution of power have always been vague, deliberately or unconsciously, in the terminology used n their arguments and the distinction between provincial autonomy, states' rights in a federal union, and a separate state have been blurred by a fog of verbiage and obfuscation. The close links that were established in more recent times between Tamil political groups, ranging from the TULF to various separatist groups, with the government and opposition in the Southern Indian state of Tamilnadu have naturally aggravated the situation, and more so the establishment of training camps in Tamilnadu for terrorist groups and guerrillas who made forays into the northern and eastern coastal regions of Sri Lanka from these. The result is that decentralization which was, and should be, a purely Sri Lankan matter has taken on a cross-national dimension of which India's role as a mediator in the recent political negotiations between the Sri Lankan government and representatives of Tamil opinion is the most conspicuous feature.

Moreover, the capacity of devolution of authority to regional units, be they districts or provinces or something larger than provinces, to reduce ethnic conflict is more limited than enthusiastic advocates of it are willing to concede. The successful operation of the system of decentralization for Sri Lanka envisaged in the *District Development Councils Act of 1980,* and now in the *Provincial Council Act*, calls for political skills of a high order and also great patience. For one thing pressure for decentralization of administration is limited to the Tamils-with whom it is almost an obsession- and largely to the Tamils living in the north and east of the island where they are either a majority or form a substantial minority. There is no pressure - on the contrary strong opposition to it - from all other ethnic groups and all other parts of the island. Quite apart from the fears of the Sinhalese majority, there are the fears of the Muslim minority, especially those living in the Eastern Province, whose pent up hostility to the Tamils has erupted with fearful ferocity in outbreaks of communal violence, Muslim against Tamil, and *vice-versa*, in the period 1985 to 1991 and has also contributed to the rise of Islamic fundamentalism as a powerful factor in the politics of the province. In other words, devolution of power to units larger than a district or a province is perceived as threatening the smaller group - the Muslims -in areas in which a larger minority - the Tamils - would be likely to dominate the affairs of a large territorial unit, a province or a regional unit linking provinces. Thus, attempts at managing Sri Lanka's ethnic rivalries and tensions through district level or provincial level councils are always caught up in the jostling among the minorities themselves as they jockey for positions of advantage in the race for political and economic gains.

NOTES

1. There has been no precision in the definition of terms used in this debate either by politicians or academics. Thus "decentralization" and "devolution" are used as interchangeable terms. In this present paper a distinction is attempted between the two. Decentralization generally refers to efforts at giving greater autonomy to regional or district level units of government departments; and to the development of informal mechanisms for delegation of authority to administrative organizations at a regional or district level. Devolution of authority generally means the transfer of power to elected regional bodies, a genuine second tier of government between the central government and local government bodies. Many scholars in other

parts of the world do not see the need for this distinction and use the term decentralization to cover both meanings. See, for example, Smith B.C., *Decentralization: The Territorial Dimension of the State* (London, 1985).

2. There were, in all, between 32 to 35 such units in the period 1815 to 1832. These were reduced to five.
3. For discussion of this see, de Silva K.M., *A History of Sri Lanka* (Delhi, 1981), 315-326.
4. See de Silva K.M., The "*Traditional Homelands" of the Tamils of Sri Lanka: A Historical Appraisal* (Kandy, 1987, International Centre for Ethnic Studies, Occasional Papers, No.1).
5. The success of the UNP at the presidential election of December 1989 does not invalidate this argument. The devolution exercise of 1987-88 and the Indo-Sri Lanka accord of July 1987 were among the key issues in the election campaign, and their salience did contribute to reducing substantially the governments' margin of victory.

REFERENCES

de Silva, K.M. 1981. *A History of Sri Lanka.* Delhi: Oxford University Press.

de Silva, K.M. 1986. *Managing Ethnic Tensions in Multi-Ethnic Societies: Sri Lanka 1980-1985.* Lanham, Md: University Press of America.

de Silva, K.M. 1987. *The "Traditional Homelands" of the Tamils of Sri Lanka: A Historical Appraisal.* Kandy: International Centre for Ethnic Studies, Occasional Papers, No. 1.

Kearney, Robert N. 1978. Language and the rise of Tamil separatism in Sri Lanka. *Asian Survey* 18: 521-24.

Kearney, Robert N. 1985. Ethnic Conflict and the Tamil separatist movement in Sri Lanka. *Asian Survey* 25: 898-917.

Leitan, G.R.T. 1979. *Local Government and Decentralized Administration in Sri Lanka.* Colombo: Lake House Investments.

Leitan, G.R.T. 1990. *Political Integration Through Decentralization and Devolution of Power. The Sri Lankan Experience.* Colombo: Department of History and Political Science, University of Colombo.

Manogaran, Chelvadurai. 1987. *Ethnic Conflict and Reconciliation in Sri Lanka.* Honolulu: University of Hawaii Press.

Tambiah, S.J. 1986. *Sri Lanka: Ethnic Fraticide and the Dismantling of*

Democracy. Chicago: University of Chicago Press.

Wijeweera, B.S. 1988. *A Colonial Administrative System in Transition: The Experience of Sri Lanka*. Colombo: Marga Publications.

Wilson, A. Jeyaratnam. 1988. *The Break-Up of Sri Lanka: The Sinhalese-Tamil Conflict*. Honolulu: University of Hawaii Press.

Chapter X

ON LIONS, TIGERS AND PEACOCKS: INDO-LANKAN ETHNO-POLITICAL RELATIONS

J.W. Björkman
Institute of Social Studies
The Hague, The Netherlands

INTRODUCTION

Endemic ethnic conflict characterizes South Asia, one of the least economically developed regions of the world. During the 20th century alone, communal and ethnic conflicts have twice fissured subcontinental polities into component parts; and persistent ethnic tensions after 1947 and 1971 have repeatedly forced the successor states to redraw their internal provincial boundaries. Since geography plays a silent but central role in the affairs of mankind, Sri Lanka can be no exception to this rule. Located near the large landmass of the Indian subcontinent, Sri Lanka's strategic situation has shaped its past and continues to influence its present. This essay examines patterns of enduring ethnic conflict with particular reference to Indo-Lankan relations. The complexity of ethnic communities in Sri Lanka as well as the subcontinental context of continuing ethnolinguistic disputes are discussed as background to ethno-politics in Sir Lanka and the parameters of Indo-Lankan *realpolitik*.

Ethno-political relations interweave two complex but subtle concepts of social science. Politics, readily recognized as the pursuit and exercise of power, entails the behavioral ability of X to make Y do (or not do) what Y does not want (or wants) to do. Power itself can be exercised in normative, utilitarian, and coercive modes (Etzioni, 1965). Normative power relies on shared values to induce (in)action; utilitarian power relies on material goods and services to reward or sanction (in)action; coercive power relies on physical force and the threat of reprisals. Arrayed along a continuum of cost and speed, normative power is cheap (talk) but slow; coercion is expensive (weaponry and material destruction) but quick; utilitarian allocations lie somewhere in between. Efficiency and effectiveness are other relevant dimensions which, like beauty and justice, lie in the eyes of the beholder. Ethno-political relations apply power to the issue of ethnicity.

At issue in ethnicity is a perceived sense of social solidarity based on ties of blood, language and culture. Religion compounds ethnic attachments, sometimes reinforcing them but at other times imposing cross-cutting cleavages which diminish social ties by providing alternative referents of attachment. These factors have long been at play in Sri Lanka as they have throughout South Asia. In recent decades they have been increasingly manifest in domestic politics. Kinship, culture and language link and reinforce each other while myths from the past support and buttress these ties.

Two major ethnic groups have long coexisted in Sri Lanka along with a variety of smaller communities. The preponderant Sinhalese people trace their origins to Prince Vijaya and his 700 lion-hearted comrades who fled from North India about 2,500 years ago. The *Mahavamsa*, a Sinhala chronicle compiled in the 6th century AD, records that Prince Vijaya arrived on the island in 543 BC on the same day that the Buddha passed into nirvana in India, but such exactitude is mythic. Most likely several waves of Aryan invasions occurred throughout the era. Sinhala, a member of the Indo-European family of languages, derives from Sanskrit and its Prakritic descendants, especially Pali. Buddhism, with its sacred texts written in Pali, was first introduced to the island from India in the 3rd century BC. Over the millennia a kind of *hinayana* ("narrow-vehicle") variant was sustained in contrast to the more eclectic *mahayana* ("broad-vehicle") version of Buddhism elsewhere.

The Tamils, too, are an ancient people whose history began on the rich alluvial plains near the southern extremity of peninsular India. Some scholars trace Tamil origins to the Indus Valley civilization which flourished three millennia before the birth of Christ but declined and disappeared at about the same time that Aryan invaders penetrated northern India. The Indus Valley script and language have never been conclusively deciphered although some archeo-linguists tentatively suggest an affinity with proto-dravidian grammar. The Tamil language is a major member of the Dravidian or South Indian family of languages which differ thoroughly from the Indo-Aryan languages of North India. While the Tamil civilization over the centuries absorbed many Aryan influences, it has evolved its own rich indentity that contributes distinctly to the Hindu heritage of India.

Whether the first settlers of Sri Lanka were Sinhalese or Tamils remains a controversial question, not so much because of ambiguous archeohistorical evidence but because of partisan passions. Some analysts appear to believe that the ethnic problems which confront Sri Lanka today can be resolved by proving that either the Tamils or the Sinhalese were the "first arrivals." Presumably the descendants of those who had arrived first would then have the right to expel the descendants of those who arrived later; equally presumably, the expellees would (and could!) then return to whichever part of India their distant ancestors once left. Neither ethnic group seems to notice its explicit acknowledgement that both of them are immigrant communities who—by logical extension of the argument—ought to vacate the Resplendent Isle in favor of its few remaining aboriginal Veddahs. Of course, the basic issues are political and mythical rather than historical and factual. But it is important for the arguments which follow that the reader be aware of the longstanding claims to empirical precedence which confound all potential solutions to the ethnic conflict.

At the heart of the dispute lie ethnic identity and mutual fear of ethnic obilteration. The overt issue focuses on language as the essential carrier of ethnic identity, but at stake is a sense of existential "being" as well as material survival. The same dilemma applies to both major protagonists in this ethnic conflict. If the dilemma can be resolved at all, the usual limited terms of discourse about the role of language must be transcended. A critical distinction must be made between an official language and a national language. An *official language* is used for the files, correspondence, announcements and authoritative decisions of a government, whether in its executive, legislative or judicial branches; the term is not synonymous with a *national language*. The latter is one in which the culture of a nation can be represented and conveyed, a language that binds the people of an ethnic group into a nation which shares values, beliefs, myths, mores and folkways. It is not inconceivable for a single person to hold several levels of such cultural identity simultaneously, but it is difficult. To do so requires tolerance, sophistication, education and a good deal of material wherewithal. The current and continuing experiences of India provide a case in point.

THE SUBCONTINENTAL CONTEXT OF ETHNO-LINGUISTIC DISPUTES

Although space is inadequate to explain the scope and depth of all South Asian ethnic, linguistic and sub-national controversies, the Census of India records over 1,600 languages or "mother-tongues" of which 15 are recognized in the Eighth Schedule of the Constitution as principal or possible official state languages (Kamat, 1980, 1053). Since the 1956 language-based States Reorganization Act which thoroughly redrew all state boundaries along linguistic contours, the demise of united India over linguistic conflicts has long been predicted but never accurately. The record speaks for itself.

In the 1960s linguistic agitations continued until Bombay State was divided into Maharashtra and Gujarat, and the Punjab was rezoned into one Punjabi - and two Hindi-speaking states. In the 1970s the entire northeast was reorganized into five successor states and two union territories (two Assamese-speaking, three English-speaking and two Bengali-speaking) in order "to save their languages and cultures from being submerged by an influx of population from other parts of India" (Gandhi, 1985, 8). And thus far during the 1980s there has been language-related political violence in Goa (between Marathi and Konkani speakers), in Belgaum district (between Marathi and Kannada speakers), in Darjeeling district (between Nepali and Bengali speakers), in Assam (between Assamese and Bengali speakers), and in Punjab/Haryana where the Punjabi/Hindi strife continues mixed with some Sikh extremists' demands for an independent Khalistan (Wallace, 1988). In its three years in office, the government of Rajiv Gandhi has signed "accords" to resolve long-standing disputes in the Punjab and in Assam. It has also tried to ignore smaller state-based linguistic issues (e.g. in Goa, Belgaum, Darjeeling) in the hope that they—like others in the past, such as the Maithili-speakers of Bihar or the demand for Jarkhand State among tribals of the Chota Nagpur plateau or the agitation for an Urdu/Telugu-speaking Telengana separate from Andhra Pradesh—will resolve themselves over time.

In India the problems of the Tamil community are not, as in Sri Lanka, a vital issue of national politics. Rather, the repercussions of Lankan policy on these problems have been felt largely in *Tamilnadu*, the state of 55 million Tamils which was once called Madras. Most of the significant public interest in India about the status of the Lankan Tamils thus exists mainly in this single south Indian state which has had a long history of "Dravidian movements," originally against the domination of the Brahmin caste and "Hindu domination" from the North, but more recently against the imposition of Hindi as the *rashtra bhasa* or national language. While Tamilnadu has had a non-Congress state government for several decades, the Union Government of India in New Delhi can hardly ignore Tamil interest in its policy decisions. In a practical sense, the implementation of Delhi's decisions often relies on the cooperation of the Tamilnadu Government; and the years of Mrs. Gandhi were marked in particular by an alliance of convenience between her *Congress (I)* party and the ruling party in Tamilnadu, the *All India Anna Dravida Munnetra Kazhagam* (AIADMK).

Furthermore, the variegated social mosaic of India is colored not only by linguistic regions but by the subtle shadings of racial divides. One of the long-standing cleavages coincides broadly with the division of India into families of languages. As mentioned earlier, there is an "Aryan North" and a "Dravidian South" which collectively comprise, along with Tibeto-Burmans in the far north and northeast and aboriginals scattered across the central interior, the multi-national state called India. There are a half-dozen Aryan languages and at least four major Dravidian languages, each with more than 20 million speakers—or more than the whole population of Sri Lanka's Sinhalese and Tamils combined. In such comparative perspective, the concerns of Sri Lanka dwindle in importance to all but the immediate protagonists.

Nonetheless, the Tamils of Tamilnadu regard themselves as the most Dravidian of Dravidians and often assert their leadership over the other Dravidian linguistic groups— sometimes to the disgust of the more numerous Telugu-speakers of Andhra Pradesh or their smaller neighbours in Karnataka (Kannada-speaking) and Kerala (Malayali-speaking). Some of the more florid, if not fiery, Tamil demagogues have advocated a "Dravidistan" composed of all four southern states to which would be added, for good measure, the irredentist communities of South Indians elsewhere in the world—quite specifically parts of Sri Lanka, Malaysia and South Africa (Kodikara, 1965, 229). While the dispassionate stance of *realpolitik* can mockingly ridicule these extravagant claims, their existence serves to justify the otherwise pointless paranoia of the Sinhalese who live in immediate proximity of the subcontinental colossus.

In recent decades when the primary issue between India and Sri Lanka (then called Ceylon) dealt with the stateless Indians who worked the tea and rubber plantations, Tamilnadu (then called Madras) had a legitimate interest in their fate. Over nine-tenths of the Indian population in Ceylon were either recent immigrants from Madras state or had descended from such immigrants; the balance were mainly Malayalees from Kerala state. Since the Indo-Ceylon Agreements of 1964 and 1974 settled the issue of these immigrant laborers by providing citizenship in either India or Sri Lanka, however, the interest of the Tamilians in Tamilnadu in the fate of those Tamils who remain in Sri Lanka as citizens must necessarily derive from emotional rather than legal grounds. Consequently, Tamilnadu politicians regularly criticize the Union Government in New Delhi for not being sufficiently concerned about nor supportive of the Lankan Tamils. Indeed, with typical hyperbole, the charge is frequently heard that the "Aryan North", which dominates the Government of India and has furnished every Prime Minister since independence, neglects the Lankan issue just because it deals only with Tamils. There is some truth in this accusation in that sustained concern with ethnic conflict in Sri Lanka diminishes in almost exact proportion of the distance from that unhappy island. The same may be said about concern for Kashmir or anger over Assam. If attentiveness and geography are linked, Nagpur may be the most neutral point in India as it lies equidistant from Pakistan, China and Sri Lanka.

In polyglot India, even the status of Hindi as the "official", much less the "national" language remains in dispute. Yet India has the benefit of over a dozen distinct 'national' languages recognized by its Constitution, none of which marks a majority of Indian citizens. The advantage is a constant jockeying among pluralistic linguistic interests which leaves everyone somewhat, if not equally, dissatisfied. The liability of a bi-lingual state such as Sri Lanka—a liability which it shares with other contemporaries like Belgium, Cyprus, Canada and Malaysia—is that the numerical majority does indeed have a "right" (if not "*the* right") to impose its ethnic language as both the official language and the national language. But "right" is not necessarily reality; sometimes it is quite the reverse.

Here, the earlier conceptualization of "power" has important implications for the issue of "rights"—human, divine, natural, or otherwise. In terms of political behavior rather than ideological posturing, a "right" is a claim made by X which is honored by Y on the basis of shared values. Without prior agreement on the "rules of the game" and the values they imply, there is no inherent merit in discussing "rights" such as self-determination or even co-existence. Talk is cheap but its misuse sometimes cheapens and coarsens communications. Without normative agreement on the content of shared rights, over which one can appeal minor variations for adjudication by higher and more learned authorities, the only "language" to apply is a Hobbesian vocabulary which delimits by force the parameters of future agreed "rights."

THE COMPLEXITY OF ETHNIC COMMUNITIES IN SRI LANKA

At no stage of its history, ancient or modern, was the island ever free from Indian influence. Except for a few hundred residual Veddahs, all its peoples migrated from the mainland during the past three millennia. The "Lion Race" of the Sinhalese trace their ancestry to North India; the Tamils clearly came from South India, whether recently or thousands of years ago; the Moors and Malays came from neighboring regions of Asia; the Burghers descend from European overlords who married into the local population. In terms of contemporary symbols, it is passing odd that the avian imagery of an Indian peacock should have such furry cousins; but the Ashokan lion-capital, carved some few centuries after the parricide Prince Vijaya fled his homeland, provides the state seal of independent India while real tigers still prowl the game sanctuaries of Mudumalai and Periyar in Tamilnadu.

Culturally Sri Lanka has always been a pluralist society. For centuries the Sinhalese and Tamils have interacted, shared customs, respected each other's gods, enjoyed each other's foods and, at least among the less traditional, married into each other's communities (Sivannandan, 1977). Nonetheless, deep-rooted in

Sinhalese consciousness lies a historical grievance against South India. "Before the advent of the Portuguese in the sixteenth century, every invasion of Ceylon invariably emanated in (sic) South India" (Kodikara, 1965, 22). As the admirably insightful historian Kingsley de Silva (1981) phrases the historical burden:

> The death and devastation wrought upon Sri Lanka by the South Indian invaders have become the stuff of folklore and mythology. Inevitably, the stories have magnified the horror of those turbulent times and have created the persistent image that the Tamils are the implacable historical enemy of the Sri Lankan nation and the Sinhala people. The Tamils are blamed for the collapse of Sri Lanka's irrigation civilization in the 13th century. But the political instability inherent within the Sinhalese kingdom during that period played an equally important part....

From as early as the third century BC when Tamil "adventurers" usurped the Sinhalese throne at Anuradhapura, until almost the end of the 15th century when the conquering Europeans arrived, the histories of South India and Ceylon remained closely linked.

The interlinked influences were not only political but also social, religious and cultural. South Asian society, whatever its geographic locale, was until the modern era essentially feudal with an economy based on agriculture and some trade. Politically, society was organized into kingdoms where personal loyalty to monarchs and dynastic rule provided the social cement for historical continuity. The relative surplus extracted from peasants and merchants provided sufficient resources for episodic warfare among the kingdoms and for the construction of religious monuments. The two major religions of Sri Lanka—Buddhism and Hinduism—were likewise imported from the subcontinent, although the former faded away in the land of its birth. As a consequence, the Sinhalese Buddhists have assumed yet another historical burden as a "chosen" people charged with a divine mission to sustain and protect Buddhism. While such a mission may appear mildly quixotic to an outside observer, history elsewhere has indicated the tenacity and temerity of "chosen" peoples howsoever self-appointed or self-anointed.

In the centuries before the European colonial powers arrived, the political histories of South Asia were largely chronicles about the rise and fall of individual kingdoms and the occasional empire. Tamil kingdoms and Sinhalese kingdoms sometimes warred against each other; sometimes they fought together against a common adversary. Periodically one kingdom would establish its hegemony, and sometimes universal dominion, over the area as illustrated by the campaigns of Dutthagamani in the 2nd century BC and the Chola Empire in the 11th century AD (Smith, 1979). Alliances occasionally became necessary and, as in Europe, royal marriage was one way by which a kingdom could be enlarged or strengthened. Sinhalese kings sometimes married Tamil princesses, as the *Mahavamsa* records Prince Vijaya himself did, and Tamil monarchs tooks Sinhalese wives. A Sri Lankan colleague once quipped that the centuries of relentless socio-political miscegination have made the likelihood of "pure blood lines" highly improbable if not downright impossible. Instead an Arya-Dravidian or Dravido-Aryan race has emerged.

One particularly ardent advocate of Eelam reaches

> the irresistible conclusion that Sinhalese emerged as a result of the ascriptive cleavage consequent upon the spread of Buddhism in the Pali language. The Sinhalese, then, in terms of their origin, are not an Aryan people as popularly claimed, but Tamil people who adopted a language which developed from Pali, an Aryan dialect. (Ponnambalam, 1983, 20).

But these are beliefs and perceptions, not scientific and historically validated genealogical analysis, that serve only to complicate current ethno-political realities.

During the nearly five centuries of European rule over the island—a period divided almost equally among the Portuguese, the Dutch , and the British—the multi-ethnic nature of Sri Lanka flourished. The modern concept of separate nationhood based on language and culture was as yet unknown. While inter-ethnic antagonisms surely persisted, the role of an external colonial power kept them at a low level of salience and instead provided a focal point for inter-ethnic cooperation and collaboration. The ethnic mosaic was further elaborated with the appearance of the Burghers (people of mixed European-Lankan parentage) and the importation of a few Malays and many Indian Tamils, the latter as plantation labor on the nineteenth century coffee and, later, tea and rubber estates.

The *Ceylonese Moors* in particular found a socio-economic niche as small traders in the rural, non-colonial, non-estate hinterland. These Muslims of initially Middle Eastern and later mixed South and West Asian origin, were sea-faring traders who took up residence on the Resplendent Isle. They now account for about seven percent of the total population (1981), yet are widely distributed around the island with a particular concentration in the Eastern Province. Even there, however, the Moors remain a numerical minority; they provide the largest plurality (42%) in Amparai District and the second-ranking plurality in Trincomalee (29%) and Batticaloa (24%) districts. Thirty percent of all Ceylon Moors live in these three arid coastal districts where no single ethnic group has a majority of the population; hence their potential political leverage is disproportionately large (Gandhi, 1985). On the other hand, only 5% of all Moors live in the Tamil-dominated Northern Province (where they comprise 5% of the population) whereas the preponderant balance live scattered among the Sinhalese-dominated areas; a quarter of the Moors live in Colombo and Kandy districts alone where they respectively comprise 8% and 10% of the populations.

To add to the social complexity, most Muslims have Tamil as their mother tongue although ethnically they are not Tamils and many are bilingual (Gupta, 1986). While not necessarily against Tamil autonomy, the prickly issue of South Asian religious communalism inhibits an enduring alliance with the Hindu Tamils. Furthermore, "aware that 70 percent of their community lives in areas where Sinhalese predominate, the Eastern Province's Muslims have often sided with the Sinhalese" (Gandhi, 1985, 8).

Nonethelesss, a *Muslim United Front* joined other Tamil groups to oppose Mrs. Bandaranaike's 1972 constitution. And today, while the *Council of Muslims in Sri Lanka* remains classically equivocal, the president of the *East Sri Lanka Muslim Front* said:

> Our grievances are the same as those of the Tamils. We are fighting the same issues as them in the areas of employment, colonisation and security. We oppose a division of the country, but we strongly believe in the north-east merger as a viable alternative to a separate state (quoted in Sebastian, 1986c, 6).

The basic issue, then, is identity and a sense of future for that collective identity, whether Tamil or Sinhalese. The problem of identity is further compounded when the ethnic group itself is neither uniform nor united. Technically about one out of every four Sri Lankans speaks Tamil as his/her mother tongue and one out of five is an ethnic Tamil. But two-thirds of all ethnic Tamils are *Ceylon Tamils* whose forebearers came to the island more than a thousand years ago while the remaining third arrived since 1850 or thereabouts. These Ceylon Tamils comprise about 11 percent of the total population of the island, speak an archaic dialect of Tamil, and are concentrated in the north. For example, 95% of Jaffna District alone are Tamils—and these 792,246 people (1981 Census) account for two-fifths of the whole Ceylon Tamil community on the island.

While just half of the Ceylon or "old" Tamils live in the Northern Province (comprised of the districts of Jaffna, Mannar, Mullaitivu and Vavuniya), the other half are widely distributed throughout the island. According to the 1981 Census, Ceylon Tamils are the majority ethnic group in only one other district, Batticaloa, located midway down the eastern coast. Otherwise, as the following maps derived from the 1981 Census indicate, the balance of the Ceylon Tamils live scattered among the majority community throughout the island (Figure 10.1). They comprise significant minorities in three other districts: 34% of Trincomalee, 20% of Amparai, and 10% of the capital Colombo itself. Many

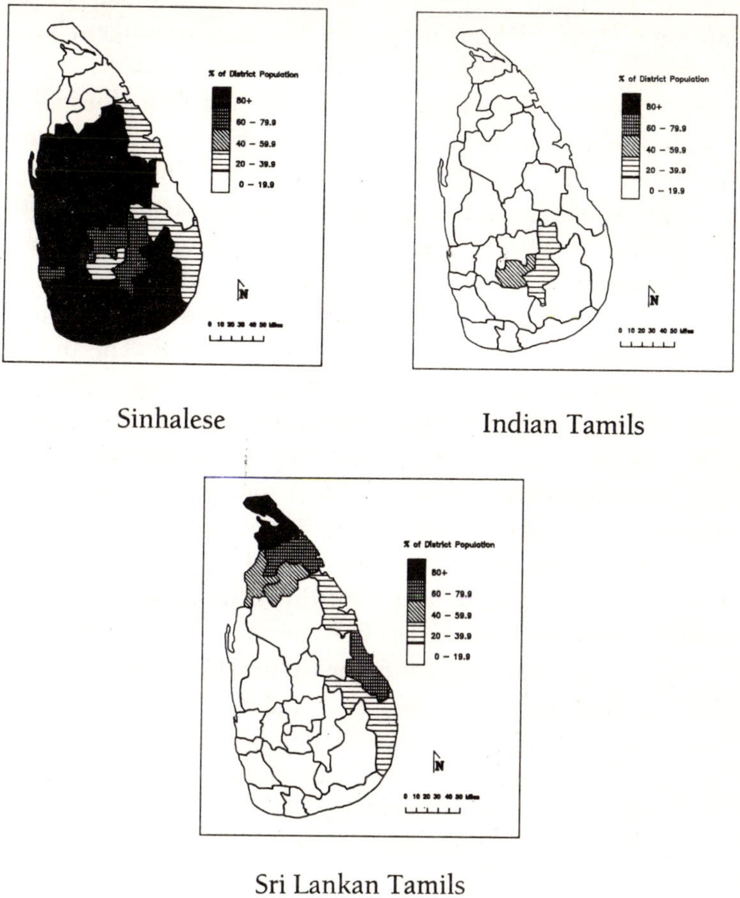

Fig. 10.1 Distribution of Ethnic Groups by District: Sri Lanka, 1981

Ceylon Tamils are noted professionals-jurists, lawyers, educators, physicians, civil servants; many others are prominent businessmen and industrialists.

In contrast to these long-rooted Ceylon Tamils are the *Indian Tamils* who now account for one-third of the ethnic Tamils and six percent of the total Sri Lankan population. Brought to Ceylon in large numbers by British planters in the 19th and 20th centuries as cheap plantation labor, the Indian or "new" Tamils are much more spatially concentrated than Ceylon Tamils. The former were, and still largely are, wage laborers on the tea and rubber estates in the sourthern part of the island. The Indian Tamil population has fluctuated considerably in size, a fact of particular importance to ethno-politics on the island. Until about 1960 Indian Tamils outnumbered Ceylon Tamils. The Indo-Ceylon Agreements of 1964 and 1974 significantly altered the relative ratio between the two ethnic Tamil communities (Table 10.1). On the other hand, the proportion of Ceylon Tamils in the total population has remained markedly stable despite trebling in absolute numbers over the last half century (Table 10.2).

Directly after independence the Citizenship Act of 1948 and the Franchise Act of 1949 declared Indian Tamils, almost to a man, to be non-citizens because their immediate kinship as well as continuing economic ties were with South India. Although (or, perhaps, because) Indian Tamils outnumbered their indigenous distant cousins, a majority of the elected Ceylon Tamil MPs in the first post-independence Parliament voted in favor of these two laws (Wilson, 1984). At that time the Tamil Congress Party was in coalition with the first United National Party government of Don Stephen Senanayake and, at least initially, the Tamil communities on the island were *not* allies but adversaries. During the subsequent fifteen years neither India nor Sri Lanka accepted these laborers as citizens so they became literally stateless. After lengthy negotiations and many ad hoc arrangements, the 1964 Indo-Ceylon Agreement (Sirima-Shastri Pact) and the subsequent 1974 Agreement (Sirima-Gandhi Pact) provided Indian and /or Lankan citizenship for all the stateless. These pacts are regularly hailed as landmarks in amicable Indo-Lankan relations

(Kumar, 1977).

Most of the Indian citizens have now been repatriated to their chosen country and re-settled while the Indian Tamils with Sri Lankan citizenship remain mainly on plantations in the central highlands. Seventy percent of the Indian Tamils (1981) live in four up-country districts where they comprise 47% of Nuwara Eliya, 21% of Badulla, 11% of Ratnapura and 9% of Kandy. The 1981 Census reçords that approximately 8% of the Indian Tamils now live in the Northern Province among the Ceylon Tamils while the balance are thinly scattered throughout the other districts of Sri Lanka. Some of these, by dint of hard work and careful husbandry, have become prosperous shopkeepers and small businessmen. Although largely low-profile, their relative success has excited envy within the ergophobic majority community and, like prosperous commercial minorities everywhere, the Indian Tamil has become a convenient scapegoat for actions taken elsewhere over which they had, and have, neither control nor responsibility. Like racial prejudice, ethnic hatred is a crude and, ironically, indiscriminate tool in the hands of the fanatic chauvinist.

The two types of Tamils have little in common. Their historical experiences differ; major caste distinctions exist between them; and they are spatially quite separate. Throughout the century since the IndianTamils began to arrive on the island, they

TABLE 10.1
Sri Lankan Tamil Populations, 1931-1981

	1931	1946	1953	1963	1971	1981
Ceylon Tamils	598,900	733,731	844,703	1,170,310	1,415,567	1,871,535
	(42%)	(48%)	(46%)	(51%)	(54%)	(69%)
Indians Tamils	818,500	780,589	974,098	1,122,850	1,196,368	825,233
	(58%)	(52%)	(54%)	(49%)	(46%)	(31%)
All Tamils	1,417,400	1,514,320	1,818,801	2,293,160	2,611,935	2,696,768
	(100%)	(100%)	(100%)	(100%)	(100%)	(100%)
Population of Island:	5,189,200	6,658,339	8,097,895	10,590,060	12,711,143	14,850,001

Source: Kodikara, 1965; Wilson, 1974; Ponnambalam, 1983; Census of Sri Lanka, 1981.

TABLE 10.2
Changes in Sri Lankan Population Distribution, 1931-1981
(Percent of Total Population)

	1931	1946	1953	1963	1971	1981
Sinhalese	67	68	69	71	72	74
Ceylon Tamils	11	11	11	11	11	13
Indian Tamils	16	12	12	11	9	6
Muslims	6	7	7	7	7	7
Others(*=<1%)	*	2	1	*	1	*

Source: See Table 10.1

had few contacts with the Ceylon Tamils. Part of the relative isolation was due to geography since the Indian Tamils remained, for the most part, on estates in the central highlands. Another reason was the lack of common interests since the immigrant laborers were illiterate and largely outcaste Untouchables compared to the better educated, higher caste, Ceylon Tamils. Ironically the Tamil language itself proved more barrier than bond since the Jaffna dialect was, and is, archaic (rather similar in its role as a linguistic relic to the French patois of Quebec, the antique English of Pitcairn Island, and the gamla Norsk of Norwegian immigrants to the American Midwest) whereas the Tamil laborers speak modern Tamil.

Consequently the two Tamil communities assume distinctly different stances on the separatism issue. Most support for a separate state comes from Ceylon Tamils whereas Indian Tamils generally support the Sri Lankan government. While the political status of the Indian Tamil had historically been subject to longstanding dispute and negotiation between mainland and island, a series of settlement agreements resolved this Indo-Ceylon problem (Kodikara, 1965). Rather it is indisputably indigenous Ceylon Tamils—or some among them—who promote the political concept of *Eelam* or an independent Tamil nation-state. Ironically, the tendency of many Sinhalese to treat all Tamils alike and not differentiate their clear differences, may still at some future date drive the two minorities together.

The majority community, who comprise 74% of the population, are predominantly Buddhists, speak Sinhala, and are the only *Sinhalese* in the world. They have no homeland elsewhere. Although a clear majority on the island, the Sinhalese see themselves as a minority endangered by the larger Tamil community in India and northern Sri Lanka. Not only is India an enormously powerful colossus, but its southernmost state of Tamilnadu alone is almost double the geographic area of Sri Lanka (130,069 versus 65,610 square kilometers) and also treble its population (48,927,456 versus 14,850,001 in 1981)—counting *all* Sri Lankans. The danger is perceived primarily in terms of the size and proximity of India which many Sinhalese fear but fully expect will invade and conquer Sri Lanka. Their only question is a rhetorical "when?"

Fears of eventual invasion were dramatically reinforced in the abortive April 1971 uprising by Sinhalese youth against the second SLFP government of Mrs. Bandaranaike. Led by the *Janatha Vimukthi Peramuna* (*JVP*) or People's Liberation Front, a militant organization of rural Buddhist youth drawn mainly from non-goigama caste-groups who were educated in the vernacular but largely unemployed, the uprising was quickly put down by the Bandaranaike government with prompt military assistance from the Government of India. Although other countries lent moral and material support, India was "first and foremost" in supplying the coercive power needed by a militarily feeble regime (de Silva 1981). Indian forces took control of the Colombo, Jaffna and Trincomalee airports and effectively sealed off the island. The ease and dispatch with which India acted plus the evident inadequacy of the Lankan armed forces supplied ample proof of South Asian *realpolitik*.

The rapidity with which Indira Gandhi heeded Sirimavo Bandaranaike's appeal for help can, of course, be partly explained by their personal rapport. But it is not insignificant that during the 1962 Sino-Indian war, the JVP had "roundly condemned India as the aggressor and maintained that 'China was legitimately defending its frontiers'" (Phadnis, 1963, 183). Even the Sri Lanka Freedom Party (SLFP) had maintained a careful neutrality, justified by its principled policy of nonalignment, while its leader sought to mediate the Asian conflict. At that time by far the strongest support for India came from the Tamil parties as both Ceylon Tamils and Indian Tamils began to organize volunteers to fight the Chinese and to raise contributions for the Indian National Defence Fund. The essential point for *realpolitik*, however, is the utter vulnerability of Sri Lanka to India's force majeure.

Despite its sense of uniqueness, the Sinhalese community is riven by internal divisions. The social distinction between low-country and high-country Sinhalese, for example, was reinforced by several centuries of history when the lowlanders were under European control while the Kingdom of Kandy remained independent. As late as the 1920s some Kandyans viewed themselves as a nationality distinct from the low-country Sinhalese and founded political associations to that end (Wilson, 1974). During those centuries, a religious cleavage also appeared because many low-country Sinhalese had accepted Christianity while the Kandyans remained devoted, if embattled, Buddhists. Although a number of Christian Sinhalese later returned to the Buddhist fold (famous recent examples being the SLPF founder, S.W.R.D. Bandaranaike, and the current President, J.R. Jayewardene), seven percent of all Sinhalese are Christian and the Catholic Church remains particularly strong. Along with the Ceylon Tamils, about a quarter of whom profess Christianity, the Sinhalese Catholics became much better educated than their Sinhalese Buddhist counterparts. Education meant not only social mobility but economic advantage for all Christians, which periodically provoked envy and anger among the Buddhists. The evident imbalance stoked the fiery furnace of chauvinism.

Finally, although the Buddhist religion proclaims egalitarian concepts of birth and status and was initially founded in order to reject the social hierarchy explicit in Hinduism, the Sinhalese society is organized into castes. While not the classic four-fold *varna* of Hinduism, Sinhalese are divided into high-ranking *Goigama* (cultivator); middle-ranking *Karava* (fisher), *Salagama* (cinnamon peeler) and *Durava* (toddy tapper); and lower-ranking *Navandanna* (artisans), *Batgam, Wahumpara, Berava, Hina, Rajaka,* etç (Wilson, 1974; Ponnambalam, 1983). The same social order permeates the Sinhalese Christian community, and it is said to be easier to arrange inter-faith caste-specific marriages than inter-caste faith-specific ones.

While Goigama are everywhere on the island (51% of low-country Sinhalese, 85% of Kandyan Sinhalese), the lower-ranking orders are more numerous outside the hill country (Jiggins, 1979; Roberts, 1982). The ambitious, upwardly mobile Karava in particular have sought to break the upper-class alliance between the Goigma and their equivalents among the Ceylon Tamils, the *Vellala*, who jointly shared the spoils of independence among themselves. The Karava became the most relentless agitators for the Sinhala-only law and spearheaded the Sinhala-only zealots. In so doing they damaged not only the Tamils but the Goigama-Vellala alliance as well. The essential point is that when examined closely, the Sinhalese reveal complex congeries of interests, layers, and divisions just like the Tamils. The social order of Sri Lanka is like a game of Chinese boxes; a further subdivision always exists within whatever division is momentarily manifest.

The majority fear is also compounded and exacerbated by socio-economic factors. For many years, the Sinhalese took some pride in their better economic conditions compared with the teeming millions of India; but in recent years the per capita gross national product in Sri Lanka has differed little from the Indian figure. Furthermore, after independence the Sinhalese found that their Ceylon Tamil compatriots dominated all the prestigious professions.in society— medicine, engineering, law, civil service, etc. Equally upsetting was the realization that the Tamil students regularly outperformed Sinhalese students in the coutrywide examinations for admission to the university, the very institution which controlled access to the professions themselves. These issues will now be explored.

ETHNO-POLITICS IN SRI LANKA: THE EDUCATIONAL ISSUE

Nationalism has been a relatively recent, basically post-independence phenomenon in Sri Lanka. The country gained its independence because of events in India and because the British Labour Party was anxious, for economic as well as ideological reasons, to shed imperial responsibilities. The few, upper-middle class, deracinated, urban, Anglophonic Sri Lankans involved in domestic politics represented an alliance of wealthy, well-educated, essentially leisured Sinhalese and Ceylon Tamils. Unlike India where "unity was forged in the fires of common struggle based on mass participation," Sri Lanka's "independence was won by negotiation and diplomacy and craft cannot altogether be excluded" (Wilson, 1974, 126). Indeed, in a mood of almost inexplicable whimsey, the British had in 1931 established parliamentary institutions and universal suffrage through the Donoughmore Constitution, and in 1948 Ceylon became the first British Crown Colony to attain (cynics say "receive") its independence. By that time the Sri Lankans had for several decades had charge of, and resources for, schools and local educational policies which by 1946 had produced an island-wide literacy rate of 57% (Weerasooria, 1981).

Despite vernacular literacy, however, an overwhelming majority of Sinhalese spoke little if any English, and that majority increasingly came to resent the domination of anglophones. Reinforced by religious revivalism the resentment began among Sinhalese Buddhists during the late 19th century but was confined to organized pressure groups throughout the first half of the 20th century. This religio-linguistic revivalism did not obtain political form until 1951 when S.W.R.D. Bandaranaike and a few of his colleagues left the United National Party to found the Sri Lanka Freedom Party (SLFP). At that time the SLFP advocated the use of both Sinhalese and Tamil languages and even had several Tamil vice-presidents (Ponnambalam, 1983). By 1955, however, "in the face of mounting pressure from Sinhalese

Buddhist militants, the party changed to 'Sinhalese only' with provision for the reasonable use of the Tamil language" (Wilson, 1974, 142).

In 1956 the SLFP in coalition with several other minor Sinhalese parties won an election by promising among other things an immediate changeover from English to Sinhala as the language of government. One of the coalition's first acts in office was to pass the Official Language Act (1956) which required all civil servants to conduct all official correspondence in Sinhala. Since many of these civil servants were Tamils who had excelled in their English examinations but knew no Sinhala, the act deprived them of promotion and equally deprived the educated Anglophonic community of its privileged access to government service. To the majority of Sinhalese the law was merely a case of long-delayed equity and national justice; to the minorities it was a form of both political and economic disfranchisement.

Christian missionaries, and particularly the Catholic Church, had long dominated education through their excellent schools. Sinhalese sentiment against this domination began a century ago when anti-Catholic agitation flared in 1883 and again in 1903. The era was ethnically tumultuous for riots against Moors also occurred in 1903 and against Muslims and Tamils in 1915. The advent of democratic politics and the institution of majority rule since the 1931 Donoughmore Constitution enabled Sinhalese nationalists and Buddhist revivalists to advance Sinhala through public policy and to extend vernacular education (de Silva, 1988). As long as the British Raj remained, however, the role of English as a unifying language among the upper and upper-middle class elites continued as the natural order.

It was only after independence that increasingly bitter clashes over language between Sinhalese and Tamils accelerated. By that time, a generation of Sinhala-only literates had emerged who expected their fair share of government jobs—and found themselves still disqualified by not knowing English. Education, instead of helping them escape a stagnant rural sector and finding gainful employment elsewhere, only served to exacerbate consciousness of their fate. The Ceylon Tamils on the other hand had cultivated their knowledge of English, excelled in English-medium education, and regularly dominated admissions to both government service and the university. They also dominated the professions. As late as 1974 "the professional Tamils who included doctors, engineers, teachers, accountants and so on, held over 25 percent of the total jobs—that is, far in excess of their share of the total population" (*Economic and Political Weekly*, 10 September 1977, 1604). Subsequently, however, recruitment by ethnic quotas and outmigration by disillusioned Tamils reduced the percentage of Tamil professionals to approximate parity with their overall population share and somewhat less among government services (Appathurai, 1983). In prescient anticipation of these effects, the Federal Party organized *satyagraha* or Gandhian nonviolent resistance against the proposed 1956 legislation which would make Sinhala the only official language, but such nonviolent restraint rapidly gave way to violent conflict. Island-wide violence again erupted against the Ceylon Tamils in 1958 and 1977, largely over the language issue (Manor, 1983). Significant conflict confined to the Tamil areas also occurred in 1961, 1974 and, most recently, the 1980s.

In addition to envy over the longterm advantages of exceptional education, the recent and more immediate source of anti-Tamil riots is all too easy to identify. Whenever the body of a Sinhalese official, policeman or soldier, killed by Tamil terrorists, is brought home for burial, an emotional triggering of anger and fear excite the Sinhalese to lash out against the nearest vulnerable Tamils. Ironically, and sadly, many of the victims of the Tamil terrorists have been moderate Tamil politicians and Tamil policemen and a variety of others (including Sarvodaya workers) who are regarded as collaborationists; yet their sacrifice on behalf of a united, integrated Sri Lanka does not arouse the same grief and anger nor the same revanchist sentiments. Equally ironically the Government of India, much less the Government of Tamilnadu, reacts to the harshness of the Sinhalese response to the Tamil terrorists rather than the actions of the latter against Sinhalese and Tamil moderates alike. The media rarely record the many heroic occasions when Sinhalese and Tamils have mutually helped, protected, assisted, and defended one another despite great personal risk-especially to reprisals by extremists within their own respective ethnic group.

Sinhalese and Tamils have legitimate grievances, if not against each other, then against a pernicious educational system. Language has been an appropriate issue because language is the basis of economic opportunity and social mobility. Sri Lankans rightly take pride in their achievement of near universal literacy and excellent social welfare activities. Yet even today, after considerable expansion of university facilities, barely one percent of the population obtain a university education. Furthermore, there has been imbalanced access to educational institutions and their channels to advancement. The 1959 Sri Lankan Universities' Committee reported that the proportion of Tamil students compared to their ethnic population was 1:320 while that of the Sinhalese was 1:3,212. Historically, while the British had not promoted education, especially English education, in the Sinhalese Buddhist districts, Christian missionaries had established good schools in the coastal areas. Whether low-country Sinhalese or Ceylon Tamils, converts to Roman Catholicism (under the Portuguese) and Protestantism (under the Dutch and later the British) had a decided comparative advantage in the English medium (Wilson, 1974). In fact, the first mission schools in Jaffna were set up by Protestant missionaries from Boston, Massachusetts, whose church at exactly the same time was Christianizing Hawaii. Such efforts gave Tamil students an extra advantage over their Sinhalese counterparts—and may explain why the Massachusetts legislature was induced to pass a resolution on Sri Lankan affairs.

Sadly enough, despite their basic literacy, most students could not aspire to enter the university because secondary schools did not offer adequate grounding in science or mathematics. In the mainly Sinhalese district of Matara, for example, the

Commission found one school with university-entrance science courses for every 103,000 inhabitants; in the Sinhalese and Indian Tamil district of Badulla, the ratio was one science-equipped school per 234,000; in the Tamil district of Jaffna, by comparison, the ratio was one school per 15,000 inhabitants. While not intended to disparage Tamil foresightfulness and planning, for which they deserve commendation, those figures meant that the Sinhalese entering the university were often precluded from programs in medicine, science or engineering.

Despite the official language change of 1956, proportionately few Sinhalese gained entry to the university. Successive discriminatory policies were therefore adopted to enhance Sinhalese enrollment at the expense of better qualified Tamil students. Not only were middle-class Tamil parents hamstrung in terms of their economic employment; their children were now being deprived of commensurate future livelihood altogether. Such "affirmative action" was doubly distressing to the Ceylon Tamils for their "natural" or "historic" areas in the north are poor, arid, and offer few economic possibilities.

After passage of the 1956 law, Tamils in government positions were given a year in which to pass an examination in Sinhala or lose their employment. A stagnating economy under a bungling SLFP government worsened the situation. While figures are difficult to obtain, Kearney (1978) reports a 1969-70 rate of unemployment in Tamil districts of 80% among those with a tenth-grade education and even higher rates for those with college degrees. Many Tamils in the professions therefore migrated to Canada, Australia, the USA and Western Europe where, for the most part, they did very well. But in Sri Lanka a generation of Tamils remain who feel grossly victimized, who lost jobs and promotions, and whose own children lost the opportunity of a university education. The removal in 1977 of the most gross discriminatory devices that excluded Tamils from the university has not really remedied the problem. This "lost generation" provides the core of the terrorist movement for "many Tamil boys who were shut out despite their high grades took to the gun and the grenade" (Gandhi, 1985, 9).

There is yet another political cost to this "impolitics" of education. Though each ethno-linguistic community had its own set of political parties, Sinhalese and Tamils used to be able to talk to each other in Parliament in English both before and after independence. Even that bridge for communication has eroded, not from loss of language skills but from absence of participants. Instead of the scheduled 1983 elections, President Jayewardene conducted a constitutionally permissible special referendum to extend the life of the sitting parliament for an additional six years. The referendum passed nationally but was heavily voted down in the Ceylon Tamil districts as well as in a few Sinhalese districts. All *Tamil United Liberation Front (TULF)* Members of Parliament decided on conscience to resign their seats at the end of the regular term because of the adverse vote in their constituencies although they also forfeit parliamentary membership by refusing to swear the loyalty oath required by the Sixth Amendment to the Constitution. These seats remain vacant, and Sinhalese politicians from Sinhalese districts have little reason to speak on behalf of the absent Tamils. Instead, politicians of the Sinhalese parties vie in espousing the Sinhalese cause and in factional infighting. It should be noted, however, that in the few anti-extension constituencies in the Sinhalese areas the *United National Party (UNP)* resigned their seats, too. Fresh elections were held and, in most cases, the UNP candidates were again returned to office so the existing government is not without legitimacy.

ETHNO-POLITICS IN SRI LANKA: THE SEPARATISM SCENARIO

Since the 1940s there has been a slow but steady growth of Tamil opinion in favor of relative autonomy. Ironically, in the 1920s the Kandyan (up-country) Sinhalese considered themselves to be a nationality distinct from both the lowland Sinhalese and the Tamils. They formed their own Kandyan Association and objected to plans of the *Ceylon National Congress (CNC)* to promote a unitary state (Ponnambalam, 1983). At that time, the Tamil leadership saw themselves as a "national minority" within a multi-ethnic state who "were content to demand 'minority rights' rather than define themselves as a nation, with rights of autonomy and self-determination" (Ponnambalam, 1983, 50). By the late 1940s, however, although the *Tamil Congress (TC)* cooperated with the first post-independence government of D.S. Senanayake (who in 1946 had transformed the CNC into the *United National Party* or *UNP*), some Tamil leaders had begun to support a federal solution for Ceylon. They had at first hand their colossal neighbor which was devising its own new federal constitution based on the Government of India Act of 1935.

In 1948 the Tamil Congress split. Formed in 1944, the TC had sought balanced representation in parliament and allied itself with the UNP after independence. Severe differences arose within the party over the proposed disfranchisement of the Indian Tamils since the conservative TC leadership supported the UNP legislation while another faction strongly dissented (Wilson, 1974). The latter left to form a new *Federal Party* (*FP*) which thereafter won overwhelming victories at the polls in the Tamil areas of the north. Through the 1960s the Federal Party, too, sought to collaborate with Sinhalese politicians of the UNP in pursuit of immediate equality within a unified polity. The Ceylon Tamils expected restoration of the status quo ante wherein Sinhalese hegemony and particularly the Sinhala-only law would be excised. This was the conservative solution to the ethnic strife. The strategy was unsuccessful, and the return of the SLFP to power in 1970 was followed by the promulgation of a new republican constitution. The latter not only cut the ties to the British Crown but also, and more importantly, removed the few constitutionally entrenched provisions for minority rights.

Even before the constituent assembly enacted the new constitution, the previously fractious Tamil political parties and pressure groups convened and in May 1972 the *Tamil United Front* (TUF) was formed. Among other things, its platform advocated secularism, a defined place for the Tamil language, fundamental rights of ethnic minorities, and decentralization of administration (Ponnambulam, 1983). Four years later to the day, the TUF reconstituted itself as the *Tamil United Liberation Front* (TULF) and resolved "that the restoration and reconstitution of the Free, Sovereign, Secular, Socialist State of Tamil Eelam based on the right of self-determination inherent in every nation has become inevitable in order to safeguard the very existence of the Tamil nation in this country" (cited in Ponnambulam, 1983, 185).

Separatism is not an easy nor indeed self-evident option for an ethnic community scattered throughout a tiny island. One component of the TUF—the *Ceylon Workers Congress (CWC)*, which represents the Indian Tamils in the central highlands — took severe exception to the founding of TULF. Indeed, the CWC joined an electoral alliance with the UNP in the 1977 elections and the CWC leader, S. Thondaman, is a minister in the Jayewardene cabinet. Yet another component, the *Muslim United Front*, also reached an understanding with the UNP which in 1977 restricted TULF to only four of the 12 seats in the Eastern Province compared to their sweep of the Northern Province (Gandhi, 1985). Meanwhile, the militant Tamils scorned the non-violent tactics and political passivity of the TULF which continues to employ liberal, legalistic, indeed constitutionalist terms of reference. In July 1984 a group of young militants disrupted a fast organized by TULF leaders to mourn the victims of the 1983 disturbance; the militants asked sarcastically what 30 years of leadership by passive parliamentarians had accomplished (*Daily News*, 25 July 1984).

Since 1980 violence has come to characterize ethno-politics within Sri Lanka and extra-parliamentary action is the norm rather than the exception. Indo-Lankan relations are necessarily involved since both refugees and rebels have received sanctuary in Tamilnadu. The proscribed TULF itself maintains its offices in Madras and more than 20 groups of Tamil militants headquarter there (Varghese, 1986). Without attempting to be exhaustive, the following list represents the relatively major organizations that promote the cause of an independent Tamil Eelam or Tamil

Eezham. only the first five have achieved any degree of public prominence and are regularly summoned by the Government of India for their views on various proposals generated by the Government of Sri Lanka and/or the Tamil United Liberation Front. The first four groups listed, which until mid-1986 collectively comprised the *Eelam National Liberation Front (ENLF)*, were "virtually frogmarched" to the Thimpu talks by the Government of India in July 1985 (Venkatramani, 1985). As a sort of "holding company" to project a unified public image, the ENLF has a variable membership because groups come and go; in early 1986 the *Liberation Organization of Tamil Eelam (LTTE)* left in disgust while part of *Peoples Liberation Tigers of Tamil Eelam (PLOTE)* joined for the first time. No verifiable figures on numerical strength of the groups exist; most can count only a few hundred active members, but the aggregate may total several thousand.

** The oldest, largest and militarily the most highly organized group calls itself the *Liberation Tigers of Tamil Eelam (LTTE)*, better known as the "Tamil Tigers." Led by Velupillai Prabakharan, it spearheads the terrorist campaign against the Sri Lankan government and yet is largely isolated (by choice as well as ostracism) from the other mainstream militant organizations. Prabakharan, a member in the early 1970s of the left-oriented Tamil Students Federation (TSF), had in 1972 formed a small organization evocatively called the Tamil New Tigers (TNT). The symbol of a tiger "seems to represent a deep-rooted nostalgia for the era of Cholas when the Tamils were supreme" (Varghese, 1986, 8). Its ferocious feline imagery also matches the Sinhalese lion which myths and the *Mahavasma* claim as an ancestor of Prince Vijaya. In 1976 TNT was renamed the Liberation Tigers of Tamil Eelam (LTTE), which began to pursue its demand for the creation of a separate Tamil state by violent means.

Prabakharan is perhaps the most controversial "Tamil Tiger" in that he unabashedly envisages one-party rule of Tamil Eelam (Hawksley, 1986) and is contemptuous of those who seek a negotiated solution (*The Hindu*, 29 September 1986). He advocates "survival of the fittest" among the militants themselves and was "reported to have crossed over to Jaffna the day before some prominent members of the moderate Tamil United Liberation Front (TULF) were brutally murdered" (Gupta *et al.*, 1985, 51). In the words of a senior Sri Lankan army officer in Colombo:

> Talks are nothing but a diversionary tactic. I cannot speak for the rest, but I have no doubts about Prabakharan's Tigers. They want Eelam and they are aware they will never get it across the table whether in Thimpu or Timbuktu (*ibidem*, 51).

Most importantly for Indo-Lankan relations, LTTE enjoys the "patronage" of Tamilnadu Chief Minister, M. G. Ramachandran, who has become Prabakharan's "patron saint" (*The Statesman*, 26 July 1986, and 27 July 1986). The Chief Minister, popularly known as MGR, has become a conduit between all the militants and the Government of India, particularly when the latter is acting as postman for proposals from the "enemy" (*The Hindu*, 30 June 1986). Unsurprisingly, given the adamant LTTE rejection of anything short of a totally independent sovereign Eelam, "the Government of India wants to utilize Mr. Ramachandran's good offices in persuading the leaders of the Tamil militant groups to study the Sri Lankan formulations and take part in the next round of talks to get into the negotiating process to press for further concessions to make the package more acceptable to them" (sic) (Reddy, 1986, 1). The price for such good will involves the usual guarantees for public, that is domestic, consumption:

> The Prime Minister, Mr. Rajiv Gandhi, assured the Chief Minister of Tamil Nadu, Mr. M. G. Ramachandran, today that the Centre had no intention at all of imposing Hindi on the people of any State against the wishes of its people. He stated quite categorically that there was no change whatsoever in the Government's language policy and that the Centre stood fully by the assurances given by both Jawaharalal Nehru and

Indira Gandhi (*ibidem*).

** The *Tamil Eelam Liberation Organization (TELO)*, a loosely-knit non-ideological group which coalesced in the early 1970s, came to prominence in July 1983 when its imprisoned leaders were massacred in Colombo's Welikada prison. Already sentenced to death the previous year for anti-state activities, they were murdered by fellow prisoners in reprisal for the LTTE-killing of 13 Sinhalese soldiers, an incident which ignited the worst anti-Tamil pogrom in Lankan history. Reportedly inclined to accommodate Indian initiatives for a peaceful settlement to the Lankan ethnic impasse, TELO was itself virtually liquidated in May 1986 by the LTTE during a week-long internecine bloodbath in Jaffna. Over 150 militants lost their lives—including the 32 year old TELO leader, Sri Sabaratnam, who was gunned down by the rival LTTE after he surrendered. Although decimated and without charismatic leadership, TELO is still reputed to have large caches of arms hidden in the Northern Province and has vowed to avenge its betrayal.

** The *Eelam People's Revolutionary Liberation Front (EPRLF)* is "a body with pretensions more intellectual than military" (Gupta, 1984, 54). This self-declared Marxist-Leninist group was founded in 1981 by its most significant unit, the General Union of Eelam Students (GUES), which coordinates Tamil students abroad. Other Front members include the *Tamil Eelam Students Organization (TESO)*, the *General Union of Youth and Students (GUYS)*, and the *Organization of Tamil Students (OTS)* (Newstime, 7 October 1986). In October 1986, after allegations of drug trafficking, EPRLF temporarily closed its *Eelam People's Information Centre (EPIC)* as a symbolic protest.

** The *Eelam Revolutionary Organization of Students (EROS)* is the smallest of the five main militant organizations and its members are better educated than the average Tamil Tiger (Varghese, 1986). EROS has no office-bearers other than a 15-member General Council who are mainly located in the West and Singapore. Founded in 1974 by Elayathamby Ratnasabhapathy, a London-based economist-journalist of Trotskyite persuasion, these far-flung expatriates originally provided ideological content and international contacts to the Tamil insurgents. Although the group condemns random killing and robbery, EROS has allied itself with LTTE and claims credit for the bomb blasts in Colombo's Lanka Oberoi Hotel and at the National Security Ministry. These activist intellectuals believe that Eelam can be established by sabotaging the Sri Lankan economy. Significantly, EROS is the only militant group to include southern areas in a map of Eelam. Although born in Jaffna, Ratnasabhapathy was raised and educated in the southern plantation districts. He is quite explicit about his passionate commitment to the Indian Tamils:

> Our concept of Eelam includes certain parts ofthe central hills like Badulla and Nuwaraelia, and hence any solution will have to take into account the future security of Tamils of Indian origin (Gopalan, 1986, 3).

** Odd-man out in the roll-call of militant groups is the *People's Liberation Organization of Tamil Eelam (PLOTE)*, which also participated in the Thimpu talks. Founded in 1980 by Uma Maheshwaran, the group is fairly large in terms of manpower and claims to have its central core trained by the Palestine Liberation Organization (PLO). Maheshwaran, himself a product of PLO training, has held membership in several Tamil organizations: first the Federal Party, then the TULF, then the LTTE. His rivalry with Prabakharan soon become so intense, however, that the two engaged in a "shooting war" in Madras (Varghese, 1986), whereafter he founded PLOTE. The oddity is that PLOTE, like the TULF, has not been party to the armed struggle against the Sri Lankan authorities. Instead it operates a clandestine radio-station called "Voice of the Tamil" and scorns the hit-and-run tactics of other groups. Although ideologically inclined and apparently well-trained, PLOTE is the most moderate of the militants (de Silva, 1985). That distinctive status may, however, be changing.

In July 1986 PLOTE fractured as nine of its 16-member Central Committee expelled Maheshwaran and resolved to join ENLF. Said a leader of the breakaway faction, "We have decided to fight from within, against the personality cult imposed on us by Mr. Maheshwaran and replace it with a democratically elected collective leadership" (*The Statesman*, 27 July 1986, 8). Significantly, PLOTE was not among the Tamil militant groups summoned to Delhi in mid-August 1986 to resume discussions with Indian officials on the ethnic crisis in Sri Lanka (*The Times of India*, 18 August 1986).

There are several self-styled "armies" among the militants, too. **The *Tamil Eelam Liberation Army (TELA)* is another small guerilla organization which cooperates largely with PLOTE. ** The *Tamil Eelam Army (TEA)*, an erstwhile ally of LTTE, achieved notoriety in 1984 through its series of sensational robberies of Sri Lankan banks. Its penchant for spectacular crime, however, has cost Tamil militants valuable sympathy in Tamilnadu. The TEA leader, Thambapillai Maheswaran, who stands accused of masterminding the August 1984 Meenambakkam Airport bomb blast that killed or maimed many Indians, jumped bail and is still at large (Venkatramani, 1986).

For all their exotic variety, subtle shades and acronymic acrobatics, the militant groups—LTTE excepted—face considerable public skepticism about their real capabilities. During the decade since their appearance, they have displayed neither coherence nor continuity. Rather, each group has tried to outmaneuver and annihilate the others in its bid to become the sole spokesman of the Tamil cause. Of the several rebel organizations in existence, some have been decimated while others have merged. Groups fight each other bitterly and even kill each other's men. In early 1986 the LTTE liquidated the TELO in murderous battles throughout northern Sri Lanka in which many innocent Tamil civilians were killed and/or maimed including some already hospitalized in Jaffna General where a major shoot-out occurred. In late 1986 the LTTE turned its guns on the EPRLF which is chiefly found in Batticaloa and the Eastern Province; dozens of militants died in internecine clashes (*Indian Express*, 15 December 1986; *Times of India*, 18 December 1986; *The Hindu*, 26 December 1986) which continued well into 1987 (*The Hindu*, 14 February 1987; *Times of India*, 18 February 1987). Such fratricidal conflict has significantly weakened militant activities outside the Jaffna peninsula and allowed the Sri Lankan armed forces to reclaim lost ground, and generally confused former advocates of Eelam. Intergroup rivalry between LTTE and EPRLF has become so intense that "there is strong suspicion that one group is colluding with the State to attack the other. In other words, some Tamil groups seem to have lost sight of who the main 'enemy' is" (*The Hindu*, 21 February 1987, 7).

Since the militants seem more divided and mutually acrimonious than ever, periodic claims about coordination among the major groups have been treated with derision by the press. As a senior police officer in Tamilnadu remarked some while ago about the many ambitious advocates of Eelam: "The problem is they have nothing in common except for a craving for fancy acronyms for their organisations and their leftist orientation" (cited in Guptas,1984, 56). And a leader of the *Tamil Eelam Supporters' Organisation* (yet another TESO) observed sourly: "Jayewardene has only one enemy (Tamils) while the Tigers have two—Jayewardene and themselves" (quoted by Sebastian, 1986a, 1). In order to obtain resources, both LTTE and TELO have even periodically kidnapped TULF leaders in Madras and held them for ransom (*The Hindu*, 29 January 1987; and 20 February 1987); such inter-Tamil extortion, however, is rarely reported as front-page news in Indian newspapers. Perhaps the most telling indictment of the inveterate rivalry among various militant groups comes from a self-critical editorial in *Tamil Information*, a privately circulated journal unaffiliated with any specific sponsor but serving the general cause of Eelam as an organ for all:

> Tamil society has also to learn to look inward. A clinical introspection is essential. Every society carries with it some canker in its vitals, which if not cleansed, can lead to its own

> destruction. Intolerance and factionalism, inability to accept a contrary point of view, self-inflated egoism, malice and mud-slinging are neither healthy nor happy attributes in a people fighting oppression and waging a struggle for liberation. If this debilitating process is not checked in time, that will be a sure way of defeating ourselves before the enemy defeats us. All guns need steady hands but if they are used in the cause of liberation they need clean hands as well (cited in Gandhi, 1985, 9).

Nonetheless, bombs still go off throughout Sri Lanka and death still stalks the Resplendent Isle. There are two distinct interpretations about the tactics of the Tamil terrorists— neither of which is without precedent elsewhere in the sordid history of embattled humanity (Rubenstein, 1987). One is that the terrorists, operating in an area where Tamils comprise a very high percentage of the population, take actions (such as killing policemen and army officers) and advocate policies (such as a separate state), which have negative short-term and long-term consequences for Tamils living in Sinhalese areas. Those with this view deplore the narrow vision of the Tamil terrorists, whom they claim do not understand the effect of their tactics elsewhere on the island. The short-term Sinhalese backlash is directed towards the nearest vulnerable Tamils, who lose lives and property and live in a climate of fear. If a separate Eelam is obtained, presumably all non-northern Tamils will be compelled to give up their jobs, property, business interests, and careers in orders to move to the North. Many—indeed a majority of all ethnic Tamils—live now in the South by choice, even against unfavorable odds. Is their freedom to be eliminated by the very Tamils who claim to pursue their better interests? Most militants assume a massive ingathering of all Lankan Tamils to their future state but, as observed above, EROS intellectual Ratnasabhapathy expects otherwise:

> Why should these (Indian Tamil) people give up their hearths

> and homes and settle in strange places? They have a right to live and prosper in their homeland and they will (Gopalan, 1986, 3).

The second view is more cynical but perhaps more realistic; it observes that the Tamil terrorists know full well what they are doing. Their goal is a separate state, and they are following tactics designed to drive the two ethnic communities farther and farther apart. Whenever Sinhalese attack the nearest Tamil in revenge, they help the terrorists drive Tamils out of the south. Every such attack bring a sympathetic response among the expatriates, who have learned to gain media attention. Every time an attack on soldiers or policemen in the north or east is followed by retaliation against Tamil citizens suspected of harboring terrorists, more support is gained for the separatist cause. The terrorists intimidate those who would disagree with them by assassinating moderate Tamils and all those regarded as collaborationists. The dual strategy chosen is deliberate....and it is working. In mid-1986, for example, LTTE leader Prabakharan "described the TULF secretary-general, Mr. A. Amirthalingam, (then) engaged in talks in Colombo with the Sri Lanka President, Mr. J R Jayewardene, to solve the ethnic crisis in the island as 'a traitor to the Tamil cause,' sending shivers down the spine of the TULF delegation" (*The Statesman*, 22 August 1986, 1). Subsequent reports that the LTTE had passed a death sentence on Amirthalingam were immediately denied as government-sponsored disinformation (*The Hindu*, 20 February 1987; 21 February 1987).

The absence of dissenting voices, of moderate voices, in the Tamil community has not gone unnoticed by the Sinhalese. It is a cause for concern among the remaining "integrationists" who still seek a united Sri Lanka. One consequence seems to be a growing unease about the reliability of all Tamils. Many public sector Tamil employees have been transferred out of Colombo or asked to go on indefinite leave of absence; the process was reportedly accelerated after a series of terrorist bomb blasts

(*Indian Express*, 18 May 1986). Earlier legal steps had been taken through a constitutional amendment which forbade advocacy of separatism, even of autonomy—thus proscribing the TULF itself. For two years thereafter the Jayewardene Government refused to talk with TULF representatives because they would not affirm their support for a united Sri Lanka. Lack of such affirmation fueled distrust, and such distrust makes any suggestion of devolution of power within the island extremely suspect. Only the constant pressure of "Big Brother" Delhi on "Little Brother" Colombo has kept an episodic dialogue alive. Yet many of the proposed governmental reforms provide structural change without any major change in content or power. The lack of substantive reform means, of course, rejection by the Tamils, which in turn seems to lead to greater suspicion by the Sinhalese.

A further complicating factor is that the Tamil districts in the north are financially deficient. Sinhalese money must be given for both ordinary costs of government as well as for development expenditures. The political question of how much is to be given for what, and who is to make decisions about the allocation of that money, is divisive in the best of times. Efforts to shift some developmental spending for roads, schools, small irrigation works, etc., to the district level have been met with the angry retort from Tamils that the amounts provided (or, rather, promised) are only a pittance (Matthews, 1987, 77). Meanwhile, in Sinhalese areas, politicians—and particularly the District Ministers, who are MPs that the Colombo government appoints to liaise with central authorities—use whatever money is provided in close cooperation with those central authorities. It is important to note that a separate Tamil state would necessarily have to be supported from the outside. At present "...the essential commodities required to run their envisaged separate state come from the Sinhalese-controlled south. Water and electricity are under government control. The salaries of the doctors, municipal employees, and teachers all come from Colombo, as does much of the food and supplies" (Hawksley, 1986, 17). Ardent Eelamites insist they would rather live off foreign aid or "do without" than continue under the yoke of Sinhalese chauvinists. If the financial issue weren't so tragic, it would almost be funny. However, the (somewhat porous) army blockade of the Jaffna peninsula in early 1987 revealed the almost total dependency of the North on southern resources. Initiated to counter and expose LTTE's claims of conducting civil administration and levying taxes, the economic blockade suspended the import of fuel, aluminum (for manufacturing weapons), and other nonessential items. Its impact was dramatic and painful (*Indian Express*, 13 January 1987; *The Hindu*, 30 January 1987).

The questions may be asked: what kind of support suffices for the advocates of Eelam? What kind of support do the terrorists have for their political goals? Outside observers as well as Sri Lankan citizens (both Tamil and Sinhalese) suggest that only a minuscule minority want a separate state. They argue that the claim for independence is a political ploy, and that most Tamils want something far less—for example, a federal system with extensive local autonomy. There is some evidence to support the latter view, but the time may be past for its actualization; and in any case, the image of Eelam may have taken root despite its prima facie improbability.

REALPOLITIK IN SOUTH ASIA: THE CENTRALITY OF INDIA

Hanging like a pendant below the peninsular subcontinent, Sri Lanka is—depending on sentiments about symbols—either a pearl or a teardrop. In terms of *realpolitik* the island is an integral part of the South Asian whole even if self-perception and history strive to establish a separate and unique status. Lying cheek by jowl to the mainland, the extricable thread of Lankan dependence on the Indian fabric was and remains evident in *the* Indo-Ceylon Problem. Throughout the 20th century, political relations were bedeviled by the status, role, and future of that most recent major wave of Tamil migrants to the island, the plantation laborers.

During the first half of the century, of course, all South Asians were subjects of His Britannic Majesty, the King-Emperor. As such, no matter where their original domicile, they were entitled to relatively free movement within the empire. The imperial economic system also facilitated the movement of money, whether investment capital, profits or remittances. Nonetheless, the interwar decades were replete with commissions, committees, reports, and proposals which addressed the issue of migrant and immigrant labor. Since the colonial governments of Ceylon (as a Crown Colony) and India had distinct status within the empire, they acted in ways remarkably analogous to their independent successors. Each colonial government regarded the immigrant laborers as essentially the responsibility of the other — and the unfortunate laborers themselves were trapped in between (Kodikara, 1965).

After independence, the policy of the Government of India about citizenship for overseas Indians remained constitutionally restrictive. The policy was not unreasonable since there were millions of overseas Indians spread worldwide from Fiji to Malaya to Mauritius, from Guyana to East Africa, from the Caribbean to Natal. From the perspective of Delhi, the Indian Tamils of Sri Lanka were a mere drop in the ocean—a perspective which, in the end, ironically helped resolve the impasse since the reabsorption of a few hundred thousand made little difference amidst the hundreds of millions on the mainland (Sivanayagam, 1986). Nonetheless, as long as Nehru lived, India held firmly to the position that all 19th century and most 20th century immigrants as well as their "natural increase" were the responsibility of Sri Lanka. Since the Government of Ceylon maintained equally firmly that whoever was not a Ceylonese citizen was an Indian citizen, the Indian Tamils became stateless (Gundevia, 1984). Periodic discussions occurred between the two governments and occasionally, as in 1954, agreements "in principle" were signed; but these agreements were always subject to conflicting and self-serving interpretations and were never implemented.

Only a few months after Nehru's death in 1964, however, his successor signed the momentous Indo-Ceylon Agreement (Sirima-

Shastri Pact) in which India accepted repatriation of the majority of Indian Tamils on the island. A decade later Indira Gandhi signed a second Indo-Ceylon Agreement with Sirimavo Bandaranaike in which the remaining 150,000 Indian Tamils (and their "natural increase") were divided equally between the two countries. Altogether India accepted some 600,000-plus Indian Tamils for repatriation to India as citizens while Sri Lanka provided citizenship to over 400,000 Indian Tamils. When the latter are added to the 134,000 persons of Indian origin already admitted to citizenship under the 1949 Indian and Pakistani (Citizenship) Act (Kodikara, 1965), more than a half million additional citizens were entered on the Sri Lankan electoral rolls. In 1986 President Jayewardene completed the process by granting the remaining stateless immediate Sri Lankan citizenship (Gemini, 1986), a gesture which paid a political debt to the Indian Tamil leaders (particularly S. Thondaman, a Minister in his government) for their electoral and coalitional support. The gesture simultaneously discomfited the Sinhalese opposition party, the SLFP, and those Ceylon Tamils who claimed that all Tamils wanted no truck with the chauvinist government (Rajappa, 1986a).

Unsurprisingly, Tamil militants pour scorn and derision on those "Uncle Tomils" who collaborate with the Sinhalese for a united future, yet the militants display uncertainty about how to proceed. Given their ambiguous status in India and dependence on Indian good will, they display an erratic pattern of public posturing and private doubts, punctuated with periodic hit-and-run forays into Sri Lanka. Their position on the 1986 negotiations is a case in point. In August, after an unsuccessful attempt to meet the Indian External Affairs Minister in New Delhi, leaders of five militant groups "arrived at a broad consensus to oppose the attempts of the Tamil United Liberation Front (TULF) to enter into an agreement with the Sri Lanka government on the ethnic issue" (*Times of India*, 21 August 1986, 9). Within a month, however, the militant movement was said to be "at the cross-roads, with opinion divided in all the militant groups on whether to follow the path of peace or continue their armed struggle against the Government for the establishment of a separate State of Eelam" (*The Hindu*, 29 September 1986, 9). Only the LTTE sustains an unrelenting military strategy, but it has experienced severe reverses in the field (*The Hindu*, 21 February 1987; Clines, 1987, 3).

Indian leverage is simultaneously evident and ephemeral. By showing a certain toughness toward the Tamil militants encamped in Tamilnadu, the Government of India helped to persuade Sri Lanka to make significant political concessions to the law-abiding Tamils. Already on record in favor of the "politics of conciliation, not of confrontation" (Gupta, 1985, 4), Rajiv Gandhi has previously expressed his displeasure with the Tamil militants "for not coming forth with 'positive suggestions to solve the ethnic problem in Sri Lanka" (*Indian Express*, 16 November 1985). In late 1986 Gandhi claimed that "India's utmost concern was restoration of peace and a life of honor for the Tamils in the island" (*Times of India*, 11 October 1986, 1). While the militant groups remain critical of the TULF leadership, they "told the (Indian) government that they would not stand in the way of a negotiated settlement that safeguards Tamil interests" (*ibidem*). In short, as long as there are signs of progress toward a negotiated settlement in Colombo, a pattern of quiet but persistent pressure on the militants has emerged. After Tamilnadu police confiscated weaponry and communications equipment from all militants (*Times of India*, 10 November 1986; and 24 November 1986), however, Prabakharan shifted his operational base out of India and back to Jaffna (*Indian Express*, 12 January 1987). Consequently the Indian authorities had less leverage to restrain the guerrillas and the armed conflict in Sri Lanka intensified in both the Eastern and Northern Provinces.

The effects of this recent pattern probably persuaded the Governments of both Sri Lanka and India of the need for disciplined coercion, which is very evident in their accord of July 1987. Indeed, since the mid-1970s, the use of violence in pursuit of the goal of Tamil Eelam steadily increased and terrorism intensified. Initially the TULF and its various predecessors were wedded to the classic Gandhian tactic of nonviolent *satyagraha.* Tamil youths, however, already subject to discriminatory ("affirmative action") policies in education in particular and in state employment in general, transmuted their frustrations into more direct form. By the early 1980s the LTTE "Tamil Tigers" were regularly employing classic terrorist tactics to further their goal. Targets included not only government institutions and personnel (the latter usually Sinhalese) but also, with increasing frequency, Tamils who have cooperated with or are sympathetic to the government (Dissanayake, 1983; Jones, 1985). As a consequence, even moderates "have been almost completely cowed into silence by Tamil terrorists; moderates who speak up often are murdered within a day" (*Christian Science Monitor*, 5 June 1986, 19). Sinhalese civilians are equally vulnerable. In November 1984 the Tigers massacred 80 settlers who were living on lands the Tamils believe belong to them. In May 1985 they attacked the second-most sacred Buddhist site on the island—the Bo Tree at Anuradhapura—where over 140 civilians were killed. In May 1986 they blew up an Air Lanka plane on the Colombo airport runway killing 16 people. In February 1987 they struck deep into Amparai District in retaliation for alleged Army atrocities in the far north (*The Hindu*, 5 February 1987). In April 1987 they massacred 26 bus passengers on Good Friday and then detonated a car-bomb in Colombo's crowded Central Bus Station several days later which killed another 113 and maimed several hundred more. The most dramatic deed, however, remains the July 1983 LTTE attack on a Sri Lankan Army unit in the north, which killed 13 Sinhalese soldiers. The whole island was quickly engulfed in the worst communal rioting the country had ever experienced, and the cynical "second view" of terrorism reaped its richest reward.

From the perspective of the Tamil militants and pro-Eelamites, the successive Indo-Lankan agreements are regarded as "the growing failure of Indian diplomacy in the post-Nehru years" (Sivanayagam, 1986, 4). They lay particular blame on C. S. Jha, the long-term Secretary of the Indian Foreign Office who had served under Prime Ministers Jawaharlal Nehru, Lal Bahadur Shastri, and Indira Gandhi. The Foreign Secretary himself concludes his chapter on the subject by saying (Jha, 1983):

> The Indo-Ceylon Agreement of 1964 removed the long-standing irritant between India and Sri Lanka. It was a good example of settlement on the basis of give and take and was a feather in Shastri's cap and a success for Mrs. Bandaranaike. ....(It) remained a model of conciliation and compromise for the solution of a chronic problem which stood in the way of friendly relations between two neighboring countries, India and Sri Lanka. For my part, as a civil servant, I regard my own contribution towards this agreement as among my most satisfying efforts in my career.

Needless to add, "North Indians" like Jha and indeed Prime Ministers Shastri and Gandhi (both from Hindi-speaking Uttar Pradesh) are held responsible for the betrayal of South Indian interests. "The sad fact remains that far too often Tamilian sentiments and views on both sides of the Palk Straits were ignored by policy makers in New Delhi, even though all bilateral issues between India and Ceylon were those that directly involved Tamilians" (Sivanayagam, 1986, 6).

Militant Tamils also lament how the current Government of India in Delhi under Prime Minister. Rajiv Gandhi repeatedly obliges the Sinhalese Government of Sri Lanka to the detriment of the Tamil people. Not only are shipments of weapons and military equipment not interdicted, but also the veteran negotiator Gopalaswami Parthasarathi (a South Indian) appointed by Indira Gandhi to facilitate communications between the disputants in Colombo was replaced by Romesh Bhandari (a North Indian). The latter was subsequently replaced by a pair of junior ministers who come from *both* North and South India. Furthermore, the Government of India practically dragooned several of the many Madras-based factions to attend the roundtables organized in Thimpu in mid-1985. In the end, after two rounds of talks, the militants walked out because the mutually agreed cease-fire had broken down under the familiar refrain: "they shot first." In the prevailing paranoic atmosphere, a lone extremist of whatever persuasion can rekindle the fires of civil war with a single bullet or bomb. Subsequently a self-appointed spokesman for the militants asserted that the "over-zealous Boy Scout diplomacy" that followed Mrs. Gandhi's death and "the accompanying razzle-dazzle not only weakened the Tamil liberation struggle, but compromised India's own position. The problem was airlifted from Sri Lanka to New Delhi via Madras and ferried onwards to a third country, Bhutan. From what was India's 'good offices' role it assumed the proportions of a mediatory role, which entailed the building of a 'neutral' mediator image, which in turn led to the clumsy and hurried deportation order on three Tamil activists..." (*ibidem*).

Since Rajiv Gandhi came to power, the Government of India has taken on a much more pro-active role in trying to resolve the ethnic conflict on Sri Lanka. The Indian attempt is impelled by more than mere altruism although there is clearly an element of such altruism, some might say "masochism," in grasping the thorny nettle of ethno-political relations once again.

Although not a unitary state per se, the Republic of India itself is a multi-national state with a quasi-federal structure tending towards a fairly high degree of centralization. As argued above, the recent history of India is replete with conflict over ethnic identities and particularly over language, both at national and state levels.

Add to this constantly bubbling linguistic cauldron the continuing controversy over Hindi as a "national" as compared to an "official" language—particularly in Tamilnadu—and one should immediately perceive two primary conditions of ethno-political statecraft according to the Government of India in New Delhi:

1) Each subnational, regional, and/or ethnic language of a

certain size deserves its due representation—but not without meeting prior conditions of geographic continuity, political commitment, and financial capacity; and

2) *No* secession from the Indian Union is acceptable.

Given such principles plus historical experiences, it seems clear that the Government of India expects a political settlement in Sri Lanka which leaves the state a coherent whole but nonetheless allows substantial devolution of political authority, decentralization of administration, and local autonomy (Khan, 1985). Its likely formula is a constitutionally entrenched quasi-federal system which delegates considerable power to subnational levels but which retains ultimate authority at the center: in other words, the Indian Constitution of 1950. Certainly this solution would not please many, if any, of the Sri Lankan disputants—but it would necessarily be more agreeable to whomever rules in Colombo (and that means Sinhalese of one political persuasion or another) than to the Ceylon Tamils. Proponents of Tamil Eelam as an independent nation-state are most likely to dislike, and reject, this broad gauge quasi-federal solution. But India cannot ask for, or expect, less without compromising its own delicately balanced ethno-political mosaic.

It is particularly hard for the Indian Government to ignore ethnic pressures since Indian compulsions are shaped by regional politics. The Sri Lankan Tamils have strong popular sympathy in the southern state of Tamilnadu. This puts the ruling state government of M.G. Ramachandran and his *All-India Anna Dravida Munnetra Kazhagam* (AIADMK) in a fix because his arch rival, and ex-colleague, M. Karunanidhi who heads the parent *Dravida Munnetra Kazhagam* (DMK) from which the AIADMK seceded, has identified totally with the Sri Lanka Tamil case. With no choice but to accommodate the Tamil militants and to allow all rebels to operate freely from Tamilnadu, MGR has become a "patron saint" to LTTE leader Prabakharan, and is described regularly as the only real influence on the latter's behavior. The domestic political picture becomes ever more complicated because the AIADMK is in quasi-alliance with the Congress Party of Prime Minister Rajiv Gandhi, who cannot afford to see his ally outflanked by an even more extremist regional party, the DMK. Already the Congress Party itself has had to face widespread propaganda in Tamilnadu that while Mrs. Indira Gandhi used force so effectively to save Bengalis persecuted by the Pakistanis in 1971, her son is now insensitive to Tamil suffering (Guptas, 1984). The propaganda ("bullets for the Bengalis but talks for the Tamils") revives the long-smouldering charge that North Indians support only each other and never the South Indians. In any case, another immediate impetus for concern by Delhi is the episodic influx of Tamil refugees who cross to India to escape the conflict and carnage and who in late 1986 numbered somewhat over 120,000 (*Times of India*, 7 November 1986) — an uncertain figure since repatriated Indian Tamils also continue to arrive (Khan 1986). However, in early 1987 several thousand refugee families returned to Sri Lanka despite the unresolved, indeed intensified, conflict; journalistic interviews cited their reasons as general homesickness and disillusionment with their Tamilnadu cousins (*The Hindu*, 31 January 1987).

There is, of course, yet another possibility: events may lurch along with neither political direction nor expectation of long lasting settlement. As a somewhat cynical sage atop Mt. Kailash is said to have quipped, "Something ignored long enough goes away." Given that sages see and speak with a sense of countless eons, such cynicism suggests that Sri Lanka is poised on the brink of prolonged civil strife. As a former TULF MP, Vettivelu Yogeswaran, described this permanent non-solution solution: "Ceylon, actually, has no future. At best we will be the Lebanon of Asia." The North Indian journalist citing his words then commented correctly: "That is the last prospect India would want to have 25 km from its shores" (Gupta 1984, 57).

Meanwhile the Sri Lankan political scene persistently provides its own obstacles to a settlement of the ethnic conflict. When Mrs. Gandhi in 1983 assigned G. Parthasarathi the task of achieving a negotiated settlement to the "Tamil problem," he organized tripartite talks involving Jayewardene's United National Party, Mrs Bandaranaike's Sri Lanka Freedom Party, and the Tamil United Liberation Front. Shortly thereafter the SLFP withdrew from the talks, which fell into the doldrums. Two years later in August 1985, "a group of Sinhalese Buddhist hardliners which included Mrs. Bandaranaike and her son Anura, formed a national front to "protect the rights and interests of the majority community at this crucial juncture in its history"(de Silva, 1985, 38). And in July 1986 the SLFP refused to participate in the Political Parties Conference (PPC) which President Jayewardene had called to discuss his proposals for the devolution of power through provincial councils. "The SLFP leader, Mrs. Sirimavo Bandaranaike, made it quite clear that the people must have the final say and, according to her, that is going to the polls" (Sebastian, 1986b, 6). Even at the cost of continued civic strife, the SLFP seems willfully ready to sabotage anything which might bring political credit to its rival, the UNP.

The United National Party in turn blames the SLFP for fanning the flames of Sinhalese chauvinism, but itself contributes to the continued alienation of the Tamil community. The guerrillas benefit enormously from the policy of the Sri Lankan Government to retain the Official Language Act. Although the 1978 Constitution did register Tamil as a national language and restore Tamil to some use in the totally Tamil territories, the 1956 law remains in force and is popularly perceived to discriminate against Tamils.

Empirical studies convincingly demonstrate the patterns of ethnic recruitment have not significantly changed in central government employment (Samarasinghe, 1984), but popular perceptions reinforced by political demagoguery run otherwise. Concern about strategic security and loyalty also make the Sri Lankan Government reluctant to promote Tamils in sensitive military and police positions although ironically the highest officials in the judicial system (the Chief Justice and the Attorney-General) are Tamils. However, given the general inability to distinguish between the rhetoric and the reality of language policy, even well-meaning moderate Tamils who prefer a negotiated settlement that sustains the integrity of the island and may actually help them economically, are driven into stances of sullen support and potential defection.

On the other hand, some signs for optimism, howsoever guarded, exist. *The Sri Lanka Mahajana Party (SLMP),* a spin-off faction from the SLFP, vociferously urges quick justice for the Tamils on the basis of full internal autonomy (Navaratne, 1986). Led by Vijaya Kumaratunga, who also happens to be Mrs. Badaranaike's son-in-law, the SLMP tries to act as a buffer between its parent SLFP and its grandparent UNP as well as a bridge between the Sinhalese and Tamil communities. In attempts to explain and promote Jayewardene's proposals for provincial autonomy, Kumaratunga has been shuttling to Madras where he meets not only fellow film star, MGR, but also most leaders of the proscribed militant groups. It should be noted that "his stance has not diminished his popularity because throughout the island large crowds continue to attend SLMP rallies where the consequences of failure (to) come to terms with Tamils are fully explained" (*Ibidem*, 16). In December 1986 Kumaratunga tried but failed to arrange direct talks between Jayewardene and Prabakharan (*Times of India*, 6 December 1986); later he arranged, but received no credit for a swap of prisoners between the government and LTTE (*Indian Express*, 20 December 1986). Other Sri Lankan political parties, including the Trotskyite *Lanka Sama Samajist Party* (LSSP) and the *Communist Party of Sri Lanka,* have also endorsed the government's proposals for autonomous provincial councils.

To complicate matters further, the expatriate Tamils who were driven abroad in search of security, education and employment, now form the hard core of Tamil Eelam support overseas. Whether based in Europe, North America or Australasia, their commitment to the cause of Eelam seems to expand geometrically according to their distance from the horrors of local civil war. While not overly rich, these expatriates contribute cash that buys some of the best political propaganda available. Tamil

Information Centers in the UK and the USA produce slick literature that is generally well-crafted and simultaneously amusing and depressing. The flood of endless lists of Sinhalese atrocities and Tamil victims is mind-numbing, and ultimately the MEGO (My Eyes Glaze Over) index of disbelief prevails. In addition to the propaganda blitz, expatriate money also buys sophisticated weaponry including Soviet Kalashnikovs and NATO-issue G-3 rifles. Just like the Irish Republican Army in Northern Ireland, the Tamil Tigers and other militants benefit enormously from their irredentist ethnic cousins elsewhere in the world.

The linkage of overseas support and domestic violence regularly reminds the Government of India about its own festering problem of Khalistan. Several years ago the *Indian Express*—significantly, a North Indian newspaper— editorialized that "terrorism in Sri Lanka cannot be treated any differently from terrorism in Punjab. Any such policy would be extremely dangerous and only recoil on this country (India) in many different ways" (8 August 1984). While this insight automatically generated outrage among South Indians, who boycotted and sometimes publicly burned the paper, the editorial continued:

> Sri Lanka is caught up in a tragic ethnic dispute and there is an understandable measure of sympathy for the minority Tamil group because of cultural affiliations across the water. Yet, the Government of India wisely decided that its best role was to try and (sic) help both sides reach an amicable settlement within a united Lanka. Nobody should be allowed to push the country off that path.

For all intents and purposes, the Government of India continues to pursue such a self-enlightened policy. Despite provocations to the contrary by Sinhalese politicians and Ceylon Tamils alike, Rajiv Gandhi repeatedly makes clear his commitment to a just political order in a unified multi-ethnic island neighbor. This is the basis for the intergovernmental accord signed in Colombo on 29 July 1987 by Gandhi and Jayewardene under dramatic circumstances.

EPILOGUE: AN IMMEDIATE PRESENT AND (IM)PROBABLE FUTURE

Indirect negotiation has been episodic between the Sri Lankan Government and the Ceylon Tamils for several years with the Government of India acting as mediator and messenger. Most of 1984 featured sessions of an All Party Conference (APC)—significantly lacking, however, both SLFP and TULF participants—which ended with ultimately unconsummated proposals for decentralized government through District Councils (APC Statement, 14 December 1984). June 1985 entailed direct talks between Sri Lankan President Junius Richard Jayewardene and Indian Prime Minister Rajiv Gandhi in Delhi, which led to unsuccessful peace talks in July and August in Bhutan between representatives of the Sri Lankan Government and Tamil leaders including militants. Subsequently the Government of Sri Lanka proposed its Provincial Councils Bill of 1985 which offered in principle a certain degree of regional autonomy to the nine regions which, although important during the British colonial period, had almost completely lost their utility by the 1960s.

In the first round of negotiations in 1986 the Sri Lankan Government proposed autonomous provincial councils which bear marked resemblance to the Union Territories in India. These would acquire legislative and executive powers through an Act of Parliament and by Presidential delegation. The councils cannot be elevated to the status of India's States except by replacing the present unitary Constitution of Sri Lanka with some form of federalism—and such a fundamental change would have to be approved by a referendum which President Jayewardene is unwilling to risk. Instead another conference of all Lankan Political parties was convened in June 1986 to discuss these proposals. Eight of the twelve recognized parties participated in this Political Parties Conference (PPC) but not, crucially, the SLFP which remains the major opposition party despite its paltry contingent in the current parliament (Rajappa, 1986b). The TULF did not participate either—technically its MPs no longer hold office, having resigned after the 1983 referendum; it also remains proscribed by the sixth Amendment which requires an oath of loyalty to a united Sri Lanka—but, under prodding from the Government of India, TULF sent a delegation to Colombo to prove its commitment to a political settlement. TULF listened to the deliberations and its good-faith proximity subsequently lead to several rounds of direct negotiations with the Sri Lankan Government.

The possibility of a third round of direct talks persisted through late 1986 and early 1987 with considerable "shuttle diplomacy" by Natwar Singh and K. Chidambaram, two junior ministers of the Government of India, ably assisted by the Indian High Commissioner (Ambassador) in Colombo, J.N. Dixit. On 19 December these Ministers and President Jayewardene tentatively agreed on proposals to resolve the ethnic dispute, proposals which included institutional linkages between the Tamil-majority Northern Province and the Tamil-plurality Eastern Province. The various factions of militants, however, persistently refused to participate in these negotiations and ignored the tentative results. Both sides in the increasingly overt military conflict insisted that its adversary first cease violent activities in the field; and as neither was willing to withdraw from what it perceives to be own advantage, the Government of India repeatedly threatened to end its role as mediator (*The Hindu*, 21 February 1987). Indeed by late Spring it had suspended its public activities and instead sent humanitarian relief supplies to Jaffna peninsula civilians (*The New York Times*, 7 June 1987).

All the Tamil groups rejected the first formulation about provincial councils as not even remotely satisfying the aspirations of the Tamil people. The Tamil Congress held that "a study of these proposals will show that they have been presented on the basis of an extension of local government administration through delegation of powers and not on the basis of real autonomy through devolution of powers" (Sebastian, 1986a, 6). The Government of India then asked the Tamil groups, both moderate and militant, to state their expectations and requirements. While the militants once again finessed the opportunity, TULF submitted a detailed set of counter-proposals to the Government of India, which passed the package on to Sri Lanka. "These TULF counter-proposals sought state autonomy for all the Tamils of the island based on the federal principle. The first part of the counter-proposals clearly laid down that "Sri Lanka, that is *Ilankai*, shall be a union of states, and the northern and eastern provinces—which are predominantly Tamil speaking —shall constitute one Tamil linguistic state." Added was a rider: "The territory of a state, once established, shall not be altered without its consent" (Venkatramani, 1986, 59). Among other demands, TULF wanted the Tamil state to have full control over education, law and order, and land settlement in its jurisdictional area.

In the second round, the Government of Sri Lanka accepted some, but not all, of the TULF demands. Regional autonomy for the Northern and Eastern Provinces; a coordinating zonal council for close cooperation between the two provincial councils; judicial self-sufficiency through a provincial High Court; authority to select students for universities in the two provinces—all have been agreed by the Sri Lankan Government. The demands not accepted are that Trincomalee (with the biggest natural harbor in the world) should be part of the Eastern Province; that all police powers should be vested at provincial level; and that all land issues should be settled locally. The respective counter-arguments are national security and ethnic composition; armed policemen easily become soldiers, should a future unilateral declaration of Eelam independence ever occur; and local land settlement powers, if granted, would ultimately drive the "nearly 27.8 percent of the Sinhala population" out of the two provinces (*Sunday Mail*, 20-26 July 1986, 8).

Likewise the demand for a single Tamil linguistic unit merging the Northern Province and parts of the Eastern Province was initially rejected (*The Statesman*, 27 July 1986), but the option was revived in the 29 July 1987 Accord which temporarily merged the two provinces subject to a confirmatory referendum in the Eastern Province before 31 December 1988. Lawyers and constitutional experts of the Government of Sri Lanka as well as the TULF thoroughly examined the proposed division of powers between delegated, reserved and concurrent lists; and the Government of India unilaterally informed the Tamil separatist groups that they would have to surrender their weapons and accept the Accord. Prabakharan, who had been flown to Delhi for consultations, remained in protective custody while Indian troops were deployed throughout the Northern Province to enforce the cease-fire and to collect the militants' weaponry with full cooperation from the Sri Lankan armed forces.

The third round of talks had been stymied by the indeterminate status of proposals worked out on 19 December 1986 between the Governments of Sri Lanka and India as "a basis" and "only a beginning point for further negotiations" (*The Hindu*, 21 February 1987, 9). Without elaborating them in detail, these proposals had mooted the removal of Amparai District (Sinhalese majority) from the Eastern Province, which would then be almost half Ceylon Tamil and 40% Muslim (who also speak Tamil). However, the complex (and differing) sets of conditions and preconditions which different participants insisted must be met before talks could resume were obviated by secret negotiations between the Government of Sri Lanka and India. The result is in the July 1987 Accord, a gamble which will be judged politically in a confirmatory referendum in the Eastern Province before the end of 1988 and then in the next mandatory parliamentary elections in Sri Lanka before May 1989. The issues are already being hotly debated throughout the island and, except for the LTTE, all parties to this ethno-political dispute repeatedly avow their respect for and reliance on democratic discussion and decisionmaking. Even the other groups of Tamil militants—especially EPRLF and EROS—express belief in political democracy if adequate safeguards for minorities are built in.

One is tempted to hope that as the rule of law is restored, the former militants will return to traditional democratic processes of negotiation, compromise and reconciliation. In this regard, the experience of India again provides useful examples. As a case in point, an extremely bloody and vicious 20-year uprising of Mizo rebels against the Union government was ended in 1986 by an "accord" between Rajiv Gandhi and the Mizo leader, Laldenga. As a result, Mizoram has become India's 24th state; democratic elections were held in which the Mizo National Front won convincingly over the Congress-I party; and Laldenga is now Chief Minister rather than chief criminal. Whether a similar transformation might occur among the LTTE is not inconceivable; it just seems improbable.

India's mediatory strategy acknowledges the dilemma faced by the militant groups. In the worlds of S.C. Chandrahasan, convener of the *Organization for the Protection of the Tamils of Eelam from Genocide (OPTEG)*:

> The militant groups are not like political parties to sit across a table and come to a mutually acceptable solution with the Sri Lanka Government. They are guerilla groups who have vowed to fight for Eelam and who have trained and committed cadres all the way down. So the leaders will run the risk of being done away with by their own cadres if they, on record, express themselves as being amenable to something short of Eelam (cited in Venkatramani, 1986, 60).

The Government of India therefore recognizes from past experience, as in the Punjab, that any kind of accord is bound to be opposed by hardline elements on both sides. A pragmatic settlement between the moderate TULF and the Sri Lanka Government would be the best bet under the circumstances. India will then deal with the recalcitrant militants, while hoping that many of them will gradually opt to go back and resume normal life. Indeed the ENLF (sans LTTE) claimed to have "not closed all options for a peaceful solution" and "reiterated its faith in the good offices of India in resolving the problem;" only the LTTE "demands a separate Eelam and nothing less" (*The Statesman*, 27 July 1986, 7). Assuming the cooperation of MGR, the Government of India is confident that it can successfully pressure both the Sri Lankan

Government and the Tamil militants to secure some kind of a settlement and gradually get it implemented. "The Sinhalese hardliners and the Buddhist clergy, not to speak of Sirimavo Bandaranaike, would be Jayewardene's headache" (Venkatramani, 1986, 60). The July 1987 Accord is predicated on these assumptions backed up by the *realpolitik* of India's own stake in a stable island neighbor with its territorial integrity guaranteed.

Sri Lanka represents yet another in the series of seemingly insoluble secessionist crises that periodically afflict the South Asian psyche. A single language is the sine qua non of a culture and its nation, but a sovereign state can (and often must) be multi-national and therefore multi-lingual. Independent India "resolved" this problem through its 1956 reorganization of internal state (non-sovereign) boundaries along linguistic lines. The resolution was and is imperfect in that subsequent reorganizations occurred and more are likely. The process is not complete since current events are characterized by periodic and occasionally very violent conflicts over language.

No South Asian country is immune to similar ethno-linguistic politics, a point which must be stressed to keep the Sri Lankan situation in perspective. The complexity of India has already been sketched in terms of its complicated ethnic equilibrium. Thus far, barring some territorial losses along its northern border and an adjudication in the Rann of Kutch, India has retained its post-Raj entity via studied policies of "unity in diversity." Its Islamic twin, Pakistan, however, experienced the ultimate in "fissiparous tendencies" in 1971 when its entire Bengali-speaking Eastern Wing seceded to become the sovereign, if utterly impoverished, nation-state of Bangladesh. Pakistan continues to confront linguistic tensions in its provinces of Sind and Baluchistan, and in late 1986 and early 1987 Karachi witnessed exceptionally savage interethnic conflict between Urdu-speaking Muhajirs and Pushtu-speaking Pathans. Bagladesh too now sustains an endemic conflict of formidable proportions in its Chittagong Hill districts.

Likewise, although few of its linguistic disputes have as yet become sufficiently vicious to merit banner headlines in world media, Nepal is replete with local ethno-politics, including objections by the Newari in Kathmandu valley itself and the Tharu in the terrai to the imposition of Gurkhali as the national Nepali language. In short, affinity to and identification with language remains one of the most powerful, potent political factors in the entire subcontinent. Ethno-politics are likely to remain for the foreseeable future with or without the sovereign state of Eelam.

This long, detailed, semi-narrative case study of one corner of the South Asian mosaic suggests a few tentative generalizations about the preconditions for political democracy in multi-ethnic states. In a simple numerical sense, all democracies are dictatorships of the majority. They have been made into decent places for everyone, including minorities, by a variety of checks and balances—the separation of powers, the flexibility of federalism, the entrenchment of individual freedoms in bills of rights. Consociational systems give a disproportionate share of power to minorities. Typical instruments of consociation include reserved seats in the cabinet, or the granting to minorities of veto power when important interests are at stake. In confederal Switzerland, for example, an informal "magic formula" keeps an intricate balance in the government between three languages, two forms of Christianity, and a clutch of different parties. In Belgium the presence in the cabinet of both French-speakers and Dutch-speakers is required by the constitution. In South Asia, India has developed a quasi-federal system with some checks and balances as well as many "cracks" or leverage points at which disaffected minorities can influence the political process (Rudolph and Rudolph 1987). Consociation may well be the best way to square the respective yearnings and fears of all Sri Lankans. There is an old adage from *The Panchatantra* that "you can't hold a tiger's tail forever." Accidentally appropriate imagery (as well as the woeful contrary case of Lebanon) notwithstanding, Sri Lankans must let go of the tiger's tail or eventually be swallowed by the tiger. The choice requires trust, creativity and leadership which, though inherently fragile, remain in tentative evidence even today on the Resplendent Isle.

Nuwara Eliya, 1987

ADDENDUM: HINDSIGHT AND AFTER-THOUGHT

While the conclusions and generalizations about Indo-Lankan ethno-political relations remain valid, my chapter is dated. Governments in both Sri Lanka and India have gone and come — sometimes several times over. Even the two signatories of the Indo-Lanka Accord no longer hold office. When Junius Jayewardene retired, Ranasinghe Premadasa was elected President of Sri Lanka. In India, Rajiv Gandhi's Congress-I Party was voted out of power in 1989; because several successor governments proved unworkable, however, general elections are again scheduled.

Other political actors have also changed. M.G. Ramchandran, Chief Minister of Tamilnadu and LTTE patron died in December 1987; subsequently, Tamilnadu has alternated between weak governments and presidential rule. Other less natural deaths have occurred. TULF leader, A. Amirthalingam, and SLMF leader, Vijay Kumaratunga, were assassinated—as were many others, most recently the UNP Deputy Defence Minister, Ranjan Wijeratne. Bombs still maim and kill innocent civilians. The JVP rose and fell again in southern Sri Lanka, in Tamil territories intermittent warfare continues, punctuated by ceasefires and ephemeral truces. During the past four years, even the Indian Army has come and gone in its Accord-sanctioned role as would be keeper of the peace.

Nonetheless, the foundations, issues, principles and options of Indo-Lakan ethno-political relations remain unchanged. *Mutatis mutandis* the endemic crisis continues. Short of writing another extended essay on current events, I reiterate the truths recounted above. Trust, creativity and leadership remain vital solvents for managing—if not fully resolving—the inherent tensions of ethnic politics in South Asia as well as thoughout the world.

The Hague, the Netherlands, March 1991.

REFERENCES

Appathurai, E. 1983. Communal politics and national integration in Sri Lanka in *National Unity: The South Asian Experience*, ed. M. Israel. New Delhi: Promilla and Company.

Clines, F.X. 1987. Rebellion in Sri Lanka becomes a deadly standoff. *The New York Times* (29 June) : 3.

de Silva, K.M. 1981. *A History of Sri Lanka.* Delhi: Oxford University Press.

de Silva, K.M. 1986. *Managing Ethnic Tensions in Multi-Ethnic Societies: Sri Lanka 1880-1985.* Lanham, Maryland: University Press of America.

de Silva, K.M. 1988. Buddhist revivalism, nationalism, and politics in modern Sri Lanka in *Fundamentalism, revivalists and violence in South Asia,* ed. J.W. Bjorkman. Riverdale, Maryland and Delhi: The Riverdale Press and Manohar Publications.

de Silva, K.M. *et al.* 1988. *Ethnic Conflict in Buddhist Societies: Sri Lanka, Thailand and Burma.* London: Pinter Publishers.

de Silva, M. 1985. The right for peace. *India Today* (31 August) : 38.

Dissanayake, T.D.S.A. 1983. *The agony of Sri Lanka.* Colombo: Swastika (Pvt), Ltd.

Etzioni, A. 1965. *Political Unification: A comparative study of leaders and forces.* New York: Holt, Rinehart and Winston, Inc.

Gandhi, R. M. 1985. Some neglected aspects of the Sri Lanka question. *Tamil Times* (December): 8-9.

Gemini. 1986. Neglected 1m 'Estate Tamils.' *Newstime* (26 September): 8.

Gopalan, T.N. 1986. India is playing its role of mediator well. *Express Magazine* (20 July): 3.

Gundevia, Y.D. 1984. *Outside the archives.* Madras: Sangam Books.

Gupta, A. 1986. Lanka's ethnic divide—I: Separatism of the Jaffna Tamils. *The Statesman* (30 April): 7.

Gupta, B.S. 1985. Rajiv's foreign policy: Changes in style and tone. *The Muslim* (31 October 1985) : 4.

Gupta, S. 1984. Sri Lanka rebels: Ominous presence in Tamil Nadu. *India Today* (31 March) : 52-57.

Gupta, S.; De Silva, M; and Venkatramani, S.H. 1985. Indian mood: New view. *India Today* (15 October) : 58.

Hawksley, H. 1986. Sri Lanka: Tamil tigers show off their strength. *Sunday Mail* (17-23 August) : 17.

Jiggins, J. 1979. *Caste and family in the politics of the Sinhalese, 1947-76.* Cambridge: Cambridge University Press.

Jha, C.S. 1983. *From Bandung to Tashkent: Glimpses of India's foreign policy.* Madras: Sangam Books.

Jones, A.K. 1985. *Time for decision: Sri Lankan Tamils in the west.* Washington, D.C.: US Committee for Refugees.

Kamat, A.R. 1980. Ethno-linguistic issues in Indian federal context. *Economic and Political Weekly* (14-21 June): 1053-66.

Kearney, R. 1978. Language and the rise of Tamil separatism in Sri Lanka. *Asian Survey* 18: 521-34.

Khan, K.A. 1985. India reaffirms support for independent unified non-aligned Sri Lanka: Text of the Minister of State for External Affairs' statement in Parliament on March 29, 1985. *India News* 21: 1 (1 April): 1.

Kodikara, S.U. 1965. *Indo-Ceylon relations since independence.* Colombo: The Ceylon Institute of World Affairs.

Kumar, L. 1977. *India and Sri Lanka: Sirimavo-Shastri pact.* New Delhi: Chetna Publications.

Manor, J. 1983. Sri Lanka: Explaining the disaster. *The World Today* 39 (November): 450-59.

Matthews, B. 1987. Devolution of power in Sri Lanka: The Problems of implementation. *The Round Table* 301: 74-92.

Navaratne, G. 1986. Yearning for peace in Sri Lanka. *The Times of India* (23 July): 16.

O'Ballance, E. 1989. *The Cyanide War: Tamil Insurrection in Sri Lanka 1973-88.* London: Brassey's (UK) Ltd.

Phadnis, U. 1963. Ceylon and the Sino-Indian border conflict. *Asian Survey* 3 (April) : 189-96.

Ponnambalam, S. 1983. *Sri Lanka: Naional conflict and the Tamil liberation struggle.* London: Zed Books, Ltd.

Rajappa, S. 1986a. Broad agreement on 2 issues at Lanka talks. *The Statesman* (19 July) :1.

Rajappa, S. 1986b. TULF to brief Tamil militants. *The Statesman* (24 July) : 1:

Reddy, G.K. 1986. MGR posted on Tamil talks—Hindi will not be imposed: P.M. *The Hindu* (2 October 1986) :1.

Roberts, M. 1982. *Caste conflict and elite formation: The rise of a Karava elite in Sri Lanka, 1500-1931.* Cambridge: Cambridge University Press.

Rubenstein, R.E. 1987. *Alchemists of revolution: Terrorism in the modern world*. New York: Basic Books.

Rudolph, L.I., and Rudolph, S.H. 1987. *In pursuit of Lakshmi: The political economy of the Indian state*. Chicago: The University of Chicago Press.

Rupesinghe, K. and Verstappen, B. 1989. *Ethnic Conflict and Human Rights in Sri Lanka: An Annotated Bibliography*. London: Hans Zell.

Samarasinghe, S.W.R. de A. 1984. Ethnic Representation in Central Government Employment and Sinhala-Tamil Relations in Sri Lanka: 1948-1981 in *From Independence to Statehood: Managing Ethnic Conflict in Five African and Asian States*, ed. R.D. Goldman and A.J. Wilson, London: Frances Pintner.

Sebastian, R. 1986a;. Lanka talks continue amid violence. *Indian Express* (19 July): 7.

Sebastian, R. 1986b. Dissenting voices. *Indian Express* (23 July): 6.

Sebastian, R. 1986c. Lanka government for political solution. *Indian Express* (29 July) : 6.

Smith, D.E. 1979. Religion, politics, and the myth of reconquest in *Modern Sri Lanka: A society in transition*, ed. T. Fernando, and R. N. Kearney. Syracuse, New York: Maxwell School of Citizenship and Public Affairs.

Sivannandan, A. 1977. Sri Lanka: Uses of racism. *Economic and Political Weekly* 12 (8 October): 1736-37.

Sivanayagam, S. 1986. Sri Lanka background briefing: Big brother small brother: A resume of Indo-Sri Lankan relations in *Tamil Information* 3 (25 March): 2-7. Madras: Tamil Information and Research Unit (TIRU).

Tambiah, S.J. 1986. *Sri Lanka, Ethnic Fratricide and the Dismantling of Democracy*. Chicago: University of Chicago Press.

Varghese, R. 1986. Fighting with Lanka and themselves. *Sunday Mail* (20-26 July) : 8.

Venkatramani, S.H. 1986. Sri Lanka: Silver lining. *India Today* (15 February): 59-60.

Wallace, P. 1988. The dilemma of Sikh revivalism: Identity versus political power in *Fundamentalism, revivalists and violence in South Asia*, ed. J.W. Bjorkman. Riverdale, Maryland and Delhi: The Riverdale Company/Manohar.

Weerasooria, W.S. 1981. *Development 1931-1981 Sri Lanka*. Colombo: Ministry of Plan Implementation.

Wilson, A.J. 1974. *Politics in Sri Lanka 1947-1973*. London: The

Macmillan Press, Ltd.

Wilson, A.J. 1988. *The Break-up of Sri-Lanka: The Sinhalese-Tamil Conflict*. Honolulu: University of Hawaii Press.

The following newspapers were also consulted: *Asiaweek* (Hongkong); *Christian Science Monitor* (Boston); *The Daily* (Bombay); *Daily Mirror* (Colombo); *The Daily News* (Colombo); Dawn (Karachi); *The Deccan Chronicle* (Hyderabad); *Economic and Political Weekly* (Bombay); *Economic Times* (Bombay); *The Economist* (London); *Financial Express* (Bombay); *The Hindu* (Madras); *Hindustan Times* (Delhi); *India News* (Washington, D.C.); *Indian Express* (New Delhi); *International Herald Tribune* (Paris); *The Island* (Colombo); *Maharashtra Herald* (Pune); *The Muslim* (Islamabad); *Newstime* (Hyderabad); *The New York Times Statesman* (Delhi and Calcutta) (New York); *The Pakistan Times* (Rawalpindi); *Saturday Review* (Jaffna); *The Sunday Mail* (New Delhi); *The Sunday Observer* (Colombo); *Tamil Information* (Madras); *The Telegraph* (London); *The Times* (London); *The Times of India* (New Delhi); *The Wall Street Journal* (New York); *Washington Post* (Washington, D.C.).

INDEX